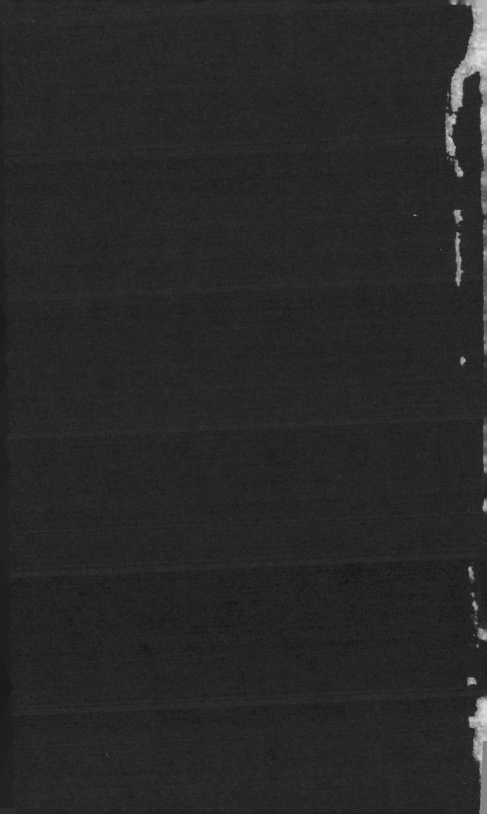

MANU
AND
YAJÑAVALKYA

MANU
AND
YAJÑAVALKYA

a comparison and a contrast

A TREATISE ON THE BASIC HINDU LAW

By

K. P. JAYASWAL

Cosmo Publications
2004 New Delhi

MANU AND YÁJÑAVALKYA

First Published by COSMO 2004

ISBN 81-7755-768-8

Published by
MRS. RANI KAPOOR
for COSMO PUBLICATIONS
Publishing Division of
GENESIS PUBLISHING PVT. LTD.
24-B, Ansari Road, Darya Ganj,
New Delhi-110 002, INDIA

Printed at
Mehra Offset Press

PREFACE

The University of Calcutta elected me to deliver twelve lectures on the subject selected by them—"*Manu and Yājñavalkya—a comparison and a contrast,*" for the Tagore Law Lectures, 1917. The scheme of the lectures, with an introductory note (which is reprinted here as the *Introduction*), indicated the line of enquiries I proposed to follow. The lectures as delivered in 1919 are printed here. A few footnotes have been newly added while the lectures have been going through the Press.

From 1911 to 1913 certain studies were published by me in the legal journal the *Calcutta Weekly Notes.* The method adopted therein found approval from Dr. Joseph Kohler, Professor of Jurisprudence at the University of Berlin, who till his death retained his position as the foremost comparative jurist of Europe[1] and who had himself written a good deal on Hindu Law. In the German Journal *Archiv für Rechts- und Wirtshafts philosophie* of which he was the Editor-in-Chief, and in the *Zeitschrift für Vgl. Rechtswissenschaft,* Prof. Kohler noticed my articles published in the *Calcutta Weekly Notes,* and observed that they marked a new stage in the history of the study of Indian law. In the present lectures I developed the same line of enquiry on the same historical method which I had already set for my studies in 1911-13. The method is briefly explained in the Introduction.

The whole body of Hindu Law, the bulk of which had been neglected, has been brought under survey in these lectures. Professor Kohler, Sir Lawrence Jenkins, Sir Ashutosh Mookerji and Sir Rashbehari Ghose were particularly keen on having an account of the complete system of Hindu Law, which had not been dealt with in its entirety.

---

[1] *Cf.* Vinogradoff, *Comparative Jurisprudence,* Encyclopaedia Britannica, XV, p. 584. (11th ed.)

As there were numerous references in these lectures to the results stated in my constitutional history (*Hindu Polity*), I deferred the printing of the lectures until the publication of the *Hindu Polity*. Immediately after the publication of the latter, these lectures were sent to the Press, but owing to the necessity of personal attention to the texts and difficulties of printing in general, the printing could not be completed earlier.

I have to thank my friends Mr. S. N. Datta and Professor H. C. Chakladar for their help in seeing the book through the Press. My acknowledgments are also due to Dr. Kali Das Nag and Prof. Arun Sen, my old pupils and friends, for their help in general and particularly for adding the index. The late Mr. Govind Das of Benares had kindly lent me several manuscripts of unpublished commentaries on Yājñavalkya. Mr. Batakrishna Ghosh has verified the references and appended some of the texts in the footnotes.

PATNA, K. P. J.
31*st October*, 1929.

N.B. Please read at page 98, *n.*[6], ix instead of xi and *anārya* for *anarya*. Minor corrections are :

At page		*Read*	*For*
5	(inset)	Dharmasūtra	Dharmsūtra
32	(inset)	codes	cods
53	(Appendix)	Brahmins	*Hramins*
81		§ 17A	§ 17
110	(f. n. 5)	**शृणुयाद्**	**शृणयाद्**
160	(inset)	of	by

CONTENTS

LECTURE X.

LECTURE XI.

INTRODUCTION.[1]

The legal literature of the Hindus is divisible into three classes: the *Dharma-Sūtras* or *Aphorisms of Law* of the different Schools, the *Dharma Śāstras* or the *Codes of Law* attributed generally to names of sages well-known in sacerdotal history, and the Commentaries and Treatises ['Digests'] by Hindu *jurisprudentes* which cover a period as lengthy as ten centuries—from about the Eighth to the Nineteenth Century of the Christian era. The third class might be regarded as being still in progress, but when we limit it to the Nineteenth Century, we mean the writings based purely on Hindu tradition and expressed in the very language which our forefathers had adopted to formulate their earliest legal conceptions, the Dharmasūtras.

Classes of Hindu Legal Literature.

2. Now this third class of work is most important from the practical point of view, for the British Law-Courts have made the opinion of the Hindu *jurisprudentes* as the ruling and binding law of Hindu Society. In this respect the Codes occupy a secondary place. Their value, however, remains very great. They are the bases of the present Hindu Law and they must be referred to where the *jurisprudentes* run amok. Unfortunately a discriminating reference to the original texts of the Codes is rare in judicial decisions of our modern Courts. This is probably due to the smallness of the number of forensic gentlemen who have devoted their time to the original texts of Hindu Law. A number of legal concepts which have been clothed with sanctity by judicial decisions but which are in fact against the spirit and text of the genuine Hindu Law, would be modified and corrected, if not wholly superseded, with

Position and Value of the Codes.

---

[1] Reprinted from the scheme of the Lectures submitted to the University of Calcutta in 1916.

more intimate discussions and attempts at an appreciation of the original C o d e s.

3. Amongst such Codes the position of the C o d e s of M a n u and Y ā j ñ a v a l k y a is pre-eminent. The former is supposed to be the foundation of the whole orthodox system of Hindu Law. Its authority is regarded as supreme by the unanimous verdict of both the lay and legal literatures of Hindu India, and as such it occupies a unique position in the legal history of the land. The latter is the present-day binding law of the majority of the Hindus. It is enough to say for its introduction, that the M i t ā k s h a r ā is a commentary on the C o d e Y ā j ñ a v a l k y a n. It has, in effect, though not in name, superseded the C o d e of M a n u. It seems clear, as we shall see later on in our lectures, that it was with the object of superseding the orthodox but unworkable provisions of the earlier Code that Yājñavalkya's Code was promulgated. It became the accepted code of law of the Hindus not only on account of its repealing virtue but also for its advanced and liberal juridical norms.

Manu and Yājña-valkya.

4. It thus becomes important to make a comparative study of the two Codes.

5. In our study, however, we cannot do without taking into account the I m p e r i a l C o d e of L a w of the M a u r y a s, embodied as we find it, in the A r t h a-Ś ā s t r a of K a u ṭ i l y a. It precedes the M ā n a v a-D h a r m a-Ś ā s t r a by about a century and a half, and there are clear traces of its great and immediate influence on the Mānava Code. The latter combats the former's view in many places, while Y ā j ñ a v a l k y a borrows bodily from the Artha-Śāstra. The *Dharmasthīyam* in the Artha-Śāstra is a unique Code in legal history. It is one of the earliest codes of law in the world, and in quality it is far superior to most of the early codes. Its authority embraced

Relation of the two Codes to the Imperial Code of the Mauryas.

an area greater than that covered by any ancient Code. It is absolutely secular. In Hindu legal literature it is the only secular Code before the N ā r a d a-S m ṛ i t i, and the Nārada-Smṛiti closely follows the *Dharmasthîyam*. You cannot have a comparative view of Manu and Yājñavalkya without reference to the Artha-Śāstra. They both are connected with it. Points which in the domain of Hindu Law appeared as so many riddles to earlier writers, can be now solved with the help of the Artha-Śāstra. The Artha-Śāstra was the missing link.

The line of a Comparative Study.

6. In our study we shall try to get a clear idea of the advance made with regard to individual laws, to note dissents of the latter Code from the former, to value the norms and principles underlying their provisions and to discover and assign historical and political reasons for advance or re-action. In my opinion, a correct appreciation of the different Codes and their different provisions without reference to the social, political and economic history of the country, is not possible. The law Codes are not so many idiocyncratic productions of Brahmins; they are children of their times.

The Dates of the two Codes.

7. A thorough enquiry, therefore, with regard to the dates of the two law Codes would be necessary. For reasons to be discussed in their proper places in the course of the lectures, the C o d e of M a n u is a product of the early days of the B r a h m i n E m p i r e, circa 150 B.C., and the C o d e of Y ā j ñ a v a l k y a followed it about three centuries later. The date of the C o d e of K a u ṭ i l y a is about 300 B.C. Our study thus covers a period of about f i v e c e n t u r i e s of legal development.

Historical explanation of the Laws.

8. The development in law has its full counterpart in developments of commerce, of political institutions and of the social welding of orthodox and Buddhistic thought. The psychology of the Hindu nation of the B r a h m i n E m p i r e is pictured in the M ā n a v a-D h a r m a-Ś ā s t r a,

and the voice of the prosperous and the liberal empire of the S ā t a v ā h a n a s is recorded in the C o d e of Y ā j ñ a v a l k y a. The B r a h m i n in the Mānava-Dharma-Śāstra claims to be the 'lord of all', he claims exemption from capital punishment, he argues for a special criminal law for his caste, and he pleads for local sovereignties as against imperialism. Look at them from the historical point of view and you begin to read these riddles. The Brahmin, when the Code of Manu was composed, was the Emperor of India, he was the lord of all, his empire recognised sub-kings, he had smarted under the Mauryan law seeking to establish uniformity and equality before the Criminal Court[1] in contravention of the common law which was based on caste. The Code of Manu practically ignores w o m a n, because that was the view of the old common law. The Code of Yājñavalkya treats her as a full legal persona : it allows her to inherit property. We can understand it if we remember that the S ā t a v ā h a n a r u l e combined orthodoxy with Buddhism and that Buddhism had made woman an equal of man. The corporation of nuns had held property as much as that of monks ; likewise, the w o m a n of the Sātavāhana régime could inherit property from her husband and father. Similarly, the privilege of the Brahmin is cut down to a minimum in Yājñavalkya. The largest space in Civil Law is given to C o n t r a c t in the latter Code. P a r t n e r s h i p of sea-traders and artisans and the law of C o r p o r a t i o n s find place in Yājñavalkya. All this is a reflection of the economic life of the country in the Sātavāhana epoch. Commerce with the West was at its zenith. The corporate life of the artisans is a known feature of the economic prosperity of the time.

9. The C o m m e n t a t o r s of Yājñavalkya narrow down the liberal provisions of the Code. This is because they write after the anti-Buddhistic reformation. For instance, they make woman only a restricted heir and owner. In places they

[1] Cf *Vyavahāra-samatā* and *daṇḍa-samatā* of Aśoka in his inscriptions,

openly disagree with the Code. Their disagreements, restrictions and enlargements (*e.g.*, in the case of adoption), become explicable if we read them with reference to their respective times and earlier literature.

10. There are some features of the two Codes which deserve our special attention, specially as, so far, they have been neglected. The Law of Procedure is a branch of Hindu Law well worth a critical study which will richly repay the student of comparative jurisprudence. It marks a high development in the legal history of the world. Then, it has also some, though rare, application and utility to our present-day Hindu Law. It is arguable that the proof of a certain matter has to be considered from the point of view of Hindu Law. An acquaintance with the Procedure Law also helps us in appreciating provisions of the Substantive Law. We shall, therefore, be devoting some time to a study of the Procedure Laws as found in the two Codes, with notices of earlier and later developments. It will be surprising to know that the procedure as to Pleadings which was prevalent in the Courts of the East India Company towards the end of the eighteenth and the beginning of the nineteenth century and which has been the subject of judicial dicta of our Courts, really came down and developed from the procedure of the Yājñavalkyan Code. A mention in Manu bears out the evidence of the *Milinda Pañho* and the Burmese Code of Manu as to the existence of professional lawyers and pleaders. The working system of the Court—the Judge and the *Sabhā*—is not to be fully gathered from the Codes, and the provisions in that respect have to be illustrated from general literature, in the light of which the Sabhā were the real Judges to whom the Judge only explained the law. The appeal to the King-in-Council is also an entertaining topic, and history helps us there in apprehending the provisions in the Codes. From history we get a picture of

Law of Procedure.

the working system of the King-in-Council sitting in appeal. It is no less interesting to note that the Codes place the Laws of Prescription and Limitation among the Laws of Procedure.

11. There is a class of law in the two Codes which up to this time the modern world has not yet placed on its statute-book but which in future is destined to be there. These are laws which we may designate as Eugenic Laws. We shall deal with them briefly for the purpose of comparison with modern views on the subject.

Eugenic Laws.

12. The Codes undertake to discuss certain Theories of Politics, the underlying idea being the inter-relation between politics and law. In these political norms also, Yājñavalkya adopts a higher standard. Manu's Code, for instance, advocates royal absolutism. This was clearly against the old tradition of the country and against the old common law. The Vedic rituals, the coronation oath and express provisions negative a theory of absolutism. But the Mānava-Dharma-Śāstra had to uphold a political revolution which was also a social revolution—a political rule by the Brahmin. The Code naturally finds relief only in a new theory. Yājñavalkya, as we shall see in detail, gives up the position of Manu. Manu's Code, however, does not allow the King to make laws as he did in the Mauryan régime. Yājñavalkya's attitude on the subject is characteristic. He does not count the King among the sources of law, yet he recognizes laws made by kings. The attitude is one of liberal conservatism throughout.

Political Theories.

13. The severity of the penal laws of Manu is a matter of standing comment. But the Criminal Law of Yājñavalkya shows a marked lenient tendency. Punishments are milder and offences have been treated as less serious. On the other hand, a number of new offences

Criminal Laws.

are added by Yājñavalkya. This marks a higher stage in differentiation and a more developed legal perception. Constructive application of law is limited, and a kindly public conscience is in evidence in the Criminal Law of Yājñavalkya's Code. Even mischief to trees and plants has been treated as assault.

The Family Laws.

13. The Family Laws in the two Codes bear more accentuated points of difference which are sometimes almost bewildering. For example, the forms of marriage prohibited by Manu are allowed by Yājñavalkya. The kinds of sons disinherited by Manu have been enfranchised by Yājñavalkya. Woman is brought in the list of heirs by the latter. Different provisions as to maintenance, succession to Strîdhana, and a number of other differences, along with the views of commentators thereon, are important studies to the lawyer of to-day. In these differences is to be found a cause of the rise of the different Schools of Hindu Law recognised by our judicial decisions. It would be interesting and not quite fruitless to examine the respective views of the *jurisprudentes* on these points of difference and to see which of them is nearest the Codes.

LECTURE I

HINDU LAW BEFORE THE CODE OF MANU

Origin of Hindu Law—the old Theory—Period of Hindu Secular Codes of Law

§ 1. The Mānava Dharma-śāstra popularly called the *Code of Manu* is the most ancient code of law still in force.[1]

Origin of Hindu Law

Before discussing the origin of that Code it would be advantageous to review the existing theory on the question of the origins of Hindu law, for it has a direct bearing on the history of the Mānava Code and the Code Yājñavalkyan.

§ 2. The current theory with which we are all familiar is that Hindu Law grew and developed in Vedic Charaṇas or Schools. The theory was propounded in the first instance by the late Professor Max Müller[2] who had based it on the analogy of the *Dharmasūtra* of the *Āpastamba* school, and was developed by the late Dr. Bühler who published translations of four Dharmasūtras in the *Sacred Books of the East* series. Bühler came to this country and studied our literature first hand. He met Brahmins who still adhered to the old Vedic learning of their particular Śākhās and could repeat from memory the Dharmasūtras along with the ritualistic sūtras of their traditional schools. He with triumphant satisfaction pointed out the extant

The old Theory

Dharmasūtras, three of which are still attached to their Kalpas, as proof positive of the theory formulated by Max Müller.[3] The same view was further em-

---

[1] In the administration of Hindu law, Manu's laws of marriage, sonship, guardianship, debt, interest, partition, succession, gifts, etc., are referred to to-day as of the first importance, whenever it is necessary to resort to first principles in order to ascertain the law (Cf. 14 M. I. A. 570).

[2] Max Müller : *Hist. Skt. Lit.* pp. 68-9.

[3] Bühler : *S. B. E.*, Vol. XXV. 1886, pp. XVIII- XLV Vol. II., Pt. I. 1897, pp. xi-xiii.

phasised by a yet greater student of Hindu Law and a former holder of this chair, Prof. Jolly of Germany.[1] It appeared as if the final word on the origin of Hindu Law had been pronounced by these scholars and the theory was accepted everywhere.

§ 3. The theory, however, was questioned for the first time in 1911, when your present lecturer suggested that there was another source of Hindu Law which seems to have been more vigorous and fruitful. That was the Artha-śāstra.[2] The Arthśāstra of Kauṭilya revealed a code of law proper, purely secular, with the express provision that the *royal law* could supersede the *dharma law*. This was not all. Passages in the Mānava Dharma-śāstra controverting some of the principles laid down in the Artha-śāṣtra, and also the Code of Yājñavalkya adopting provisions and principles of Kauṭilya's code were pointed out. The Code of Nārada which had been regarded as the first Hindu Code of pure law turned out to be largely based on the Code of the Artha-śāstra.[3]

§ 4. The date of the Artha-śāstra has been declared by competent critics—those who have made special studies in Maurya history, history of Hindu Law, the inscriptions of Aśoka, and comparative literature of the period—to be the time of Chandragupta and Kauṭilya[4]. The period therefore of the Hindu Code of law in its modern sense, *i. e.*, of secular and municipal law, has to be shifted back from the 4th and 5th century A. C.—the date of the Code of Nārada, to *cir.* 320 B. C. We have a purely secular code of about that date in the book entitled Dharmasthīyam or 'the Code for the Royal Judges' of the Artha-śāstra, which is nothing but purely secular laws to be administered by Royal

Period of Hindu secular Codes of Law

[1] Jolly : *S. B. E.*, Vol. VII.. 1880., pp. x, xx--xxii.

[2] 15 *Calcutta Weekly Note.*, cclxxiv (274), ccxc (290), ccxix (299); see also 16 C.W.N. clxx (170).

[3] *Ind. Ant.*, 1913, p. 306.

[4] Fleet— Foreword to Kauṭilya's Arthaśāstra, Translation by Shama Shastry, Mysore 1909, V. Smith—*Early History of India* (4th ed.). 160 ; Jacobi, *Ind. Ant.*, 1918 ; *Cf.* Jayaswal : *Hindu Polity*, pp., 203-14, V. Thomas : *J. R. A. S.*, 1925, p. 520.

Judges. And the Dharmasthīyam is without doubt anterior to the Codes of the Mānava and Yājñavalkya Dharmas.[1]

§ 5. Pure municipal law, however, did not originate with Kauṭilya and Chandragupta. The Artha-śāstra is avowedly based on previous works of its class—treatises and codes on the applied science of government called Daṇḍanītis and Arthaśāstras. The Code of Law of Kauṭilya likewise is based on the laws formulated and promulgated by the former schools of politicians and former codes of statesmen. Kauṭilya throughout his work cites earlier authorities—schools of politicians and individual political scientists. Such cited authorities are about 18 in number. Eighteen or nineteen prdecessors would cover about 400 years at a modest calculation. In his Code of Law he refers to the laws of such former statesmen and schools of politicians. And it may be marked that he does not refer to any writer of the Dharmaśāstra school, nor does he quote any Dharma-sūtra. It may therefore be taken that long before 320 B. C., the time of Kauṭilya, municipal law had developed in the schools of politicians and statesmen. The law which was laid down in that Imperial Code of Government, the Artha-śāstra, for administration by Judges, was the law which the statesmen and politicians had evolved and developed for centuries in the past.

Corroboration from Dharma-sūtras

§ 6. The Dharma-śāstra literature corroborates this view. It knows and recognises the authority of the Artha-śāstras. Āpastamba's Dharma-sūtra is pre-Pāṇinian in its language and oldest in form.[2]

[Bühler on purely external considerations took it to be the latest of the published Dharma-sūtras, and those which ought to have been dated centuries after were placed before it. Prof. Jolly corrected the mistake regarding the date of the Āpastamba

---

[1] Jayaswal: *op. cit.*, pp. 207-14.
[2] Bühler: *S. B. E.*, Vol. II. Pt. I. 1897, pp. xii—xix.

Sūtras which he placed about the fifth century B. C. After a careful analysis of the Sūtra law* I am glad to say that I came to the conclusion which confirms Prof. Jolly's view of the date of Āpastamba, but I regret that I cannot follow him or Prof. Macdonell in accepting the higher antiquity of the Dharma Sūtras of G a u t a m a and B a u d h ā y a n a . In their present shape they cannot go further back than 350 B. C. and 200 B. C. respectively. Nor can they be placed later. V a s i s h ṭ h a ' s Dharmasūtra was put in its present shape about 100 B. C.* These three had their second editions about these dates. Their first forms would have been much earlier, *cir.* 500 B. C. to 300 B. C., Baudhāyana being the earliest of the group. The language of Gautama is younger and there is undeniable evidence that it was revised ; Baudhāyana salutes 'Baudhāyana' amongst *sūtra-kāras* and Vasishṭha quotes a verse of Vasishṭha and has a language more recent than Gautama. All these at the same time bear traces of earlier editions.]

Ā p a s t a m b a lays down that the royal priest (who had to try certain cases of spiritual jurisdiction), was to be, to quote Bühler's translation, 'learned in the law and the science of government : राजा पुरोहितं धर्मार्थशास्त्रकुशलम् (II. 5. 10, 14) "the king (should send these transgressors—II. 5. 10, 13) to the *Purohita* who should be an expert in the D h a r m a- and the A r t h a - ś ā s t r a s." The V i s h ṇ u-d h a r m a-s ū t r a has a similar injunction : वेदेतिहासधर्म-शास्त्रार्थकुशलं कुलीनमव्यङ्गतपस्विनं पुरोहितं च वरयेत् (III. 70) : "He was to be well-versed in the V e d a, I t i h ā s a, D h a r m a - ś ā s t r a and A r t h a - ś ā s t r a." The Arthaśāstra literature and the Artha-śāstra laws which the Purohita was required to know had been thus in existence before Āpastamba's work *i. e.*, before the 5th century B. C., and before the Sūtras of Vishṇu.

The V i s h ṇ n - S m ṛ i t i is based on the Dharmasūtras of the

* See appendix A.

Kāṭhaka school and is influenced by our Mānava Dharma Śāstra in its present shape. As the latter does not recognise the validity of the Artha-śāstra laws, the provision in Vishṇu should be referred to the original Kāṭhaka Dharma-Sūtra. The Kāṭhaka Dharma is mentioned by Patañjali as the first of its class, *i. e.*, it must have been regarded as ancient by him.[1] The Artha-Śāstras would thus be contemporary with the earliest Dharma-sūtras, if not anterior to them. [There are passages in Jātakas where the technical term artha has been used in connection with the meaning of *government*.[2] It is not unlikely that some of the early works on Arthaśāstra existed in the time of the Jātakas.]

Corroboration from Mānava and Yājñavalkya Codes

§ 7. The Mānava Dharma-śāstra refers to it as artha and daṇḍa-nīti though it does not require the Purohita to know it and does not recognise its authority.[3] The Yājñavalkya uses the other term for Artha-śāstra, Daṇḍanīti, and requires the Purohita to be versed in it.[4] Yājñavalkya, as we shall see later, also uses the term *Artha-śāstra* in discussing its authority as against the Dharma-śāstra.

Real province of the Dharmsûtras

§ 8. An analysis of Āpastamba's Dharma-sūtras reveals the fact that the Dharma laws were originally concerned with ceremonial and religious conduct, with the infliction of penances as the spiritual counterpart of the royal or Artha-śāstra administration of criminal law, with the administration of the hermitage and the regulation of hermit life, and with the ceremonies on death and the obligation of the successor to perform

[1] Jolly : *S. B. E.* Vol. VII. p. xiv. *Mahābhāshya*, Benares Ed., IV, fols. 82 b and 75b; Kielhorn II. 315.

[2] J. II.30, J4.

[3] M., VII 43 and 60; II. 13; 15 C. W. N., CCXC (290); CCXCIX (299).

[4] *Yājñavalkyasmṛiti*, 1. 313 :

पुरोहितं प्रकुर्वीत दैवज्ञमुदितोदितम् ।
दण्डनीत्यां च कुशलमथर्वाङ्गिरसे तथा ॥ Cf. also 1·311.

those rites, and only consequently and subsequently with the rights of the twice-born regarding the succession itself. It is interesting to note that the Vaikhānasa Dharma Praśna published recently by the Travancore state, which probably is the earliest Dharma-sūtra, yet published,[1] does not touch the subject of succession. But discussions quoted by Yāska (III. 1.) prove that the question of inheritance was a favourite subject of speculation amongst Vedic scholars and that technical terms of the law of inheritance had already come in vogue. Probably in the beginning, inheritance was not a topic of the Dharma literature and it found place there later. This is suggested by its position in Gautama where it comes as the very last, even after the Penances.[2]

§ 9. The Vaikhānasa-dharma lays down the duties of the Kshatriya as one of the Varṇas, but it says nothing about the king or administration. Āpastamba discussing the *Dharma* for the Kshatriya as a householder, prescribes only five rules of political import. I may better quote them here as it is in their place that chapters on law and legal administration have been introduced in later Dharmasūtras and Dharmaśāstras :—

(1) The Kshatriya shall act in war according to the canons laid down by military authors : 'युद्धे उद्योगा यथोपायमुपदिशन्ति तथा प्रतिपत्तव्यम् ।' (II. 5, 10, 10).

Further a principle is emphasised or introduced by the Dharma school in this connection in these words :

"The Hindus (Āryas) forbid the slaughter of those who have laid down arms, of those who (beg for peace) with flying hair or joined hands, and of fugitives" (II. 5. 10. 11).

A violation of this Hindu law of war was brought by

---

[1] Cf. *the Vaikhānasadharmapraśna*, Ed. Gaṇapati Śāśtrī, Trivandrum, 1913, pp.1-51. *Vaikhānasa-mata* is mentioned by the Mānava Dh. Ś. VI. 21. It is cited by Baudhāyana, Dh. Ś., II. 6, 11., 14-15, III 3. 15. 17. (Bühler, XXV, 28 Intro.). A comparison of the book of Vikhanas now published with Baudhāyana shows that the book was before Baudhāyana when he wrote his Dharmaśāstra.

[2] Stenzler : *The Institutes of Gautama*, London, 1876, pp. 32-4.

D h a r m a - S ū t r a - k ā r a s under the spiritual or ecclesiastical jurisdiction of Dharma. The violation was to be taken as a violation of Dharma law entailing the spiritual punishment of penance. The law in fact directed against the wantonness of the conquering soldier (Kshatriya), and it is not necessarily a law for the king.

The next provision is very important as it shows the junction of the Dharma and Artha (royal) jurisdictions :

(2) "The spiritual guide shall order those who (whilst) participating according to the Śāstras (Dharma) have gone astray through the weakness of their appetites, to perform penances proportionate to their (sinful) acts as laid down (in the Śāstra) (III, 5. 11. 12.). If they (such persons) disobey the Śāstra (injunctions) he (the Āchārya, spritual guide) shall take him to the King (13). The King shall (send them) to the Purohita *versed* in the D h a r m a and A r t h a (śāstras) (14) who shall order the Brahmin culprits to do the penance (15) and reduce them to obedience by methods short of killing and slavery according to their physical strength(16). In the case of other castes, the king after having examined their acts may punish them up to death (II. 5. 11. 1)."

Thus we see that the D h a r m a j u r i s d i c t i o n is seeking the help of the r o y a l j u r i s d i c t i o n and the jurisdiction of law proper to enforce the sanction of Dharma, or in the alternative, to give the recalcitrant over to law for both his crime and sin. The king had the authority to rule and punish (2. 5. 10. 6.).[1] It is not that an alternative jurisdiction in favour of the king was being created. A man committing a crime was in any case responsible to the King's law, the Artha law. But he had to do his penance independently. The penance-punishment was a sacerdotal punishment. It was awarded by sacerdotal leaders

[1] Bühler : *Āpastambīya-Dharmasūtram.*, p. 67. (2. 5. 10. 6)—
एतान्येव क्षत्रियस्याध्यापनयाजनप्रतिग्रहणानीति परिहाप्य दण्डयुद्धाधिकानि ।

and these leaders took the help of the king when they were not obeyed.

When the Dharma law thus joined hands with the Artha law, the former had to suggest and emphasise certain principles of the Dharma school. For example, Āpastamba next adds :

(3) "No one (apparently referring to the people thus brought before the king) shall be punished in case of doubt" न च सन्देहे दण्डं कुर्यात्। (II. 5. 11. 2).

(4) "Having searchingly investigated through cross-examination and ordeals, the king may convict : सुविचितं विचित्या दैवप्रश्नेभ्यो राजा दण्डाय प्रतिपद्येत (II. 5. 11. 3). The king who acts thus succeeds in both the worlds" (II. 5. 11. 6).

That no one should be punished in a case of doubt was an equitable doctrine of the Dharma school which would have probably found approval in the Artha school. But the latter never allowed ordeals in their proof. They are not allowed in Kauṭilya's Artha-śāstra laws ;[1] they have not been even shown the courtesy of being discussed and then rejected. After the Brahmin political and social revival under the Śuṅgas and Kāṇvas the cause of the ordeals was vigorously advocated. A century or two later a political revolution is dramatised as the result of the courts not allowing the ordeal trial to a Brahmin accused in a murder case. The dharma school which dealt with matters divine advocated the divine mode of proof even in the law court and they coaxed the king with the promise of the other world. But the school of political thinkers who recognised superstition only to exploit it for revenue, and one of whom even went the length of declaring the Vedas as a sort of useful screen for politicians,[2] would not sanction such a superstitious mode of proof in the law courts.

[1] Sastri, R. Shama, *The Arthaśāstra of Kauṭilya*, 1909, pp. 140-50.

[2] *Ibid.*, p. 6.

वार्त्ता दण्डनीतिश्चेति बार्हस्पत्याः—संवरणमात्रं हि त्रयी लोकयात्राविद इति।

The above are all the Dharma-laws for the king in the chapter on the duties of the Varṇas in Āpastamba's Dharmasūtra. But Āpastamba further adds a sort of appendix, after exhausting the topics of the Dharma law, on the d u t i e s of the k i n g from the Dharma point of view :

"The general and special duties of all castes have been explained. But we will now declare those of the k i n g in particular".
—(II.10.25.1).[1]

The rules which follow in 5 chapters (II. 10.25.26.27.28.29) are on subjects which came under the Dharma jurisdiction or are principles which the Dharma lawyer wanted to be taken notice of by the administrators of the Artha or Secular law. The rules may be summarised as follows :

1. That amongst the public buildings of the king, there should be a building for the *śrotriya* (ritualist) Brahmins who may chance to come from outside to the capital (25).

2. That gambling should be brought under state-control (25). (Apparently the Dharma school regarded it as a vice to be discouraged).

3. Likewise, gladiatoring, singing, dancing and music were to be controlled by government (25).

4. That it was the king's duty to protect those who suffer from want in the kingdom (25).

5. That it was his duty to see that nowhere in his kingdom theft was committed (25). (Theft was regarded as a heinous sin by the Dharma lawyers.)

6. That the king should not live on more than his religious and political chiefs (25). The Dharma lawyers advocate an equal remuneration. In their view the office of the king did not entail greater labour and responsibility than that of the religious and political chiefs of the state. Probably the Artha School which

---

[1] व्याख्याताः सर्ववर्णानां साधारण-वैशेषिका धर्माः ।
राज्ञस्तु विशेषाद्वक्ष्यामः ॥१॥

had a regular civil list as evidenced by the Kauṭilîya, was in favour of allowing a larger allowance to the king.[1]

7. That the king may give gifts to the Brahmins on condition that the officers of state do not oppose it. (26.1). This rule was a check on the royal power even in the case of charity. As an example we may recall the opposition of the ministers to the extravagant giving of property to the Buddhist Saṅgha by Aśoka. The Chancellor Rādha-Gupta did what the Dharma lawyer called "Uparodha", refusing to ratify the gift.[2] All the deeds of gifts in copper-plates are countersigned by a Minister in Hindu India[2]. The Artha Śāstra also enjoins that the Ministers' opinion should be followed.[2]

8. That the administration was responsible for the crime of theft (26.6-9). This was a rule of Dharma not to be found in the Artha-Śāstras. The Dharma school emphasised the responsibility from the Dharma point of view. The king would in their opinion become liable to penance if he did not keep the kingdom free from theft.

9 (a). That bravery in protecting the realm was the real performance of sacrifice by the king, and his reward was spiritual (26.2).

9 (b). That the taxes sanctioned by the Dharma Śāstra alone should be realised, and students, women, working people, learners, Brahmin ascetics, and those disqualified to succeed were to be exempted from all taxation (26. 10. 17.)

10. Certain rules regarding adultery. Adultery was a sin to which the Dharma administration paid special attention. Minute rules about penance-penalties and expiation are given. The Dharma school claimed jurisdiction over it, as the marriage itself was a creation of the Dharma law "धर्माद्धि संबन्धः" (II.10.27.1). The Dharma school extends the law to some new cases and brings the rules (II. 10. 26., 18-24. II.10.27.,1-13) to the notice of the king's administration.

---

[1] *Cf.* AŚ. ch. 91; *Hindu Polity,* II. p. 136.

[2] *H. P.* II, pp. 143, 150.

11. Repressive punishment against the Śūdras who showed contempt to the members of the Dharma school. (II 10. 27. 14.) The rules were necessitated by the rise of heterodoxy. Aśvaghosha, though much later, criticising the Dharma school says that the Buddhist Śūdras were as learned as the Brahmins and they were as good as the Brahmins.[1] As the Buddhists were not under the control of Dharma jurisdiction, the help of the state was sought. No such law against the Śūdra is found in the Vaikhānasa Dharma-sūtra which is referred to in Manu's Code and is evidently a work of the pre-Buddhist period.[2]

12. The Brahmins were also brought under the king's jurisdiction both for serious and minor offences (II. 10. 27. 11, 17—20).

13. Abuse of the privilege of seeking the "*sacred shelter*" of the royal priest and the *Snātaka* and the king was discouraged. Refuge was to be ineffectual in capital offences (27. 20).

14. The rules in chapter 28 refer to the offences committed in the "Araṇya" area, that is, the area set apart for the colony of the people in the third (*Vāna-prastha*) *Āśrama*. They lived outside the city in an enclosed area which was an artificial forest.[3] There was culturable land for raising modest crops of grain and vegetables for the hermits, some of whom cultivated themselves while others had sub-cultivators and labourers. The rules given here are intended to protect them from unruly herdsmen and sub-cultivators and labourers who disregarded their contracts. Even the hermits, for their acts which offended against the peace of the colony, were put under the king's jurisdiction. "He who takes the property of another—fuel, water, roots, flowers, fruits, incense, fodder or vegetables, if he is not a learned man, is to be beaten by words (reprimanded) ; if he is learned, he shall be deprived of his

[1] Aśvaghosha's *Vajrachchhedikā*.
[2] Cf. The *Vaikhānasadharmapraśna*, op. cit. See *Manu*, Ch. VI. 21.
[3] *Āpastamba*, *op. cit.*, p. 95....अरण्ये ...2. 11. 28. 8. AŚ., Ch. 23.

cloth.[1] And if the king does not punish when (these) offences are committed he shall become guilty".

15. Next follow two Dharma principles on the commission of offences : he who makes another, he who counsels another, to commit an offence and he who commits the offence, are all sharers in the guilt. One repeating an offence is specially guilty.

16. That both husband and wife have mastery over property, that is, there can be no offence by one against the other in respect of their property. Agents employed by either are lawful.

17. That cases of Dharma law should be decided by the educated elders coming of good stock, gifted with intelligence and jealous of maintaining the Dharmas. In doubtful cases they should rely on ordeals and inference.

18. Oaths which have been treated by Hindu lawyers as a species of ordeal, came under the province of the Dharma thinkers. They recommend its application to all witnesses in the king's courts, and Āpastamba prescribes special formulæ to be administered (II.11. 29.7-10).

19. In matters not provided for, only such Dharma laws are to be accepted about which all the Aryan countries are unanimous.

The above analysis covers all the 'l a w s' in Āpastamba, which have been treated as "Royal duties: the Civil and Criminal Laws". But in fact they are not secular laws. Some are political and legal principles from the Dharma point of view and others are special rules on the offences which fell under the Dharma jurisdiction. There is not, for instance, a word about sale, mortgage, and other contracts, not a word about the majority of crimes. B a u d h ā y a n a 's Dharma rules are far fewer, resembling in bulk the original rules of Āpastamba about the king and his laws : (a) that the king should not use poisoned and forked arrows, and that he should not turn back from the battle-field; (b) that Dharma

[1] *Ibid.* p. 95. विदुषो वाससः परिमोषणम् । 2. 11. 28. 11.

allows only certain taxes which are the salary of the king, and that he should not be oppressive and arbitrary in taxation ; (c) the king should protect ownerless properties for a year, and then take them if they did not belong to a Brahmin ; (d) royal punishment for the Brahmins ; (e) punishment and penances in slaughter of men and lower animals ; (f) oath formulæ for witnesses.

The meaning of Vyavahāra and its province.

§ 10. An analysis of Gautama's Dharma laws will reveal a similar result.[1] All these provisions which have been taken by European scholars to have been civil and criminal laws are not so. They are really part of the *Dharma* or penance law. Then, where were the real and regular civil and criminal laws of the country ? My answer is : they were in the Arthaśāstras or the Codes of Administration.

There are indications that the secular and municipal laws were called the *Vyavahāra laws.* The Mahā-Bhārata[2] declares that the authority of the Vyavahāra laws is as sacred and great as that of the Dharma law. The Dharma law, it says, has its origin in the Vedic lore, and the Vyavahāra has its origin in political governance and the king, that governance is a sacred act, being ordained by the Creator, its laws (Vyavahāra law) consequently are sacred :

भर्तृप्रत्यय उत्पन्नो व्यवहारस्तथाविधः । (50)
उक्तो यश्चापि दण्डोऽसौ भर्तृप्रत्यय-लक्षणः ।
ज्ञेयो नः स नरेन्द्रस्थो दण्डः प्रत्यय एव च ॥ (52)

"*Vyavahāra* in that way rises from the Master (Sovereign). It is also called '*Daṇḍa*' or *Governance* as its authority is from the Master. It is known to be established in the King. *Daṇḍa* (Daṇḍanīti, Artha-śāstra) is also that authority."

---

[1] Vasishṭha must be left out of consideration, it being clearly much later.
[2] XII. 121.

व्यवहारः स्मृतो यश्च स वेदविषयात्मकः । (53)

यश्च वेदप्रसूतात्मा सधर्मो गुणदर्शनः ॥ (54)

व्यवहारः प्रजागोप्ता ब्रह्मदिष्टो युधिष्ठिर ।

त्रीन्धारयति लोकान् सत्यात्मा भूतिवर्धनः ॥ (55)

"That *Vyavahāra* Law which is *Smṛita*, deals with Vedic subjects; that which is derived from the Vedas is *Dharma.* It regulates *guṇas* (appetites) (while) the *Vyavahāra is the protector of the subjects.* O Yudhishṭhira ! it is enjoined by the Creator. It upholds the three worlds, truth is its soul; it ensures prosperity of the animate world."

The commentator explaining "dharma" in the above verse says, प्रायश्चित्तदण्डो धर्म एव, "*Dharma* (is law) inasmuch as it awards the punishment of *Penance*".

यश्च दण्डः स दृष्टो नो व्यवहारः सनातनः ।

व्यवहारश्च दृष्टो यः स वेद इति नः श्रुतिः ॥ (56)

"That what is the 'Daṇḍa' (nīti) is laid down as our traditional Vyavahāra (law). The Vyavahāra thus laid down is our Veda—that is, our (of the Rulers) sacred tradition".

This saying of Bhīshma that the Vyavahāra as laid down in the Daṇḍa-Nīti is the Veda for the Kshatriya is an emphatic assertion of the authority of the Vyavahāra law. It implies that the D h a r m a is s a c e r d o t a l and the V y a v a h ā r a s e c u l a r.

§ 11. Kauṭilya says that *Dharma*, *Vyavahāra*, *Customs* and *Royal ordinance* are the four legs of law suits, that the latter in each case may supersede the former.[1] He further contemplates the possibility of a conflict occurring between the Dharma-śāstra and the Vyavahāra-śāstra, and there the Dharma-śāstra had

[1] *Arthaśāstra., op. cit.* p. 150 (ch. 58).

धर्मश्च व्यवहारश्च चरित्रं राजशासनम् ।

विवादार्थश्चतुष्पादः पश्चिमः पूर्वबाधकः ॥

to be followed if not opposed to reason. Here the Vyavahāra-śāstra is contrasted with the Dharma-śāstra. It clearly implies a body of secular law.

As we have seen, there were rules recommended by the Dharma school about the offences primarily of their jurisdiction. They as well as the equitable principles of that school must have been followed and also the penances must have been enforced by royal law-courts. It would be to all these that Kauṭilya refers to under Dharma-śāstra.

Kauṭilya indicates the province of the Dharma and Vyavahāra laws (p. 150). He mentions 'truth' (oaths), as an example of Dharma and as an example of Vyavahāra he mentions the law about the evidence of witnesses which seems to have been a creation of the secular law. In other places in the Kauṭilīya the use of the word Vyavahāra denotes civil law: विवाहपूर्वो व्यवहारः[1] where it means the rights of civil law, प्राप्तव्यवहाराः[2] 'those to whom legal rights are available', and व्यावहारिकानर्थान्[3] where 'Vyavahāra' is 'legal'. In *Vyavahāra-sthāpanā*[4], Vyavahāra means the law of contract. Probably it was the law of contract, which was the chief feature of the Artha-śāstra and which the Artha-śāstra lawyers developed exclusively, that gave the name to their system of secular law.

Kauṭilya, again, refers to a Dharma-rule in a way that it throws a flood of light on the distinction between the Dharma and the Vyavahāra laws. He says that interest allowed by the Dharma law is $1\frac{1}{4}\%$ monthly. After stating this he mentions the rate allowed by 'Vyavahāra' (*viz.* 5%) सपादपणा धर्म्या मासवृद्धिः पणशतस्य, पञ्चपणा व्यावहारिकी । (ch. 8). Now referring to the Dharma Sūtras

---

[1] *Arthaśāstra, op. cit.* p. 151. ch. 59.
[2] *Arthaśāstra, op. cit.*, p. 154.

द्वादशवर्षा स्त्री प्राप्तव्यवहारा भवति ... ।

[3] *Arthaśāstra, op. cit.*, p. 147.

... ... व्यावहारिकानर्थान् कुर्युः ।

[4] *Arthaśāstra, op. cit.*, pp. 147-8.

(Baudhāyana[1] and Gautama[2]), we do find that they allow only $1\frac{1}{4}\%$. But the Dharma-śāstra of Manu, though it emphasises the $1\frac{1}{4}\%$ rule, allows also the Vyavahāra law rate and so does Yājñavalkya.[3] The latter two therefore recognise the rate which had been sanctioned by the Vyavahāra and allowed by the law courts.

§ 12. In the time of the Buddha the royal judge is called the *Vyāvahārika*. He is called so, I think, also in Aśoka's inscriptions. Khāravela's inscription distinguishes between *vyavahāra* and *vidhi*. The former, no doubt, means municipal law and the latter, *dharma*. At the same time *dharma* is occasionally used to denote law generally in Buddhist literature and also in Kauṭilya (e.g. *dharmastha* for a judge).

§ 13. Yājñavalkya calls the law proper portion of his work the *Vyavahāra-adhyāya* 'the book on secular laws' (Book II). The Nārada-smṛiti uses the word in the sense of secular laws.

§ 14. In the definite sense of secular law it occurs in Gautama for the first time amongst the Dharma sūtras:

तस्य व्यवहारो वेदो धर्मशास्त्राण्यङ्गानि पुराणम् ।
देश-जाति कुल-धर्माश्चाम्नायैरविरुद्धा प्रमाणम् ॥ XI. 19·20.

"For him (the king) the *Vyavahāra*, the Veda, the Dharma-śāstras, the Aṅgas, the Purāṇas, and also the laws of the country, castes and *kulas*, which are not opposed to the (sacred records), are authority". It may be marked that the Vyavahāra here is of the highest authority, being placed first. By Gautama's time the Artha-laws apparently acquired the technical name 'Vyavahāra'. Formerly they seem to have been referred to by the term '*Artha*' or '*Artha-śāstra*' and *Daṇḍa*.

---

[1] *Baudhāyana*, 1.5.10.22.
[2] *Gautama*, *op. cit.* p 16. (12.29)—

कुसीदवृद्धिर्धर्म्या विंशतिः पञ्चमाषकी मासम् ।

[3] M. VIII. 140, 142, 152 ; Y. II. 37.

§ 15. The *artha* laws were king's laws or *rājaśāsana* in the language of Kauṭilya. That the authority of the king's or *artha* laws was supreme, is seen from a passage of the orthodox *Mahā-Bhāshya* (*cir.* 150 B.C.) which says 'this is neither ordained by the ruler, nor by the *dharmasūtra-kāras* ("authors of the Dharma-Sūtras")—नेवेश्वर आज्ञापयति नापि धर्मसूत्रकाराः पठन्ति (P. 1. 1. 46).[1]

Secular laws and King's law in the Sūtra period.

Here the royal authority is superior to the Dharma-sūtras according to Sanskrit syntax. It is mentioned first and the Dharma-sūtras are placed after.

Vasishṭha writing about the administration of law begins with: "Now about the *Vyavahāras* (laws),"[2] and directs that the king's administration of law should be impartial and guided by the rules of the sciences of the first two castes आद्यवर्णयोर्विद्यान्तत:, that is, the Dharma-vidyā and the Artha-vidyā (or, as Bühler says, the Daṇḍa-nīti).

§ 16. *The above data conclusively establish the fact that the secular laws or king's laws in the sūtra period were different from the Dharma law.* They were to be found in an independent class of literature—the Artha-śāstras. The Dharma-law, though it greatly influenced the municipal law, cannot be treated as the real or main origin of Hindu Law. The provinces of the Dharma and the Artha laws were separate. In secular matters the authority of the latter and the kingly enactments was the only binding authority. But in the *Mānava-dharma-śāstra*, for the first time, we find the Dharma-śāstra invading upon and appropriating the province of the Artha law and making the latter only an appanage to its own system. The reason was, as we shall see presently, that the sacerdotal power became also the political power in the country. The law of the politician, therefore, got merged into the law of the sacerdotalist. This invasion of the law proper by the Dharma-

The Secular and Dharma systems in the Mānava Code.

[1] On *Iśvara*, 'Ruler', see *Mahābhāshya* on P. 6.1.2. (9), Kielhorn, III. 7; *cf. Iśvara-kāmita* in Vātsyāyana, Chakladar, *Studies in Vāts.*; p. 31 (1929). [2] *Vasishṭha*, XVI. 1.

śāstra explains the sudden appearance of a fully developed system of law in the Dharma literature in the shape of the Mānava Code. The portions of the Dharmasūtras which former scholars treated as law proper, but which, as we have seen, are not so, cover only three or four pages in print, while Manu's Code gives 982 out of its 2684 verses to the king and the law to be administered by him. It divides the legal subjects in eighteen 'Titles'. The 'Eighteen Titles' are really the 'eighteen titles' of Kauṭilya's 'Code for Judges', with slight modifications. In ignorance of these circumstances, which we now know, Bühler tried in vain to explain the origin of the Mānava Code by reference to a hypothetical 'Mānava-dharma-sūtra.' His study to establish that thesis covers over 100 pages of one of the volumes of the *Sacred Books of the East* ('The Laws of Manu'). It is a monument of research and wide scholarship, but it fails in its object. The very arguments of that learned writer go to show that there was no such work as 'Mānava-dharma-sūtra' as a precursor to the Mānava-dharma-śāstra[1].

The Dharma literature before the Mānava Code.

§ 17. But before we go into the latter subject we may briefly survey the history of the early Dharma literature.

Long before Kauṭilya and also Āpastamba, there had been Dharma-sūtras in existence. Pāṇini gives a special rule for the Dharma-books, चरणेभ्यो धर्मवत् (IV.2.46). According to this rule the Vedic *charaṇas* or schools had their Dharma books which were called after their names.

The Dharma books of several charaṇas are named by Patañjali, to wit[2]:

the Kāṭhaka Dharma,
the Kālāpaka ,,
the Maudaka ,,
the Paippalādaka ,,

---

[1] See Lecture II below.
[2] P. IV. 3. 120.

and the Ā t h a r v a ṇ a (Atharva-vedic) Dharma (P.IV.3. 131). That all these were in sūtras is proved by Patañjali's comment cited above, 'nor do the authors of the Dharma-sūtras read(enjoin) this'. But like Āpastamba and Kauṭilya, Patañjali calls them collectively the 'śāstra' or 'dharma-śāstra' (P.6.1.84 ; 1.2.64 (39). The term *Dharma-śāstra* does not necessarily imply that the literature under that name must be in verses, as supposed by some scholars. The "Artha-śāstra" of Kauṭilya and Gautama's "Dharma-śāstra" dislodge that assumption.

§ 18. Before the time of Patañjali, text-books independent of Vedic schools, had been already in existence in sūtra style (intermixed with *ślokas*), for there were people who devoted themselves solely to the study of the D h a r m a - v i d y ā (*Mahābhāshya* on P. IV.2.60). I may point out that G a u t a m a ' s Sūtra and V a s i s h ṭ h a ' s Sūtra are good examples of this class of literature. The Dharma-śāstra had already separated itself from the A ṅ g a *s* at the time when the Gautama-sūtras assumed the present form. In the *sūtra* quoted above *dharmaśāstra* is mentioned as independent of the Aṅgas which also are mentioned along with them.

§ 19. Principles of Dharma or principles allied to Dharma were to be found in a P u r ā ṇ a literature which was contemporaneous with the *sūtras*. The evidence of the Gautama-dharma-sūtra is decisive on the point : **तस्य व्यवहारो वेदो धर्मशास्त्राण्यङ्गानि पुराणम्.** This is also confirmed by Āpastamba, who like Gautama, mentions the Purāṇa. Āpastamba in one place definitely names it and quotes a *sūtra* from it. It was the *Bhavishyat Purāṇa.*[1] The Purāṇa was drawn upon very often by the Dharma-sūtra-kāra*s*. Several principles of purely equitable nature were borrowed from the Purāṇa by the Dharma-sūtra-kāra*s*, who regarded it with respect and as a source of *Dharma*. Such was the condition of the D h a r m a l i t e r a t u r e when the M ā n a v a C o d e made its appearance on the scene.

---

[1] II. 9. 24. (6). Cf. 1. 6. 19 (13) where *ślokas* from the Purāṇa are quoted, which are also found in Manu (IV, 248-40). *Cf.* also *ibid.* (14) and (15) = M., IV. 211—2, VIII. 317.

LECTURE II

DATE AND ORIGIN OF THE CODE OF MANU

Earlier views on its date—Manu the political writer different from Manu the lawyer—Mānava Gṛihya—Mānava Srāddha-kalpa—Vishnu-Smṛiti—Earliest mention of the Code of Manu—Parthians—Patañjali—definition of the Āryāvarta—Political character of our Code—Code's Orthodoxy—its political reason—Mānava a Suṅgan Code—its real author—no Mānava Dharmasūtra—Mānava Code and Gîtā.

Necessity of fixing the date of the Mānava Code.

§ 1. Let us now proceed to discuss the date of the Mānava Code. It is very important to find out its date. By discovering it, we may refer this epoch-making work to the circumstances under which it was produced. The Code of Napoleon becomes explicable only when we know the facts and the circumstances of the French Revolution. Is there any method by which we can acquaint ourselves with the circumstances under which the "Code of Manu" was promulgated and accepted? The only method is to discover its definite date.

Earlier views on its date.

§ 2. Max Müller would place the Code later than the fourth century A.C. This view was, however, based not on any material in the Mānava Dharma Sāstra but on a verse of the Vṛiddha Manu or the "Enlarged Manu."[1] The view has been disposed of by Bühler.[2] Professor Macdonell in his *History of Sanskrit Literature* (p. 428) says that the Code probably assumed its present shape not much later than 200 A.C. But he gives no reason. Dr. Jolly after deprecating the fashion of "undue depreciation of the antiquity

---

[1] Max Müller: *India, What can it teach us?*, p. 366.

[2] Bühler: *Manu, S.B.E., op. cit.*, p. cxvii.

and historical importance of the Code of Manu" that had "become rather common in these days," (Tagore Lectures, 1883, p. 43), assigns it to a period before that of Yājñavalkya which "cannot be referred to an earlier date than the first centuries A.D." (p. 49). Bühler placed it within comparatively definite limits. He spent great time over a critical study of the Code, and came to the conclusion that the Code, as we have it, existed in the second century of the Christian era, and was to be dated between the second century B.C. and the beginning of the second century A.C. or somewhat earlier.[1] We may, now, with the result of recent researches into Indian history and fresh data, narrow down these limits, extending over four centuries, to a reasonable span, and refer the work to a definite chapter of Indian history.

§ 3. Let us first separate our Manu from the other Manus of Sanskrit literature.

Other Manus.

Manu's name is associated by Kāmandaka[2] with certain opinions which are not to be traced in our Mānava Dharma. Bühler was inclined to disregard the evidence as proving the existence of a treatise on political subjects, independent of the Mānava-Dharma Code.[3] Bühler's view is no more maintainable after the discovery of Kauṭilya's work. Kauṭilya mentions, as I have already pointed out[4], that he was drawing upon former Artha-śāstras and he quotes passages from them. One of his authorities was a work of a school of politicians called the School of the Mānavas[5], from which he cites passages in *sūtras* and rejects its opinions. The existence, thus, of a Mānava Artha Śāstra or Mānava Rāja-śāstra [or M. Rāja-dharma] is a historical fact beyond all doubt. Kāmandaka[6], who follows

[1] Bühler : *Manu, S. B. E., op. cit.* pp. cxvii-viii.
[2] Kāmandaka : *Nītisāra*, II.3 ; XI.67.
[3] Bühler : *Manu, S. B. E., op. cit.* pp. xxxvi-viii.
[4] *Hindu Polity*, i, p. 4.
[5] They may not be necessarily identical with the Vedic school of the Mānavas.
[6] *Kauṭilya's Arthaśāstra, op. cit.*, p. 6.

Kauṭilya also refers to that work.[1] In addition to the actual quotations from the Mānava Artha-śāstra in Kauṭilya we have this work quoted also in the Mahā-Bhārata. In the Mahā-Bhārata[2] instead of Kauṭilya's (school of the) "M ā n a v a *s*" it is attributed to a M a n u, M a n u P r ā c h e t a s a. Probably the work itself stood under the name of one author, like our Āpastamba Dharma-sūtra, but it was known to be the work of a school as treated by Kauṭilya. Manu Prāchetasa is described as one of the authors of the Rāja-śāstras or Politics, along with Bṛihaspati, Uśanas, Viśālāksha, Indra, the author of the Bāhudantaka, and one Gauraśiras, all of whom, except the last, have been quoted by Kauṭilya.[3] T h e Mahā-Bhārata has a tendency to exaggerate these human and historical authors into divine and mythical personages. V i ś ā l ā k s h a, a favourite authority of Kauṭilya, who was not even the founder of a school, has been converted into a god = Śiva of 'large eyes.'[4] Likewise, the author of the "B ā h u d a n t a k a" A r t h a-ś ā s t r a, a work not mentioned by name in Kauṭilya, but mentioned in the Mahā-Bhārata, has been cited by Kauṭilya as Bāhudantî-putra,[5] an ancient style of reference. The Mahā-Bhārata converts him into 'the thousand-eyed Indra.'[6] The Artha-śāstra of the Mānavas, which was referable to a human Manu or a Mānavāchārya, was likewise attributed to the son of Prachetas, to distinguish him, no doubt, from Manu Svāyambhuva, the reputed author of our code of law. The same author or rather the same work is alluded to by the writer of the P a ñ c h a-T a n t r a when he enumerates Manu amongst his political authorities, the authors of the N a y a ś ā s t r a *s* (Codes on Polity)[7] : Manu, V ā c h a s p a t i (Bṛihaspati), Ś u k r a (Uśanas), P a r ā ś a r a, and his son, and Chāṇakya (Kauṭilya). The two P a r ā ś a r a s

---

1 *Kāmandaka, op. cit. supra.*
2 *Mahābhārata*, XII. 57. 2.
3 *Kauṭilya's Arthaśāstra, op. cit.*, pp. viii, 6, 14.
4 *Mahā-Bhārata*, XII. 57. 1-2.
5 *Kauṭilya's Arthaśāstra, op. cit.*, p. 14.
6 *MBh.*, XII. 57-2.
7 *Pañchatantra*, I.

are also quoted by Kauṭilya[1], and so are the Bārhaspatya and Auśanasa *Arthasāstras.*[2]

§ 4. The work of Manu, the politician, was extant as late as the tenth century A.C., for I see a quotation from it in sūtra, in Somadeva's[3] work, which says that even the ascetics must pay the legal tax to the king. This is a view quite opposed to our Mānava Dharmaśāstra.[4] Similarly, the opinions quoted in sūtras by Kauṭilya from the Mānava work on Politics and the two verses quoted by the Mahā-Bhārata have not the remotest connection with our Mānava Dharma Code. On the other hand, contrary provisions are to be had in that Code. Thus, then, there was no affinity between the pre-Kauṭilya Mānava Rāja-śāstra and the Mānava Dharma-śāstra. Nor does the latter allude to the former in any way.

§ 5. We should bear in mind this distinction between this political treatise of the historical Mānava school and our Dharma-śāstra attributed to the Adam of the Hindu race. The distinction would save us from much confusion. We must, likewise, distinguish the latter from the historical Mānvāchārya, the author of the Mānava Gṛihya-sūtra, from whom a school of the Krishṇa Yajurveda derives its name (Mānava charaṇa). The Mānava Gṛihya-sūtra is still current in Western India and has been published in Russia. The Ṭīkākāra [commentator] Ashṭāvakra-deva gives the name of the author as above, and the original name of his Gṛihya-sūtra as the Bṛihad-dharma. This name is also to be carefully noted. It proves that there was no separate Dharma-sūtra of the school written, according to the tradition of that school.

Our Code and the Mānava Gṛihya-sūtra.

Two competent European scholars, Jolly and Bradke, who made a study of the Mānava Gṛihya-sūtra, have declared that

[1] *Kauṭ. AS'.* op. cit. p. 32.
[2] *Kauṭ. AS'.* op. cit. p. 6.
[3] *Somadeva, Nītivākyāmṛita, VI.* See *HP.*, i. p. 8 *n.* for the quotation.
[4] *Manu,* VII. 133-137.

no affinity between it and our Manu's Dharma-śāstra could be traced.[1] Utterly dissimilar doctrines on important questions like marriage were met with. It is thus evident that no connection between our Mānava Dharma-śāstra and the Vedic school founded by Mānava existed.

§ 6. Bühler thought that he found the missing link between the Mānava Dharma-śāstra and the Vedic Mānava School in the Śrāddha-kalpa. But this book is not a regular part of the literature of the Mānava school. It is not always connected with it[2]. Bhāsa[3] treated it as an independent manual, and like the Artha-śāstra of the Mānavas, it was distinguished from the Manu of our Dharma-śāstra and from the Mānavas of the Vedic school by being attributed to Manu Prāchetasa (*Pratimā*, p. 79), 'प्राचेतसं श्राद्धकल्पम्'. Its adoption by the present Yajurvedī Mānavas is not invariable and seems to be recent. Above all, the connection alleged by Bühler, is very slight, consisting of only seven verses which are common to both.[4] The 'connection' is more than neutralised by otherwise total disagreement. The seven verses might have been very well introduced from our Dharma-śāstra. Then, again, Jolly and Bühler sought to establish a connection through the Vishṇu-smṛiti.[5] The latter is founded on the Dharma-sūtras of the Kaṭha school of the Krishṇa Yajus, and very many doctrines are common to Vishṇu and our Manu. By this community a connection between the two Vedic schools of Kaṭha and Mānava and a consequential affinity between our Manu's doctrines and the Mānava school have been presumed. The process is too far-fetched to be convincing. The Vishṇu Smṛiti is admittedly later than Manu's

---

1 Jolly : *S. B. E.*, vol. vii. *Introduction.*
Von Bradke : *Z.D.M.G.*, vol. xxxvi, 1882, pp. 417-477, (*Über das Mānava Gṛihya Sūtra*)

2 Bühler : *Manu, S. B. E., op. cit.*, pp. xl-xlii.

3 Bhāsa : *Pratimā*, Trivandum, 1915, p. 79.

4 Bühler : *Manu, op. cit.* p. xliii.

5 *Ibid.*, p. xliv. Jolly, *S. B. E.*, vol. VII. p. xxv-xxvii.

Code and the similarity can be explained in the natural way by supposing the influence of the former on the latter work[1]. Nor, as Bradke[2] pointed out, have we the original Kāṭhaka before us to warrant the theory.

§ 7. Although we have no trace that the Code is based on any work of the Mānava school, nor is there any trace (as we shall see hereafter) of a Mānava-dharma-sūtra, still in the light of new evidence it is now certain that the Code is the work of a historical person who called himself and was called by others a Mānava.

Earliest mention.

§ 8. The chief feature of our Code is that it is attributed to the primeval Manu, Manu-Svāyambhuva, son of Svayambhū or the Creator. There could not have been two Mānava-dharma-śāstras with this claim. The Dharma-śāstra therefore referred to in Vātsyāyana's Kāma-sūtra, a work of about the third century A.C.[3], must have reference to this Code. It is related there that Prajāpati or the Creator composed a huge work (in 100,000 chapters) for the conduct of the society respecting the three divisions of life, the Dharma, Artha, and Kāma,[4] and that future authors drew upon that for their respective subjects. The same tradition is given in the Mahā-Bhārata also, and even an index of this encyclopædia attributed to the Creator is summarised. The name of the book there is the Daṇḍanīti.[5] Vātsyāyana says that Manu Svāyambhuva separated from this encyclopædia of Prajāpati its portion on dharma,[6] as Bṛihaspati derived his Artha-śāstra from its book on

---

[1] *S.B.E.* vol. 24, p. xliv.

[2] Bradke: *Z.D.M.G.*, vol. XXXVI, p. 417 ff.

[3] Chakladar, *Studies in the Kāmasutra*, J.B.O.R.S., Vol. 1919, p. 205.

[4] प्रजापतिर्हि प्रजाः सृष्ट्वा तासां स्थिति-निबन्धनं त्रिवर्गस्य साधनमध्यायानां शतसहस्रेणाग्रे प्रोवाच।
Kāmasūtra, Chowkhamba Sanskrit Series, p. 4: Kāmasūtra, op. cit. p. 4.

[5] *M.B.H.* XII. 57. 7.

[6] तस्यैकदेशं स्वायंभुवो मनुर्धर्माधिकारिकं पृथक्चकार। बृहस्पतिरर्थाधिकारिकम्।

artha. This story of the alleged plagiarism by Manu Svāyambhuva from the book of the first Patriarch does not deserve serious thought. But it establishes the fact that the Mānava Dharmaśāstra, already attributed to Manu Svāyambhuva, was in existence in the time of Vātsyāyana and had already become a standard book like the Artha-śāstra of Bṛihaspati. It must have been promulgated some time before Vātsyāyana. Vātsyāyana is mentioned in the Pañcha-Tantra (Cir. 300 A.C.) and quoted by Kālidāsa (5th century A.C.). Vātsyāyana mentions a Sātavāhana[1] of the early first century A.C. We can therefore place him about 200 A.C. Similarly the Mahā-Bhārata (Śānti Parvan) knows the work of Manu Svāyambhuva.[2]

§ 9. We come to the same conclusion as to the high and established authority of the Mānava Dharma-śāstra before the second century A.C. by Aśvaghosha's (*Vajrasūchī*) quotations from the Mānava-Dharma for the purposes of criticising the caste system. Aśvaghosha's time is nearly certain. Literature and art both place him *cir.* 100 A.C. On the basis of these pieces of evidence we can confidently say that our Code was in existence before 100 A.C., as some time must have elapsed after its compilation for its authority to become so established as to be quoted as the chief work of the orthodox school. Its latest date therefore would be about the first century B.C. or the beginning of the first century A.C. Aśvaghosha's quotations also prove the fact that no part of the Mānava-Dharma was in sūtra.

Parthians in the Code.

§ 10. Its earliest date cannot go beyond the time of the Parthians who along with the Pauṇḍras, Choḍas Yavanas, Śakas and others are described in the Code (X. 43-44) as excluded by the Hindus on account of their non-adherence

---

1 *Kāmasūtra, op. cit.*, p. 149,
कर्तर्या कुन्तलः शातकर्णिः शातवाहनो महादेवीं मलयवतीम्।

2 *M.Bh.*, XII. 59, 1-4

to Hindu rites and Brahmins.[1] The Parthian kingdom was founded by A r s a k e s in 248 B. C. and within a short time it developed into a mighty empire. Under emperor M i t h r a-d a t e s I (171-138 B.C.) the Parthian power, ousting the Indo-Greeks (*cir.* 150 B.C.), reached the banks of the Indus and probably crossed it. The region to the west of the Indus became part of the Parthian empire. The Parthians called themselves P a r t h a v a and the Iranian form of that name was P a h l a v a. The P a h l a v a form occurs in Indian inscriptions of the first century. The Parthian kings had become identified with Persian civilisation, as is evidenced by their names (*e.g.* M i t h r a d a t e s, given by God M i t h r a), and coins, before they came in contact with India. It may be taken that with their entry into the trans-Indus region there came in the Persian form of their name, a Prakrit equivalent of P a r t h a v a as P a h r a v a. The Nāṭya-śāstra of Bharata has the form P a h r a v a. The Mss. of Medhātithi's Bhāshya on Manu's Code read P a n h a v a which could be an easy mis-reading for P a r h a v a. They are treated by the Mānava Code as Śūdras like the Śakas and the Yavanas. Now P a t a ñ j a l i[2] who wrote his commentary in the early part of the reign of P u s h y a m i t r a (*cir.* 188 B.C.—150 B.C.), regards the Śakas and the Yavanas in the same manner as 'Manu' does.[3] He treats them

---

[1] *Manu*, X. 43-4:

शनकैस्तु क्रियालोपादिमाः क्षत्रियजातयः ।
वृषलत्वं गता लोके ब्राह्मणादर्शनेन च ॥ X. 43.
पौण्ड्रकाश्चौड्रद्रविडाः काम्बोजा यवनाः शकाः ।
पारदाःपह्लवाश्चीनाः किराता दरदाः खशाः ॥ X. 44,
मुखबाहूरुपज्जानां या लोके जातयो बहिः ।
म्लेच्छवाचश्चार्यवाचः सर्वे ते दस्यवः स्मृताः ॥ X. 45.

[2] *Mahābhāshya*, III. 2. 123:
इह पुष्यमित्रं याजयामः ।

[3] Patañjali, *Mahābhāshya* on P. II. 4. 10.

as Śūdras, whom the natives of the Āryavarta would allow to eat in their plates. In other words, although technically they were Śūdras, they were considered higher than Śūdras. Manu explains their social position which was reaching śūdra-hood by presupposing a Kshatriya origin in the remote past. Ethnic civilisations have the tendency to account for other races by reference to the theories on their own race origins. You can verify this by consulting the Jewish records. It is a common belief amongst many Hindus of to-day that the Japanese were originally Kshatriyas of the Solar race. And the belief grew up within such a short period as since the Russo-Japanese war, when the Japanese first became known to the mass of the Hindus. Aśoka was similarly seeking affinity when he made the curious remark in his inscriptions that every nation has got Brahmaṇas and Śramaṇas except the Yavanas (*i.e.*, the Greeks).[1] But there was something more than ethnic egoism at the bottom of the identification of the Śakas and the Palhavas as former Hindus. Patañjali gives the description of a Brahmin: 'white, fair and fair-haired.'[2] The Yavanas and the Śakas, who were also Aryan like the Brahmins and the Kshatriyas, were painted fair on the stage according to the Nāṭya-śāstra.[3] With them the "Parhavas" *i.e.* Parthians, too, whom many historians regard as of the Śaka stock, were to be painted fair like the fair castes of the Hindus. Other races mentioned by Manu were ancient neighbours of the Āryāvarta and were ruling castes. According to the Hindu theory the Kshatriya ought to rule. But the contrary fact was there and the best way to reconcile the Dharma-śāstra theory was to pre-suppose an ancient origin and a fallen present. Patañjali's enumeration of the Śūdra-foreigners

Patañjali.

[1] Inscriptions of Aśoka, R.E. XIII.

[2] Patañjali: *Mahābhāshya*—P. II. 2. 6; V. 1. 115:

तथा गौरः शुच्याचारः पिङ्गलः कपिलकेश इत्येतानप्यभ्यन्तरान्ब्राह्मण्ये गुणान्कुर्वन्ति ।

[3] *Nāṭyaśāstra*, XXI. 89—90, p. 233 (ed. Kāvyamālâ).

on the frontiers of the Āryāvarta does not contain the Pahlavas. Patañjali wrote very near 188 B.C. (the beginning of the Śuṅga regime), as the Imperial *yajña* performed by Pushyamitra was co-eval with the composition of the Mahābhāshya.[1] The Parthians come on the scene, according to history, two decades later. The highest age-limit of our Code therefore would be after the Mahābhāshya, say after 188-170 B.C. The Mahābhāshya does not cite the authority of the Mānava-dharma-śāstra but knows only 'Dharma-śūtra-kāras.'[2] The Code thus was composed within these 170 years of the pre-Christ period.

§ 11. This was the period of Brahminical revival and actual Brahmin political rule in India. The Śuṅgas and their successors Kāṇvāyanas were Brahmins. We may notice here that the Śuṅga family were Bhāradvājas, according to Pāṇini[3], that is, they were followers of the Kṛishṇa Yajur Veda.

§ 12. There are other indications that Manu's Code is referable to the early part of this period. The definition of Hindu India (Āryāvarta) given in Manu's Code is significant. The oldest definition is that of the Vedic school of the Bhāllavins given by them in a work of theirs called the Nidāna.[4] 'In the west the boundary is the Indus; in the east, the Sūryodayana; (as to the north and south), the habitat of the black antelope.'[4] Zoology proves that the *habitat* of the black antelope is between the Himalayas and the Vindhyas.[5] Baudhāyana fixes the western and eastern limits as 'the Vinaśana ('the river which disappears,' *i.e.*, the Sarasvatī in the Patiala

Āryāvarta of Manu.

[1] Patañjali : *Mahābhāshya*, III. 2. 123 :

वर्तमाने लट् ॥३।२।१२३॥ इह पुष्यमित्रं याजयामः ।

[2] Patañjali, *Mahābhāshya*, P. I. 1. 47, p. 115.
[3] Pāṇini, IV, 1. 117. JBORS. 1918, '*Brahmin Empire*'.
[4] Vasishṭha, I. 14-15 ; Baudhāyana, I. 1. 2. 29-30.
[5] Jayaswal, *Modern Review*, 1913, p. 329 (*Black antelope*).

District) and the K ā l a k a v a n a, the Himalayas and the Vindhyas (P ā r i y ā t r a) as the northern and the southern boundaries.[1] Vasishtha[2] and Patañjali[3] vary the western limit and make it the Ādarśa (mountain). According to Varāhamihira the Ā d a r ś a s lived amongst the Himalayan peoples. Patañjali further says that the Yavanas and the Śakas have been driven out beyond the limits of Āryāvarta. We know from history that P u s h y a m i t r a did defeat the Greeks and took the Punjab from them. Vasishtha's and Patañjali's definition referring to the north-western frontier, therefore, relates to the political boundary of the time of Pushyamitra, and Baudhāyana's to the time when the Punjab had passed out of the hands of the Hindus in the later Maurya period. Manu[4] adopts the geographical description of the Bhāllavins, the habitat of the black antelope, but he neither adopts their western boundary (the Indus), nor the Ādarśa of Patañjali. 'From s e a to s e a in the east and west, and from mountain to mountain (the Himalayas and the Vindhyas) is the Ā r y ā v a r t a according to the learned.' 'The country of the M l e c h c h h a s is beyond that.' Pushyamitra's dominions included Bengal, as Patañjali says that on the order of the sovereign Brahmins from the towns to the east of A ṅ g a cannot be produced, for there are none there.[5] The eastern limit as the B a y of B e n g a l, therefore, could be referred to the Śuṅga times. The K ā l a k a v a n a or the F o r e s t

---

[1] *Baudhāyana*, op. cit. I, 1, 227,

[2] *Vasishtha*, I. 8:

आर्यावर्तः प्रागादर्शात्प्रत्यक्कालकवनादुदक्पारियात्राद्दक्षिणेन हिमवतः ।

[3] Patañjali : *Mahābhāshya* on P, II, 4,10,

[4] *Manu*, II. 22-23:

आसमुद्रात्तु वै पूर्वादासमुद्राच्च पश्चिमात् ।
तयोरेवान्तरं गिर्योरार्यावर्तं विदुर्बुधाः ॥ II. 22.

कृष्णसारस्तु चरति मृगो यत्र स्वभावतः ।
स ज्ञेयो यज्ञियो देशो म्लेच्छदेशस्त्वतः परः ॥ II. 23.

[5] *Mahābhāshya* on P. VI. 1. 2 (9).

of Death would have been some forest in Bengal. But Manu's vagueness in his western limit, the Arabian Sea, suggests that he was not sure of the Punjab. He does not go beyond the Sarasvatī (II. 17). He defines the Brahmāvarta[1] (a definition not known to earlier literature), and its part the Brahmarshideśa.[2] The latter, the land of authority in matters of orthodox conduct, was comprised of the Kurukshetra, Matsya (western Rajputana), Pāñchāla and Śūrasena (around Mathurā) countries. A short time after the appearance of the Parthians on the Indus we find Mathurā as the seat of foreign Satraps, about 120 B.C. We know from the inscription of Khāravela that Mathurā was under a Yavana invader who ultimately had to retire back to his country, in the time of Bṛihaspati (Pushya) Mitra.[3]

§ 13. That these definitions of Hindu India had reference to political events was the view of former Hindu lawyers also. For instance, Medhātithi commenting on these verses (II. 22-24) says :

"Āryāvarta—where they (the Āryas) become supreme again and again and where the Mlechchhas even after repeated attacks fail to become permanent settlers आर्यावर्तः ··· तत्र पुनः पुनरुद्भवन्त्य आक्रम्याक्रम्यापि न चिरं तत्र म्लेच्छाः स्थातारो भवन्ति. Medhātithi further explains the political significance of the verses which according to him imply a political definition. If the country came under the Mlechchhas (यदि कथंचिद् ब्रह्मावर्त्तादिदेशमपि म्लेच्छा आक्रमेयुः तत्रैवावस्थानं कुर्युर्भवेदेवासौ म्लेच्छदेशः ।) this becomes

---

1 *Manu*, II. 17,

सरस्वतीदृषद्वत्योर्देवनद्योर्यदन्तरम् ।
तं देवनिर्मितं देशं ब्रह्मावर्तं प्रचक्षते ॥

2 Manu, II. 19,

कुरुक्षेत्रं च मत्स्याश्च पञ्चालाः शूरसेनकाः ।
एष ब्रह्मर्षिदेशो वै ब्रह्मावर्तादनन्तरः ॥

3 Jayaswal, J, B, O, R, S, 1919, (1927),

a Mlechchha country. Likewise he explains, if a Hindu king establishes dominion over a Mlechchha country and introduces Hindu community there, it becomes a sacred Hindu-land (II. 23). Land is not itself guilty. M l e c h c h h a-d e śa-i s m has reference to men. यतो न भूमिः स्वतो दुष्टा (II. 23) पुरुषसंसर्गेन म्लेच्छदेशता (II. 24). 'Āryāvartaism does not relate to the land defined' (II. 22).

The Śūrasena country would not have been counted amongst the pre-eminently Aryan countries if it had already passed under the Mlechchha Satraps. The Code, consequently, has to be assigned to a period after the Mahā-Bhāshya but not much later than 150 B.C., say to 150 B.C.—120 B.C. At the same time it precedes our Mahā-bhārata, for the latter knows that Mathurā was under outlandish people like the Yavanas and Kāmbojas (meaning Śakas) who had a special mode of fighting (Śānti P. 101.) "The Yavanas, the Kāmbojas, and those that live around Mathurā, are well-skilled in cavalry fight."

Political character of the Code.

§ 14. There are passages in the Code which reflect the political character of its time. In Ch. XII which is the last chapter of the Code, there is a verse towards the close (100) which declares: सेनापत्यं च राज्यं च दण्डनेतृत्वमेव च । सर्वलोकाधिपत्यं च वेदशास्त्रविदर्हति ।" "The post of the Commander-in-chief and the kingdom, the very Headship of Government, the complete e m p i r e over everyone, are deserved by the knower of the Vedic-Science" (100). This comes in the manuscript after the verses 106-108 of the printed copies, (Bühler, p. 507). Verses 106 and 107, apparently, and the 108th, avowedly, refer to Brahmins. The above quoted verse coming after the 108th leaves no doubt that its '*Veda-vit*' ('knower of Veda') means a Brahmin. We have here now the amazing advocacy of the Brahmin claim to become Senāpati, to obtain

[1] M.Bh. *Śānti P.*, 101, 5:

तथा यवनकाम्भोजा मथुरामभितश्च ये । एते नियुद्धकुशला दाक्षिणात्यासिचर्मिणः ।—ed. Kumb.

the kingdom, to be the ruler and the emperor. I cannot resist the temptation to suggest that the claim is reproducing the precedence established by Pushyamitra Śuṅga in recent history. He was the Senāpati under the Mauryas, he obtained the kingdom and the rulership and established his empire. The fact seems to be alluded to as the great achievement of Vedic orthodoxy. Otherwise it is not easy to explain how the knowledge of Vedic science deserves Senāpatya, Rājya, and Sarvalokādhipatya. No such statement is to be traced anywhere else. This is not all. The following verse frees him from all sins. "He the knower of the Veda throws off the taint of his deeds, as a powerful fire destroys even green trees"[1] (101). The sins which he might have committed in his senāpatya (Pushyamitra was a regicide) and rule (numerous Buddhist monks, according to Tāranātha, were killed by him) are burnt down automatically because he is a *Veda-vit.* Again, elsewhere, XI, 261-62, it is declared that the Brahmin (*vipra*) who has killed even the peoples of the three worlds, is completely freed from all sins on reciting three times the Rik, Yajur or Sāma-Veda with the Upanishads.[2] Why should such provisions find place in a Dharma-śāstra? Such provisions are unknown to earlier Dharma-śāstras. Manu's XI, 262, is given in Vasishṭha in a portion (27.3) which is pronounced by Bühler to be a late addition.[3] Baudhāyana's IV, 5.29, has been changed into Manu's XI, 263. Baudhāyana's passage really

---

[1] *Manu*, XII. 101:

यथा जातबलो वह्निर्दहत्यार्द्रानपि द्रुमान् ।
तथा दहति वेदज्ञः कर्मजं दोषमात्मनः ॥

[2] *Manu*, XI. 261-2:

हत्वा लोकानपीमांस्त्रीनश्नन्नपि यतस्ततः ।
ऋग्वेदं धारयन्विप्रो नैनः प्राप्नोति किञ्चन ॥ 261.
ऋक्संहितां त्रिरभ्यस्य यजुषां वा समाहितः ।
साम्नां वा सरहस्यानां सर्वपापैः प्रमुच्यते ॥ 262.

[3] Bühler: *Vasishṭha, S.B.E.*, Vol. XIV., Pt. II., pp. xviii-xix.

applied to very minor sins of eating, not to killing. Why should killing on a large scale by a Brahmin be presumed at all? Disease must precede remedy. Large killing by Brahmin Pushyamitra had been already committed.

§ 15. The old Dharma-sūtras had prohibited even the touch of a weapon to a Brahmin. 'A Brahmin shall not take up a weapon in his hand though he be only desirous of examining it', "परीक्षार्थोऽपि ब्राह्मण आयुधं नाददीत ।"—Āpastamba, 1.10.29, 6. The same was the view of Gautama as quoted in Baudhāyana[1]. But Gautama was revised and this has been taken out and exactly the opposite provision put in (VII, 6),[2] that he might lawfully take to the profession of arms! We might pause to think why and when this revision took place. It must have taken place when the Brahmin-warrior became a general social institution. That is a society which succeeded or co-existed with the early Śuṅga period. It took place to give sanction to the institution which from the old Dharma point of view was an abnormal growth. Baudhāyana's sūtra which in its present shape is only a revised edition of an earlier work[3], allows the profession of arms to the Brahmin.[4] Vasishṭha and even Vishṇu still remained silent on the point. Baudhāyana further quotes an opinion to justify this departure (II. 2. 4, 18) :—

"For the protection of cows, Brahmins, or in the case of a confusion of the Varṇas, Brahmins and Vaiśyas (also) should take up arms out of consideration for the Dharma."

This was not an ancient view. It is not found in Āpastamba, Gautama, or the present Vishṇu-sūtra. The necessity had not arisen before. The omission of the Kshatriya in the

---

[1] Baudhayana, II. 2. 4. 17.

[2] *Gautama*, op. cit. VII. 6 (तदलाभे क्षत्रियवृत्तिः) ।

[3] It salutes Baudhāyana *i.e.*, the earlier author, and knows Āpastamba the author of the Sūtra (II. 9, 14).

[4] Bau. II. 2. 4. 16.

above *sūtra* is important. We understand the significance of the 'Varṇa-saṅkara' confusion and the whole verse by a reference to the M a h ā - B h ā r a t a .

§ 16. A doubtful question is put for solution in the S ā n t i (88.35-37). If the Kshtriyas become decadent and the country is invaded and taken by foreigners (Dasyus = foreign tribes, as defined in Sānti, 65[1]), and confusion of castes ensues consequential on their rule, could a non-Kshatriya undertake to drive them out and assume kingship and under these circumstances could he, a Brahmin, Vaiśya or Sūdra, be a lawful sovereign, or does he remain under the disability imposed by the Dharma-śāstra ? The answer of the Mahā-Bhārata is that he would be a lawful sovereign.[2] Such a discussion could not have arisen before the decay of the Kshatriya power in India which was complete a little before Alexander's time. Further, such a discussion would not have arisen before the assumption of sovereignty by a non-Kshatriya. The M a u r y a s as Sūdras and the S u ṅ g a s as Brahmins, both extremes had taken up such position between 325 and 188 B.C. Both had succeeded against the 'Dasyus' and both in the beginning were orthodox. Now Baudhāyana's quotation omits both the Kshatriyas and the Sūdras, and allows such privilege only to the Brahmins and the Vaiśyas. The Kshatriya

---

[1] And M., X. 45. *M.Bh.* XII. 65. 31 :

अप्रतच्चिरे सर्वे स्वधर्मं च ददुस्तेन: ।

'वर्णिनश्चाश्रमाश्चैव म्लेच्छाः सर्वे च दस्यवः' ॥

[2] M.Bh. XII. 78. 12-3 ; XII. 78. 36 :

अथ तात यदा सर्वाः शस्त्रमाददते प्रजाः ।

व्युत्क्रमन्ते स्वधर्मेभ्यः क्षत्रस्य चीयते बलम् ॥ 12.

तदा त्राता नु को नु स्यात्को धर्मः किं परायणम् ।

एतं मे संशयं ब्रूहि विस्तरेण पितामह ॥ 13.

* * *

ब्राह्मणो यदि वा वैश्यः शूद्रो वा राजसत्तम ।

दस्युभ्यो यः प्रजा रक्षेद्दण्डं धर्मेण धारयत ॥ 36.

is omitted for his incompetency; the Sūdra is omitted because of his heterodox view. The orthodox people would have the society saved by the Brahmin and the Vaiśya and not the Śūdra. They apparently have had the experience of the Buddhist Mauryas.

§ 17. The Dharma theory which advocated the taking-up of arms by the two castes for Dharma, justified it by the help of a doctrine which the Dharma school had already adopted. Āpastamba by a general rule and Gautama by a special one allowed an exception to the general prohibition: when in danger of life or limb a Brahmin may use force in self-defence. This was an equitable doctrine introduced from the Purāṇa into the Dharma law by Āpastamba[1], who used it as a rider to the unrelenting rule of the Dharma penalty in cases of murder. But this was in favour of every caste. Gautama prescribed: प्राण-संशये ब्राह्मणोपि शस्त्रमाददीत । 7. 25. :—

"Even a Brahmin should take up arms in danger of life." Vasishṭha adopts the opinion without any discussion as settled law. The only difference is that instead of the 'confusion of castes' it gives the 'invasion upon Dharma': धर्मसंवर्ग *Vas.* III. 24. But our Manu goes a step further. It sanctifies an armed rebellion against an internal, social and religious revolution. (VIII, 348):[2]

"The twice born should take up arms in the circumstances of the Dharma being obstructed and of a revolution of the twice-born castes produced by Time."

The revolution complained against is a revolution not of the

---

[1] See Lecture IX below.

[2] *Manu*, VIII. 349-50:

शस्त्रं द्विजातिभिर्ग्राह्यं धर्मो यत्रोपरुध्यते ।।

द्विजातीनां च वर्णानां विप्लवे कालकारिते ।। 349.

आत्मनश्च परित्राणे दक्षिणानां संगरे ।।

स्त्रीविप्राभ्युपपत्तौ च घ्नन्धर्मेण न दुष्यति ।। 350.

four-fold *varṇa* system, as such, but which had shaken the upper three classes only. The revolution had been brought about in course of time or by Time. The sacred law of the *dvijātis* had been superseded. It seems to me that these characteristics point to an internal revolution which is known to have been produced in the time of the heterodox (later) Mauryas who did stop the *dharma* (*yajñas*, sacrifices) of *dvijātis*.[1] The injunction that a Snātaka should not live in the kingdom of a Śūdra, IV. 61[2], an injunction met with for the first time only in this Dharma-śāstra, and equally the new dictum that the kingdom where the Śūdra decides matters of law (Dharma, M. 8. 21)[3] sinks down, must follow the facts of a Śūdra rule and Śūdra justice. "The kingdom is distressed like a cow in the mire before the very eyes of the ruler for whom a Śūdra administers justice." The event must have been recent to be alluded to. The kingdom of the Mauryas had nearly sunk down and did struggle like a cow in the mire, when it was pressed under the Indo-Greeks and probably also the Śakas as implied by Patañjali.[4] It was orthodoxy under the Śuṅga which liberated 'the sinking cow.'

§ 18. The exaggerated and new claims for the Brahmin caste, *e.g.*, that a Brahmin only in name is competent to judge (8.20) ;[5] that the Brahmin is the lord of all—*Sarvasyādhi-patir-hi saḥ*,[6] become explicable in the light of the political age when the Code was promulgated.

---

[1] Aśoka, R. E. I.

[2] न शूद्रराज्ये निवसेन्नाधार्मिकजनावृते । न पाषण्डिगणाक्रान्ते नोपसृष्टेऽन्त्यजैर्नृभिः ।

[3] *Manu*, VIII. 21 :

यस्य शूद्रस्तु कुरुते राज्ञो धर्मविवेचनम् ।

तस्य सीदति तद्राष्ट्रं पङ्के गौरिव पश्यतः ॥

[4] Patañjali, *Mahābhāshya*. on P. II. 4. 10

[5] *Manu*, VIII. 20 :

जातिमात्रोपजीवी वा कामं स्याद्ब्राह्मणब्रुवः ।

धर्मप्रवक्ता नृपतेर्न तु शूद्रः कथंचन ॥

[6] *Manu*, VIII. 37.

§ 19. The Code is marked throughout with an aggressive orthodoxy. The heretics, *e.g.*, the Buddhists and Jainas, were to be banished from the capital and were as bad as thieves (9.225-26)[1] ; no oblations were to be offered to the soul of those who had joined the ascetic orders of mixed castes in vain, and to women who had joined heretical orders (*i.e.*, become nuns) like those who had committed suicide or fallen morally (V. 89-90). A heretic (*e.g.*, a Buddhist, c.f. Kullūka and S. Nārāyaṇa[2]) was not to be honoured even in speech by a Brahminical student (IV.30). "All those traditions (*smṛitis*). and all those despicable systems of philosophy, which are not based on the Veda, produce no reward after death ; for they are declared to be founded on Darkness. All those doctrines which from other sources spring up and fall, are worthless and false, they being of modern date."[3] (XII.95-96).

The Code's orthodoxy and its explanation.

§ 20. The expression '*of modern date*' (arvāk-kālika) should be particularly marked. The reference to modern systems is to the heterodox systems of Buddhism and Jainism. Nuns

---

[1] *Manu*, IX. 224-28 :

द्यूतं समाह्वयं चैव यः कुर्यात् कारयेत वा ।
तान्सर्वान्घातयेद्राजा शूद्रांश्च द्विजलिङ्गिनः ॥ 224.
कितवान्कुशीलवान्क्रूरान्पाषण्डस्थांश्च मानवान् ।
विकर्मस्थान् शौण्डिकांश्च क्षिप्रं निर्वासयेत्पुरात् ॥ 225.
एते राष्ट्रे वर्तमाना राज्ञः प्रच्छन्नतस्कराः ।
विकर्मक्रियया नित्यं बाधन्ते भद्रिकाः प्रजाः ॥ 226.

[2] पाषण्डिनो……शाक्यभिक्षुकक्षपणकादयः (Ku.). पाषण्डिनो बौद्धादीन् (S. Narä.)

[3] *Manu*, XII. 95-96 :

या वेदबाह्याः स्मृतयो याश्च काश्च कुदृष्टयः ।
सर्वास्ता निष्फलाः प्रेत्य तमोनिष्ठा हि ताः स्मृताः । 95
उत्पद्यन्ते च्यवन्ते च यान्यतोऽन्यानि कानिचित् ।
तान्यर्वाक्कालिकतया निष्फलान्यनृतानि च ॥ 96.

were for the first time in Hindu Society permitted by the heretical sect of the Buddhists. The orthodox system allowed women to go into the V ā n a p r a s t h a or hermit-life with their husbands. But they could not join the next order, the ascetic. The publication of V i k h a n a s' D h a r m a which takes us to the society before Buddha's time, makes the question of the fourth order and its relation to Buddhism perfectly clear. All the three upper castes could go into the Vāna-prastha and live in enclosures outside the city set apart as artificial jungles and divided into seven groups, named after the gotra-names of the seven patriarchal Ṛishis.[1] (We know that the B u d d h a after leaving home went to one of such colonies). Having lived there the life called Ś r a m a ṇ a k a *i.e.*, the t o i l-s o m e, 'because of the austerities' (Vikhanas), the hermit, *if he is a Brahmin*, can take to the fourth life, and leaving the enclosure (Pravrajyā) may become a B h i k s h u, monk.[2] What the Buddha did was to abolish the hermit stage which required undergoing austerities, keeping the sacred fires with Vedic *mantras* and doing the *Śrāddha*, and to take himself and to invite and admit others, who were not Brahmins, to the fourth order. Not only he opened up the fourth order to all castes but to all ages. There had been fairly an old age-limit, as we find in Vikhanas, to enter the fourth order.[3] This too was abolished by the Buddha. Further the order was thrown open to both sexes. For these reasons, as we find in the Buddhist *sūtras*, Brahmins never addressed the Buddha with the respect due to an orthodox Bhikshu.

§ 21. The orthodox community and the Dharma-śāstras naturally fought against this. They emphasised the d u t y of m a r r y i n g, made it compulsory and went to the length of even extolling the married and family life as higher than all other orders (including the Vānaprastha and the Bhikshu). But nobody

---

[1] *Vaikhānasa Dharma-praśna* (Trivandrum, 1913) I. 6-8 ; II, AŚ., xiii. p. 49.
[2] *Vaikhānasa*, I. 9. 3, II, 1.
[3] Above 70 years, *Ibid.* II. 8. 1

fought so vehemently as the author of our Mānava Code.[1] He declared that the intermixed *pravrajyā* (Manu VI. 130) (ascetic order) 'of all castes', that is, the Buddhists, as vain, and bad as suicides, the nuns as fallen women, and as we shall see in a subsequent lecture, enjoined suppression of heterodoxy by law and force.

§ 22. The Code is consistently hostile against heretical Indian Republics. He treats the Mallas and the Lichchhavis as degraded Aryans.[2] The sūtrakāras forbid Brahmins to accept the generosity of the Gaṇas.[3] But no one except Manu names the Lichchhavis and the Mallas. We know them becoming important only in the Buddhist and Jain history.

§ 23. The fact of the heretical doctrines being called of modern date throws further light on the date of the Code. The legislator could not have flourished very long after the rise and fall of Buddhism in its first stage, to mention the doctrines 'of modern date' and 'those which spring up and fall.' People must have remembered then the date of the birth of those systems, which they also saw declining.

§ 24. The features of the orthodox counter-revolution in the Code are not limited to social matters only.

Manu and the Artha-śāstra.

The principles of law which had been in vogue in the period before the Śuṅgas have been combated and condemned where they depart from the strict principles of the Dharma school. The Artha-śāstra, for instance, provides that the king-made law may override the Dharma

---

[1] *Manu*, VI. 34-35; VI. 37:

आश्रमादाश्रमं गत्वा हुतहोमो जितेन्द्रियः ।
भिक्षाबलिपरिश्रान्तः प्रव्रजन् प्रेत्य वर्धते ॥ VI. 34.
ऋणानि त्रीण्यपाकृत्य...मोक्षं तु सेवमानो व्रजत्यधः ॥ VI. 35.
अनधीत्य द्विजो वेदाननुत्पाद्य तथा प्रजाम् ।
अनिष्ट्वा चैव यज्ञैश्च मोक्षमिच्छन् व्रजत्यधः ॥ VI. 37.

[2] *Manu*, X 22.

[3] Cf. *Apastamba*, I. 6. 18, 16.

law and that in the case of a conflict between the d h a r m a-p r o-v i s i o n s and d h a r m a-n y ā y a the deciding factor is n y ā-y a (reason or justice): 'before Nyāya, the text must fail.—'Nyāyastatra pramāṇam syāt tatra pāṭho hi naśyati.'[1] Nyāya or legal interpretation was formerly employed to explain away texts. An example occurs in Āpastamba (II.6.14.13), where a Vedic text has been explained away in favour of a Dharma doctrine. But Kauṭilya provides for a conflict between Nyāya and Dharma, and puts the latter entirely under Nyāya or Dharma-nyāya, which would openly put aside a Dharma text. Apparently here principles of consideration of justice are implied. 'Manu', on the other hand, claims that Dharma laws coming, as they do, out of the Vedas (Vedic literature) and 'Dharma-śāstra' (probably including the Gṛihya-sūtras), cannot be over-ridden.[1] To subject them to reason would be subjecting their two sources (Veda and Dharma-śāstra) to the Canons of Reason (II.10.11), and the Brahmin who does so is to be treated as a scoffer at the Veda, and his opinion should be excluded.[3] 'The knowledge of the Dharma resides in those who are not given over to Artha and Kāma. For those who want to make enquiry about the Dharma the authority is the S r u t i. Where Śruti conflicts (with another S r u t i text, or with Dharma text), both are held to be law; for both are pronounced by the wise to be law' (II. 13. 14).

As 'Dharma' stands for the Dharma-śāstra, so 'Artha' stands for the Artha-śāstra and 'Kāma' for the Kāma-śāstra. This interpretation is supported by a use in this code itself, '*dharmārtha-kāma-kovidam*', VII. 26, which Rāghavānanda does explain as '*Smṛiti-Vātsyāyana-nīti-śāstrānām vettāram.*' Vātsyāyana gives a

---

[1] AŚ. Ch: 58, p. 150.

[2] *Manu*, II. 10:

श्रुतिस्तु वेदो विज्ञेयो धर्मशास्त्रं तु वै स्मृतिः ।
ते सर्वार्थेष्वमीमांस्ये ताभ्यां धर्मो हि निर्बभौ ॥

[3] *Manu*, II. 11:

योऽवमन्येत ते मूले हेतुशास्त्राश्रयाद्द्विजः ।
स साधुभिर्बहिष्कार्यो नास्तिको वेदनिन्दकः ॥

series of his predecessors amongst whom A r u ṇ i-U d d ā l a k a ' s son, S v e t a k e t u headed the list of writers on Kāma.[1] He is an ancient teacher. B ā b h r a v y a of Pañchāla, whose opinions are often quoted by Vātsyāyana, had written a very heavy volume on Kāma.[2] It would have been one of the authorities of Vātsyāyana, whose work, or the Kāma literature in general, was meant by "Kāma" in the above verse.

It is apparent that 'Manu' is attacking the Artha-śāstra doctrines, in mentioning *artha* in the above verse. As we proceed further we shall see his differences from the Artha-śāstra. Here it is enough to note the above difference on a main principle, which is put down in the opening portion of the discussion on the sources of law in Manu's Code.

§ 25. The Mānava Code thus suffers from its political, social and sacerdotal prejudices. It is a code as well as a controversy. But if we transfer ourselves to its times, we can imagine how ready approval it would have received from the race to which it was preached. Buddhism and Buddhist State stood discredited. The G ā r g a - s a ṁ h i t ā, mentioning a successer of Śāliśuka Maurya, says that the fool would establish a "so-called conquest by Dharma" while Sāketa, Mathurā and Pañchāla would be passing off to the viciously valiant Greeks, Pāṭaliputra itself being in danger and the whole country in consternation.[3] The policy of c o n q u e s t by D h a r m a (Buddhism), was a written legacy to his descendants by A ś o k a who prohibited further conquests by the sword.[4] The last of his line was talking of this 'sublime nonsense' of his forefather to make the conquest of Dharma, while the very existence of the country was in jeopardy. The astronomer

---

[1] *Kāma. op. cit.*, p. 5 :

तदेव तु पञ्चभिरध्यायशतैरौद्दालकिः श्वेतकेतुः संचिक्षेप । I. 9.

[2] *Ibid.* :

सप्तभिरधिकरणैर्बाभ्रव्यः पाञ्चालः संचिक्षेप । I. 10.

[3] [For the Gārgasaṁhitā see now J.B.O.S., 1928 and 1929 where the whole of the historical portion has been edited by me.]

[4] Aśoka Inscriptions, RE. XIII.

G ā r g a summed up the sentiment of the time in his characterisation of the last Maurya emperor : *dharmavādî adhārmikaḥ*, and *mohātmā*, 'talking of dharma that anti-dharma' king, 'the fool'. In their eyes he was the religious Nero who looked on with equanimity at the gradual consumption of Hindu civilisation (*dharma*) by the vicious Greeks. The Brahmin (Pushyamitra) took up the sword in this 'V i p l a v a of D h a r m a', and not only saved the dharma for the time being but also rehabilitated it. He liberated the whole country and completely destroyed the power which had threatened confusion in the holy land of the Āryas. He proved to them by his valour that the land for the Mlechchhas was beyond Āryāvartta. The Śuṅgan Manu translated into terms of dharma-law the contempt for the Śūdra and heterodox ruler before whose very eyes the kingdom was sinking like a cow in the mire, and the exultation of the Brahmin orthodoxy over its achievements. His Code is the mirror reflecting the national sentiment of the time. His absurd claims for Brahminism were admitted at the time, for they were based on the facts of the time. The Brahmin, in fact, was 'the lord of everything' at the moment

Brahmin as the political saviour.

§ 26. This seems to have been the basis of the high authority which it soon acquired. At the end of the first century Manu's Code is *the* Dharma-śāstra. There is no such indication of such a position of any book at the time of the Mahā-Bhāshya. This rapidity in its acceptance is also due to a probable royal recognition. Prof. Jolly has given instances how law-codes in later Hindu times were promulgated.[1] Kings, ministers or dharma-ministers wrote, or had written, treatises on law which became the authority in the state. The books were sent even to friendly states where occasionally they were adopted. Very probably

The Mānava—a Śungan Code.

[1] Jolly : Tagore Lectures, pp. 27-28.

the Mānava-dharma Code became the approved code of the Śuṅgan régime.

§ 27. The name alone of 'M a n u' would not have given the code such a permanent authority. In the first two pre-Christian centuries, nobody could have been deceived by the name. In fact the name of the real author, as we shall see presently, was well-known. Nobody in those early days could have believed, as M e d h ā t i t h i did not believe in later days,[1] that the book itself was to be referred to Manu, the father of the race. The book undoubtedly sought the prestige of the great name of Manu, but the name was adopted to stand as a symbol of conservatism, the tradition of yore. Hence in numerous verses the repitition 'so spoke Manu,' the first law giver. Other authors have assumed still greater names, *e.g.*, P r a j ā p a t i or V i s h ṇ u, but their books never acquired the universal obedience of the race, as tendered to Manu's Code.

Real author.

§ 28. The author of the N ā r a d a - s m ṛ i t i writing in or about the 4th century of the Christian era, states that one S u m a t i B h ā r g a v a composed 'the Code of Manu.' S u m a t i B h ā r g a v a is not a legendary name. He must, therefore, be taken to be a historical entity. The author of the Nāradîya is not uncorroborated. The Code itself is signed in the family name of B h ṛ i g u, which was the ancient custom current up to the first century of the Christian era. "T h e T e x t c o m p o s e d b y B h ṛ i g u (entitled) 't h e D h a r m a C o d e o f M a n u'" is the real title of the work, subscribed to the end of every chapter of 'Manu's Code' itself.[2]

§ 29. The N ā r a d î y a, however, in accordance with the theory of the later Dharma school, which does not recognise human

---

[1] मनुर्नाम कश्चित् पुरुषविशेषः (on M. I. 1, 'Manu a certain individual'. *Cf.* Bühler, p. xiii-xiv. See also Jayaswal, 15 *Calcutta Weekly Notes*, 299 *n*).

[2] *Manu*, end of every Chapter :—

इति मानवे धर्मशास्त्रे भृगुप्रोक्तायां संहितायां प्रथमोऽध्यायः,° द्वितीयोऽध्यायः, etc.

authorship of Dharma-śāstras, says that Sumati Bhārgava abstracted his code from the encyclopædic work of a hundred thousand chapters of the primæval Manu.[1] We have seen that the earlier tradition was that there was such a huge book by the Father of the Universe (Prajāpati) and not by the Father of Man. Vātsyāyana says that Manu's Dharma-śāstra was an abstract of the law portion of this enclyclopædia and it is to this tradition that Medhātithi refers. But the author who wrote under the name of Nārada was in a difficulty. The school of the Dharma-śāstrins knew full well the tradition current amongst them that "Manu's Dharma Code" was composed by Sumati, and there was no room for an intermediary edition, hence the alleged original source of the Dharma, Artha and Kāma śāstras, was itself turned into the encyclopædia of Manu Svāyambhuva from that of Prajāpati. The authorship of the parent book of all the Śāstras was transferred from the father of the universe to the father of man. This new tradition was adopted by later books like the Skanda Purāṇa[2] which says that the original ordinance (śāstra) of Manu had four successors, the Bhārgavī, the Nāradîyā, the Bārhaspatyā and Āṅgirasî saṁhitās.[3] The lost Bṛihaspati-smṛiti, from its collected quotations, has been proved by Prof. Jolly to have been a sort of commentary on Manu's Code. About two editions by Nārada, the tradition is given by the pseudo-Nārada himself.[4] He professes to follow Sumati's Code, but in fact he does not do so. The Skanda shows that the Āṅgirasa-smṛiti was also a later composition, evidently later than Nārada's and Bṛihaspati's Codes.

§ 30. The value of these traditions lies in the fact shewing that at a time when the name of the real author of Manu's Dharma

---

1 *Nārada*, his r se introduction, 1-5.
2 Mandlik, *V. Mayûkha*, p. xlvii.
3 "भार्गवी नारदीया च बार्हस्पत्याङ्गिरस्यपि । स्वायम्भुवस्य शास्त्रस्य चतस्रः संहिता मताः ।"
4 Sūtra introduction to the NS.

Code was still remembered, our Sumati's Mānava Dharma was taken to have been the first Saṁhitā of Manu's ordinance. Sumati's Code was the first historical 'Code of Manu's laws' in their eyes.

§ 31. The analysis which I have made confirms the tradition. There was no other book on Dharma law attributed to Manu.

No 'Mānava Dharma-sūtra.'

Nor was there any Dharma-sūtra of the school of the Vedic Mānavas. The late Dr. Bühler was led into the belief, on the analogy of the current metrical editions of several Dharma-śāstras after the names of the original Dharma-sūtras, that there must have been a sūtra original for the metrical Mānava Dharma-śāstra as well.[1] Further, finding too great an advance in the legal portion of Manu's Code in comparison with the old Dharma-sūtras, Bühler with the instinct of a historian supposed an original behind it. But the original, as it now turns out, is not to be sought in a lost Dharma-sūtra but in the laws of the Artha-śāstra. Bühler after a very searching enquiry ultimately based his whole argument of the pre-existence of a supposed 'Mānava Dharma Sūtra' on a passage of Vasishṭha, IV. 5-6, which stands as follows :—

पितृदेवतातिथिपूजायामप्येव पशुं हिंस्यादिति मानवम् ॥ Ch. IV. 5.
मधुपर्के च यज्ञे च पितृदैवतकर्मणि ।
अत्रैव च पशुं हिंस्यान्नान्यथेत्यब्रवीन्मनुः ॥ 6
नाकृत्वा प्राणिनां हिंसां मांसमुत्पद्यते क्वचित् ।
न च प्राणिवधः स्वर्ग्यस्तस्माद्यागे वधोऽवधः[2] ॥ 7.
अथापि ब्राह्मणाय वा राजन्याय वाभ्यागताय महोक्षाणं वा महाजं वा
पचेदेवमस्मा आतिथ्यं कुर्वन्तीति ॥ 8.

In his translation of Vasishṭha's D h a r m a-s ū t r a (*S.B.E.* xiv, p. 26, *n.*) Bühler took 'M ā n a v a m' to mean a M ā n a v a-s ū t r a, and expressed the opinion that the sūtra marked with *iti* may indicate either a direct quotation or a summary of the opinion given in 'the Mānava Sūtra.' He believed that the

---

[1] *The Laws of Manu*, p. xix.

[2] A sure sign of the post-Buddhistic conscience.

whole passage, sūtras 5 to 8, has been taken bodily from the ancient Dharma sūtra, adding: "if my view is correct, it follows that the lost Mānava Dharma-sūtra consisted, like nearly all the known works of this class, partly of prose and partly of verse." This is the sheet-anchor of the theory asserting the pre-existence of a lost dharma-sūtra of the Mānavas which has been universally accepted. In his introduction to Manu (*S. B. E.* 25) Dr. Bühler argued with complete confidence that the passage stands as a quotation and proves his thesis thereby: "As has been stated in the introduction to Vasishṭha all the four sūtras must be taken as a quotation because the particle *iti*, 'thus,' occurs at the end of IV. 8, and because the identity of Śūtra 6 with Manu, 5.41, as well as the close resemblance of Śūtra 7 to Manu V. 48, show that the quotation is not finished with Sūtra 5. If we accept this explanation we have in one passage the usual arrangement followed in the Dharma-sūtras. First comes the prose rule, next the verses which confirm it, and finally a Vedic passage on which both the rule and the verses rest."[1] An analysis of the argument and the method of Vasishṭha obliges me to say that I cannot accept Bühler's view. First of all, the subject in Vasishṭha begins with sūtra 5 and ends with sūtra 8. If the whole lot is a quotation, then where is the opinion of Vasishṭha himself ? The sūtra-kāras first state their rule and then either quote others to confirm their own opinion or to explain away an adverse opinion. A quotation cannot stand in the air. The system itself relied on by Bühler proves that the first sūtra (*i.e.*, Vasishṭha, IV. 5) must be Vasishṭha's own opinion which is supported by Manu's verses and a Vedic text. This view is confirmed by the text adopted in the Anandāśrama edition (the Smṛiti-samuchchaya, p. 194) which runs—पितृदेवतातिथिपूजायां पशुं

[1] Bühler: *Manu*, op. cit. p. xxx—xxxii.

हिंस्यात्, where no *iti* is attached to the end of the sūtra. This text is found in 6 out of the 7 MSS. used by the Poona editor (Mr. Hari Nārāyana Apte). Further, Vasiṣhṭha never puts the Mānava quotations in this form. He has got the set form मानवं चात्र श्लोकमुदाहरन्ति (3.2 ; 13.16 ; 17.37 ; 20.18) ; and he never departs from it. And he puts only those verses of Manu under quotation which are not already attributed to Manu in the text itself. (1.17 ; 11.23 ; 12.16 ; 23.43 ; 26.8). This too is a fixed system. So the quotation-mark if there was one (for, *all* his verses which are found in our Mānava Code as well, are not acknowledged by Vasishṭha as borrowings), would have been against sūtra 7. In that case it could never have been in the form it is given, 'इति मानवम्', which would not only be quite contrary to the system of Vasishṭha but also against the system of the whole sūtra literature. The Sūtra-kāras put their references, if to a book (*e.g.*, Purāṇa, Veda) in the locative, and if to another Sūtra-kāra, in the nominative singular or plural. The reference to a work is never in the nominative. For these reasons I accept the text of the Ānandāśrama edition which gives no quotation mark. As pointed out by Bühler himself, the text on which he based his translation bears traces of having been conjecturally restored in later times. 'इति मानवम्' was one of those conjectural emendations in accordance with the present-day notions of Sanskrit composition, which intended to mean, as Kṛishna Paṇḍita Dharmādhikārin says, 'Manu-matam' ('Manu's opinion'), and not a quotation. It is a faithful summary of the following verse (Sūtra 6) attributed to Manu in the body of the text itself.

Thus the very foundation of the theory does not exist. No evidence of a former Dharma-sūtra of the school of the Mānavas exists. On the other hand, the materials on record negative such a conclusion.

§ 32. If such a work had in fact existed we would have found it more than once quoted in the sūtras. Āpastamba does not quote a single sūtra from Manu, nor does Baudhāyana. Baudhāyana enumerates all the Dharma-sūtras of his Veda[1]. But the name of Āchārya Mānava or Manu is not there. As the Mānavas belonged to the same Veda, one would expect the 'Mānava Sūtra-kāra' in the list, if such a sūtra of dharma did exist. Gautama also does not cite any such sūtra. The present, recast Vasishṭha and Sumati's Code seem to be nearly contemporaries. Their mutual borrowings also point to the same conclusion. The three earlier Dharma Sūtras do not know him at all. And in fact there is no quotation therein from a Mānava Dharma Sūtra.[2]

Revision of Manu's Code.

§ 33. Again, we cannot agree with Bühler that the present Mānava Code existed in its very shape before the second century A.C.[2] The major portion of the quotation is in the V a j r a-s ū c h î of A ś v a g h o s h a are identified in our present Manu, but verses which gave the history of questionable origins of certain Ṛishis and a verse in a metre other than *Anushṭubh* are noc to be found in our Manu; which is, as you know, exclusively in *Anushṭubhs*. Occasionally different and archaic metres are found even in the Mahā-Bhārata. The original Sumati's Manu Code also had them. This is also proved by a quotation in Vasishṭha in *Trishṭubh*, which is now found condensed into *Anushṭubhs* in our present code.[3] We may not attach too much importance to what Nārada says about the volume of Sumati's work of 4000 Ślokas, as there is a vein of exaggeration there throughout. Yet the evidence of Aśvaghosha, Vasishṭha, and certain differences in the Mahā-Bhārata and the present-day Mānava versions of the same passages compel us to come to the conclusion that changes were made at least once. The changes.

---

[1] Baudhāyana, 5. 9. (14).

[2] References and appeals to Manu's name and authority in Vedic literature and other early records are allusions to the seer of the Vedic *mantras* and the wise father of mankind, not to the author of a law-book. The matter is fully discussed by Bühler, *The Laws of Manu*, pp. xvi, lx.

[3] V. xix. 37=M. vii. 133, 138, viii. 391 (*andho°* etc.)

however, could not have been great in view of the large number of identified verses. The verses in different metres were certainly altered into anushṭubh and some verses, probably considered unnecessary, were left out. We, however, could not be sure that no material change was introduced, though it does not seem to be likely. Its authoritative character from the beginning would have prevented great material changes, and there is no great evidence of such changes.

§ 34. The alteration must have been complete before Y ā j ñ a-v a l k y a's C o d e, which follows the system of having only one metre—the heroic. Yājñavalkya follows Manu, the language of Manu yet remains markedly of an earlier epoch. The coins and monetary system retain their old character in Manu. While for practical purposes the main date may be regarded to be *circa* 150 B.C., the final revision and the present form would have been fixed by 100-150 A.C., not later. The oldest commentators who have been quoted by Medhātithi and who might go back to the Gupta times, seem to have found it in its present shape, for Medhātithi does not raise any question as to any serious discrepancy except the ordinary variant readings.

§ 34. It is to be noticed that the Code retains its human and historical character throughout the book, except in the beginning where it is attributed to Manu. In all other places it is purely a human work. It quotes other authors (Vasishṭha, Gautama, Atri[1], etc.). If the work had been attributed to Manu in its original scheme no sūtra-kāra*s* would have been mentioned. It would not have referred, as it does, to D a ṇ ḍ a-n ī t i, Arthaśāstra, 'recent' smṛitis, and old *kalpas*.[2] The addition of Manu's name in the preface must also be placed in the period of revision subsequent to Aśva-ghosha and anterior to Vātsyāyana. Aśvaghosha does not know Manu, he knows only the Mānava Dharma Śāstra.

---

[1] M. VIII. 140=V. II. 51; M. III. 16.
[2] M. II. 140 (*Kalpa*).

§ 35. It seems that Sumati Bhārgava, the real author, belonged to the school of the Mānavas, hence he calls his work the Mānava Dharma-śāstra. In ch. XII he calls himself a "Mānava" *i.e.*, the follower of the Vedic school of the Mānavas. It was the title of his work, the Mānava-dharma, which suggested the legend of the authorship of the primeval Manu. A new evidence proves that the work was known as the 'Mānavīya Dharma-śāstra'. Bhāsa describing the education of a learned Brahmin, enumerates after the Vedas and the Aṅgas[1]:

Sumati a Mānava.

the Mānavīya Dharma-śāstra,
the Bārhaspatya Artha-śāstra,
the Māheśvara Yoga-śāstra,
Medhātithi's Nyāya-śāstra, and
the Prāchetasa Śrāddha-kalpa.

The enumeration shows that the Mānavīya Dharma-śāstra was not a part of the Kalpasūtras (Aṅgas) but a separate treatise. It could not therefore have been a sūtra work. It was a standard work like Bṛihaspati's Arthaśāstra (quoted in Kauṭilya and the Mahā-Bhārata[2]). It must have been, therefore, our Dharma-śāstra, whose author was a Mānava. It seems that Sumati Bhārgava, himself a Mānava, wrote the book, not as a handbook of the Mānavas, but as a general treatise. Hence, it was not incorporated in the Mānava literature of the school, nor was it based on the principles of the *kalpa* of that school. Throughout the book there is no special leaning towards the Veda (Black Yajus) of the school. One faint indication merely would suggest that the author belonged to that Veda, but the work never assumes a definite school tendency.

§ 36. It is at the same time noteworthy that the work is the product of a time when the Black Yajus was repeated in every

---

[1] *Pratimā*, p. 79.
[2] Śānti P. (Kumbkonam ed.), C. 55 (Cal 57)., 38; [cf. *ibid.*, 67 (Cal. 68). 7-61.]

village throughout the Āryāvarta, and when the ruling power was a follower of the same Veda. I have shown elsewhere that Bhāsa belonged to the time of the Kāṇva dynasty who succeeded the Śuṅgas.[1] Bhāsa knows the Code before it had been attributed to Manu. His mention also proves that Sumati's Code was the ruling authority in the Kāṇva times. Bhāsa's Brahmin is a militant Brahmin, he is always armed. The Dharma Code of the militant Brahmin was the Code of the Mānava Dharma Śāstra, and the Mānava Dharma Śāstra is militant throughout.

Manu's Code and the Gītā.

§ 37. The last chapter of Manu bears a striking resemblance to the doctrines of the Gītā in several places. The Bhavishya Purāṇa which describes Pushyamitra as the saviour of Hindu society and Dharma[2] and as subjugating Kali, makes him also a special student of the Gītā. The Gītā is a gospel of war composed to combat the Buddhist doctrine of 'no war.' It is very likely that the Gītā was not only a favourite of Pushyamitra but a work of his period. This doctrinal affinity between Manu and the Gītā is easily explicable. The Śuṅga period, in the light of recent studies has to be counted as the epoch of the first Sanskrit revival, and of great literary activity.[3] The revision of the Rāmāyaṇa, which in adding a description of Ayodhyā, gave it the description of Pāṭaliputra of massive *sāl* palisades (*mahatî sāla-mekhalā*) and ditches,[4] and which called the "Tathāgata Buddha" a thief[5], and placed the ruler of Magadha in the days of Rāma and called him 'the emperor',[6] goes back to that period. So does the brahminisation of the Mahā-Bhārata. Sanskrit histrionics, the beginnings of the Kāvya style, Sanskrit inscriptions, and fuller Sanskritic

---

[1] JASB., 1913.
[2] Pratisarga P., XXIII, 18—40.
[3] Jayaswal, JBORS., 1918. (*Revised Notes on Brahmin Empire*)
[4] R. 1. 5. 12.—14
[5] R. II. 109. 34.
[6] R. 1. 13. 26. (See 24 and 25 for the use of '*Rājasiṁha*', 'His majesty,' as fn Bhāsa).

forms on coins and seals which appear for the first time in that period, all indicate a great Sanskrit literary upheaval in the period, which even Buddhism, the great advocate of Prakrit, does not escape. During and after the Śuṅga epoch even the Buddhists had to adopt Sanskrit as the medium to spread their cult.

The Mānava Code studied as part of the literature of the Śuṅga revival becomes explicable in its character.

APPENDIX A (to Lects. I & II).

The age of the Dharmasūtras.

Āpastamba, I. 6. 18, gives two rules (31-32), *avidhinā cha pravrajitaḥ—yaschāgnîna-pāsyati*, 'And a person who has become an ascetic without the *vidhi* (procedure laid down). And one who forsakes the (sacred) fires[5]'. These refer to heretical bhikshus who did not follow the sacred, orthodox sūtras in leaving home or the third stage. This will indicate a time about the rise of Buddhism and Jainism. In fact, the Buddha discarding the orthodox law threw open the *bhikshu* or the fourth stage to all castes and all ages and both sexes. [*Cf. Bau.* II. 10. 17; *Vaikhānasa,* I. 1. 10-11.] It was only after the rise of Buddhism that un-authorised *pravrajyā* became prominent enough to require provisions against it. Kauṭilya also enjoins secular penalties against it [AŚ, II. 1, p. 48]. We should notice that Āpastamba's provision against *Saṅghānna* (food of Saṅghas) would also indicate a time after 500 B.C. Apart from these indications every other index is for an earlier date. That it has retained its original form is proved by the text of the Hiraṇyakeśin school. Gautama by counting *yavana* as one of the Hindu castes (IV. 21) fixes his own time. The Indian *yavana* comes on the scene with his colony on the Kabul river under the early Persian rule, as I have shown in *Hindu Polity* (I. pp. 147-148). His social system which knows no *Hrahmins*, noticed in Aśoka's ins-cription, was a well known matter in the third century B.C. And it must be earlier when his caste is the subject of speculation amongst the authorities on caste-system.—Gautama gives the opinion on his (yavana's) origin, as yet not fully established (पारशव-यवन-करण-शूद्राञ्छूद्रेत्येके) as the opinion of 'some.' We cannot, therefore, along with other con-siderations, assign the sūtra, as we find it, earlier than 300 or 350 B.C. Gautama, whose book was revised as proved by the quotation in Baudhāyana about Brahmins taking to the profession of arms, gives a passage which cannot but be from Āpastamba who em-ployed it in a special discussion. The present edition would be dated about 200 B.C. One revision of Baudhāyana is clearly detectable. He salutes Baudhāyana himself, and Āpastamba who really was later than the original Baudhāyana amongst the Dharma-sūtra-kāras. Some of his chapters are regarded as late. It seems that the revision took place in the early Śuṅga period or very little before that. The original edition would have been before

Āpastamba, *i.e.*, before 450 B.C. or 500 B.C., (see also § 6 of Lect. IV below, On Bau. and Vasishṭha's definitions of Aryan India of their times see Lect. II. § 12). Vasishṭha's sūtra in its present shape is admittedly very late. There was, no doubt, an earlier edition, traces of which are prominent, but the present Vasishṭha cannot be earlier than 100 B.C. and might be later. It borrows largely from the present edition of Baudhāyana.

Vaikhānasa dharma-Praśna is a regular dharmasūtra, still a part of a Kalpa sūtra. [*Cf.* Jolly, *RS.*, § 3]. Being the most important authority of the Sūtra period on the hermit and ascetic āśramas, it has been used as a manual by the Sannyāsins. And for that reason, it has suffered in one respect : the worship and cult of Nārāyaṇa which has been the ruling practice and belief of the Sannyāsins has been engrafted on to the Sūtra. But fortunately there is no other change, and the added material can be easily detected. Baudhāyana in II. 6. 11, II. 7. 12, and II. 10. 17, II. 10. 18, III. 1. quotes from the *Vaikhānasaśāstra*, and a comparison will prove that Baudhāyana had the present sūtra before him minus the lines about Nārāyaṇa. The edition of M. M. Gaṇapati Sastri (1913) has a purer text than what the Vienna MS possesses. It has no fourth *praśna*, and *budhavāra* (Tuesday) [Jolly, RS.] is not found in it. The work is undoubtedly pre-Buddhistic. The *Vānaprasthin* kept *śrāmaṇaka* fire (II. 5) and observed various austerities or *tapasyā*. On account of this hard life (*śrama*), it was called *śrāmaṇaka*. Meat-eating was allowed. But to the *Bhikshu* (one in the fourth āśrama) it was prohibited. The Bhikshu shaved his head and so did the hermit. A Parama-Haṃsa ascetic may be without clothes (I. 9. 5).

A householder had to kill animals at his sacrifices (I. V. 3). Quotations in Bau. are so close that in some places the text of the printed edition can be corrected—at p. 8 (I. VII. 9) *unmattako* is to be restored from Baudhāyana as *unmajjako* (Bau. III. 3. 11). The interval between Vikhanas and Baudhāyana is so great that the Vānaprasthins are called Vaikhānasas (Bau. III. 3), after the name of the author of this treatise owing to the special feature of his work in dealing with the subject of their life. It is significant that amongst the living Buddhists (*e.g.*, in Ceylon) a distinction is made between *Sramaneras* and *Bhikkhus.* The Buddhists evidently borrowed the terms from Vikhanas. The Sūtra of Vikhanas is the only pre-Buddha Dharma-sūtra.

LECTURE III

DATE AND CHARACTER OF THE CODE OF YĀJNAVALKYA

Division—Style—interpolated parts—the Author and his sources—Date of the Code—criticism of the earlier view—Scientific character of the Code—its advancement—its conservatism—other Codes between Manu and Yājñvalkya.

§ 1. The second Code of our study, the *Yājñavalkya-Smṛiti*, belongs to the class of Sumati's Mānava Code. Like the latter, the Code of Yājñavalkya is a Dharma-Vyavahāra Code covering the whole area of the law secular as well as the law canonical. The stage had yet to come when this unhistorical amalgamation was to be rejected and law proper restored to its original entity. Although this achievement was still reserved for Nārada and his followers, Bṛihaspati[1] and Kātyāyana,[2] our author 'Yājñāvalkya' made an immense advance in that direction by making sharp divisions of his Code into Āchāra (I), Vyavahāra (II), and Prāyaśchitta (III). The first and the last were the real subjects of the Dharma-śāstra. The third one (law proper) was introduced in the middle, as a sort of appendix to the Āchāra of the king. This was in conformity with the practice of the later Dharma-sūtras. But Yājñavalkya makes quite a distinct division and treats law proper as an independent

[1] For the translation of *Nārada* and *Bṛihaspati*, see Jolly, *S.B.E*, xxxiii. Bṛihaspati's Code was restored, from fragments in quotations by Jolly, but it was not published. [Prof. Chakladar has prepared a larger edition.]

[2] [As a result of these lectures, Mr. N. C. Bandopādhyāya (Calcutta) has collected fragments of Kātyāyana and rendered them in the form of a Smṛiti Code.]

An example of converting a purely Dharma-book into a legal-canonical code is the *Parāśara-Mādhavīya* of recent history. Mādhava, the Prime Minister and the great Brahmin scholar of the Vijayanagara kingdom, did what Sumati, and the author of the Vishṇu Smṛiti and Yājñavalkya did in ancient days. He combined the two subjects in one code.

subject in the fashion of a finished lawyer. He does not give lectures on secular law from the Dharma-lawyer's point of view, he lays down clean-cut provisions of law into, so to say, so many sections. Nor does he devote a preponderating space to ā c h ā r a as in Manu. He gave it only as much space, as he gives to V y a v a h ā r a, if not less. The style is severe, like that of the Sūtra-works, and it is so marked that interpolations in three places are easily detected. In the last book (on the Penances), the author first deals with funeral impurity in 34 verses, with expiation for abnormal life in distress in 10 verses (35-44),[1] and with the severe life of penances of the hermit-stage (Vānaprastha) in 11 verses (45-55). Then follow another 11 verses (56-66) on the life of the ascetic (the fourth Āśrama). After them, into the same section, 137 verses (67-203) have been introduced giving anatomy of human body and a long discourse on *Yoga*, which are no part of a Dharma-śāstra. The interpolated nature is evident from the facts (1) that the last verse, 205, of the section, which is a regular Dharma-śāstra view against asceticism,[2] and which ought to be just after the ascetic description, reappears at the end of the Yoga disquisition.[1] It seems to have been cut away from its original position immediately after verse 66. (2) The style is loose, the whole disquisition is a dialogue,[3]

Divisions and Style.

Additions.

[1] References are to Mr. V. N. Mandlik's edition (*The Vyavahāra-Mayūkha and the Yājñavalkya Smṛiti*, I, Bombay, 1880).

[2] The dharmaśāstras discourage the fourth stage and give riders to that effect. Yajñavalkya likewise says, "Even a house-holder who has acquired his fortune honestly, who diligently pursues knowledge, who is hospitable to guests, who worships his departed ancestors periodically, and who speaks the truth, can obtain final emancipation"

न्यायागतधनस्तत्त्वज्ञाननिष्ठोऽतिथिप्रियः ।
श्राद्धकृत्सत्यवादी च गृहस्थोऽपि हि मुच्यते ॥ III 205.

[3] *Yājñ.* III. 117-8, 129: अनादिरात्मा कथितस्तस्यादिस्तु शरीरकम् ।
आत्मनस्तु जगत्सर्वं जगतश्चात्मसंभवः ॥ 117.
कथमेतद्विमुह्यामः सदेवासुरमानवम् ।
जगदुद्भूतमात्मा च कथं तस्मिन्वदस्व नः ॥ 118.
यद्येवं स कथं ब्रह्मन्पापयोनिषु जायते ।
ईश्वरः स कथं भावैरनिष्टैः संप्रयुज्यते ॥ 129.

a characteristic not to be found anywhere else in the body of the Code. (3) It bears traces of having belonged to another treatise. The expounder is addressed as "Brahman," and he describes his Yoga system as having been learnt from the Sun, and to be regarded as sacred as an Āraṇyaka. According to the Gîtā (4.1) the Sun taught Yoga to Manu. The very doctrines quoted in our second Code are attributed to Vishṇu in the Vishṇu Smṛiti. It is thus apparent that the *Yogaśāstra* introduced into the Code is the work of some other writer who had combined the teachings of the Gîtā[1] and the standard Māheśvara Yoga. The discussions indicated by verse 118 are only to be found in part in the Code, which shows the interpolated and borrowed nature of the subject. Likewise the colophon (329 to 335), which mentions the closing of the assembly and their thanks to Yājña-valkya, is apocryphal and is so admittedly. The original book on Penances thus had some 192 verses (335-137-6).

§ 2. In the Introduction, the first two verses, relating the circumstances under which Yājñavalkya composed the Code, are admittedly later. The next verse, like the opening in the Dharma-sūtras, mentions the sources of law. But the following two verses (4-5) break the subject by introducing the names of the Dharma-śāstras in which even the name of Yājñavalkya himself is given and works of later date (*viz.*, Vyāsa, Bṛihaspati) are also given.[2] These two verses are not only out of place but clearly later. Verse 6 is a verse on gift which has no connection with the subject. Verse 7

[1] *Cf.* the *Hārīta-Sūtra* citing verses in the Gītā style from a *Kāma-Gīti* [Aparārka, p. 211]. (Ānandāśrama *ed.*, 1903). The style of Hārîta is like that of Kauṭilya, e.g. आहवयुद्धो मस्त्युद्धिरित्याचार्याः. Hârîta is considered to be the oldest Dharma-sūtra [Jolly, *Recht und Sitte*, § 3].

[2] *Yājñavalkya*, I. 4-5 :

मन्वत्रिविष्णुहारीतयाज्ञवल्क्योशनोऽङ्गिराः ।
यमापस्तम्बसंवर्ताः कात्यायनबृहस्पती ॥ 4.
पराशरव्यासशङ्खलिखिता दक्षगौतमौ ।
शातातपो वसिष्ठश्च धर्मशास्त्रप्रयोजकाः ॥ 5.

again takes up the sources of law and is a quotation from the Mānava Code. Verse 8 enumerates good conduct and mentions the practice of Yoga as dharma, which again is out of place and has nothing to do with the sources of the Dharma-law, and must have been added at the time of the addition of the Yoga disquisition. The next and the last verse (9) of the Introduction is again a regular doctrine of the Dharma school on the sources of the Dharma law : the assembly (Parshat) is to lay down law on mute points. Thus 6 out of the 9 verses of the Introduction are clumsy interpolations. Apart from this there is no trace of later additions in the book. If we separate these, the number of verses in each book would stand as follows :—

Āchāra	301,
Kingly duties	60,
Vyavahāra	307,
Penances	192,

which make up the round number of 860, against the present number 1010.

§ 3. Yājñavalkya was a family name, like Bhārgava in Sumati Bhārgava. The personal name of the author is lost. The Introduction calls him Yājñavalkya, the prince of Yogins, but that has reference to the disquisition on Yoga. His alleged association with Mithilā may be based on historical fact, but occurring in the legendary and apocryphal part of the Introduction the allegation loses its value. The Yājñavalkya family was associated with Mithilā and Videha but it cannot be said that the Yājñavalkyas never went out of North Bihar and that they were not to be found in other parts of the country. Yājñavalkya's

The Author and his sources.

treatment of the Yajurveda with marked partiality,[1] his leaning towards the Mantras of the White Yajus, and some analogies between the doctrines of Pāraskara's Gṛihya Sūtra and our Code,

[1] *Yājñ.* I, 42.

would warrant us in saying that the author belonged to the White Yajurveda and that he adhered to the Vedic school of his family. But we cannot go further and assert, as was done by Jolly and others[1] that the analogies prove the existence of a Dharma-sūtra which was the basis of the Yājñavalkya Code. No such Dharma-sūtra is mentioned anywhere. We can only say that the Code is based on (1) the Mānava Code as pointed out by Stenzler, (2) the Vishṇu-Smṛiti, as pointed out by Jolly, and lastly, and for law proper mainly, on the Arthaśāstra of Kauṭilya, as we shall see in the course of the present lectures.

§ 4. On the date of Yājñavalkya's Code, it has been argued that as the code refers to the Grahas or planets, it must be later than the 2nd century A.C.[2] But as Bühler has pointed out, that it is not proved that a work having reference to the Greek astronomy must be dated in the 4th century A.C. The publication of fresh Babylonian tablets has destroyed the old argument that Ptolemy was the founder of the so-called Greek astrology. Bühler's demur to accept the argument is now fully supported. Then, it is wrong to say that the earlier Dharmaśāstras do not know the Grahas mentioned in Yājñavalkya. Baudhāyana's Dharma-sūtra not only knows them but places them in the same order as Yājñavalkya with the same addition of Rāhu and Ketu.[3] Baudhāyana offers them Tarpaṇa (pacification). Yājñavalkya has simply taken them from Baudhāyana. The prominence in Yājñavalkya only shows that the belief had become stronger.

Similarly reference to the worship of Gaṇeśa or Gaṇapati does not prove any late date of Yājñavalkya. Baudhāyana knows Gaṇapati and the different forms of Vināyaka.[4] Gaṇapati is found carved in temples of Gupta times. It is to be noted that Gaṇe'a in the Gupta period is a

[1] Jolly, *Recht und Sitte*, §6.
[2] Jolly, *The Institutes of Vishṇu*, S.B.E. VII. pp. xx-xxi.
[3] Jayaswal, *I.A.*, 1918, p. 112; *Baudhāyana*, I. 5. 9. (9).
[4] *Bau.*, I. 5. 9 (7)

benevolent deity but in Yājñavalkya he is malignant and dreadful.

§ 5. Yājñavalkya counts the Nakshatras from Kṛittikā as the first[1], which was an ancient system. In the Gupta period the system had been given up and the Nakshatras were reckoned from Aśvinî. These facts indicate a period anterior to the Guptas. So do the political and social data. Yājñavalkya does not give any definition of 'Āryāvarta.' In the period before the rise of the Guptas the very centres of Aryan culture and orthodoxy had been under the Mlechchhas. An ethnic definition like that of Manu was impossible. The heretic is still tabooed,[2] but degrading provisions against nuns have been removed. Meat-śrāddha[3] is still allowed, and bull-sacrifice in honour of a guest still sanctioned (I. 109), though it is omitted from the Śrāddha list where rhinoceros is still retained.[4] Meat-eating is at the same time discouraged for the Brahmin (I. 181). The Atharvan, as a Veda, is yet not fully admitted. (I. 101, I. 3, 9).

§ 6. The punishment provided for the forgery of coin called here Nāṇaka,[5] proves that the work has to be referred to the closing period of the Sātavāhanas and about the middle of the Kushan period. Kanishka who founded his dynasty about the end of the first century A.C. had the word Nānā on his gold coins. The dynasty was Hinduised; their coins were generally Śivite. 'Nāṇaka' became the other name for the Śivite Coin, and coin in general.[6] Kanishka's rule extended up to Benares and Ayodhyā, without doubt, and probably up to Pāṭaliputra. His and his successors' coins gave the name Nāṇaka to the gold-coins of the time, like the Āśrafî of the Muhammedan times. Contemporary sub-kings

---

[1] *Yājñavalkya*, I. 267. [2] *Yājñavalkya*, III. 6. [3] *Ibid.*, I. 46, 258-60.

[4] *Ibid.*, I. 259. Bṛihaspati says that bulls were eaten only in the Madhya country, and implies that it was considered sinful in other parts. *Vyavahāra Mayūkha* (ed. Mandlik). p. 8,

[5] *Yājñ.*, II. 240-54.

[6] Y. I 241, and in the *Mṛichchhakaṭika* (I. 23) (*nāṇaka-mūshikā*. The commentator Pṛithvîdhara says, *nāṇaṁ Śivāṅkaṁ ṭaṅkādi-vittaṁ*). *Cf.* Bṛihaspati (Vîr. M., p. 383).

might have had their own Nāṇakas or might have adopted the Kushan Nāṇaka in their currency. The period of the Code, in view of the above data, therefore, would be about 150-200 A.C. It cannot be earlier, and it cannot be much later.

§ 7. The highly developed stage of trade, evidenced by the laws in the Code about partnerships and contract and foreign commerce,[1] also takes us to the Andhra-Kushan period which is noted for the oversea (Roman, Alexandrian, and Chinese) commerce.

§ 8. Yājñavalkya probably wrote somewhere in the Madhyadeśa, for had he written his work in Western India where the Sātavāhanas were supreme, he would not have mentioned 'nāṇaka.' And as he contemplates the existence of an orthodox prince,[2] apparently in Madhyadeśa, he would have written the Code in the kingdom of some small prince of the Madhyadeśa. It is significant that Manu's prohibition of gifts from non-Kshatriya kings have been omitted by Yājñavalkya.

Scientific character of the Code.

Nor is there any pointed hostility to the Mlechchhas. He wrote at a time when the Mlechchhas were evidently ruling. But his work being a purely scientific book, the scientific attitude and freedom from prejudice made the work acceptable throughout India. It was not a mere chance that jurists like Vijñāneśvara and Aparārka selected it as the basis of their writings. Religious schools have also given it unstinted honour. The Ṛig-Vedins have adopted the work, although it does not belong to their Veda.

§ 9. The Code of Yājñavalkya reduced the fanatical penances of Manu to very reasonable limits. It raises the position of the Śūdra, allows him Chāndrāyaṇa penance which had been open only to the twice-born, enjoins respect to be shown to him when gifted with knowledge, and allows trade to him.[3] The extravagant

Its social laws.

1 These laws will be discussed in a subsequent Lecture (on Contract, Lect. X).
2 *Ibid.*, I. 311, 3 Y. III. 262, 268; I.. 886; 120; 166 see also III. 22.

punishments for his suppression are omitted. Likewise, the extravagant claims of the Brahmin for total immunity is set aside, and he is brought under the king's law. The profession of arms is once more forbidden to the Brahmin.[1] His claim to sovereignty is ignored.

§ 10. As we shall see later, Yājñavalkya bears the stamp of the kindly conscience bequeathed by Buddhism during its past revolution. Punishments are, like penances, much less severe, and here the Code is an advancement not only on Manu but also upon Kauṭilya. Laws about women are brought in conformity with their social position, already immensely raised by Buddhism. Their right to inherit was fully admitted.[2] It is possible that it received imperial recognition during the early Gupta times, and in their reign, we may presume, it extended to Western India where it has remained the ruling authority. The Code may be taken to have replaced and repealed Manu's Code throughout the land of Aryan civilisation.

Its advancement.

§ 11. Yājñavalkya with his progressive tendency still retains orthodox conservatism. It is due to this feature that it outlived the true codes of law like that of Nārada. The orthodox school favoured Yājñavalkya. Yājñavalkya may be credited to have given a permanent life to the Dharma-Vyavahāra mixed system of law in the country. Without him probably today we would have been more used to Nārada, or Bṛihaspati and Kātyāyana, and we would not have lost the latter two.

Its conservatism.

§ 12. We have already seen that the Dharma-sūtra of Vasishṭha was revised a little after the Mānava Code. Vasishṭha is the first example of the attempt to convert a Dharmasūtra into a canonical-secular law-book after the pattern of the Mānava

Law-books between Manu and Yājñavalkya.

[1] Cf. III. 35 Discussed in a subsequent Lecture below.
[2] See Lecture on Family Law below.

Code. The attempt is repeated in the form of the Vishṇu-dharma-śāstra.[1] The frame work of this Dharmaśāstra is a sūtra work, whereon there is a super-imposition of the Vyavahāra-law. The mixture is concealed under the name of God Vishṇu. This is the first attempt to attribute a law-book to a divine origin. We do not know when the work was ascribed to Vishṇu. There are three stages in the development of this work. The first is the framework of a Dharmasūtra belonging to a school of the Kṛishṇa Yajus, very probably to the Kaṭhas as contended for by Jolly. The subject-matter of this stage is certainly older than the Mānava Code and the present Vasishṭha. The second stage is marked by the usurpation of the function of dictating secular laws. This stage belongs to the intermediary period between the two Codes. The third seems to be one when it is given a sectarian Vaishṇava clothing, with the inclusion of a lot of non-dharmaśāstra matters. This is post-Yājñavalkyan. The strictly legal portion is important for the purposes of comparison. Vishnu follows Manu, and Yājñavalkya seems to be conscious of Vishnu's laws, though in places there are clear cases of borrowing by Vishṇu from Yājñavalkya. We can, with the help of Vishṇu and Vasishṭha, detect some of the changes introduced in Manu in its revision, and can mark also the process of development of law in Yājñavalkya. Take, for instance, the dharma-provision in Manu, prohibiting to the Brahmin gifts from and food from certain classes of people[2]. Vishṇu[3] gives the classes which are peculiar to Manu, except the king. Vasishṭha also has no prohibition against gifts from kings[4]. Vishṇu on the other hand expressly sanctions it[5]. The prohibition relates really to the king, who was greedy and who discarded the śāstras and who was not a Kshatriya.[6] Yājñavalkya follows closely Manu: he gives only the classes interdicted in Manu, and prohibits the gift of the greedy and the Śāstra-hating king and the food of a

[1] See colophon, p. 213 (ed. Jolly).
[2] M. IV. 205-218, 219-221.
[3] Vi., LI. 7-16.
[4] *Cf.* Va. V. 30, VI. 27-29.
[5] *Cf.* Vi. III. 84.
[6] *Cf.* Aparārka, on Y, I. 164, भूपो नतु चत्रियः ।

cruel king.[1] It is thus evident that the prohibition against the king's gift was not in the original Mānava Code. It was inserted in the revision, and at that time there were undoubtedly a number of Śāstra-hating and non-Kshatriya kings in the country. Yājñavalkya adopts the spirit and leaves out the caste-criterion, looking at the confused state of the society around him.

These intermediary law-books never obtained the status of authoritative Codes. As law-books they were too poor to attain that position.

[1] Y. I. 161-165, 164 नृशंसराजं° Viśvarūpa : नृशंसः···राजविशेषणं वा ।

APPENDIX B to LECTURE III.

On the Age of the later Dharma-śāstras.

Codes of Nārada, Brihaspati and Kātyāyana. In Lecture IV, § 10 gives new data for Nārada's date. It is noteworthy that verses 1-4 and 5 of Yājñavalkya which enumerate 20 authors of DharmaŚāstras do not include Nārada, although they mention Vishṇu. Viśvarūpa has these verses in their oldest form.[1] Instead of 'Yājñavalkya' we have 'I' there, and placed last. Vijnāneśvara had the other text, and Aparārka gives both.[2] Viśvarūpa (p. 10) cited another ('enlarged') edition of Yājñavalkya ('*Vriddha-Yā°*') wherein Nārada is included. The only conclusion we can draw from this is that Nārada's was not regarded as a dharma-code when Yājñavalkya's code was added to or revised, as it has the later writers Vyāsa, Kātyāyana, Bṛihaspati etc. Omission of Baudhāyana from the list is significant. Probably the verses only meant metrical treatises. It seems that Nārada being purely a Vyavahāra author was omitted. Under the name of *Kātyāyana*, there were probably more than one work on dharma subjects.[3] *Brihaspati's* independent work on law proper, like that of Nārada, is known to have existed in manuscripts till recent times.[4] On the analogy of Bṛihaspati's *vyavahāra* code, with which *Kātyāyana* forms a twin, we may assume that Kātyāyana had a work purely on Vyavahāra.[5] These two must be very near the time of Nārada. The Commentators of the eighth or ninth century A.C. fix the lower limit of Bṛihaspati and Kātyāyana—they could not be later than the seventh century. The tradition in the Skanda Purāṇa places Nārada before the composition of Bṛihaspati's Code. This agrees with the date proposed by me on internal evidence, namely, that Nārada belongs to early Gupta times.[6] The provisions of Bṛihaspati and Kātyāyana themselves show that Bṛihaspati developed the laws of Nārada, and that Kātyāyana further improved upon Bṛihaspati. By allowance of time for the natural process we would have to place Nārada in the fourth or fifth century B.C. It is noteworthy that all these three Gupta Codes use the word *Dināra*[7] to denote the current gold coin. They evidently belong to one political period, the period of the same currency. Except the Gupta period there is no other political period long enough to afford time to the rise of their law codes.

The *Vishṇu Smṛiti's* definition of Āryāvarta discloses the unsettled political state of the author's time :—

'The country in which the caste-system (four-fold varṇas) does not obtain is the mlechchha-country. Āryāvarta is beyond that.' The knowledge is general that beyond India there was nowhere the caste system. But the author in place of Manu's description that the land beyond Āryāvarta was mlechchha-deśa, inverts the order and describes Āryāvarta by describing the mlechchha-land. His meaning is what Medhātithi says. Even if in India there are foreigners anywhere, *that part* ceases to be Āryāvarta. Yājñavalkya similarly in not attempting a territorial description follows Vishṇu.

[1] Trivandrum Sanskrit Series LXXIV (ed. Ganapati Sastri, 1922), p. 9.

[2] Ānandāśrama, 1903, p. 7, *n.*

[3] Jolly, *Right and Sitte*, § 8.

[4] *Ibid.*, § 9.

[5] *Cf.* Jolly, *Rect*, §§ 8-9.

[6] *Cf.* Jolly, *RS.*, § 9, who would place Bṛihaspati in the 6th or 7th Century A.C.

[7] *Ibid*

LECTURE IV

THEORY OF SOURCES AND ADMINISTRATION OF LAW

Origins of Dharma-law according to our Codes and earlier Samayas—Vedas—Smriti—Purana—Kalpa—Nyaya—'Aryan Practice'—Vedic rituals—King-made laws—'Charitra'—Parishad—Rule of Reason and Good Conscience —Danda—Theory of Punishment—Caste and Administration of Law.

Origins of Dharma Law :

§ 1. Āpastamba describes the dharma-laws as those which regulate conduct and which are based on resolutions or Samaya*s*.[1] The word *samaya*, which has been translated by European scholars as 'agreement,' really means a resolution passed by corporate bodies[2]. The dharma-samaya*s* were thus laws resolved upon by certain popular bodies. These popular bodies were the bodies of the Vedic schools, collectively or individually. Āpastamba here gives the real origin of the dharma-rules. They were originally communal rules agreed upon in assemblies. The same origin is implied by Āpastamba in his last Sūtras, where he says that authoritative works do not exhaust the dharma-laws and hence the unanimous practice of all the Aryan countries is to be referred to[3].

Samaya*s*

§ 2. Āpastamba lays down : "The Resolution of the dharma-knowing (assembly) is Authority". "And the Vedas".[4] Texts for sacraments in the Grihya-sūtras go back to the Vedas. Further, if you refer to Ch. III of Yāska you would find that the dharma-lawyers had recourse to Vedic passages for their legal principles of inheritance. This is really what is meant by the Vedas as the source of the dharma-law. It is noteworthy that this reference to the Vedic literature on questions of the dharma-law was placed by

Veda*s*

---

1 अथातः सामयाचारिकान् धर्मान् व्याख्यास्यामः ॥ I. 1, 1, 1.

2 *Hindu Polity*, I. p. 124 ; *Vīramitrodaya*, (Calcutta 1875), pp. 423-25.

3 II, 11. 29. 13-14 .

4 धर्मज्ञसमयः प्रमाणम् ॥ २ ॥ वेदाश्च ॥ ३ ॥ I. 1, 1, (2-3).

Āpastamba next to the resolutions, in authority. Yāska gives contradictory views on inheritance ; it seems that some agreement in the Vedic schools had to be arrived at by resolutions and common agreement.

'Smṛiti'

The later Dharmasūtras, however, mention the Vedas as the chief source. The "Samaya" source which was the main in Āpastamba, disappears in the later sūtras. The laws had already been settled and no need of the Samayas remained. In place of the *Samaya*, we get Smṛiti, that is, the literature which had grown up on the dharma-laws. Literature takes the place of the living organism. Baudhāyana says : "Dharma is laid down in respective Vedas ; the Smṛiti (dharma-law) is the second source." [1] Gautama says: "Veda is the source of dharma, Smṛiti of the Veda-knowers (Vedic schools) is another source."[2]

Smṛiti [3] here signifies, as interpreted by the commentators, the Gṛihya and Dharmasūtras of the Vedic schools. The Dharma-sūtra being the last addition to the Kalpasūtra (Aṅga) and being in portions independent of the Vedic rites, soon developed into a separate literature. Hence Gautama has Dharmaśāstras apart from the *Aṅgas*.[4]

'Dharma-śāstra'

§ 3. Sumati Bhārgava equates Smṛiti with Dharma-Śāstra and makes *Śruti* (Veda) and *Dharmaśāstra* the only sources of the dharma-law [5]. He would not go to the historic basis of the

---

[1] I. 1. (1) : उपदिष्टो धर्मः प्रतिवेदम् ॥ १ ॥ स्मार्तो द्वितीयः ॥ २ ॥

[2] I. 1-2 : वेदो धर्ममूलम् ॥ १ ॥ तद्विदां च स्मृतिशीले ॥ २ ।

[3] "Tradition" probably is not a happy translation. The *Smriti* is contra-distinguished from *Śruti.* The latter is the Vedic literature proper, the recitation of which by itself was considered meritorious. Its passages were '*heard*' at sacrifices and sacraments. But the Kalpa literature, which directed the methods of ceremonies, was not to be recited but to be *remembered.* This is the real distinction.

Cf. Viśvarūpa on Y. I. 4-5.

[4] Gautama-Dharma-Sāstra, XI. 19 ; धर्मशास्त्राण्यङ्गान्युपवेदाः पुराणम् ।

[5] *Manu*, II. 10 : श्रुतिस्तु वेदो विज्ञेयो धर्मशास्त्रं तु वै स्मृतिः ।
ते सर्वार्थेष्वमीमांस्ये ताभ्यां धर्मो हि निर्बभौ ॥

Dharma-laws, but would limit himself to the Dharma-literature. P a t a ñ j a l i also recognises only the literature authority of the Dharma-sūtras, collectively calling it the *Dharmaśāstra.*[1] But this view of literature-sources, thus narrowed down to two, was not in accordance with the earlier view of the Dharma-school. S u m a t i B h ā r g a v a not only neglected the K a l p a s ū t r a *s* but also another literature. The P u r ā ṇ a is treated by Āpastamba as a source, for he quotes from it.[2] G a u t a m a expressly counts it.[3] Y ā j ñ a v a l k y a goes back to the ancient tradition[4] and takes not only the A ṅ g a *s* (which include the K a l p a *i.e.* the Śrauta, Gṛihya and Dharma sūtras) but also the P u r ā ṇ a, as the sources of the Dharma-law.

P u r ā ṇ a

K a l p a

§ 4. We find already Ā p a s t a m b a employing *Nyāya* in the interpretation of the dharma-laws.[5] K a u ṭ i l y a gives it the position of the determining authority in considering dharma texts.[6] S u m a t i condemns the very employment of the *Hetu-Śāstra*[7] against sacred texts. Y ā j ñ a v a l k y a[8] accepts both *Nyāya* and *Mīmāṃsā*, the latter of which had been already tacitly accepted in

N y ā y a

---

[1] Patañjali, *Mahābhāshya*, I, 2. 3, (on Vārttika 39 to P. 1. 2. 64),

धर्मशास्त्रं च तथा ।

[2] *Āpastamba*, Dharma-sūtra (I. 6,19), II. 9 (6) cf. Gautama, DhŚ. XI. 49.

[3] *Gautama*, VIII, 6 ;

वाकोवाक्येतिहासपुराणकुशलः ।

See also foot-note [2].

[4] *Yājñavalkya*, I. 3 :

पुराणन्यायमीमांसाधर्मशास्त्राङ्गमिश्रिताः ।
वेदाः स्थानानि विद्यानां धर्मस्य च चतुर्दश ॥

[5] *Āpastamba*, II, 6. 14. 13 :

अथापि नित्यानुवादमविधिमाहुर्न्यायविदो यथा
तस्मादजावयः पशूनां सह चरन्तीति । तस्मात्
स्नातकस्य मुखं रेफायतीव ।

[6] *Arthaśāstra*, ch. 58, p. 150 :

न्यायस्तत्र प्रमाणं स्यात् तत्र पाठो हि नश्यति ।

[7] *Manu*, II. 11 :

योऽवमन्येत ते तूभे हेतुशास्त्राश्रयाद्द्विजः ।
स साधुभिर्बहिष्कार्यो नास्तिको वेदनिन्दकः ॥

[8] See foot-note [4].

Baudhāyana.[1] Gautama also recognises it.[2] In cases of conflict, Gautama[3] makes Vedic scholars authority, as against Kauṭilya's Nyāya.[4] But Sumati puts forward an amazing proposal : both the conflicting texts are law (both must be followed)[5]. Yājñavalkya would not adopt such an attitude of senseless orthodoxy. He lays down that when two Smṛiti texts are in conflict, the authority of Nyāya will prevail; but he limits this rule to the Vyavahāra or the law portion proper of the Dharmaśāstra [6]. He remains silent on the question of a conflict in the Dharma-laws. At the same time, he makes it clear that the laws of the Dharmaśāstra are in authority superior to the laws of the Artha-Śāstra in general [7]. In place of 'Vyavahāra' of Kauṭilya's Code, Yājñavalkya puts down 'Artha-Śāstra', which in the light of our interpretation of *Vyavahāra*, is identical with the 'Vyavahāra laws.' The views of Kauṭilya and Yājñavalkya thus agree, except that the authority of Nyāya is limited by the latter to the Vyavahāra portion of the Smṛiti. This was done to meet halfway the orthodox, though illogical, view of Sumati.

§ 5. From these literary sources of law, we now pass on to other sources. Communal assembly was the primary

---

[1] *Baudhāyana*, I. 1, 1,8. *Cf. Manu*, XII. 111, and Kullūka's comment thereon.

[2] *Gautama*, XI, 23 ;

न्यायाधिगमे तर्कोऽभ्युपायः।

[3] *Gautama*, XI. 25 :

विप्रतिपत्तौ त्रैविद्यवृद्धेभ्यः प्रत्यवहृत्य निष्ठां गमयेत्।

[4] *Kauṭilya*, ch. 58, p. 150:

न्यायस्तत्र प्रमाणं स्यात् etc.

[5] *Manu*, II, 14 :

श्रुतिद्वैधं तु यत्र स्यात्तत्र धर्मावुभौ स्मृतौ।
उभावपि हि तौ धर्मौ सम्यगुक्तौ मनीषिभिः॥

[6] *Yājñavalkya*, II. 20 :

स्मृत्योर्विरोधे न्यायस्तु बलवान् व्यवहारतः।

[7] *Ibid.* II. 21.

authority in matters of *dharma*. We have also seen that Āpastamba enjoins that where written dharma-law was found insufficient, the unanimous practice of Aryan Countries was to be accepted as binding.

'Aryan Practice'

This position is greatly modified by the time of our Codes. The decisions of a communal assembly had long ceased to be a source of dharma. As to the practice of Aryan communities or countries, Gautama does not accept any country as the seat of authority. According to him, the Veda is the root of the *dharma*; the Smṛiti of 'the Veda-knowers' (Vedic schools. *i.e.* Kalpasūtras) and their practice are also the sources[1]. But in the next line he utters a caution as to the "practice." The practice had changed. The practice of old times, he says, is contrary to the dharma-law. But the (ancient) people were great, and their arbitrariness was no precedent for the present times. Where courses of practice of two equally great authorities are conflicting, one may be followed at pleasure[2]. Gautama confines "the practice" to precedents—practice as found in history, and not living practice. Society had changed and Gautama was conscious of the historical process of the change. He, therefore, would not launch himself into difficulty by recognising the living practice. He would confine himself to the written law. This, of course, is the position adopted in the present edition of Gautama. But there is an indication that the earlier edition had a similar doctrine. The quotation in Baudhāyana from Gautama to discredit the view which recognises localism in "Aryan practice", leans to it.[3]

§ 6. Baudhāyana limits the "practice" to the Śishtas or the Brahmins who observe Vedic discipline in their conduct.

---

[1] *Gautama*. I. 1-2 :
वेदो धर्ममूलम् । १ । तद्विदां च स्मृतिशीले । २ ।

[2] *Ibid.* I. 3-6:
दृष्टो धर्मव्यतिक्रमः । साहसं च महतां । न तु दृष्टार्थे
ऽवरदौर्बल्यात् । तुल्यबलविरोधे विकल्पः ।

[3] *Baudhāyana*, I. 24-25.

From communal he makes it individual "practice" of Vedic Brahmins. V a s i s h ṭ h a does the same with further modifications.[1] He introduces a doctrine of the M ī m ā ṃ s ā school in the discussion on the sources and applies it in a curious way. The Mīmāṃsā doctrine is that the dharma-law cannot be referred to human reasons. This was a description of the dharma-law. Vasishṭha uses it as a definition. Hence the authority of the practice of communities is naturally dislodged. Both Baudhāyana and Vasishṭha give the old doctrine of the binding force of the practice of the Āryāvarta, but they give it half-heartedly. After giving their own definitions of the Aryan India they go on to throw doubt by quoting definitions of much narrower limits and otherwise differing definitions of the ancients. Baudhāyana further weakens the territorial practice by pointing out that the people of the north and the west—the Āraṭṭas, the Kāraskaras, the Sauvīras, the Sindhus, the Saurāshṭras, and many communities of the Āryāvarta, had already become mixed in blood.[2] V a s i s h ṭ h a clearly says that the dharmas of the *pratilomas* (mixed) were no authority.[3]

Our M ā n a v a C o d e, however, echoes the ancient tradition. It reiterates that the l i v i n g p r a c t i c e of the Aryan countries is a source by itself, but it limits the territories to those between the rivers S a r a s v a t ī and D ṛ i s h a d v a t ī,—K u r u k s h e t r a, M a t s y a, P a ñ c h ā l a, Ś ū r a s e n, a and the next adjoining country the B r a h m ā v a r t a.[4]

---

[1] *Vasishṭha*, I. 5-7 :

सदलाभे शिष्टाचारः प्रमाणम् ॥ ५ ॥
शिष्टः पुनरकामात्मा ॥ ६ ॥
अगृह्यमाणकारणो धर्मः ॥ ७ ॥

[2] *Baudhāyana*, I. 1. 30-32.

[3] *Vasishṭha*. I. 11 :

न त्वन्ये प्रतिलोमकधर्माणाम्।

[4] *Manu*, II. 17-18 ;

सरस्वती दृषद्वत्योर्देवनद्योर्यदन्तरम्।
तं देवनिर्मितं देशं ब्रह्मावर्तं प्रचक्षते ॥
तस्मिन्देशे य आचारः पारंपर्यक्रमागतः।
वर्णानां सान्तरालानां स सदाचार उच्यते ॥

This was the sacred land of the Yajus and still in Sumati's time it was the land of pure Aryans. Sumati knows the limitation placed by Gautama, as he quotes his very words (वेदोऽखिलो धर्ममूलं स्मृतिशीले च तद्विदाम् । II. 6) : and he also knows the limitation placed by Baudhāyana, as he adds आचारश्चैव साधूनाम्, but he avowedly and distinctly calls the living practice of the Aryan communities to be an independent source.[1] He, unlike Vasishṭha, does not confine it to the case of *abhāva* (vacuum) or to the practice of individuals. Sumati could still count on a living, orthodox society, though only in one part, who were nearer the Vedic age and Vedic mode of living than the rest. Yājñavalkya found no such oasis of early society left around him.[2]

Vedic rituals if a Dharma Source ?

§ 8. The Mānava sets forth a controversy[3] as to whether acts which are based on 'desires' can be subject of Dharma. It says that it can be, because no action logically can be 'desire-less', and because the Vedas allow 'desirous-ness' by allowing sacrifices. We can understand its significance if we transport ourselves to the stock controversies of the heterodox schools of the time. Desire, according to them, was the chain which tied men to this world of misery. Maṅkhali Gosāla, the Jainas and the Buddhists were all unanimous on this reasoning to condemn Vedic sacrifices and to preach detachment. If attachment of itself stood condemned, how could the lofty term dharma be employed to rituals and ceremonials which were calculated to fulfil the objects of attachment ? The Mānava Code, like the Bhagavad-Gītā, fights this agrument

[1] *Ibid.* II. 17-18 : II. 19-20 ;

तस्मिन्देशे य आचारः etc.; एतद्देशप्रसूतस्य etc.

[2] *Cf. Yājñavalkya*, I. 7. See also Aparārka's comment thereon.

[3] *Manu*, II. 3-4 ;

संकल्पमूलः कामो वै यज्ञाः संकल्पसंभवाः ।
व्रतानि यमधर्माश्च सर्वे संकल्पजाः स्मृताः ॥
अकामस्य क्रिया काचिद्दृश्यते नेह कर्हिचित् ।
यद्यद्धि कुरुते किंचित्तत्कामस्य चेष्टितम् ॥

by saying that man cannot be 'without desire.' "K a r m a-y o g a" therefore, says the Mānava, like the Gītā, is allowed by orthodoxy [1]. The conclusion is that ritualistic matters are the subject of Dharma and the Dharma-laws. This controversy is for the first time raised and answered in the Mānava amongst our Dharma-law books. The C o d e of Y ā j ñ a v a l k y a adopts the theory without any controversy [2].

King-made Laws and the Artha-Śāstras

§ 9. The position of the k i n g - m a d e l a w in the Codes is significant. The king-made law in the A r t h a-Ś ā s t r a[3] is the highest kind of law. Even P a t a ñ j a l i places the 'order of the Ruler' as of higher authority than the Dharma-sūtra-kāras [4]. But the M ā n a v a would not accept the position. The Dharma was sacred, and the Vyavahāra was now merged in it. Nothing superior to his all-wide Dharma could be admitted by Sumati. He enumerates the eighteen classes of actions at law and says definitely that he takes the division from the Vyavahāra law.[5] We do get it in the Vyavahāra law of the Arthaśāstra of Kauṭilya. But at the same time Manu enjoins that in judging causes only "traditional Dharma" was to be followed [6]. The traditional Dharma, naturally, excludes the king-

---

[1] *Ibid.* II. 2 ; II. 5 ;

कामात्मता न प्रशस्ता न चैवेहास्त्यकामता ।
काम्यो हि वेदाधिगमः कर्मयोगश्च वैदिकः ॥ 2.
तेषु सम्यग्वर्तमानो गच्छत्यमरलोकताम् ।
यथा संकल्पितांश्चेह सर्वान्कामान्समश्नुते ॥ 5.

[2] *Yājñavalkya*, I. 7 ;

श्रुतिः स्मृतिः सदाचारः स्वस्य च प्रियमात्मनः ।
सम्यक् संकल्पजः कामो धर्ममूलमिदं स्मृतम् ॥

[3] *Kauṭilya*, op. cit., p. 150.

धर्मश्च व्यवहारश्च चरित्रं राजशासनम् ।
विवादार्थश्चतुष्पादः पश्चिमः पूर्वबाधकः ॥

[4] *Mahābhāshya*, on Pāṇini I, 1, 47.

[5] *Manu*, VIII. 7 ;

स्त्रीपुंधर्मो विभागश्च द्यूतमाह्वय एव च ।
पदान्यष्टादशैतानि व्यवहारस्थिताविह ॥

[6] *Ibid.* 8 ;

एषु स्थानेषु भूयिष्ठं विवादं चरतां नृणाम् ।
धर्मं शाश्वतमाश्रित्य कुर्यात्कार्यविनिर्णयम् ॥

made laws. Y ā j ñ a v a l k y a, on the other hand, recognises the authority of '*dharmo rājakritaścha yaḥ*', 'the l a w that is m a d e by the k i n g'[1], although he follows Sumati in his system of making the Vyavahāra subject to, and part of, the Dharma. He, like Sumati, would have justice administered in accordance with what he calls 'D h a r m a-Ś ā s t r a'—धर्मशास्त्रानुसारेण[2] (in place of Sumati's "Dharma").[3] While Sumati put it in the abstract, Yājñavalkya is putting it in the concrete. A D h a r m a-V y a v a h ā r a C o d e in the shape of S u m t i's M ā n a v a D h a r m a C o d e had now been established, and Yājñavalkya could very well refer to the 'D h a r m a C o d e.' The main difference between the two Codes is with regard to the position of the king-made law. Sumati ignores it. But king-made laws could not be ignored. The laws of the M a u r y a s, for instance, were too current to be ignored and some of them were too good to be ignored. They were cited as late as the time of D a ṇ ḍ i n, the author of the Daśakumāracharita, who mentions a special law of the Maurya times which prescribed that capital punishment was to be excused in cases of merchants found guilty of possessing stolen property[4]. The underlying principle seems to have been to presume very strongly fair dealing in a merchant, and presume him not to be a receiver of stolen property. Such an equitable provision outlived political and religious revolutions. Y ā j ñ a v a l k y a with the true spirit of the lawyer could not bar royal laws when such laws existed. In fact, he, as we shall see, incorporated many of such laws in his Code.

---

1 *Yājñavalkya*, II. 186.

निजधर्माविरोधेन यस्तु सामयिको भवेत् ।
सोऽपि यत्नेन संरक्ष्यो धर्मो राजकृतश्च यः ॥

2 *Ibid.* II. 1. व्यवहारान्नृपः पश्येद्विद्वद्भिर्ब्राह्मणैः सह ।
धर्मशास्त्रानुसारेण क्रोधलोभविवर्जितः ॥

3 *Manu*, VIII. 8. *supra.*

4 *Daśa-kumāra-charita*, Uttarakhaṇḍa, 2nd. Uchchhvāsa, 44. मौर्यदत्त एष वरो वणिजाम्, ईदृशेषु अपराधेषु नास्ति असुभिः अभियोगः । *Cf. A.Ś.*, ch. 87, p. 226.

King-made law and the Code of Nārada.

§ 10. At the same time Yājñavalkya does not admit that the authority of the royal laws could be higher than that of the Dharma-laws. We would not expect a Dharma-Śāstra admitting it. But curiously enough the N ā r a d a - S m ṛ i t i does admit it,[1] and admits it in the very terms of Kauṭilya. The Nāradan Code bears strong traces of a monarchist legislation. It is a work of the G u p t a t i m e s, and evidently a Gupta minister of law adopted the process described in the Ś u k r a - N i t i : "The P a ṇ ḍ i t a - A m ā t y a (called also D h a r m ā d h i k ā r i n) having considered what ancient and present laws are followed by the community and which of them are approved in the Codes and which of them are at present opposed to the Codes, which, again, are against (the opinion of) the community and against jurisprudence, may recommend to the king those of them which will secure behoof both here and hereafter."[2] The form of recommendation was undoubtedly a new code, under an old name, of course, like the P a r ā ś a r a C o d e by S u v r a t a and then by the minister M ā d h a v a.

Pseudo-Nārada not only recognises the king-made law but gives arguments for it : As the king has obtained lordship, he has to be obeyed. Polity depends on him.[3] Then his official duties[4] are compared with those of certain gods in terms of Manu, IX. 303—310. These are, properly speaking, in the nature of quotations. But his next provision lays down that non-compliance with king's laws would be punished with death,[5] which meant in those days, according to Fa-Hian, a heavy fine.

As to the age of the Nārada Code, there are traces of a recent political revolution in the Code of Nārada (xviii. 9 ; 45).

---

[1] *Nārada*, I. 10, 11.

[2] *Śukra-Nīti-sāra*, II. 99-100.

[3] *Nārada*, XVIII. 25.

तपःक्रीताः प्रजा राज्ञा प्रभुरासां ततो नृपः ।
ततस्तद्वचसि स्थेयं वार्ता चासां तदाश्रया ॥

[4] *Ibid.*. XVIII. 26-31.

[5] *Nārada*, XVIII. 32, तं नावजानीयात्···आज्ञायां चास्य तिष्ठेत मृत्युः ।

The Punjab was outside the jurisdiction of the Nārada Code (App. 39), the whole of the Prāchī (Magadha), and the Deccan were under its survey (App. 57). D ī n ā r a was a new coin, evidently the one struck in India after the Roman *denarius*.[1] All this, taken together, points to the time of Samudragupta and his immediate successors.[2] At that time people began to recall to their mind the political traditions of Chandragupta Maurya. Queens named their sons after him. Viśākhadatta dramatised the victory of C h a n d r a g u p t a M a u r y a over foreigners. Kāmandaka sought to popularise Chandraguptan politics in easy verses. Authors praised the Mauryan laws and Mauryan Code of polity. All eyes turned towards the history of Chandragupta Maurya and his system. The air was thick with what I may term *Chandraguptaism*, particularly at the beginning of the Gupta period. In that ferment pseudo-Nārada re-established with force the authority of the king-made law, the great legal principle of Chandraguptan system. He did not stop short with one provision, he undertook to re-enact largely the laws of Chandragupta the Great.

C h a r i t r a

§ 11. Another source of law in the Mauryan Code is C h a r i t r a, commonly translated as 'custom.' This has an engrossing history. Under the Mauryan empire there was a book or r e g i s t e r called S a ṅ g r a h a, in which Dharma-laws, Vyavahāra-laws, and C h a r i t r a ["conduct", "acts"] of 'D e ś a', 'G r ā m a', 'J ā t i', 'K u l a', and S a ṅ g h a s had been collected and kept up-to-date,[3]

---

[1] Jolly, SBE. 33, p. xviii.

[2] In discussing the date of the Code of Nārada, Bühler and Jolly (SBE. vol. 25, p. cvii *n.*, vol. 33, p. xviii) have said that Bāṇa mentions Nārada's law-book in a passage of his Kādambarī, but that passage refers to the *Nāradīya Rāja-Dharma* or *Artha-Śāstra*. Its existence has now been traced [Rāja-Nīti-Ratnākara, J. B. O. R S, 1924]. The main result of Dr. Jolly is that Nārada's law-book cannot be later than 400 or 500 A. C. (p. xviii).

[3] *Kauṭilya*, *op-cit*. p. 62 ,—
देश-ग्राम-जाति-कुल-सङ्घातानां धर्मव्यवहारचरित्रसंस्थानम्'' निबन्धपुस्तकस्थं कारयेत्. See Aparārka (p. 593) on Y. II. 1, (citing Nārada 'चरित्रं पुस्तकरणे'), चरित्रं देशग्रामकुलधर्मः तत्पुस्तकरणे ।

that is, the state had held a legal survey of India. It is now disclosed by recent researches that the "D e ś a" here denotes the J ā n a p a d a - c o r p o r a t i o n, as 'G r ā m a' means the t o w n - c o r p o r a t i o n,[1] J ā t i denotes the corporate bodies of castes, and K u l a was a body politic which had the system of oligarchy or aristocracy.[2] These were all corporate bodies which exercised the power of legislation and had their own laws, called S a m a y a and S a ṁ v i d.[3] The Mauryan law code recognised the special laws of these corporate bodies. They were declared to be of inferior authority, if they came in conflict with the common Dharma-laws; and they were, like any other law, subject to the statutes of the king.[4]

§ 12. In the light of these researches and the data of the Artha Śāstra, let us see the position of the so-called "c u s t o m a r y l a w s" in Manu and Yājñavalkya. They were, in fact, laws, regulations, bye-laws, and conventions of corporate associations. They were not customary laws; nor were they individual customs of families or local customs of a country. In other words, they were not what we call today K u l ā c h ā r a and D e ś ā c h ā r a in Anglo-Indian decisions.

§ 13. The Mānava in VIII. 41 enjoins upon the dharma lawyer to take notice of, and be guided by, the dharmas of the *Jāti*, of the *Jānapada*, of the *Śreṇī* (trade-guild) and the *Kula*. These were all corporate associations and possessed powers of legislation. Their laws as already pointed out, were called *samaya* and *saṁvid* and at times even *dharma*. The Mānava, again, accepts them in VIII. 219. Yājñavalkya (I. 360) follows Manu. It is to be marked that *deśa* in Manu, VIII. 219, is the Deśa-corporation, the same as

---

1 *Hindu Polity*, Pt. II, pp. 62ff : *Indian Antiquary*, 1929, p. 139.

2 *Hindu Polity*, Pt. II, pp. 65f. ; *Ibid.* Pt. I, pp. 85, 128. See also AS. ch. 129, p. 328; सङ्घानां सङ्घधर्मिणां च राजकुलानां etc.

Hindu Polity, Pt. II, pp. 65, 66, 106. AS. ch. 64, p. 165 : ch. 67, p. 173

AS.. ch. 68. p. 150. संस्थया''' नश्यति ।

the *Jānapada* of Yājñavalkya. The same thing is meant by d e ś a in Manu, VIII. 46.

Now all these bodies were institutions which could legislate. Their laws have been therefore recognised. Existence of the power of legislation was the test for such recognition. When we find that the laws of a country, which has been conquered, are to be upheld, the test is the same.[1] It was once a country with legislative powers. The Ā c h ā r a of a country was separate from the V y a v a h ā r a of a country. Ā c h ā r a related to sacerdotal matters, it was the sacerdotal Āchāra and conduct. The d e ś ā c h ā r a was not what we understand by it to-day, viz., the customary law of a country. The other phrase made after the model of *deśāchāra, viz.,* the 'K u l ā c h ā r a ', has no existence in the codes. They do not know such a thing as special laws or special customs of a family. No family as a family could legislate, it could have no laws of its own. There could be 'dharma' (traditional law) or statute law (S a m a y a and S a ṁ v i d) of tribes or castes, of guilds, of municipalities, and of a J ā n a p a d a or 'country association.' But the special law or customs of a particular family is unknown to these codes we are discussing. The K u l a of the codes was not a family, but a form of government.[2]

§ 14. M a n u and Y ā j ñ a v a l k y a, putting the *Jānapadas* and *Deśa-Saṅghas* in plural, indicate a time when several Jānapada assemblies existed under one ruler, when there was one emperor, but at the same time the empire was split up in country-units. This is exactly what the Mānava preaches. This is exactly what the Mauryas did not tolerate. In the records of A ś o k a we have only one J ā n a p a d a for the whole country.[3] But M a n u stands for the old tradition which would not allow the

---

[1] *Yājñ.* I, 342;

किन्तु यस्मिन् य आचारो व्यवहारः कुलस्थितिः ।
तथैव परिपाल्योऽसौ यदा वशमुपागतः ॥

[2] *Hiudu Polity*, Pt. II, p.65.

[3] Rock Edict, VIII. The *AŚ.* advocates an all-India empire (ch. 122, p. 338).

abolition of the separate territorial entities. The Mānava in effect condemns centralised imperialism.[1]

§ 15. The old national assembly, the Vedic Parishad,[2] or Samiti, was the body which originally, as Āpastamba implies, settled what the Dharma-law ought to be. But in an age when the Dharma-law had grown in literature, the provision for the determination of law by the assembly, the assembly as the source of law, came to be limited to the cases where text-books were silent. The assembly which still retained the Vedic name Parishad, was also narrowed down in its strength. The number was early fixed at ten, as the quotation in Baudhāyana[3] and the provision in Vasishṭha,[4] prove. This was a Parishad of experts: four men representing the four Vedas. one Mīmāṃsaka, one reciter of the dharma-texts, one knowing the Aṅgas, and three Brahmins representing the three orders. There had been, however, a tendency to limit the number still further (Baud. I. 1, 1. 9), the minimum being a Parishad of three[5]. The odd number three was based on the principle of voting. The Buddhists followed the system of the country when they laid down that the minimum strength of a Saṅgha quorum should be three.[6] Bṛihaspati (I. 11) also gives the same minimum to the town-corporation and other bodies. Yājñavalkya adheres to this rule when he prescribes the Parishad of three.[7] But in place of the assembly of ten, an ancient quorum, Yājñavalkya puts down "four who know the dharma-laws of each Veda."[8] As we know from Patañjali,[9] even the Atharva-Veda had its own dharma-sūtras. Yājñavalkya

Parishad

---

[1] *Manu*, VII. 201-203.

[2] *Hindu Polity*, Pt, I, pp. 11-16.

[3] I. 1, 1, 8.

[4] III. 20, त्र्यवरा परिषज्ज्ञेया etc.

[5] See *Manu*, XII, 112.

[6] *Hindu Polity*, Pt. I, p. 110, *n*.

[7] *Yājñ*., I, 9.

[8] *Ibid*.

[9] *Mahābhāshya* on P. IV. 3, 131.

bases his P a r i s h a d on the representation of the f o u r V e d i c s c h o o l s. As an inferior Parishad he allows a Parishad representing the three Vedas.[1] The latter rule was in accordance with the rule of the Mānava, XII. 112. But the former was not. The Mānava did not include the representative of the Atharvan in the Parishad. Nor was the constitution of the Mānava's Parishad based on the Vedas only. The Mānava excluded the Atharvan, while the view cited by Baudhāyana was for the inclusion of that school. The established position of the Dharma-sūtras of the Atharvan is noticed, as we have seen, by Patañjali. But the Mānava's attitude is consistent throughout.[2] Its attitude is conservatism. In the time of K a u ṭ i l y a, the Atharva-Veda was still struggling to be admitted as a canonical Veda, and K a u ṭ i l y a did not admit it as such.[3] The author of the Mānava is doing what Kauṭilya had done. The view quoted by B a u d h ā y a n a cannot be earlier than the time of the Mānava, and evidently represents the other school noticed by Kauṭilya who did recognise the Atharvan. B a u d h ā y a n a's next provision, on the condemnation of the people of the Punjab as being of mixed origin, also indicates the period of about 200 B. C., the period of Buddhism and foreign settlement in the Punjab[4]. Yājñavalkya found the opinion about the position of the Atharva-Veda too well established in literature and in actual life to be ignored.

§ 16. The P a r i s h a d in the period as a source of law, was not the Parishad of yore, the community. It was reduced to

---

[1] *Yājñ.*, I. 9.

[2] See *Manu*, XI. 261-264.

[3] AS., ch, 3. p. 7 :

सामर्ग्यजुर्वेदास्त्रयस्त्रयी। अथर्ववेदेतिहासवेदौ च वेदाः।

[4] *Cf.* Similar opinion on the Punjab people in the Mahābhārata, Karṇa Parvan, Chs. 40 and 44, where they are described in the same terms as in Baudhāyana, with the further information that they had lost the Vedic religion, and that the whole of the Punjab was under one ruler at Śākala, evidently referring to the Buddhist time under the Indo-Greeks. (*Hindu Polity*. i. pp. 38, *n*. 93).

experts, and even one man's opinion was deemed sufficeint (Manu XII, 113; Yājñavalkya 1. 9). Large assemblies are openly condemned (Manu, XII, 114. *Cf.* Baudhāyana, I, 1,1 13; 17). A probable cause of the latter tendency may have been heterodoxy which was gaining ground amongst the Brahmins.

Rules of Reason and Good Conscience

§ 17. We may recall Kauṭilya's provision that if the Dharma-text is found opposed to judicial reason the dharma-text fails (*naśyati*) and there the authority of reason prevails.[1] It is possible to translate *naśyati* by 'is missing' as against 'fails'. But Yājñavalkya's discussion excludes this interpretation. He says where there is a conflict between two Smṛiti texts, "Reason [or *Equity*, as Mandlik puts it,[2]] is there stronger." Yājñavalkya does not permit a possibility of conflict between Reason and Text. He limits the superiority of Reason or Equity to a conflict between the Śāstras themselves. That Yājñavalkya had before him the discussion of the Artha Śāstra is evident from his immediate rider:

"But than the Artha Śāstra (=the Vyavahāra law) the Dharma Śāstra is stronger: this is the law."[3]

The point is that Yājñavalkya accepts Kauṭilya's doctrine that Nyāya is an independent element by itself, which should be followed in the administration of justice (*nyāyena cha chaturthena*), though he does not give it the scope allowed by Kauṭilya and later on accepted by Nārada and Bṛihaspati.[4] In accepting

---

1 *Artha-śāstra*, ch. 58, p. 150:

अनुशासद्धि धर्मेण व्यवहारेण संस्थया। न्यायेन च चतुर्थेन चतुरन्तां महीं जयेत् ॥
संस्थया धर्मशास्त्रेण शास्त्रं वा व्यावहारिकम्। यस्मिन्नर्थे विरुध्येत धर्मेणार्थं विनिश्चयेत् ॥
शास्त्रं विप्रतिपद्येत धर्मन्यायेन केनचित्। न्यायस्तत्र प्रमाणं स्यात् तत्र पाठो हि नश्यति ॥

2 Translation of *Yājñ.* II, 21:

3 *Yājñ.* II, 21:

अर्थशास्त्रात्तु बलवद्धर्मशास्त्रमिति स्थितिः।

4 Quoted in *Vīramitrodaya*, pp. 17-18,

धर्मशास्त्रविरोधे तु युक्तियुक्तो विधिः स्मृतः। (Nārada p. 17)
केवलं शास्त्रमाश्रित्य न कर्तव्यो हि निर्णयः।
युक्तिहीनविचारे हि धर्महानिः प्रजायते ॥ Bṛihaspati (p. 18).

the position of Nyāya, he made a great advance on S u m a t i. Sumati Bhārgava does not allow its operation in law court. Even if two texts conflict both are law and both are good (M. II. 14). On the most liberal interpretation, this would mean that option was given, but option is not 'reason'. The spirit in which the provision was laid is gathered if we refer to the previous verse : 'law is not a thing for those engaged in the Artha (Śāstras) and Kāma (Śāstras).[1]

§ 17. S u m a t i, at the same time, introduces a new juridical principle in the administration of law, which very much approximates to the Nyāya doctrine of the Artha-Śāstra. It is 'the satisfaction of c o n s c i e n c e' (*ātmanastushṭiḥ*) (II. 6), 'agreement with conscience' (*svasya cha priyamātmanaḥ* II. 12) or what one's heart permits' (*hṛidayenābhyanujñātaḥ* II). This factor is treated next to the sources of law (II, 6, 12). Sumati was a great lawyer, his defect is due more to the controversy of his time than to his insight as a lawyer. He would not have the name of R e a s o n because it was used by the Code of the hated and deposed power. But he would not easily deny to his age the benefit of jurisprudence already established. Y ā j ñ a v a l k y a naturally accepts the new doctrine.[2]

§ 18. The M ā n a v a C o d e has the theory that the a d m i n i s t r a t i o n of j u s t i c e (*daṇḍa*) is the r e a l k i n g, the r e a l r u l e r, the real government (VII. 17), that it destroys even the king if he goes against the law (VII. 28). In other-words, the king is brought under the law : the rule of law, the sovereignty of law, is preached with the greatest vigour.[3] As a corollary to this theory, it is further laid down in the M ā n a v a that justice is never to be administered by the king personally.[4]

D a ṇ ḍ a

---

1 *Manu*, II, 13 : अर्थकामेष्वसक्तानां धर्मज्ञानं विधीयते ।

2 *Yājñ* I, 7. श्रुतिस्मृतिः सदाचारः स्वस्य च प्रियमात्मनः ।
सम्यक्सङ्कल्पजः कामो धर्ममूलमिदं स्मृतम् ॥

3 VII. 14-28.

4 *Manu*, VII, 30, to be read with VII. 27-29.

"It (administration of law) cannot (*na śakyaḥ)* be carried on (*netuṁ*) with justice by the king personally, or by a king, foolish, greedy, arbitrary, and given to personal appetites."

And,

"It can be carried on by a king fully assisted, by a king honest and true to his (coronation) oath, following the path of the Śāstras and the wise."

The 'assistance' enjoined here is the S a b h ā or the j u r y, and the j u d g e.

We know from the drama M ṛ i c h h a k a ṭ i k a that the judge pronounced the guilt or innocence of the prisoner, and that he pronounced also the legal sentence, and that the execution of that sentence was vested in the king.[1] Other Codes make it clear that the king when he sat himself in court had to accept the opinion of the Lord Chief Justice. The Codes of N ā r a d a[2] and B ṛ i h a s p a t i[3] clearly record the duty and jurisdiction of the Sabhā or Jury. It was they who found a man guilty or otherwise. The Mānava is not clear on the point, but the jurisdiction is indicated by the enjoined necessity that they must speak out, and that if they spoke unjustly, they would be committing sin, and that the jurors' share of the guilt is equal to that of the king in case of injustice (VIII. 18). The theory was a settled principle of Hindu jurisprudence and Yājñavalkya was too zealous a lawyer to leave it out. He adopted it (I. 354-56) almost in terms of the Mānava. He emphasises that the same law obtains for the Crown Prince, the king's brother, father-in-law or uncle, as for an ordinary citizen, that no one was exempt from the operation of the law (I. 357-58).

---

[1] *Mṛichchakaṭika*, ix. 39. निर्णये वयं प्रमाणं शेषे तु राजा ।

[2] Quoted in *Vīramitrodaya*, p. 36. pp. 41-42.

[3] Bṛihaspati, who is regarded to have followed the Mānava Code and written a Vṛitti, so to say, on it, defines the provinces of the constituents of the court in these terms :

"The judge is the speaker, the king enforces sanction, the jury are the examiners of the cause, the common law gives decision—victory, recovery or punishment."

§ 19. The object of law (dharma) and its administration, according to the M ā n a v a, is the maintenance of p e a c e and o r d e r in the community. (M., VII. 22 ; 18 ; 20). A man honest by nature is rare (VII. 22) ; society is controlled by the administration of law. Without that the stronger would roast the weaker like fish on a spit (20), and all social embankments would collapse (24). In other words, the object is m u n i c i p a l p e a c e. Man by nature is such that he is to be controlled by law. There is no sacerdotal element in the *telos* defined by Sumati.

Object of the Administration of Law

Y ā j ñ a v a l k y a remains silent on the point. While the king is the agent of the administration of law and source of justice, according to S u m a t i (VII. 26) and according to Kauṭilya (p. 150), Y ā j ñ a v a l k y a would make ascetics as the prime movers of law (III. 186).[1] Evidently this is a trace of the influence of monastic Buddhism and its claim about the 'dharma'. Here he tends to be a sacerdotalist rather than a lawyer.

The guiding principle in awarding punishment is laid down in the Mānava Code, in VIII. 126. The following matters were to be taken into consideration with thorough analysis (*tatvataḥ*):—

Theory of Punishment.

(1) the a n u b a n d h a or m o t i v e ;

(2) the place and time, that is, the c i r c u m s t a n c e s under which the offence was committed,

(3) the capacity of the criminal, and

(4) the crime itself.

Anubandha is explained by Medhātithi as repeatedness of the offence (paunaḥpunyenaiva pravṛittiḥ) or the cause of the act (pravṛittiḥ karaṇaṃ vā anubadhyate prayujyate yena). That the second meaning of Medhātithi is the technical sense of *anubandha* is proved by A ś o k a's inscription.[2] In view of the first meaning the punishment would be invariably severer,

1 अष्टाशीति सहस्राणि मुनयो···धर्मप्रवर्त्तकाः ।

2 'Pillar Edict' IV.

while in that of the latter it may be lighter. Aśoka uses the term *anubandha* in connexion with remission of punishment. His officers of the dharma department were to examine and reduce punishments awarded to prisoners on the consideration of :—(1) anubandha, (2) the children of the prisoner (to be supported), (3) absence of free agency, and (4) old age.

The M ā n a v a provision in VII. 16 also shows that 'anubandha' had the sense of m o t i v e, after its general meaning 'sentiment.' In the latter place the points to be considered are (1) the place and time, (2) the capacity, (3) and 'knowledge' (vidyā) or consciousness.

The last element corresponds to *anubandha.* It, thus, undoubtedly refers to mentality.

§ 20. It is necessary to look into the previous history of this element. According to Gautama (XII. 51), thorough ascertainment is to be made about:—(1) the doer (purusha) (probably his status), (2) the capacity of the culprit, (3) the crime itself, and (4) the motive (anubandha).

K a u ṭ i l y a[1] (p. 226) has—(1) the doer, (2) the offence, (3) the agency (karaṇaṃ) and the part played by it, (4) the motive (anubandha), (5) the circumstances present at the time of the offence, and the (6) place and time.

Āpastamba divides the shares in an offence[2] amongst the employer, advisor and doer.

§ 21. The tendency of legislators had been to narrow these considerations into four fixed points: (1) the motive, (2) the magnitude of crime, (3) the capacity of the culprit whether or not to do the full amount of mischief, and to bear punishment, and (4) the circumstances. Consideration regarding agency tended to be omitted ; the culprit was regarded to be fully responsible for the act

---

Arthaśāstra, p. 226;

पुरुषं चापराधं च कारणं गुरुलाघवम् ।
अनुबन्धं तदात्वं च देशकालौ समीक्ष्य च ॥

Āpastamba, II. 11, 29, 1:

प्रयोजयिता मन्ता कर्तेति स्वर्गनरकफलेषु कर्मसु भागिनः ।

whether propelled by others or by himself to commit the crime. But Y ā j ñ a v a l k y a omits *anubandha* altogether :—

"*Dhik*-censure, severe language, wealth-punishment (fine and forfeiture), and corporal punishment—some or all may be employed according to the nature of the offence, taking into consideration (1) the place and time when the offence was committed, (2) the strength of the offender (capacity), (3) the age of the offender, (4) the actual act of offence, and (5) the wealth of the offender (capacity to bear pecuniary punishment) (I. 367).[1]

Probably the act itself in his opinion was the evidence of motive.

§ 22. He is of opinion that r e p e a t e d o f f e n c e s are to be dealt with more severely. This is implied in his I. 367, read with Manu, VIII. 129-30.[2] Here he followed the ancient and the established law.[3]

Position of Brahmin at law

§ 23. The p o s i t i o n of the B r a h m i n in the two Codes is a point of great importance. A privilege is claimed in the M ā n a v a C o d e which practically places him above c r i m i n a l p e n a l t y in felony. He is to be (1) allowed to leave the country, (2) without a wound on him, and (3) with all his property, in proved offences of capital punishment (VIII. 378-81). Neither forfeiture and fine, nor corporal punishment, is to be sentenced on him. He suffered only what Hobbes called a "change of air" after having committed the most heinous crimes,[4] acts of treason,

---

[1] *Yājñ.* I, 366 :

धिग्दण्डस्त्वथ वाग्दण्डो धनदण्डो वधस्तथा ।
योज्या व्यस्ताः समस्ता वा ह्यपराधवशादिमे ॥

[2] *Ibid.* 366:

ज्ञात्वापराधं देशं च कालं बलमथापि वा ।
वयः कर्म च वित्तं च दण्डं दण्ड्येषु पातयेत् ॥

Cf. *Manu* VIII, 373.

[3] *Āpastamba*, II, 11, 29. 2:

यो भूय आरभते तस्मिन् फलविशेषः ।
पुनरपराधे द्विगुणं । *Arthaśāstra*, p. 223.

[4] राष्ट्रादेनं बहिः कुर्यात् समग्रधनमक्षतम् । (*M.* VIII,380)
···अस्य वधं राजा मनसापि न चिन्तयेत् । (*Ibid.* 381)

murder, etc.! The claim was made by the Brahmin when the Brahmin was on the throne. But was it allowed? The Mṛichchhakaṭika shows that it was not. Yājñavalkya does not allude to it even distantly. He places no one above the law.

§ 24. As to the previous history of the claim, there are two genuine land-marks:—the Arthaśāstra (c. 300 B. C.) of Kauṭilya and Āpastamba's Dharmasūtra. Without the Arthaśāstra we would have never known the real position of the Brahmin in Hindu Law before the Mānava Code. There, in a code covering two books of the Arthaśāstra—longer in matter than the Mānava and Yāñavalkya on law proper put together, there is no trace of such an exception. In the actual administration of law under the Mauryas the exception was unknown. A Brahmin culprit if convicted of treason to the state was to have the most ignominious form of capital punishment: he was to be drowned.[1] In some cases he was subjected to severer punishments than men of other castes, as he stood on the highest rung of the social and intellectual ladder, punishment varying in inverse ratio to social inequality.[2]

It is noteworthy that Vasishṭha has no such claim. Nor has Āpastamba. The claim had a very slight foundation in earlier law. The earlier law was this. Where offence was sought to be proved by circumstantial evidence, and no direct evidence was available but there was a general repute of bad character or guilt of a person, the law allowed apprehension of such a person, and trial before the criminal court. The presumption in such cases was against the prisoner and he had to clear his character. In some of such cases the prisoner was subjected to mild torture to obtain confession. This was abolished by the Mauryas, on the ground that prisoners, to avoid pain, admit guilt; hence conclusive evidence must be adduced; torture or 'hard labour' was allowed only

[1] *Arthaśāstra*, p. 227:

ब्राह्मणं तमपः प्रवेशयेत् ।

[3] *Arthaśāstra*, ch. 83, p. 218:

वैश्यं द्विगुणः, क्षत्रियं त्रिगुणः, ब्राह्मणं चतुर्गुणः (दण्डः) ।

"when guilt has been established".[1] In other words, torture was not allowed to obtain confession, but when in dark cases, difficult of proof, guilt was established by evidence, the preliminary punishment of the old law must be inflicted ; he had a chance of total escape, but when found guilty he was to be subjected to severe punishment. These severe punishments consisted of whipping, suspension, heating (for a day), or exposure (for a night), and water-tubing.[2] When spies proved the guilt, at the trial, the prisoner could be subjected to whipping, etc. (p. 219). To this, exception was made in the case of (a) certain women, (b) B r a h m i n s optionally, (c) the learned and (d) ascetics. A Brahmin was to be subjected to either the same amount of pain as a healthy woman, or he was only to be subjected to the 't o r t u r e of c r o s s - e x a m i n a t i o n', while the learned and the ascetics were not to be subjected to any pain whatsoever, their guilt had simply to be proved by the evidence of detectives. In after-trial punishments, a Brahmin was not subjected to tortures, yet as a substitute for tortures, on his forehead the degrading symbol of his offence was to be stamped as a deterrent. And, then, he had to serve out his sentence in hard work, e.g., at the mines. If the offence was heinous, the mark of degradation was to be cut into him and he was made to work at the rand, or if the ruler liked (thought him to be too contaminating even in prison or at the rand) declared him " c o u n t r y-l e s s " after a public proclamation. This was quite in keeping with the Hindu principle of the o b j e c t of p u n i s h m e n t. Originally punishments were devised to be " m e n t a l c h a s t i s e m e n t" (p r ā y a ś c h i t t a) and to be deterrent *(pratyādeśaya)*. The Brahmin culprit was subjected to pointed ignominy in addition to his punishment. Owing to learning and birth he was only spared physical tortures.

---

1 *Ibid.* p. 219 :

आप्तदोषं कर्म कारयेत्।

2 *Ibid.*,

व्यावहारिकं कर्म चतुष्कं
षड्दण्डाः, सप्तकशाः, द्वावुपरिनिबन्धौ, उदकनालीका च। etc.

In effect the branding operated as a severer punishment. No one including his family members, could hold any social intercourse with a branded man; all legal rights were denied to him. He became a social and a legal outcast, an out-law, not to be greeted, not to be associated with, not to be sympathised with, not to be heard in law courts.[1]

If turned out of the country, he was worse off; at the mines or in prison he could get food, but when turned out he had to die of starvation; making 'c o u n t r y-l e s s' or 'h o m e-l e s s' (*vivāsa*) entailed loss and forfeiture of property (M. IX. 242; Baudhāyana).

§ 25 The e a r l i e r l a w inclined to be harsher on the Brahmin. For instance, Ā p a s t a m b a, II. 10. 27, which deals with Penances to be enforced by the king, prescribes in homicide, theft, and misappropriation of land,

(a) in the case of a Śūdra, no penance but torture,

(b) in the case of a Brahmin, 'blinding' until he agreed to undergo the required penance,

(c) in the case of other castes (i. e., Vaiśya and Kshatriya), solitary confinement until the culprit agreed to undergo penance.

In default, all were equally banished (14-20). Solitary confinement was given to a Brahmin in lesser offences (19). Thus the punishment to him was harsher. What he got for lesser offences, the other two castes got for the higher ones. Likewise, severer punishments are expressly laid down for him in the Arthaśāstra.

The beginning of the change started with a change in policy on the law of t h e f t. Theft was originally punished with death. It was one of the seven most heinous crime-sins, which were, according to Yāska[2], theft, defiling Guru's bed, *brahmahatyā* (probably

---

[1] *Manu*, IX. 238-239;
असंभोज्या ह्यसंयाज्या असंपाठ्याविवाहिनः। चरेयुः पृथिवीं दीनाः सर्वधर्मबहिष्कृताः॥
ज्ञातिसंबन्धिभिस्त्वेते त्यक्तव्याः कृतलक्षणाः। निर्दया निर्नमस्कारास्तन्मनोरनुशासनम्॥

[2] *Nirukta*, VI, 27:
स्तेयं तल्पारोहणं ब्रह्महत्यां भ्रूणहत्यां सुरापानं दुष्कृतस्य कर्मणः पुनः पुनः सेवां पातकेऽनृतोद्यमिति।

'full killing'), abortion, drinking of surā (liquor), repetition of crime, instigating men to criminal sins. Capital punishment was in course of time limited to theft of gold. But even there and in all cases of theft capital punishment was practically abolished in the Arthaśāstra.[1] Yet torture-punishment was dealt to prisoners in thefts of serious and aggravated nature. This was abolished in favour of the Brahmins, ascetics and sick women, under Chandragupta. Similarly there was a change in the law of a d u l t e r y. It had been punished with death. The punishment was reduced to tortures which in turn, under Chandragupta, were reduced to simple imprisonment and fine.[2] The new laws on the reduction of punishment in theft and adultery are found in two chapters in the Arthaśāstra[3]. Under the Śuṅgas there was a tendency to go back to the old punishment of torture for adultery, but the Brahmin was exempted.[4] Likewise there had been a tendency to make distinction in cases of m u r d e r. The Arthaśāstra divided manslaughter into three classes. If immediate death was caused by an assault the culprit was tortured to death; where death in consequence of a wound resulted after seven days, the culprit was given s i m p l e c a p i t a l p u n i s h m e n t. If death ensued after a fortnight, it became a matter for imprisonment, and if after a month, a matter for fine. Torture had been administered in cases of bad culprits; this was abolished under the M a u r y a s, and t o r t u r e d d e a t h s were replaced by s i m p l e c a p i t a l p u n i s h m e n t.[5] In case of the Brahmin, in adultery, theft, and homicide, instead of torture, branding[6] was insisted upon as a severer measure, in accordance with the Artha view that a Brahmin ought to be punished more severly[7]. He did hard labour all the same (like others) according to Kauṭilya and Gautama; he

---

[1] Aś.. ch. 87, p. 224, See p. 226 (for theft of gold).

[2] Aś., *ibid.*, see also the last verse at p. 228 (ch. 88)

[3] *Arthaśāstra*, IV, 10-11.

[4] Cf. *Manu*, VIII, 377ff.

[5] Aś., ch. 88 p. 227

[6] Aś., ch. 85. p. 220

[7] Cf. Kātyāyana (who generally reverts to Kauṭiliya laws) : येन दोषेण शूद्रस्य दण्डो भवति धर्मतः । तेन चेत् क्षत्रविप्राणां द्विगुणो द्विगुणो भवेत् ॥ Smṛiti Ch., p. 298.

according to them was put in solitary confinement[1]. All the U t t a m a-s ā h a s a punishments (confiscation, banishment, labour, branding) were inflicted on him except torture. Capital punishment on a Brahmin is not prohibited in Ā p a s t a m b a.

§ 11. Under the Ś u ṅ g a s when the Brahmin became the ruling caste, he made these claims :

(a) no branding,
(b) no capital punishment,
(c) no torture,
(d) no confiscation,
—in adultery, in rape, in theft, and otherwise (*i.e.*, murder).

After the Śuṅga rule, in the Code of Y ā j ñ a v a l k y a, (a) was not entertained ; branding was reiterated. And as there was a substitute for tortures, and as tortures were dying away, the claim (c) was allowed, but (d) was not allowed ; nor was (b)[2]. In theft[3] and adultery, punishment had ceased to be severe. In cases of cold-blooded murder a Brahmin was given the highest punishment.[4]

Some curious changes happened during the B r a h m i n revolution under the Śuṅgas. Theft which primarily was considered heinous but latterly had ceased to be so, was again declared to be heinous but only when of a B r a h m i n ' s p r o p e r t y. H o m i c i d e as a heinous sin of the old times was changed into the *killing of a Brahmin.*[5] The same crime if committed by a Brahmin entailed a much milder punishment. That all these changes were new is evident from a comparison of the law in Kauṭilya, Āpastamba and Gautama, on the one hand, and in the Mānava Dharmaśāstra, on the other.

---

1 Aś., p. 219-20 ; *Gautama* XII, 46-47: न शारीरो ब्राह्मणस्य दण्डः । कर्मवियोगविख्यापन विवासनाङ्ककरणानि ।

2 Yājñ. II, 230 ; I. 356-57.

3 See Y. III. 257, where 'a Brahmin, who has stolen gold, should confess to the king...when beaten or discharged by the king, he will be purified.'

4 Ibid., Cf, Aś. ch. 85, ch. 88, p. 222.

5 M. IX. 235, XI. 26.

§ 12. Further, the seat of the judge in the Mānava is claimed for the Brahmin caste.[1] This is again contrary to the previous history. But this was excusable. The claim was made only with regard to the Civil Court, where under the Mānava, Dharma and Vyavahāra were now mixed matters, and Dharma had been almost an exclusive province of the Brahmin from olden times. The Mānava does not say that the *Kaṇṭaka--Śodhana* (Criminal) courts were also to be presided over by the Brahmin.

Judgeship and Brahmin

§ 13. The Śūdra had been at a great disadvantage in early law. The Ārya is opposed to the Śūdra who is black and almost alien in Āpastamba.[2] His position from 400 B.C. to 300 B. C. suddenly and greatly changed. This might have been due to the spread of Buddhism. Buddhism was especially identified, in the parlance of the orthodox people in 400-300 B. C. and later, with the Śūdra, for instance, an ascetic of Buddhism was called a Śūdra ascetic, never minding what his original caste was.[3] Kauṭilya, though orthodox, is very favourable to the Śūdra.[4] The evolution of a large political (imperial) nationality and the fact of Śūdra rulers were responsible for this change in politicians. His position is favourable also in Gautama. But with the Brahmin revolution, and with the hostility to the Śūdra dynasty (i. e., Mauryas) and Śūdra religion *(i.e.,* Buddhism), the Śūdra greatly suffers in the Mānava Code. With the fall of the Śuṅgas, his position is so much improved as he had never attained before. Yājñavalkya has no repressive law against a Śūdra disputing with the Brahmins, or against a Śūdra teaching, a Śūdra owning property and so forth. Manu's hostility to the Śūdra is primarily towards the learned Śūdra, towards the controvertialist

Position of Sūdra at law

---

[1] *Manu,* VIII, 9, 20-21.
[2] Cf. Āp., II, 2, 4, 19 ; 10, 26, 15 etc.
[3] Aś., ch. 77, p. 199.
[4] Cf. Aś., ch. 70, p. 181ff.

Śūdra, claiming equality and freedom. That claim is almost tacitly allowed in Yājñavalkya. And herein lies the greatness of Yājñavalkya as a lawyer. He accepted facts and bowed to the change that had taken place. [1]

[1] Aśvaghosha in the *Vajra-suchi* expressly states that there were learned Śūdras, and he finds no difference between them and Brahmins.

LECTURE V.

CONSTITUTIONAL NORMS OF MANU AND YAJNAVALKYA.

Theory of State—Kingship—Divine theory—Fatalism in Politics interdicted—Brahmin—Ownership in land—Conqueror—Laws of War—Republics—Puritanism.

§ 1. The Dharma-śāstra made certain constitutional laws as part of its legal system. These were the first principles of the Hindu Code of Polity, a code which was as binding[1] on kings and ministers as any law on private individuals. The two Dharma Codes lay down these laws before touching the subject of the municipal law. The Dharma-śāstra of S u m a t i[2] in adopting those principles sought to depose the Code of Polity from its position of authority. Sumati gave a combined code of Dharma, Artha and Vyavahāra to the Śuṅga times, and presumably also to the Śuṅga administration. Beyond itself no Artha Code or Vyavahāra Code was recognised as authoritative by his Code. This feature of a common code was the originality of Sumati. And in no small degree did it contribute to the Code's first position as a Hindu Code of Law—a Code for the Hindu as a king, as a subject, and as a member of society—containing, as it does, laws constitutional, municipal, social and sacerdotal.

Mānava Code and Constitutional Laws

The constitutional laws which were thus made an integral part of this approved Code of Sumati's 'Dharma' are highly important. They for all ages were now clothed by the Dharma authority with a sanctity as supreme as that of any branch of Dharma. They were, so to say, made sacred, and became binding on kings and statesmen

---

[1] Cf. *Śānti-Parvan*, LIX, 107:

यश्चात्र धर्मोनीत्युक्तो दण्डनीतिव्यपाश्रयः etc.

[2] *Manu*, II, 12-13. see also Lecture I above.

with all the sanction and halo of Dharma. Apart from the rules, there are certain theories discussed in the Codes. Let us notice them here.

§ 2. Both Sumati and Yājñavalkya know the State as composed of seven elements[1]. But Sumati discloses acquaintance with a very ancient theory. According to that the

Theory of State

State is composed of five component parts or Prakṛitis,[2] 'the bases', which are called the limbs (*aṅgas*) of the state by Yājñavalkya[3] (I. 353). They, according to Sumati, were [omitting the king] :—

(1) the ministry,
(3) the country,
(2) the capital,
(4) the revenue, and
(5) the army.

There cannot be a state without these limbs. The first of these, it may be noted, represents the ruling power.[4] The theory of the five *prakṛitis*, according to Kāmandaka[5], was the earliest (K. VIII. 4). Bṛihaspati[6], the author of the famous *Bārhaspatya-Artha-śāstra* proposed an amendment to this theory.

---

[1] M. VII. 157-158 Y., I. 353; M., later on, and out of place, in IX. 294-7.

[2] M. VII. 156-7:

एताः प्रकृतयो मूलं॰ ।
अमात्यराष्ट्रदुर्गार्थदण्डाख्याः पञ्च चापराः ।
प्रत्येकं कथिता ह्येताः॰ ॥

[3] Y., I. 353:

स्वाम्यमात्यौ जनो दुर्गं कोशो दण्डस्तथैव च ।
मित्राण्येताः प्रकृतयो राज्यं सप्ताङ्गमुच्यते ॥

[4] See *Hindu Polity*, Pt. II, pp. 115-51.

[5] K. VIII, 4:

अमात्यराष्ट्रदुर्गाणि कोशो दण्डश्च पञ्चमः ।
एताः प्रकृतयस्तज्ज्ञैर्विजिगीषोरुदाहृताः ॥

[6] K., VIII. 5:

एताः पञ्च तथा मित्रं सप्तमः पृथिवीपतिः ।
सप्तप्रकृतिकं राज्यमित्युवाच बृहस्पतिः ॥
[K. Trivandrum, 1912 p. 10].

He postulated that the state is composed of s e v e n elements (सप्तप्रकृतिकं राज्यम् इत्युवाच बृहस्पतिः, Kāmandaka, VIII. 5), that is, (6) the K i n g should be counted as an element or limb, and so also (7) the A l l y . In his opinion a l l i a n c e was a vital source of strength or weakness of a state. Now the position of the H i n d u M i n i s t r y and its origin have to be taken into consideration to understand the controversy whether the king was or was not an essential limb, a vital seat in the organism of Hindu State. I have shown it elsewhere[1] that the Hindu ministry had a popular origin and were vested with the power of ruling, according to the constitution of Hindu Monarchy. The king was bound to accept their advice which the ministers themselves translated into action and executed in the king's name. Bṛihaspati's opinion had become accepted before the time of Sumati. Kauṭilya[2] gives it as the universally accepted view without any controversy.

§ 3. S u m a t i takes the state to consist of s i x e l e m e n t s, for he gives the calculation of 72 parts in the circle of 12 states (M. VII. 156-7). He takes the ally as a component element of the circle of states, called m a ṇ ḍ a l a, with reference to foreign policy and the policy of establishing a balance of power. Sumati in his m a ṇ ḍ a l a theory[3] adopts the earliest view. A maṇḍala consists according to that theory of four neighbouring states[4]. This was the earliest view of political scientists. The later view, *viz.*, of K a u ṭ i l y a and others, Sumati did adopt later in Ch. IX (294-97) while discussing their relative importance and the importance of the king in national crises. Here he accepts Kauṭilya's decision (VIII. 127, p. 319), that every preceding prakriti is more important than the succeeding one, but gives his

---

[1] See *Hindu Polity*, Pt. II. pp. 115-51.

[2] *Artha-śāstra* VI. 1; 96 p. 255:

स्वाम्यमात्यजनपददुर्गकोशदण्डमित्राणि प्रकृतयः ॥

[Mysore, 1909, p. 255.]

[3] *Manu*. VII, 157.

[4] Cf. *Kāmandaka*, VIII. 20, p. 108:

मूलप्रकृतयस्त्वेताश्चतस्रः परिकीर्तिताः ।

प्राहैतत् तन्त्रकुशलश्चतुष्कं मण्डलं मयः ॥

own reason for holding that for their individual functions each one and all conjointly, are equally important

§ 4. Yājñavalkya follow the view of Kauṭilya (p. 257) that the state consisted of seven limbs, counting the king and the ally amongst the limbs (I. 352-3) :

(1) the Svāmin or Sovereign
(2) the Ministry or Government,
(3) the Nation (Jana),
(4) the Capital,
(5) the Exchequer,
(6) the Army, and
(7) the Ally.[1]

This he adopts in the very language of Kauṭilya[2], only shortening the 'Janapada' as Jana, but he leaves out the unnecessary discussion of their relative importance.

Theory of kingship.

§ 5. The Hindu theory of kingship as I have shown in detail elesewhere[3], had been from the earliest times that the king is a servant of the people, that his title rests on a contract between him and the subjects, he agreeing to protect them and to secure to them prosperity, and to receive in return taxes as wages of government. Sumati for the first time introduced a new theory. He said that the king was a deity made by gods out of their own portions, that he could burn and destroy those opposing him, and that nobody could question the laws made by him in favour of those he liked and against those he disliked.[4] This was a divine

---

1 Y., I. 352-3 :

हिरण्यभूमिलाभेभ्योमित्रलब्धिर्वरा यतः ।
अतो यतेत तत्प्राप्त्यै रक्षेत्सत्यं समाहितः ॥
स्वाम्यमात्यो जनो दुर्गं कोशो दण्डस्तथैव च ।
मित्राण्येताः प्रकृतयो राज्यं सप्ताङ्गमुच्यते ॥

Cf. *Artha-śāstra*, VI, 1 . 96, p. 255.

2 See, *n.* 2, p. 95 above.

3 *Hindu Polity*, Pt. II, pp. 135, 163, 185.

4 *Manu*, VII. 3-13.

theory of kingship with the right of perfect arbitrariness. This was opposed to all traditions, Vedic rituals of kingship and coronation, and the very spirit of Hindu Law which refuses to place even gods above the law and which distinctly places the king under it. The great jurist Medhātithi commenting on verse 6—'nor can any body gaze on him'—refers to the Vedic text of coronation that the king by sacrament of coronation becomes superior to all and he explains away all the verses of the Mānava Code attributing divinity to the king as mere words, having no force of law, they being mere arthavāda to the Vedic '*vidhi*' about the royal position as being superior to that of the subjects [1].

Medhātithi on the theory

Not only this. On verse 13 which attributes right of arbitrariness he says, that it can mean only lawful orders of the king, otherwise the provision would be contrary to the spirit of Hindu law [2]. The orders and laws of kings referred to in the verses of 'Manu' could be according to Medhātithi, orders on trifling and innocent matters, as for instance, general rejoicing on a marriage in the Prime Minister's family, prevention of killing of animals by soldiers on certain days and the like, and that only such orders were to be obeyed. Other commentators also refuse to accept the dictum of Manu and explain it away as meaning the contrary of what he says. No Hindu lawyer acquainted with the spirit of the ancient law and constitution of his country could accept a theory of divine irresponsibility in Hindu kingship.

§ 6. Yājñavalkya contemptuously ignores the theory. In its stead he tells the king that illegal actions on his part are to carry the result of forfeiture of majesty and banishment with his

---

[1] *Medh.* on Manu, VII, 9. अस्य विधेरर्थवादश्लोका एते ।

[2] *Medh.* on *Manu* VII. 13:

...न त्वग्निहोत्रादिधर्मव्यवस्थायै वर्णाश्रमिणां राजा प्रभवति । स्मृत्यन्तरविरोधप्रसङ्गात् । अविरोधे चास्मिन् विषये—वचनस्यार्थवत्त्वात् ।

whole family,[1] that acts of oppression to the subject were to entail not only deprivation of majesty and condemnation of the dynasty, but also infliction of the highest punishment[2]. And in fact to this the Hindu king had agreed by the coronation oath[3]. Yājñavalkya was only translating the undertaking of the coronation oath.

Theory of Daṇḍa

§ 7. The Mānava Code itself, evidently on its revision, fully contradicted the theory by another theory placed just below the divine theory (VII. 14-31), whereby it declared that law and justice (law's administration, 'daṇḍa') was created by the Creator as His own son. It was that which was the real king and not the king himself, that it was empowered to destroy the king if he behaved illegally and arbitrarily, if he was not true to the coronation oath[4]; that the king must follow the opinion of the ministers and act in accordance with the śāstras. The coronation oath, as we know from other sources,[5] also imposed the condition to follow the law strictly, to maintain it and to regard the country as god. Yājñavalkya canonised this latter principle which was the ancient principle of constitution.

§ 8. The Code of Sumati had to support a usurper,[6] a revolutionary dynasty. To preach that 'he was

---

1 *Yājñavalkya*. I, 340: अन्यायेन नृपो राष्ट्रात् स्वकोशं योभिवर्धयेत् ।
सोऽचिराद्विगतश्रीको नाशमेति सबान्धवः ॥

2 *Yājñavalkya*. I. 341 : प्रजापीडनसंतापात्समुद्भूतो हुताशनः ।
राज्ञः कुलं श्रियं प्राणांश्चादग्ध्वा न निवर्तते ॥

3 *Hindu Polity*, pt. II, pp. 6, 49-50.

4 *Manu*, VII. 28 : दण्डो हि सुमहत्तेजो दुर्धरश्चाकृतात्मभिः ।
धर्माद्विचलितं हन्ति नृपमेव सबान्धवम् ॥ (read with 31. 'सत्यसन्धेन').

5 *Hindu Polity*. pt II, pp. 49ff.

6 Hence the claim that the Brahmins had the right of regicide, and the right to destroy the royal army (XI. 313), alluding, of course, to the murder of Brihadratha Maurya. This impious claim of right, put amongst constitutional laws, was never repeated in subsequent codes, and is not to be found earlier. The regicidal action of Pushyamitra was condemned by Bāṇa as 'un-Hindu' (*anarya*).

not to be treated lightly, or insulted' (M. VII. 5) he had to invent a a divine theory. The author of the Code of Manu went, as every Hindu lawyer did when he wanted to re-examine the legal position of the king, to the ritual of coronation, the very basis of Hindu kingship. He by a little distortion converted the gods invoked to help the new king in his new situation into manufacturers of a new divinity—the king. Both jurists and political scientists rejected this trick, as it was against the sacred *śruti* itself which most emphatically declared the king to be a mere human being entering into an office on contract.[1]

Explanation of the invention of the divine theory

§ 9. Yājñavalkya goes a step further and limits the prerogative of the king even in a conquered country. He says that conquest gives exactly the same right to, and imposes the same duties on, the king with regard to the new subjects as the king has got in his own country. The conqueror could not even introduce new laws there. The new subjects have to be ruled in the same way as the subjects of his own country.[2] This had been already the view of the *Mīmāṃsā school* and the view was deduced from the legal position of the king. *Śabara* commenting on a Sūtra of *Jaimini* points out that the king's right is only magisterial. He acquires no right of property in the kingdom except in the personal effects of the ex-king. The conqueror acquires right of property only in the latter and succeeds merely to the right and duty of ruling.[3] Yājñavalkya *canonises this constitutional theory* as *law* and as an *integral part of Hindu Dharma Code.*

King's Right on conquest.

---

1 *Hindu Polity*, Pt. II, pp. 14-41.

2 *Yājñavalkya*, I. 342-43 :

य एव नृपतेर्धर्मः स्वराष्ट्रपरिपालने ।
तमेव कृत्स्नमाप्नोति परराष्ट्रं वशं नयन् ॥
यस्मिन्देशे य आचारो व्यवहारः कुलस्थितिः ।
तथैव परिपाल्योऽसौ यदा वशमुपागतः ॥

3 *Śabara* on *Jaimini* 6, 7, 3. see also *Hindu Polity*, Pt. II. p, 175 *n*, 2.

'Legitimacy' in Politics.

§ 10. Sumati introduces a provision on the principle known in European politics as the doctrine of legitimacy. The old dynasty in a conquered country must be restored. Some member of the ruling family is to be placed on the throne. But in doing so "the wishes of the whole people is to be ascertained by the brief procedure" as to the selection, and the very member selected by the people is to be put on the throne.[1] The Hindu constitution of monarchy enjoined that a new succession had to be approved or rather decided upon by the people through two Assemblies the Paura and Jānapada.

Sumati requires the conqueror to conform to that law of constitution. Medhātithi says that by the people here "the Paura etc. are meant" (पौरादीनामभिप्रायः). The commentator Rāmachandra explains the expression 'brief method' (samāsena) as 'through assembly' (samudāyena). Before that a general amnesty (*abhaya* proclamation of No-Fear') was to be issued (VII. 201), which was addressed according to Medhātithi to the Paura, the Jānapada, and the army.[3] That this law was followed and acted upon in practice is seen from the record (copper plate) left by Dharma-Pāla who on conquering Mahodaya or Kānyakubja accepted the opinion of the Elders of Pañchāla (the whole country) and placed a prince of the old dynasty on the throne of Pañchāla.[4]

§ 11. This law of reinstallation of the old dynasty is not found repeated in Yājñavalkya probably due to the then non-

---

[1] *Manu*, VII. 202 :

सर्वेषां तु विदित्वैषां समासेन चिकीर्षितम्।
स्थापयेत्तत्र तद्वंश्यं कुर्याच्च समयक्रियाम्॥

[2] *Hindu Polity*, pt. II, chs. XXVII-XXVIII.

[3] Medhātithi on *Manu* VII. 202 :

एष पौरादीनामभिप्रायः संक्षेपेण ज्ञात्वा नैतदेवमिच्छति। तत्कुलीनं कर्तुमिच्छत्ययमेव तस्मिन्देशे तद्वंश्यं मृदुमलंप्रियसुखकलत्रं तेन संहततत्प्रकृतिभिश्च प्रधानादिभिः समयं कुर्यात् समकोशदानादि परिमाणं च भवता मम दैवाकारेण पापेन भवितव्यं कार्यकालेन स्वयमुपस्थातव्य-मुभयतो दण्डेन कोशेन चेत्यादि॥

[4] *Epi. Indica*, IV, p. 248.

Hindu (Kushan) imperial rule, but that it became the established law of the Hindus is proved by the history of the conquest of Samudragupta and other references. The Vishṇu Smṛiti[1] had already adopted the same law (III. 47-48) with the exception that the old dynasty should be abolished only when it is of low descent (49), evidently referring to the Śūdra dynasties of the past. Yājñavalkya seems to have been too much either under the influence of the Kauṭilīya Arthaśāstra, or the facts of his own time—the Kushan rule—made him ignore the Mānava code on the point. He talks of a conquered country as if it would be incorporated into the conquering country, as a matter of course. Yājñavalkya, of course, follows Sumati when he enjoins that the laws of the conquered country are not to be interfered with.[2]

Fatalism in politics interdicted.

§ 12. Both Manu and Yājñavalkya condemn fatalism in politics.[3] The Buddhist theory of 'Karma' had taken a hold on the philosophic mind of the nation ; it had been sown broadcast by the Buddha and his contemporaries. Earlier politicians had only to fight against astrology. For instance, Kauṭilya, in whose days the theory of Karma had not yet become universal, says that "it is politics which fights politics ; what would the stars do in matter of politics ? A fool who believes in them is rejected by

---

1 *Vishṇu*, III. 47-49 :

राजा परपुरावाप्तौ तु तत्र तत्कुलीनमभिषिञ्चेत् ।
न राजकुलमुच्छिन्द्यात् ।
अन्यत्राकुलीनराजकुलात् ।

2 Yājñavalkya, I, 340-341 :

य एव नृपतेर्धर्मः स्वराष्ट्रप्रतिपालने ।
तमेव कृच्छ्रमाप्नोति परराष्ट्रं वशं नयन् ॥
किन्तु यस्मिन् य आचारो व्यवहारः कुलस्थितिः ।
तथैव परिपाल्योऽसौ यदा वशमुपागतः ॥

3 *Manu*. VII, 205, 221-215.
Yājñ. I. 349, 351.

politics" (p. 349).[1] But the evil effect of the star calculation was limited. It concerned with the beginnings of an undertaking. But the fatalism of the iron theory of Karma (past doings producing the present) was ubiquitous and ever-present. If applied to politics it would paralyze the state in foreign relations. Evidently the Buddhist rule did introduce it into politics. Sumati declares 'the ordering of fate' to be *achintya*, 'to be ignored as it is in man that action is vested'[2]. Kauṭilya says that an enemy-country which is a believer in Fate is a source of strength (सम्पत्, 'asset',) to the conqueror[3]; it is a fit country to be invaded and conquered. Yājña-valkya probably finding fatalism badly established puts it somewhat mildly that Fate cannot be realized without the human architect (I, 350-351)[4]. Fatalism had become too securely established to be condemned downright.

§ 13. The position of the Brahmin in this part of our Codes calls for a special notice. The Brahmin in the M ā n a v a is called

Brahmin Sovereignty

1. I ś a in the sense of the ruler of the whole 'world', IX. 245;
2. I ś v a r a which in the Śuṅga period means 'ruler' as in the Mahābhāshya, 'for the protection of the treasure of Dharma' (I. 99);
3. "A d h i p a t i of the whole" (VIII. 37);

---

[1] *Kauṭilya*, p. 349:
नक्षत्रमतिपृच्छन्तं बालमर्थोऽतिवर्तते ।
अर्थो ह्यर्थस्य नक्षत्रं किं करिष्यन्ति तारकाः ॥

[2] *Manu*, VII. 205:
सर्वं कर्मेदमायत्तं विधाने दैवमानुषे ।
तयोर्दैवमचिन्त्यन्तु मानुषे विद्यते क्रिया ॥

[3] Arthaśāstra. VI, 1 97; pp, 256:
व्यसनी, निरुत्साहो, दैवप्रमाणो···अमित्रसम्पत् ।

[4] *Yājñavalkya*, I. 350-51:
केचिद्दैवात् स्वभावाद्वा कालात् पुरुषकारतः ।
संयोगे केचिदिच्छन्ति फलं कुशलबुद्धयः ॥
यथाह्येकेन चक्रेण रथस्य न गतिर्भवेत् ।
एवं पुरुषकारेण विना दैवं न सिध्यति ॥

and is described : 4. "Whatever exists in the world is the property of the Brahmin ; on account of the excellence of his origin the Brahmin is indeed entitled to it." (I. 100)

Passage no. (3) refers to treasure-trove, and on proper construction only means that he himself is the under-surface protector of the whole treasure-trove which had been buried by his fore-fathers (p ū r v o p a n i h i t a)[1]. As a learned Brahmin was free from the tax of protection and as he is the discoverer (विद्वांस्तु ब्राह्मणो दृष्ट्वा) of the treasure to which he is entitled as heir, he is to be deemed as the protector and is not to pay any tax-share to the king as others had to do (VIII. 33) [see above]. The king is called, two verses below, (VIII. 39) the "a d h i p a t i of l a n d" 'one who is the protector of the sub-soil.' But the Brahmin is not called so. Passage no. (1) refers to a moral ruler. But the passage of Book I (No. 2) claims the Brahmin to be both the m o r a l r u l e r and the p o l i t i c a l r u l e r. The term is technical, a political term of the time, meaning a political ruler. The verse with the next one (101) probably ended the first book in the original edition, as the succeeding portion after v. 101 begins suddenly to attribute the work to Manu, praises the complete book and gives a table of contents[2]. No mention of Manu's authorship is found after that except in the closing portion of the work (XII. 107-126), which is no part of the book by context. Verse 101, B. K 1, carries the c l a i m of r u l e r s h i p further :—

"The Brahmin eats but his own food, wears but his own

---

[1] *Manu*, VIII. 37 :

विद्वांस्तु ब्राह्मणो दृष्ट्वा पूर्वोपनिहितं निधिम् ।
अशेषतोऽप्यादवीत सर्वस्याधिपतिर्हि सः ॥

[2] *Ibid.* I. 102 :

तस्य कर्मविवेकार्थं शेषाणामनुपूर्वशः ।
स्वायंभुवो मनुर्धीमानिदं शास्त्रमकल्पयत् ॥

apparel, bestows but his own in alms, other men subsist through the benevolence of the Brahmin."[1]

Here is a claim of sovereignty, which was true in the Śuṅga times for the first time in history. Yājña-valkya naturally does not adopt any portion of this claim of Brahmin sovereignty.

As to paying taxes, a Vedic priest was free from paying dues, *e. g.*, at ferry. This was an ancient claim. The Vedic priest was supposed to pay taxes in the shape of religious service. This exception was sought to be extended in case of treasure troves. The old theory had been that the king took a treasure-trove as it belonged to none, and the king was the heir of one who had no heirs. In the Mānava an entirely new theory was introduced that the king takes a treasure-trove as his wages for protecting the land. The old law had been that the king paid $\frac{1}{6}$ to the discoverer, and was not to take any thing at all when the heir was found. Under the new theory, the king was allowed a tax of protection in each case, whether owner was found or not. His tax varied from $\frac{1}{6}$ to $\frac{1}{2}$, $\frac{1}{2}$ where no heir was forthcoming. He was to give the other half to the Brahmins. The Brahmin here was taking the place of the Buddhist monk who had been given everything under the later Mauryas. The law-books only claim that a Vedic priest should not be taxed and this was claimed in the Brāhmaṇas, the reason given being, as Vasishṭha says, that the priest allows one-sixth of his spiritual deeds to the king[2]. Even this seems to have been disputed, as the Mānava Arthaśāstra says that even ascetics who live by picking up acorns in fields give $\frac{1}{6}$ of the gleanings to the king for protection.[3]

Brahmin and taxation.

---

1 *Ibid.* I. 101 :

स्वमेव ब्राह्मणो भुङ्क्ते स्वं वस्ते स्वं ददाति च ।
आनृशंस्याद्ब्राह्मणस्य भुञ्जते हीतरे जनाः ॥

2 *Vasishṭha*, I. 42—44.

3 *Hindu Polity*, I. p 8.

§ 14. It is to be noted that Sumati does not anywhere postulate that sovereignty included o w n e r s h i p in l a n d. The only passage which has been taken to indicate that (भूमेरधिपतिर्हि सः) expressly refers to 'protection' and not 'ownership.' Bühler and others have given it the value of 'lordship' in utter disregard of the express text and the commentators' exposition. A correct appreciation of the Hindu theory of taxation would leave no room for doubt as to the impossibility of a theory of sovereign's proprietary right in land. The king gets a sixth and other shares of commodities not as 'royalty', not because it grows out of the land in the kingdom, but because it is produced under the p r o t e c t i o n offered by him. Manufactures, and commodities brought from outside also give "shares"[1] just like the land-produce. After fixing the shares,[2] and after saying that the king being too busy, should place public affairs in the hands of the Prime Minister (141), Sumati proceeds to lay down : "In this way he shall arrange all the affairs of government, (taxation etc.), and his duty shall be 'to be under harness', and to protect with care the subjects. The king is to be taken as d e a d when the subjects are being looted and are complaining while the monarch and his servants are helpless. The ruler's first duty is to protect the subjects. As he enjoys the prescribed amount of the fruits of production (taxes), the king is bound by law (to do his duty). (VII. 142-144). The Mahā-Bhārata says that the taxes ('shares') are 'wages' of the king for protection[3]. The orthodox theory cited in Kauṭilya declared that the original king contracted to govern and protect on the condition of receiving the prescribed taxes.

Ownership in land

The natural deduction is that the man appointed to protect

---

[1] M. VII., 130.

[2] *Ibid.* VII, 127-40.

[3] *MBh.*, XII, 71, 10:

बलिषष्ठेन शुल्केन दण्डेनाथापराधिनाम्।
शास्त्रानीतेन लिप्सेथा वेतनेन धनागमम्॥

internally and externally cannot claim any right of ownership in the objects placed under his guard and trust[1].

This contractual theory was so strong that it affected the law of theft in a curious way. If one party—the king—to the contract took taxes as wages of protection, the other party—the subject—should claim and obtain compensation when he lost property on account of theft in the kingdom. On this reasoning which is known to the Artha-śāstra,[2] we actually find a law stated in Manu[3] and Yājñavalkya,[4] and carried on to later codes e.g. Nārada, Kātyāyana[5] etc., that the King must give compensation to the subject when theft occurs and the property is not traced. Manu gives it amongst the constitutional laws, while Yājñavalkya and Nārada place it in the municipal law.

§ 15. Yājñavalkya omits all directions about m i l i t a r y m a t t e r s. He evidently thinks that they are outside the scope of constitutional law. Matters of strategy and tactics were subjects, in a general way, of the Arthaśāstras, yet the Dharma writers always asserted their claim to speak on the rights of fighters in the field. We have seen this in the analysis of Āpastamba. Both Yājñavalkya and Sumati deal with those rights, and it was necessary to do so, as matters arising out of war could come before a court of law or dharma, or a common court of law and dharma.

Laws of War

§ 16. The origin of these laws which imposed 'c i v i l i z e d w a r f a r e' (d h a r m a-y u d d h a), was the D h a r m a S c h o o l. The Artha School is not keen to define these laws. Sumati enumerates these laws as follows :—

---

[1] *Hindu Polity*, Pt. II, pp. 174-83.

[2] AŚ. I. XIII. 9 etc.

[3] M. VIII. 40, Y. II. 36. Cf. *Gautama* X. 46-47, *Āpastamba*, II. 26 (8), *Vishṇu*, III, 66-67,

[4] *Nārada*, XIV. 23: स्तेनेष्वलभ्यमानेषु राजा दद्यात् स्वकाद्गृहात् ।
Kātyāyana: स्वदेशे यस्य वा किञ्चित् हृतं देयं नृपेन तत् ।
—cited by Chaṇḍeśvara in *V. Ratnā*. p. 345.

1. Treacherous weapons shall not be employed against the enemy (VII. 90) ;
2. Nor barbed arrows, nor poisoned ones, nor points ablaze with fire (VII. 90) ;
3. Nor shall a soldier be killed who has lost his horse or vehicle ;
4. Nor a non-fighter (e. g. 'a hermaphrodite') nor one who is coming to surrender, nor one who has fallen ;
5. Nor one who has lost his coat-of-mail, nor one who has his limb fractured ('bhagnaṁ') ;
6. Nor one who is unarmed, nor shall a spectator be killed (92) ;
7. Nor a fighter whose weapons have failed him, nor one who is in distress, nor one who is badly wounded (93) ;
8. Nor one in fear, nor one who is retreating (91).

Out of these according to Yājñavalkya, treacherous or deceptive weapons were permissible, though looked upon with disfavour in his time (I. 324). The other provisions of Sumati have full force of law in Yājñavalkya.

Republics

§ 17. In the time of Sumati the laws of Gaṇas or republics do not form the subject of his survey. Sumati knows them only to prohibit Brahmin students going to their country and Brahmins from being entertained by them, for the simple reason that Sumati's republican neighbours were heterodox and as such he regards them as *nāstika jana* [1]. But he has nothing to do with their laws. In the time of Yājñavalkya the Gaṇas had been, in the majority, conquered, and their laws came under the purview of the royal courts. Yājñavalkya is not hostile to them. [2]

---

[1] *Manu*, IV, 63, 163.

[2] *Yājñ*. I, 360-361.

कुलानि जातीः श्रेणीश्च गणान् जानपदानपि ।
स्वधर्माच्चलितान् राजा विनीय स्थापयेत् पथि ॥

Ibid, II, 187 :

गणद्रव्यं हरेद्यस्तु···तं राष्ट्राद्विप्रवासयेत् ।

§ 18. A point of difference between the two Codes illustrates the attitude of each on practical administration. G a m b l i n g, especially b e t t i n g, was a national vice of the Hindus from the Vedic times. Āpastamba, admitting the evil, provided for its royal control.[1] Kauṭilya made it a state monopoly and derived revenue from it.[2] Sumati condemns it and prohibits it altogether in the kingdom.[3] It could not be allowed on the principle that gambling was a species of t h e f t,[4] 'a n o p e n t h e f t', where people are deprived of their property openly. Yājñavalkya goes back to the Maurya laws and the state monopoly of gambling (II. 199-202).[5] He adopts the law almost in the same language.

Gambling

§ 19. Sumati expects the state to be puritanical and of correct morals, while Yājñavalkya expects the king to be more practical, to reduce the vice by administrative methods rather than by a moral crusade. The difference is due to the surroundings of Sumati. The Ś u ṅ g a r e v o l u t i o n succeeded the puritan Buddhist descendants of A ś o k a, the knight-errants of morality. The Mauryas stopped *samāja* or what Sumati calls *Samāhvaya*, fighting together' between living beings—between animals, or between animals and men. This was gladiatoring and similar duels' between animals, which were a feature of national amusement at the time of Megasthenes. Aśoka stopped it, and allowed only *ekatya samajas*[6] or shows of 'single' performances. Sumati

Sumati's political puritanism imitated from Aśokan

---

1 *Āpastamba*, II, 10, 25, 12:
सभाया मध्येऽधिदेवनमुद्धृत्यावोक्ष्याक्षान्निवपेद्युग्मान्वै भीतकान्यथाथान् ।

2 *Artha-Śastra*, III, 20, 74.

3 *Manu*, IX, 221. द्यूतं समाह्वयं चैव राजा राष्ट्रान्निवारयेत् ।

4 *Ibid.* 222. प्रकाशमेतत्तास्कर्यम् ।

5 *Yājñ.* ग्लहे शतिकवृद्धेस्तु सभिकः पञ्चकं शतम् ।
गृह्णीयाद्धूर्तकितवादितराद्दशकं शतम् ॥
स सम्यक्पालितो भागं राज्ञ दद्याद्यथाश्रुतम् ।
Kauṭ. जितद्रव्याद्ध्यक्षः पञ्चकं शतमाददीत ।

6 Aśoka. Rock Edict I.

on account of the betting which accompanied it, counted it as gambling, and not only stopped that but also gambling otherwise. The Code of the Śuṅga vied with the Buddhist rule of the Mauryas in puritanism. It denounced royal hunting allowed by all political writers, drinking, dancing and music with the severity of the Buddhist. [1] It allowed extravagant liberality like the Mauryas, with the difference that it substituted *Brahmin* for *Bhikkhu* and would give all and every thing to the new political parasite to make him grow fat on the state as the monks had done in the *ancien regime.* Śuṅga puritanism emphatically differed only when there arose the question of sacrifice and meat-eating. There it declared that it was Vedic and sacred; it must be done. Even ordinary meat-eating it justified on the ground of natural tendency, rendering at the same time tribute to the Religion of Mercy by the admission that to desist from it was meritorious.[2]

§ 20. Without taking into consideration the great social revolution already wrought in the previous régime, it is not possible to appreciate the eccentricities and peculiarities of the laws of Sumati. Sumati was not only a lawyer and law-giver, but also an advocate and preacher of the anti-Buddhist Brahmin revolution.

---

1 *Manu*, VII, 47, 50.

2 *Ibid.* V, 16, 18, 22-23, 27-33, 36. 39-42.

LECTURE VI

THE LAW COURT AND PLEADINGS

Court House—Sabha—King's Penal Authority—Caste Courts in Districts—King's Cases—Pleading—Counter Cases

Court House.

§ 1. We are in possession of some information about the Court House. The information, though scanty, is important. It relates to the court building at the capital. It was called the *Dharma-Sthīyam* under the Mauryas and probably also earlier. It was generally located near the great building called the *Mahā-Mātrīyam* or the Chancellary, the Downing Street of those days. The office of the Ministry and the Imperial High Court stood in independent blocks.[1] Near the High Court Buildings was a Hall fitted with necessary accessories for the convenience of the Judges and the Jurymen, e.g. a bath-house etc., and there stood also the deity.[2] The building of importance was the H a l l. A Hall (*Śālā*) signified that it was a public place. Evidently it is this Śālā which is called S a b h ā by Sumati and others.[3] *Sabhā* and *Śālā* as buildings are identical in earlier literature. Āpastamba defines *Sabhā* as a house 'which can be seen through from one side to the other'—from outside and inside.[4]

§ 2. A principle laid down with emphasis was that n o c a s e should be heard i n c a m e r a.[5] The character of the Hall of Justice is based on the same principle of publicity.

---

[1] Aś. ch. 26. p, 58. पृथग्धर्मस्थीयं महामात्रीयम् ।

[2] *Ibid.* सर्वेषां शालाखातोदपानवच्च स्नानगृहाग्निविषत्राणमार्जारनकुलारक्षास्वादैवपूजनवृत्ताः कारयेत् ।

[3] *Manu*, VIII. 11 यस्मिन्देशे निषीदन्ति विप्रा वेदविदस्त्रयः । राज्ञश्चाधिकृतो विद्वान् ब्राह्मणास्तां सभां विदुः ॥

[4] *Āp.* II, 10, 25, 5 यथोभयां संदृश्येत बहिरन्तरं चेति ।

[5] *Śukranīti*, IV, 5, 7.

नैकः पश्येच्च कार्याणि वादिनोः शृणुयाद् वचः ।
रहसि च नृपः प्राज्ञः सभ्याश्चैव कदाचन ॥

§3. The Court Building, according to Bṛihaspati, was at the central place in the capital. It had its independent water supply, as in the Maurya Civil Buildings (AŚ. p. 58). It was decorated with plants and trees ; it bore its a r m s (*lakshaṇāni*). Internally it was decorated with g a r l a n d s.[1] That the Sabhā-hall really was so beautiful is proved by sculptured representations of the Second century B.C. on Sanchi and Bharhut reliefs. It was adorned with s t a t u e s and p i c t u r e s,[2] a description which tallies with the description of the royal hall in Jātaka VI. It had further, according to Bṛihaspati, i m a g e s of g o d s, a detail which is implied also by the Arthaśāstra.[3] F i r e was placed there both according to Āpastamba[4] and Bṛihaspati.[5] It was supposed to be an entity like a Hindu house with its deity and its sacred fire.[6] The constant Fire meant constant life, never for a moment deserted. It had a t h r o n e according to Bṛihaspati, as in theory the king presided over the court. There was a curious symbolism : 'Seed-gems' were placed before the Court.[7] It seems to me that this refers to ordeals. According to other passages,[8] the l a w-b o o k s (Dharmaśāstrāṇi) formed part of the equipment. This must have been true of the time of Sumati, for he fully emphasises the value of 'reading' his Code.[1]

---

1 *Bṛihaspati*, II. 18-19 (quoted in VM. p. 10.)

दुर्गमध्ये गृहं कुर्याज्जलवृक्षान्वितं पृथक् ।
प्रागृदिशि प्राङ्मुखीन्तस्य लक्षणयाङ्कल्पयेत् सभाम् ॥
माल्यभूपासनोपेतां बीजरत्नसमन्वितताम् ।
प्रतिमालेख्यदेवैश्च युक्तामग्न्यम्बुना तथा ।
लक्षणयां वास्तुशास्त्रोक्तलक्षणैा तु लक्षिताम् ॥

2 See foot-note 1.

3 Foot-note 2, p. 110 *ante*.

4 *Āp*. 11. 10, 25, 6. सर्वेष्वेवाजस्रा अग्नयः स्युः ।

5 *Bṛih* II, 19. *Supra*.

6 Cf *Āp*. II. 10, 25. 7. अग्निपूजा च नित्या यथा गृहमेधे ।

7 बीजरत्नसमन्विताम् । See *Bṛih*. quoted above.

8 *Bṛihaspati*, I, 17.

Codes were a feature of the time, and Sumati refers to conflict between Smṛitis. Several manuscripts must have been ready at hand. Vasishṭha like the Jātakas refers to precedents, and acknowledges their authority.[2] Under these circumstances the *Dharmaśāstras* which were a feature of the court in later times presumably were placed in the Court Hall in the time of Sumati. According to Bṛihaspati the Sabhā faced east, while according to Āpastamba a Śālā (in general) ran from north to south and faced south.[3]

§4. The Court sat in the forenoon[1] and rose before the last division (the 8th) commenced,[5] altogether for about 4½ hours. This again was evidently an ancient practice. Four days in the month the Court remained closed—the 14th and the 15th of the dark fortnight, the full moon day, and the following 8th of the month.[6] If the 14th and 8th refer to both fortnights, the holidays would be 6 in every 30 days, which could not be considered excessive. The seats were arranged in this way :—

The Bench Clerk

The King or the Chief Justice

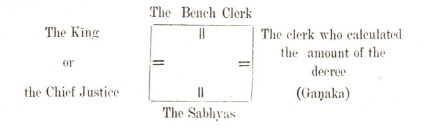

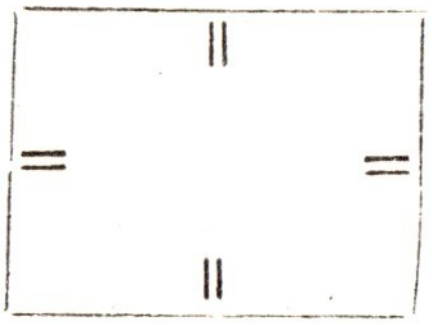

The clerk who calculated the amount of the decree (Gaṇaka)

The Sabhyas

§5. The constitutional positition of the Sabhyas who are called assessors by Bühler and others, should be ascertained. The number

---

[1] *Manu.* XII. 126 इत्येतन्मानवं शास्त्रं भृगुप्रोक्तं पठन् द्विजः ।

[2] *Vasishṭha*, XIX. 10,

[3] *Brih.* II. 18 प्राग्दिशि प्राङ्मुखीन् तस्य *Āp.* II. 10, 25, 5. दक्षिणेन पुरं सभा दक्षिणोदग्द्वारा etc.

[4] *Kātyāyana* in *Mayūkha*, p, 3.

[5] *Kātyāyana, ibid.*

[6] *Saṁvarta*, quoted in *Mayūkha*, p. 3.

of the Sabhyas, *i.e.*, those who formed the Sabhā, was always uneven, 7 or 5 or 3.[1] Seven was the maximum and three the minimum. As Mitra-Miśra correctly explains, it was for the purpose of obtaining a majority in the event of a difference of opinion that the uneven number was insisted upon.[2] According to the Mānava (VIII. 10) number three was the favourite.[3] It was so under Chandragupta, as Kauṭilya's code of administration directs that *three* dharmasthas should preside along with royal officers.[4] Were these Sabhyas mere ornamental advisors, or had their opinion, ascertained by "the method of majority," any binding force? Bṛihaspati is clear. Whether the King sat or his representative—the Chief Justice (or in other courts, a 'minister' as Kauṭilya, Yājñavalkya, and others call the Government servant, that is, the 'judge'), he had to "abide by the opinion of the Sabhyas".[5] This is again confirmed by the defined authority of the Sabhyas, the Royal Judge and the King:

Sabhā

"The President (Chief Justice or Judge) is the mouth-piece ('Speaker'); the King executes punishment; the Sabhyas are the examiners of the case."[6] The etymological explanation given of the word Prāḍvivāka (Chief Justice) is 'one who is the foremost in speaking,'[7] which, as the Hindu lawyers say, relates to his jurisdiction to examine and cross-examine witnesses, etc. The people who decided the case were the Sabhyas. Hence when there is miscarriage of justice, the codes blame the Sabhyas and not the royal judge.[8] Bühler in agreement

Royal Judges and King's Penal Authority

---

1 See *Hindu Polity*, pt. I. 110, *n.* 2

2 *VM.* p. 35. त्रिभ्योऽन्यूनाः सप्तभ्योऽधिकाश्च न कार्या इत्यत्र तात्पयम्। संख्यावैषम्यन्तु भूयोऽल्पविरोधे भूयसां स्यात्।

3 सभ्यैरेव त्रिभिर्वृतः।

4 *AŚ*, Ch. 58, p. 147 धर्मस्थास्त्रयस्त्रयोऽमात्याः।

5 *Bṛih.*, I. 24 (Jolly).

6 *Bṛih.*, quoted in VM., p. 42:

वक्ताध्यक्षो नृपः शास्ता सभ्याः कार्य्यपरीक्षकाः।

7 See VM., p. 32.

8 *Yājñ.*, II, 4; *Manu*, VII. 14, 19

with the spirit of the term, renders it as 'Judges.' The Sabhyas were the real Judges. The Sabhyas were not servants of the Crown. It is clear from various references where the *Sabhyas* are opposed to the 'king's servant'.[1] They very much resemble the present Jury ; in spirit both are the same. Yet both had different origin and history. The English Jury first came in as witnesses of the neighbourhood. But the *Sabhā* was a remnant of the national assembly of the Vedic times. The Sabhyas represented the constitutional sovereign authority of the Nation, and at the same time they were distinguished men. In the law-codes the qualification of being 'knowers of law' is coupled with the distinction of honesty and birth. The *Sabhā* and the English Jury are essentially different in genesis, though they both arrive at the same judicial goal and perform there the same function.

Caste

§6. Under the Mauryas the Court consisted of three Dharmasthas[2] and three ministers, one of them was undoubtedly the president who did all the questioning. The jury was thus of three, or of five if the ministers' votes were also counted. In the time of the Buddha the judges of the Supreme Court of Śrāvastī were called 'the Great Ministers.' Both Sumati[3] and Yājñavalkya[4] enjoin that the royal judge should be only one and that he should be a Brahmin. No such caste rule existed under the Mauryas, who appointed ministers on merits ; nor is such a caste rule found in Āpastamba (II. 11.29,5). At the same time, the prāyaśchitta cases went to the Purohita.[5] Now as Sumati amalgamated Dharma and Vyavahāra into one, the insistence on the condition that the royal judge should be a Brahmin by caste was probably not without historical justification. But when Sumati

---

1 राजा सत्पुरुषाः सभ्याः शास्त्रं गणकलेखकौ ;
नृपोऽधिकृतसभ्याश्च स्मृतिर्गणकलेखकौ (*Bṛih.*, etc., cited in Digests.)

2 *Manu*, VIII, uses the word *Dharmastha*.

3 *Manu*, VIII [*e.g.*, 57], 9. नियुञ्ज्याद्विद्वांसं ब्राह्मणं कार्य्यदर्शने ।

4 *Yājñ.*, II. 3. नियोक्तव्यो ब्राह्मणः ।

5 *Āp.*, II. 10. 27. 1. चरिते यथापुरं धर्मोद्धि संबन्धः ।

requires the jurymen also to be Brahmins, he goes too far (VIII. 1,11). Yājñavalkya did not accept it (II. 2,3). Authors of the other Codes allowed jurymen to be of all castes except Śūdra. This exception they make in view of Sumati's animated prohibition.[1] Sumati uses the words Vṛishala and Śūdra as denoting the same thing. Vṛishala according to the Mahā-Bhārata and the Artha-śāstra meant a Buddhist. The corresponding provision in Bṛihaspati in place of Śūdra gives atheists.[2] Sumati implies it by qualifying Śūdras as 'atheists' (VIII. 22). The whole attack is on the later Mauryan system. Buddhism declined to recognise caste distinction. The Buddhist rule of the descendants of Aśoka opened the jury to learned Śūdras and Buddhists. Sumati points out the divine punishment—famines and disease—if the country be *Śūdra-bhūyishṭha,* having a *majority of Śūdras*, atheists and non-twice-borns, *i.e.*, in a jury Śūdras by religion and Śūdras by birth preponderating.[3] In Maurya times there had been prolonged famines. To a Śūdra juror, Sumati will prefer an unlettered Brahmin (VIII. 20).

There were cases where a special jury was summoned, *e.g.* cases of theatricals who were regarded as Śūdras. Such cases were decided by a jury recruited from the very class of men having technical knowledge (Gautama, XI. 21-22).[4]

§ 7. Sumati says that petitions should be entertained in order of caste.[5] But Yājñavalkya and earlier writers have not got this rule. According to Bṛihaspati[6] (Mayūkha, 3-4), who closely follows the

---

[1] *Manu*, VIII. 16, 20-23.

[2] See *Bṛih.* quoted by Aparārka on *Yājñ.*, II. 2.

[3] *Manu*. VIII. 22. यद्राष्ट्रं शूद्रभूयिष्ठं विनश्यत्याशु तत्...दुर्भिक्षव्याधिपीडितम्
Medh. comments : प्रकरणाच्च शूद्रभूयिष्ठता विवादनिर्णये तु शूद्रविषया द्रष्टव्या। यत्र शूद्रा भूयांसो विवादनिर्णयकारास्तद्राष्ट्रमाशु विनश्यति, etc.

[4] *Cf. Śukranīti*, IV. 5, 18-23.

[5] *Manu*, VIII. 24. वर्णक्रमेण सर्वाणि पश्येत् कार्याणि।

[6] See quotation in *Mayūkha*, *pp. 3-4.*

Mānava, this rule means that when both parties appear in a criminal matter with counter-cases, the caste or marks of injury should decide precedence.

§ 8. In every town under the Mauryas there was the Dharmathīya Court on the same model—a bench of five and one president, and there were such courts on the frontiers which were apart from the town and district areas.[1] These courts were the common-law courts. They decided all the cases as coming under 17 or 18 Heads of the Vyavahāra law. The division had been originally made by the Arthaśāstra codifiers. The heads were 17 according to Kauṭilya :

Courts in Mofussil

1. Concerning Marriage and its rights	8. Concerning Companies
2. „ Inheritance	9. „ Sales and Purchases
3. „ Lands and Houses	10. „ Gift and its Resumption
4. „ Non-performance of Samayas and Agreements	11. „ Res nullius
	12. „ Ownership
	13. „ Sāhasa
	14. „ Assault
5. „ Debts	15. „ Defamation
6. „ Deposits	16. „ Gambling and Betting
7. „ Slaves and Labour	17. „ Miscellaneous Matters

Sumati adopted the classification (VIII. 4-7) and added Adultery to it. Adultery was dealt with in Mauryan times by the *Courts of Kaṇṭaka-Śodhana.* This court was presided over by royal officers only, three ministers. They were Criminal Courts.[2] They dealt with offences which did not come under the 17 classes, those which were offences according to statutes or regulations of the king, (*e.g.*, rules of road), or which had then come from the Dharma jurisdiction into the king's jurisdiction. Adultery was one of the latter class ; and so was theft. Sumati also has

---

[1] *AŚ.*, ch. 58, pp. 147-150.

[2] *Ibid.*, ch., 78, p. 200. प्रदेष्टारस्त्रयस्त्रयो वाऽमात्याः कण्टकशोधनं कुर्युः ।

the Kaṇṭaka Courts [1] and has them presided over by 'ministers' [2] (IX. 234). All offences under their jurisdiction are placed separately as in Kauṭilya. The latter portion of Chapter IX of the Mānava Code is devoted to them. Yājñavalkya also makes a division of offences in the manner of the Arthaśāstra division with reference to Dharmasthīya offences and Kaṇṭaka-śodhana ('Thorn-treating' Court) offences. Thus after Sāhasa he again takes up Guilds, then Adultery, and finally Bribery, etc. (II. 259-307). All these came according to the Arthaśāstra under the 'Kaṇṭaka-curing' or Magisterial Courts.

Under the Mauryas the Magisterial Courts had great powers. They adjudged cases including those of theft, bribery, adultery, abduction and treason amongst serious offences, and offences against rules of road and other administrative laws. They inflicted capital punishment, tortures, imprisonments, fines, in fact they could give all classes of sentences. And this they did without a jury.

§ 9. Sumati amalgamated the two jurisdictions and transferred all serious offences to the Court of Jurors. Only minor offences, *e.g.*, those about rules of road etc., were left to Magistrates, and those common-law petty offences which the Court of Jurors tried sitting as a court of miscellaneous offences, were transferred to them. This is clear from the treatment of offences in the Mānava and Yājñavalkya. The magisterial courts were left also to execute punishments. That this amalgamation continued is evidenced by Bṛihaspati who declares the Sabhyas to be Judges and the King as executing punishments. [3] Bṛihaspati calls the High Court (the Court of the Chief Justice) the Court of the Royal Signet Seal, and the court presided over by

---

[1] *Manu*, IX. 252-253:

कण्टकोद्धरणं नित्यमातिष्ठेद्यत्नमुत्तमम् ॥
रक्षणादार्यवृत्तानां कण्टकानाञ्च शोधनात् ।
नरेन्द्रास्त्रिदिवं यान्ति, etc.

[2] *Manu*, IX. 234.

[3] See p. 113 *ante*.

the King, 'Śāstritā Court' or the Ruler's Court.[1] Mofussil Courts went on circuit according to the same authority[2].

§ 10. Great dignity and formality attached to the Bench. The dress and demeanour of the King (Manu VIII. 1,2), and *a fortiori* of the Judge, was to be dignified, not ostentatious. The King taking his seat uncovered his right hand (VII. 2) as on all ceremonial occasions. The President (VII. 10) remained standing in certain cases, while in others he was seated. The Judge had to maintain a pleasant presence even before the worst criminal. He must have a smile on his face before he spoke.[3] This is a lesson which judges in all ages ought to take to heart. The Judge was required never to lose patience and never to show temper.

Dignity and Impartiality

Those persons were selected as Sabhyas who were equally impartial to friend and foe[4]. Dharma depended on them; if the Sabhyas remained neutral or did not utter what was lawful, they would be shot down by injustice.[5] There was no one who could be held above the law, even the king's relatives--his brother, his son, his teacher, his father-in-law or uncle—everybody, was liable to trial before the Court.[6]

---

[1] *Bṛihaspati*, I. 2 (Jolly); see quotation in *Smṛitichandrikā*, Vyavahārakāṇḍa, p. 41.

प्रतिष्ठिताऽप्रतिष्ठता मुद्रिता शास्त्रिता तथा ।
चतुर्विधा सभा प्रोक्ता सभ्याश्चैव तथाविधाः ॥

[2] *Ibid.*, I. 3 (Jolly). See quotation, *ibid.*

प्रतिष्ठिता पुरे ग्रामे चला नामाऽप्रतिष्ठिता ।
मुद्रिताऽध्यक्षसंयुक्ता राजयुक्ता तु शास्त्रिता ॥

[3] *Vishṇu*, III, 63-64. स्मितपूर्वभाषी स्यात् । वध्येष्वपि न भ्रुकुटिमाचरेत्

[4] *Yājñ.*, II. 2. राज्ञा सभासदः कार्या रिपौ मित्रे च ये समाः ।

[5] *Manu*, VIII. 12-13:

धर्मो विद्धस्त्वधर्मेण सभां यत्रोपतिष्ठते ।
शल्यञ्चास्य न कृन्तन्ति विद्धास्तत्र सभासदः ॥
सभा वा न प्रवेष्टव्या वक्तव्यं वा समञ्जसम् ।
अब्रुवन् विब्रुवन् वापि नरो भवति किल्बिषी ॥

[6] *Yājñ.* I. 357. अपि भ्राता सुतोऽर्घ्यो वा श्वशुरो मातुलोऽपि वा ।
नादण्ड्यो नाम राज्ञोऽस्ति धर्माद्विचलितः स्वकात् ॥

This was such a settled principle of Hindu law that even Kauṭilya, the great advocate of royalty, lays down without any controversy or hesitation that the Court could punish even the king as he could punish the subject (prakṛiti)[1]. This was mandatory even on the Criminal Judge (*Pradeshṭā*) who was a servant of the Crown. Recorded cases show that impartial justice of this standard was in fact administered (Lect. XIII).

§ 11. A very salutary rule existed to keep under check irresponsible propensity of the Judges. Where negligence of the Judge in giving decision was found by the King in appeal, the learned Judge was fined up to 1000 (gold or silver pieces according to offence).[2] This was a sort of compensation to the poor litigant who had to suffer for the foolishness of the Judge. Yājñavalkya, however, makes the Jury liable only in case of perversity through fear, partiality or avarice : there they are separately fined double the amount of the value of the suit.[3] Sumati in that case deprived the Jurors and the Judge of their whole property.[4] Kauṭilya[5] imposed a fine of eight times the value ; and if dishonestly a man was corporeally punished, the same punishment was imposed on the

---

1 *AŚ.*, ch. 87. p. 226 :

उत्तमापरमध्यत्वं प्रदेष्टा दण्डकर्मणि ।
राज्ञश्च प्रकृतीनां च कल्पयेदन्तरान्वितः ॥

2 *Manu*, IX. 234, अमात्याः प्राड्विवाको वा यत् कुर्युः कार्यमन्यथा ।
तत् स्वयं नृपतिः कुर्यात् तान् सहस्रञ्च दण्डयेत् ॥

See also the comments of Nārāyaṇa and Rāghavānanda Cf. also IX, 231.

3 *Yājñ*, II. 4. रागाल्लोभाद्भयाद्वापि स्मृत्यपेतादिकारिणः ।
सभ्याः पृथक् पृथग् दण्ड्या विवादाद्द्विगुणं दमम् ॥

4 *Manu*, IX. 231 ; *Vishṇu*, V. 180 ; *Bṛih.*, XXII. 10.

5 *AŚ.*, ch. 86. p. 223. धर्मस्थः प्रदेष्टा वा हैरण्यमदण्ड्यं क्षिपति क्षेपद्विगुणमस्मै दण्डं कुर्यात् ।
हीनातिरिक्ताष्टगुणं वा शारीरदण्डं क्षिपति, शारीरमेव दण्डं भजेत ।
निष्क्रयद्विगुणं वा ।

Jurors or the Magistrate (Pradeshṭā) or double the commutation-fine. Ordinary fines were imposed on those Jurors who threatened or browbeat, sent out or unjustly silenced a disputant or defamed him.[1] The last provision will very much appeal to our own times. Fines realised from the King were given away in charity, according to Kauṭilya.[2]

King's Cases

§ 12. The King (in Council) heard appeals as the highest court of appeal[3]. But he had also original jurisdiction, according to the Śukra-Nīti, in matters of contempt committed in his Court[4] (IV.5). The King himself was supposed to be party in cases of treason, forgery of state seals, coinage, and other state offences. Ten classes of offences—offences against statues, torture of women, bastardy, adultery, women's misconduct, theft, abortion, assault by deed, assault by words,—were also cases where the King was the complainant[5]. These cases were instituted at the instance of the state. They cover almost all important criminal offences.

Actions

§ 13. The state took cognizance of civil grievance where the wronged parties were minors, gods, ascetics, and other helpless people[6] (AŚ. p. 200). Otherwise without a complainant or plaintiff's own motion no case could be entertained.[7] It was illegal if the Government prompted

---

[1] AŚ. ch. 86, p. 222. धर्मस्थश्चेद्विवदमानं पुरुषं तर्जयति, भर्त्सयत्यपसारयति, अभिग्रसते वा, पूर्वमस्मै साहसदण्डं कुर्यात्। वाक्पारुष्ये द्विगुणम्।

[2] *Ibid.* ch. 90; p. 234.

[3] Cf. *Manu*, IX, 234.

[4] *Śukranīti*, IV, 5.

[5] *Ibid.* IV. 5, 83ff.

[6] AŚ., ch. 77, p. 200:

देवब्राह्मणतपस्विस्त्रीबालवृद्धव्याधितानामनाथानामनभिसरतां धर्मस्थाः कार्याणि कुर्युः।

[7] *Manu*, VIII, 43:

नोत्पादयेत् स्वयं कार्यं राजा नाप्यस्य पूरुषः

न च प्रापितमन्येन ग्रसेतार्थं कथञ्चन॥

people to come to court as suitors. The actions were classed according to the classification of the 'Eighteen Titles'.

§ 14. The proceeding began with certain questions put by the Judge to the suitor coming to his court. This initial procedure we do not know from our early codes, but according to Kātyāyana it was as follows : The suitor, when his turn arrived, stood before the court and bowed. The Judge addressed the suitor in these words :

> '*What is thy business? What is thy grievance?*
> *Fear not! Speak out, O Man!*'[1]

—an address in full conformity with the high traditions of Hindu Judiciary, and worthy of being followed in any age and civilization.

§ 15. To bring an action and obtain relief, when he proved his cause, was the suitor's right (Cf. Manu, VIII. 12-13). Judges who tired the patience of the suitors and who would not take down a plaint were liable to punishment.[2]

§ 16. The Mānava does not give any rules of pleadings. But such rules had been fixed. Probably Sumati had no change to offer and he allowed the current practice. According to the Arthaśāstra, these details were necessary in a plaint :—(1) the date (of the cause of action) which was expressed in "the year (regnal year of the king), the ṛitu (season), the month, the fortnight, the day"; (2) the cause of action (karaṇa) ; (3) the statement of the case ; (4) the amount of claim ; (5) the fact that the plaintiff and the defendant are capable of suing and being sued ; (6) their residence, country, town, caste, family name and business.[3]

Pleadings

The plaint was stated in Court by the plaintiff and it was taken

---

[1] काले कार्यार्थिनं पृच्छेत् प्रणतं पुरतः स्थितम्। किं कार्यं, का च ते पीडा, मा भैषीर्ब्रूहि मानव ॥—cited in *Smṛitichandrikā* (Mysore, 1914 III (1). p. 70).

[2] *AŚ* : ch. 87, p. 222.

[3] *AŚ*.. ch, 58, p. 149. संवत्सरमृतुं मासं पक्षं दिवसं करणमधिकरणमृणं वेदकावेदकयोः कृतसमर्थावस्थयोर्देशग्रामजातिगोत्रनामकर्माणि चाभिलिख्य

down in the presence of both the parties. The Artha Śāstra and Yājñavalkya[1] assume both parties present. Kātyāyana and others supply the information that before pleadings were taken down, the defendant was summoned either by a writ under seal or through the bailiff[2]. Yājñavalkya (II. 6) says that the plaint should be taken down in the presence of the defendant (pratyarthin) 'as the plaintiff states', 'marked with the year, the month, the fortnight, the day, the name, the caste, and the like."[3] Kātyāyana says on the same : (a) the date—year, month, fortninght, hour—province, district, place, caste, person and age (whether of age or not), (b) the case *(sādhya*, that which is sought to be proved), (c) the measure *(pramāṇa)*, (d) subject-matter *(dravya)* in dispute and its number (saṅkhyā), (e), one's own *nāma* (description), if the property be immovable, then the *nāma* of the field, etc., its nature—if hereditary, the reign of the king when the property was acquired, etc., are to be given. [4]

Then the answer of the defendant was taken down, according to Yājñavalkya (II. 1) and others, in the presence of the plaintiff. The plaintiff's coming to court, according to Yājñavalkya, was called the First Step in the case, the recording of the pleadings, the 'Second Step,' that of evidence, the Third, and the Judgment was the Fourth[5]. For putting in his defence the defendant could take adjournments, except in common law criminal cases[6]. This was the practice also under the Mauryas.

---

[1] *AŚ.*, ch. 87, p. 222 वादिप्रतिवादिप्रश्नानर्थानुपूर्व्यान्निवेशयेत्। Cf. Yājñ., II. 6-7.

[2] *Smṛitichandrikā*, Vol. III, p. 72, quotes Kātyāyana—मुद्रां वा निक्षिपेत्तस्मिन् पुरुषं वा समादिशेत्। तस्मिन्नावेदके। पुरुषः साध्यपालः।—Devaṇṇabhaṭṭa. Cf. *Bṛih.*, (Jolly, II. 33)—यस्याभियोगं कुरुते तथ्येनाशङ्कयाथवा। तमेवानाययेद्राजा मुद्रया पुरुषेण वा।

[3] *Yājñ.*, II. 6. समामासतदर्धाहर्नामजात्यादिचिह्नितम्।

[4] See quotation from Kātyāyana in Aparārka's commentary on *Yājñ.*, II. 6.

[5] See *Yājñ.*, II. 5—8

[6] *Ibid.* 12 साहसस्तेयपारुष्यगोभिशापात्यये स्त्रियाम्।
विवादयेत् सद्य एव कालोऽन्यत्रेच्छया स्मृतः॥

Time for lodging Defence

§ 17 'The defendant may be allowed 3 or 7 nights to prepare his defence.' If he was late he was fined lightly. Three fortnights' time was the longest limit.[1]

§ 18 Kauṭilya (p. 149), Sumati (VIII. 25-26) and Yājñavalkya (II.13-15) also imply that the plaintiff was thoroughly examined, like witnesses, and his movements and behaviour marked. But they do not deal with the rules of pleadings which we find so vastly developed and minutely considered with technical details in Nārada, Bṛihaspati and Kātyāyana. In fact, the modern world has not improved upon them. Kauṭilya only says that the plaint and the written statement should be scrutinised,[2] but gives no rules of guidance. It seems that these rules grew after Yājñavalkya. It is noteworthy that Nārada contemplates plaints prepared by the plaintiff at home (I.13-14) which was filed by him in court. When that practice was allowed, technical rules would have evolved and could be insisted upon and taken advantage of.

The plaintiff had to depose in reply to the statement of the defendant (or 'written statement') the very day it was put in, as, says Kauṭilya, 'the plaintiff knows the cause and its determination is sought by him.'[3] This is implied in Yājñavalkya II. 7 : 'after (defendant's reply) the plaintiff shall at once cause to be taken down the case which is known to him and its proof.'[4]

Counter-Cases

§ 19 Counter-cases were not allowed. Yājñavalkya says :

---

1 *AŚ.*, ch. 58, p. 149 :

तस्याप्रतिब्रुवतस्त्रिरात्रं सप्तरात्रमिति। अत ऊर्ध्वं त्रिपणावराध्यं द्वादशपणापरं दण्डं कुर्यात्। त्रिपक्षादूर्ध्वं···परोक्तदण्डं कृत्वा, etc.

2 *AŚ.*, ch. 58 p. 149 निविष्टांश्चावेक्षेत।

3 *Ibid.*, p. 149 :

अभियोक्ता चेत् प्रत्युक्तस्तदहरेव न प्रतिब्रूयात्, परोक्तः स्यात्।
कृतकार्यविनिश्चयो ह्यभिनियोक्ता, नाभियुक्तः।

4 *Yājñ.*, II. 7.

श्रुतार्थस्योत्तरं लेख्यं पूर्वावेदकसन्निधौ।
ततोऽर्थी लेखयेत् सद्यः प्रतिज्ञातार्थसाधनम्॥

'Until the plaintiff's case is disposed of, no counter-case shall be allowed to be brought against him, nor shall any one else be allowed to bring another case against the defendant in reply'. 'But in quarrels (*kalaha*), assaults, and sāhasa a counter-case will be allowable'[1]

This was an ancient law of procedure as Kauṭilya provides :

"In cases other than *kalaha* and *sāhasa,* and in cases amongst guilds of merchants and corporate bodies, the defendant shall bring no counter-case. Nor can there be a counter-case against the defendant."[2]

Evidently Sumati does not subscribe to this view. Nārada, however, adopts it (1. 55) : so does Bṛihaspati (Jolly IV. 10).

In connexion with counter-cases in criminal complaints, it seems that there had been a different view before 300 B. C. For,

"Authorities think that in *kalaha* one who is the first to complain wins, as the pain makes him run to Court."

"But Kauṭilya says, Not so. Whether the complaint is lodged first or last, it is the evidence of witnesses that must be depended upon." [3]

---

[1] *Yājñ.*, II, 9—10.

अभियोगमनिस्तीर्य नैनं प्रत्यभियोजयेत् ।
अभियुक्तञ्च नान्येन नोक्तं विप्रकृतिं नयेत् ॥
कुर्यात् प्रत्यभियोगञ्च कलहे साहसेषु च ।
उभयोः प्रतिभूर्ग्राह्यः समर्थः कार्यनिर्णये ॥

[2] *AŚ.*, ch. 58, p. 149 :

अभियुक्तो न प्रत्यभियुञ्जीत अन्यत्र कलहसाहससार्थसमवायेभ्यः ।
न चाभियुक्तेऽभियोगोऽस्ति ।

[3] *AŚ.*, ch. 76, p. 196 :

कलहे पूर्वागतो जयत्यक्षममाणो हि प्रधावति इत्याचार्याः ।
नेति कौटिल्यः । पूर्व पश्चाद्वाऽऽगतस्य साक्षिणः प्रमाणम् ॥

LECTURE VII.

LAW OF EVIDENCE.

Burden of proof—Contrary Pleadings—Possession—Witnesses —their Examination—Witness-box—Cross-examination—Oath —Ordeals—not recognised by Kauṭilya—Ordeals in the Mānava Code—in Yājñavalkya—in Drama Mṛichchhakaṭika — Perjury—Witness-Jury—Costs to witnesses— Documentary Evidence.

§ 1. Yājñavalkya[1] gives the direction for determining the question of the burden of proof. 'As soon as the defendant's reply, taken down in his presence, is read out to him, the plaintiff must depose as to the *pratijñāta* and proof in the case.'

Burden of Proof.

Nārada says that the pratijñā is the essence of a law suit (**सारस्तु व्यवहाराणां प्रतिज्ञा समुदाहृता**) if he fails in it, the plaintiff loses his case, if he goes across it, he reaches his object.[2] Yājñavalkya in similar language had described the effect of the *pratijñāta* ('undertaking'):

"On proving that, he wins, otherwise he fails."[3]

The *pratijñā* or *pratijñāta* ('promise', 'undertaking') was the issue joined by the plaintiff. The *siddhi* or burden of proof lay on the plaintiff on his issue. It is not to be taken that in every case he had to 'undertake' pratijñā. The Mānava Code (VIII. 60) says that only when the defendant denies the

---

1 *Yājñ.*, II,, 7. श्रुतार्थस्योत्तरं लेख्यं पूर्वावेदकसंनिधौ ।
ततोऽर्थी लेखयेत् सद्यः प्रतिज्ञातार्थसाधनम् ॥

2 *Nārada* quoted by Aparārka on *Yājñ*, II., 8.
सारस्तु व्यवहाराणां प्रतिज्ञा समुदाहृता ।
तद्धानौ हीयते वादी तरंस्तामुत्तरो भवेत् ॥ (Nār. I, 6.)

3 *Yājñ.*, II., 8. तत्सिद्धौ सिद्धिमाप्नोति विपरीतमतोऽन्यथा ।

claim, the plaintiff had to adduce evidence: "On being asked, only when the defendant denies, the claimant shall prove his case by at least three witnesses before the king and Brahmins."[1] In other words, Yājñavalkya's procedure refers to the stage when the Reply (our 'written statement') is in what the later codes call, mithyā-uttara or Denial.

Yājñavalkya contemplates the defence of 'confession and avoidance. This the later authorities called *pratyavaskanda*. For he says in II. 17:

> "When both parties have called witnesses the first party's witnesses shall be examined. When the case of the first party (according to commentators, 'the issue') becomes latter, the witnesses of the second party depose first."[2]

The import of the latter portion has been missed by Mandlik and others. *Pūrvapakshe adharî-bhūte*, 'when the issue of the first party becomes latter' is explained by Aparārka by quoting parallel and explicit passages from Nārada and Kātyāyana.[3]

Kātyāyana says:

> "The first party's case attains latter-ness by Kāraṇa (a special case pleaded in defence). Hence it is said that burden of proof is always discharged by the case of the first party (*i.e.*, although a defendant technically, he becomes plaintiff by his pleading)."

---

[1] *Manu*, VIII., 60. पृष्टोऽपव्ययमानस्तु कृतावस्थो धनैषिणा ।
त्र्यवरैः साक्षिभिर्भाव्यो नृपब्राह्मणसंनिधौ ॥

[2] *Yājñ.*, II., 17. साक्षिषूभयतः सत्सु साक्षिणः पूर्ववादिनः ।
पूर्वपक्षेऽधरीभूते भवन्त्युत्तरवादिनः ॥

[3] *Aparārka* on *Yājñ.*, II., 17 (p. 624).

Kātyāyana—कारणात् पूर्वपक्षोऽपि ह्युत्तरत्वं प्रपद्यते ।
अतः क्रिया सदा प्रोक्ता पूर्वपक्षप्रसाधनी ॥

Nārada— आधर्यं पूर्वपक्षस्य यस्मिन्नर्थवशाद्भवेत् ।
विवादे साक्षिणस्तत्र प्रष्टव्याः प्रतिवादिनः ॥

Nārada:

"By reason of the cause pleaded when the case of the first party attains latterness, the witnesses of the defendants are to be examined."

This is preceded by:

"When both parties allege their cases and both call witnesses, his witnesses will begin whose issue becomes first."[1]

This would be the case when, for instance, the plea of bar by former judgment is taken (*prāṅ-nyāya*). Yājñavalkya does not mention these technical pleas but he implies them. Here the onus is shifted. And, as another rule of Yājñavalkya proves, the plaintiff is entitled to prove his case even from the mouth of the defendant's witnesses: (II. 79 with Aparārka)

"The party whose witnesses (or) whose adversaries' witnesses prove his *pratijñā* to be true, wins, otherwise his defeat is certain."

Aparārka:

"One whose witnesses, or one whose vādin's *i.e.*, defendant's (*prativādinaḥ*) witnesses prove the issue to be true, is the victor."[2]

§ 2. The rules show a very developed stage of pleadings. The language of Yājñavalkya which is terse like that of the sūtra-writers, makes their appreciation difficult. His procedure law becomes clear only when we make a comparative study of the subject and give value to each of his syllables. Here Aparārka excels even the great Vijñāneśvara and

[1] *Ibid.* द्वयोर्विवदतोरर्थे द्वयोः सत्सु च साक्षिषु ।
पूर्वपक्षो भवेद्यस्य भवेयुस्तस्य साक्षिणः ॥

[2] *Yājñ.* I., 79. यस्योचुः साक्षिणः सत्यां प्रतिज्ञां स जयी भवेत् ।
अन्यथावादिनो यस्य ध्रुवस्तस्य पराजयः ॥

Aparārka on it: यस्य वादिनः प्रतिवादिनो वा प्रतिज्ञां साक्षिणः सत्यामाहुः स जयी भवति ।

the acute Mitra-Miśra. Yājñavalkya's law of procedure is far in advance of Kauṭilya and Sumati. Yet he does not reach the level attained by Nārada and Bṛihaspati, whom the most technical rules of pleadings of modern Europe have not yet surpassed. In our courts at present, for instance, it is to be argued and the judge has to be convinced by the authority of English cases that plaintiff's right cannot be affected by 'fraud of speech' in his plaint. But in Nārada's time the matter was placed beyond controversy.

Contrary pleadings.

"One who further abandoning his first case, takes stand on another, on account of shifting his ground, is called one of 'Hîna' ('Inferior') pleading. In all civil cases on account of fraud-in-speech the right is not lost."

As Nîlakaṇṭha puts it, the plaintiff may be fined for perjury, but his civil right remains intact and relief cannot be denied to him.[1]

§ 3. Adverse possession in the eye of the Artha Law was a case of abandonment of ownership by the real owner. It is treated by Kauṭilya in connection with abandonment and loss of ownership. He states that 10 years' adverse possession to the full knowledge of the owner would estop him from claiming chattel, and twenty years', land and buildings. The property of the king or a minor could not be acquired by prescription. Neither of them can be deemed to have abandoned it. At best it is permissive possession in case of the king's property. In case of the minor, it is stealth. According to this view, further, no one could prescribe against one who had left his property and country during a revolution.[2]

Possession.

But Yājñavalkya has a different standpoint. He gives the same law, but regards it as part of the law on

---

[1] *Vyavahāramayūkha* of Nīlakaṇṭha, ed. by Mandlik, p. 7.
[2] Arthaśāstra, p. 191.

evidence.[1] It is a matter of proof, a right created by the procedure of proof, and not a substantive right. He does not allow any proof of title where possession has been hereditary.[2] The Dharma lawyers of later times gives a reason for it. A lost title is presumed in the possessor (see Aparārka and quotations therein). They have a doctrine of smārta smaraṇakāla, literally, 'legal memory' which is limited by the man's memory fixed at twenty or sixty years (three generations).[3] Vishṇu gives generations instead of years (*V.* 187). Yājñavalkya acts on the principle clearly when in II. 28 he says that the question of titles being put in issue, the owner can recover the property, but not his son or grandson." By this doctrine of presuming title in the possessor it was sought to reconcile the Artha Law which had been the law of the country, with the Dharma doctrine that there could be no prescription in case of land.[4] The Mānava went back to the Dharma law and declared that possession can never mature into title. 'Possession is no proof. This is the settled law.'[5] The Dharma law regarded misappropriation of land as a sin, and theft of land as a great sin. It could not legalise a sin. Adverse possession and theft of land were identical in their doctrine of mental cure. Where there is intention of misappropriation there is theft according to their definition of the sin of theft. They were shocked at the Artha-śāstra law of acquiring title by adverse possession. As they did not allow adverse possession of land in

---

[1] *Yājñ.*, II., 24. पश्यतोऽब्रुवतो भूमेर्हानिर्विंशतिवार्षिकी ।
परेण भुज्यमानाया धनस्य दशवार्षिकी ॥

[2] *Ibid.* 28. आगमस्तु कृतो येन सोऽभियुक्तस्तमुद्धरेत् ।
न तत्सुतस्तत्सुतो वा भुक्तिस्तत्र गरीयसी ॥

[3] Aparārka on *Yājñ.*, II., 28 :
अन्यवौत्सर्गिकं स्वस्वामिभाव एव प्रामाण्यमिति आगमकर्तुः सुतस्यापि भुक्त्यैव स्वाम्यसिद्धिरिष्यते । सा स्मार्तकालातिक्रमे सति द्रष्टव्या । स्मार्तश्च कालः पुरुषत्रयभुक्तिकालात्मकः ।

[4] *Gautama*, XII., 39. पशुभूमिस्त्रीणामनतिभोगः ।

[5] *Manu*, VIII., 200 संभोगो यत्र दृश्येत न दृश्येतागमः क्वचित् ।
आगमः कारणं तत्र न संभोग इति स्थितिः ॥

favour of a private citizen, so they did not allow it in favour of the king either ; they could not make an exception to the doctrine. The king could not prescribe (Gautama XII., 39) as no one could prescribe against the king. A thief in the eye of the Dharma was always a trustee ; he must return the property and undergo penance. How could the king, the general trustee, prescribe against a subject ? How could he act like a thief ? This was the reasoning of the Dharma law. Yājñavalkya solved the juridical difficulty. He transferred the controversy from law to procedure, and cut the knot.

Witnesses.

§ 4. The earlier term for witnesses in a civil transaction was śrotṛi, 'hearer.' In early law when a man completed a transaction by uttering a solemn pronouncement, *e.g.*, in gift, contract etc., the witnesses were asked 'to hear' that. The eye-witness 'Sākshin', ('with one's eyes') is a later term, and originally probably was a term of criminal or sin law. They were not asked or appointed *to hear* a matter. They *saw* a deed. The term Śrotṛi occurs in the Artha-Śāstra[1] where *Sākshin* is replacing it. It goes out of use in the Mānava and later Codes. Yet it survives in literature longer. Bhāsa uses it in its technical sense.[2]

Witnesses required in a civil action to prove a case were at least three. This had been the law before the Mānava Code, and this remained the law in subsequent times. As a general rule one witness was not sufficient to prove one issue. One witness, however, was sufficient where the parties agreed to abide by his evidence ; or two, in debts, but never one.[3]

The following persons were disqualified to be cited as witnesses, according to (1) Kauṭilya, (2) Sumati, and (3) Yājñavalkya

---

[1] *E.g.*, Ch. 58, p. 147.

[2] *Bhāsa*, Pratimā, p. 70.

[3] *Arthaśāstra*, Ch. 68, p. 175. प्रात्ययिकाः शुचयोऽनुमता वा त्रयोऽवरार्ध्याः ।
पक्षानुमतौ वा द्वौ, ऋणं प्रति न त्वेवैकः ॥

respectively and treated of by all these authorities under Recovery of Debt :—

(1) (a) *Not to be called*, (pp. 175-6)	(2) (VIII. 64—72)	(3) (II. 70-73)
1. wife's brothers,	'Artha-Saṁbandhins',	the same
2. friends (or partners),	the same,	
3. prisoners,	tainted,	forger
4. creditors } 5. debtors },	'Artha-Sambandhins',	the same
6. enemies,	'Artha-Sambandhins',	
7. 'Aṅgadhṛita',	afflicted with disease,	deformed
8. convicts (for perjury),	the same,	the same
Not to be made witnesses	(2)	(3)
9. the king,	the same	
10 Vedic priest,	the same	
11. persons maintained by the town,	theatricals and artizans,	'Kitava'
12. lepers,	'vikalendriya'	
13. outcasts,	'with marks of outcast'	'Abhiśasta patita'
14. chāṇḍāla,	'Antya'	
15. the blind, the deaf, the dumb and egoistic idiot.	Vikalendriya, old, child, dependent, one of bad fame, 'Dasyu', one of prohibited occupation, one not in fit state of mind (66)	old, child, mad
16. females,	the same	the same
17 government servants,		
(a) *Except in transactions of their class*		
Other exceptions :		
(b) In criminal cases of the classes of theft, assault (by deed or words), adultery, and rape all these could be witnesses except Nos. 2, and 6	the same (72)	the same (72) and with no exception
(c) In secret transactions, even only one person could be a witness, or one who has overheard or seen by chance, *except* the king and an ascetic,	—'anubhavin' (69)	'pākhaṇḍin'
(d) The prosecution could call even masters against servants, teachers and priests against pupils and clients, parents against son, and others,	the same (70)	

The Mānava follows the Kauṭilîya almost with verbal faithfulness, using only in a few cases later terms. Yājñavalkya cuts down the list and includes ascetics and hermits whom the first two authorities excuse and exclude. Yājñavalkya thinks that they are the best witnesses and that they can be summoned.[1] The rule

[1] *Yājñ.*, II., 68.

about one witness by consent is adopted by both.[1] The Artha-śāstra helps us to explain many disputed terms in the list, and it can now be seen that Manu's obscure language has got the same divisions as I have shown in the Kauṭilîya.

Manu verbally takes the rule of the Kauṭilîya about contradiction in the evidence of witnesses that the majority should be believed.[2] Yājñavalkya also adopts it.[3] It is noteworthy that Yājñavalkya does not except the king from his list.

§ 5. The rules about secondary evidence in cases where documents are lost, or in cases where men are abroad, etc., which we find in Nārada and later, are not found in the codes under review. Nārada marks the highest development of the law of evidence. The period from about 400 A.C. to 600 A.C. seems to have been the greatest for the blossoming of the Hindu legal genius. It was the period of the Gupta Empire.

Examining witnesses.

§ 6. A long address to the witnesses to speak the truth is given in the Mānava.[4] Yājñavalkya in its place gives two of the verses which Manu gives, almost in the same language.[5] Evidently, as Nārada implies,[6] the exhortation was taken from one of the Purāṇas, two of which we know by name: the Bhavishyat is quoted by Āpastamba (II. 9. 24. 6) and the Vāyu by the Mānava (IX. 42). In the address, it is curious that the Ganges and Kuru (Kshetra) already appear as places of pilgrimage.[7]

Witness-box.

§ 7. The witnesses went inside the square formed by the members of the court (Manu VIII. 79). This position of the court or some special place seems to be alluded to in the Śukra-Nîti as the *a-rahaḥ*[8] where

---

[1] *Manu*, VIII., 77; *Yājñ.*, II., 72.

[2] *Manu*, VIII., 73.

[3] *Yājñ.*, II., 78.

[4] *Manu*, VIII., 80-101.

[5] *Yājñ.*, II., 73-75.

[6] See Aparārka's quotation on *Yājñ.*, II., 75:

पुराणैर्धर्मवचनैः सत्यमाहात्म्यकीर्तनैः ।
अनृतस्यापवादैश्च भृशमुत्त्रासयेदपि ॥

[7] *Manu*, VIII., 92.

[8] *Śukranîtisāra*, IV. 5. 203. (Jîvānanda, 1890).

the witness after going inside the court stepped in to give evidence. The word means 'non-private.' It was evidently the place marked out for the witness as a witness-box.

Cross-examination.

§ 8. The Judge (President) administered oath to the witness, recited the address of truth, and cross-examined him. The cross-examination is mentioned as early as Āpastamba.[1] It was severe, for it has been treated as a form of 'torture' in the Artha-Śāstra.[2] Even the accused was cross-examined. The Burmese Code of Manu gives a curious story of the origin of cross-examination: It was accidentally discovered, according to it, in the time of Manu. Some boys were playing and one of them by his questionings was seen to discover the truth.

Oath.

§ 9. A change seems to have taken place between the time of Kauṭilya and that of the Mānava Code in the history of oath. The Brahmin, according to Kauṭilya's rule, was asked: 'Tell the truth,' but no oath was administered. Another and a common formula was directed both to the Kshatriya and the Vaiśya, in which reference to their bravery was made; and no oath was repeated by the witness. This shows that the Vaiśya was still a fighter and his position was equal to that of the Kshatriya. The formula must have been ancient to contemplate such equality. The Śūdra was addressed with superstitious threats and threats of fine. But he too was not made; to swear.[3] In Manu's Code the picture is different. The Brahmin is not put on oath and has still the same formula addressed to him. But as to the Kshatriya and the Vaiśya and the Śūdra, each is put on an oath specially designed for his caste and vocation.[4] The equality of the Vaiśya is gone, and superiority

[1] *Āp.*, II. 5, 11, 3. सुविचितं विचित्या दैवप्रश्नेभ्यो राजा दण्डाय प्रतिपद्येत।

[2] *Artha-Śāstra*, Ch. 85, p. 219. वाक्यानुयोगो वा।

[3] *Artha-Śāstra*, Ch. 68, p. 176.

[4] *Manu*, VIII., 113-114.

18

of the Brahmin is emphasised. This is an index of a great social revolution. The old age with Vedic vestiges sharply changed —a dividing line, as it were, was drawn with the Śunga revolution and the Code of Sumati Mānava. The Mānava does not look back to a golden age, it rather condemns some of the old practices. But soon after, the Hindu Nation began to look back with longing eyes to their golden age, now separated by the Chinese wall of a Code of Dharma laws under the sceptre of the Brahmin king.

Ordeals.

§ 10. The Artha-Śāstra laws never recognised the use of ordeal in Vyavahāra or the trial at law. It was, however, a mode of proof or disproof in trials at dharma. It had been so for ages. Āpastamba advises the king to employ it in dharma trials in doubtful cases.[1] The Mānava is at pains to show why ordeals should be recognised. It cites old cases from Vedic literature that ordeals had been gone through.[2] Now as Vyavahāra was made a handmaid of dharma, ordeal was imposed on the law. True, it was confined to the old prāyaśchitta cases, cases of heinous sins, and was limited in employment to cases where no other proof was available. Yet it became a recognised institution. Not a line, not a word, in controversy or otherwise, is mentioned about the proof by ordeal in the Artha Śāstra. And all works of the tradition of the Artha-Śāstra discourage it. Nārada[3] discourages it, and the Śukra Nîti[4] points out very limited utility. That the Artha-Śāstra could not recognise it stands to reason. The Artha-Śāstra school held that law was a human creation, a creation of society, of thinkers, as asserted by the Śukra-Nîti in clearest accents.[5] Why should they allow gods to come in and interfere with them ?

Manu, VIII. 109, reads :

"If two parties dispute about matters for which no witnesses

[1] *Āpastamba,* II., 11., 29, 6. सन्दें हे लिङ्गतो दैवेनेति विचित्य।
[2] Cf. *Manu,* VIII., 116.
[3] Nārada, *Intro.*, 30, 41; I., 245-6.
[4] *Śukranîti* IV, 5. 164 ff.
[5] *Ibid* IV. 5. 4.

are available, and it is difficult to ascertain the truth, it should be discovered even by oath."[1]

This indicates the nature and origin of oath. It stood on the same footing as an ordeal, or ordeal was only a form of oath ('Śapatha'). Such a thing was not allowed in a trial at Vyavahāra. As the Mānava is introducing it, he proceeds to give his reason. 'Both by great sages and gods, oaths have been taken in proof, even V a s i s h ṭ h a took an o a t h before K i n g P a i j a v a n a (Sudās)."[2] This appeal to history is an appeal to the Veda itself. In Ṛ i g v e d a, VII. 104, 15, the oath taken by V a s i s h ṭ h a before king S u d ā s is recorded. On the accusation of V i ś v ā m i t r a, that the former was a malignant spirit (Rākshasa), and as such he had destroyed his hundred sons, Vasishṭha swore: 'I will fall dead on the spot if I am a Rākshasa.'[3]

Absence of Ordeal in Artha-Śāstra.

§ 11. Hindu lawyers have unanimously and rightly classed oath under D i v i n e E v i d e n c e or O r d e a l. The Mānava places oath, to be administered to each witness, together with ordeals (VIII. 113). He sanctions two o r d e a l s, that o f w a t e r and that o f f i r e. Along with them a third one, of s w e a r i n g by the head of wife and children, is given (VIII. 114-115). Once again he proceeds to give reasons for this new legislation. V a t s a took the o r d e a l of f i r e. This is quite authoritative, it being related in the Pañchavimśa Brāhmaṇa, XIV. 6. 6. His descent had been questioned and he took the ordeal. Now it should be noted that the Mānava Code in these passages is introducing, on Vedic texts, ordeals both in civil and criminal evidence. The Mānava takes up the law of Kauṭilya in its sequential order, step by step, and introduces his new

---

[1] असाक्षिकेषु त्वर्थेषु मिथो विवदमानयोः ।
न विन्दंस्तत्वतः सत्यं शपथेनापि लम्भयेत् ॥

[2] *Manu*, VIII., 110. महर्षिभिश्च देवैश्च कार्यार्थं शपथाः कृताः ।
वसिष्ठश्चापि शपथं शेपे पैजवने नृपे ॥

[3] See Sāyaṇa on Ṛigveda VII., 104, 15, and Medhātithi on Manu, VIII., 110.

section on the ordeals at the close of the civil subject as dealt with in Kauṭilya, closing his own treatment by resuming a subject (Debt) already finished. You can feel the interpolation if you make an analysis. The Mānava undertakes to reproduce the section on pleadings (149) and on witnesses of the Maurya Code of Law.[1] Kauṭilya's Code does not contemplate that the king has to take any part in the judicial proceedings. His code is called the Dharmasthîyam, 'the Book for the Dharmsthîya Courts,' and the 'Kaṇṭaka-Śodhanam', 'the Book for the Kanṭaka Śodhana Courts'. But Sumati, according to the traditions of the Dharma School, requires the king to do justice, and if he is unable to do it, then his substitutes should do it. This he details in the first six verses of Chapter VIII. He makes the king in theory the dispenser of justice according to the view of the Dharma School. Then he takes up the subject of Debt, while Kauṭilya begins with contracts of debt and other contracts, then deals with marriage and family law of property and then with Debt. In the latter chapter (64) Kauṭilya treats of the subject of witnesses and proof. Sumati having treated of marriage beyond the province of civil law, deals with Debt first, and in doing so he introduces the principles of the *Dharma* which he opposes with that of *Vyavahāra*. The Dharma law method of procedure open to a creditor was to realise his debt by self-help or by sitting in *dharanā*. This, says Sumati, should be allowed and the king should not stop it.[2] Then the Vyavahāra

---

[1] See *AŚ.*, Ch. 58 (p. 149) and Ch. 68 (p. 175) respectively.

[2] Cf. *Manu*, VIII., 48-50:

यैर्यैरुपायैरर्थं स्वं प्राप्नुयादुत्तमर्णिकः ।
तैस्तैरुपायैः संगृह्य दापयेदधमर्णिकम् ॥
धर्मेण व्यवहारेण छलेनाचरितेन च ।
प्रयुक्तं साधयेदर्थं पञ्चमेन बलेन च ॥
यः स्वयं साधयेदर्थमुत्तमर्णोऽधमर्णिकात् ।
न स राज्ञाभियोक्तव्यः स्वकं संसाधयन्धनम् ॥

method here called 'procedure at Artha' (Artha-Śāstra),[1] is described. Verses 52-60 agree with the Artha-Śāstra, p. 149. Then 'Manu' goes on to say, 'I will fully declare what kind of witnesses in suits by creditors should be called'.[2] Verse 62 simply says that free men are competent witnesses. Verses 63-77 are reproduction in younger language of the S ā k s h y a S e c t i o n of Kauṭilya, with a faithfulness which can only be explained as a result of direct borrowing. Kauṭilya gives after S ā k s h y a, directions about addressing formulæ to the witnesses. This subject is immediately taken up in verse 79 and the Purāṇic address runs up to 101. Verses 103 and 106 give the exception of the Dharma School where untruth is excusable (in cases where truth might lead to an unjust capital punishment). Verse 107 gives the Artha law on a d j o u r n m e n t in the very words of Kauṭilya.[3] The next rule (108) is that if in s e v e n d a y s a misfortune happens to the witness, he will be considered to have perjured himself. This Dharma superstition of the oath-ordeal was substituted for the rule in Kauṭilya about a r e v i s i o n of the j u d g m e n t if conspiracy and falsehood of witnesses be found out in seven nights ![4] The next rule of Kauṭilya is already reproduced as verse VIII. 72 in Manu,.[5] The subject proper comes to an end in Kauṭilya. In the Mānava the subject of o a t h s and o r d e a l s is taken up which we have already

---

[1] *Manu*, VIII., 51. अर्थेऽपव्ययमानं तु करणेन विभावितम् ।

[2] *Manu*, VIII., 61. यादृशा धनिभिः कार्य्या व्यवहारेषु साक्षिणः ।
तादृशान् सम्प्रवक्ष्यामि यथा वाच्यमृतञ्च तैः ॥

[3] *Kauṭ.*, Ch. 58, p. 149:
त्रिपक्षादूर्ध्वमप्रतिब्रुवतः परोक्तदण्डं कृत्वा यान्यस्य द्रव्याणि स्युस्ततोऽभियोक्तारं प्रतिपादयेदन्यत्र प्रत्युपकरणेभ्यः ।

Manu, VIII., 107. विपक्षादब्रुवन् साक्ष्यमृणादिषु नरोऽगदः ।
तदृणं प्राप्नुयात् सर्वं दशबन्धञ्च सर्वतः ॥

[4] *AŚ.*, Ch. 68, p. 176. एकमन्त्राः सत्यमनुपहरतेऽनुपहरतां सप्तरात्रादूर्ध्वं द्वादशपणो दण्डः ।

[5] *Ibid.*, Ch. 68, p. 176. पारुष्यस्तेयसंग्रहणेषु तु वैरिस्यालसहायवर्ज्याः ।

Cf. *Manu*, VIII., 72. साहसेषु च सर्वेषु स्तेयसंग्रहणेषु च ।
वाग्दण्डयोश्च पारुष्ये न परीक्षेत साक्षिणः ॥

seen (109-116). Then the revision law (117) is given, and the question of sentence for false deposition, and then the Debt (140) is again resumed.

§ 12. Vishṇu calls ordeals Samaya, (Samayas were resolutions on oath of corporate bodies). Vishṇu treats them as oaths[1] (IX). He limits their application to old ordeal-cases: treason, which was supposed to be a great sin, 'sāhasa', and denial of a deposit being the only civil case included.[2] The last one was probably regarded as a great sin, being on the footing of a bad form of theft. Number of ordeals increases to 5 or 6 in Vishṇu. They had evidently existed, but as Sumati was innovating, he would not include the whole lot.

Ordeal in Yājña-valkya.

Yājñavalkya sanctions five, but only in 'great accusations', which Aparārka explains as the 'Major Sins', or in case of consent of both parties, and in the sin of treason.[3]

Drama Mṛichchha-kaṭika and ordeal.

§ 13. That ordeals became popular is evidenced by the drama Mṛichchhakaṭika. The Mṛichchhakaṭika dramatises a revolt at a bad administration of law, the faults of which were :—

(1) refusal to act on Manu's exemption to the Brahmin from capital punishment, although the court recommended it,

(2) refusal to allow ordeal, and

(3) acting on circumstantial evidence.

The last had been condemned under the Mauryas. It seems that there was a revival of it in the second or the third century

---

[1] Cf. *Vishṇu*, IX., 1. अथ समयक्रिया ।

[2] *Ibid.*, IX., 2-3. राजद्रोहसाहसेषु यथाकामम् । निक्षेपस्तेयेष्वर्थप्रमाणम् ।

[3] *Yājñ.*, II. 95-96. तुलाग्न्यापो विषं कोषो दिव्यानीह विशुद्धये ।
महाभियोगेष्वेतानि शीर्षकस्थेऽभियोक्तरि ॥
रुच्या वान्यतरः कुर्यादितरो वर्तयेच्छिरः ।
विनापि शीर्षकात् कुर्यान्नृपद्रोहेऽथ पातके ॥

A. C. The drama knows the coin Nāṇaka as current in its time.[1] Its Tîkākāra (commentator) and a passage in the Kāśikā[2] show that it was marked with the legend *Nānā* which we do find on Kushan coins. They were current in the second and the third centuries of the Christian era. Buddhism was flourishing and was looked upon with favour in the time of the drama. These facts indicate a time before the rise of the Gupta power. It is important to notice that the Brahmin was not then exempt from capital punishment. And Yājñavalkya about that time does not admit the claim. Ordeals were very popular at the time. Four out of the five of Yājñavalkya's ordeals are enumerated in the drama.[3] Evidently people had an easy escape thereby.

Perjury.

§ 14. The Dharma school regarded perjury as a heinous sin, equal to the drinking of liquor by a Brahmin, or the murder of a friend, or blasphemy.[4] The Artha-Śāstra punishment for it was fine up to the amount of the value of the suit or banishment in criminal cases.[5] Yājñavalkya doubles the fine, and prescribes banishment for a perjured Brahmin.[6] Manu (VIII. 120-123) has heavy fines plus banishment for others and only banishment for the Brahmin. There is always a higher punishment in the Mānava than in the Kauṭilîya. The Dharma advocate Sumati sought to bring about a better state of affairs by severer punishments. In spite of kindly punishments, as we know on the historical testimony of Megasthenes, false evidence, untruth, and theft were practically non-existent in the time of Chandragupta. The vices were rare and the punishments tended to be milder.

---

1 *Mṛichchhakaṭika*, I. 23.

2 *Kāśikā, on* P. IV., 3. 80.

3 '*Trial of Chārudatta*' 16 *C.W.N. ii.*

4 *Manu*, XI., 57. ब्रह्मोज्झता वेदनिन्दा कौटसाक्ष्यं सुहृद्वधः ।
गर्हितानाद्ययोर्जग्धिः सुरापानसमानि षट् ॥

5 *Artha-Śāstra*, p. 176 ; 209 (IV. 4.)

6 *Yājñ.*, II. 81. पृथक् पृथग दण्डनीयाः कूटकृत् साक्षिणस्तथा ।
विवादाद्द्विगुणं द्रव्यं विवास्यो ब्राह्मणः स्मृतः ॥

Witness-Jury.

§ 15. A provision is found both in the Artha-Śāstra[1] and our Codes[2] that in boundary disputes in villages, witness-jury, the neighbours, could decide the cause. This was a relic of archaic law preserved in an advanced society. There was a curious procedure for them which Manu (VIII. 256) and Yājñavalkya (II. 152) give. They put on red dresses and chaplets of red flowers and took up earth and placed it on their head, and then pronounced their evidence-verdict.

Costs to Witnesses.

§ 16. The Artha-Śāstra shows that witnesses were given allowances for their journey and diet and that the cost was added to the decree,[3] the losing party had to bear it finally. Witnesses, who were in the neighbourhood, were brought by the parties, but those who were far off or who would not come, were summoned by the judge and were punished for default. They were summoned in the name of the king.[4]

Documentary Evidence.

§ 17. Kauṭilya and Sumati are alive to the importance of documentary evidence. For instance, Kauṭilya says that where, on account of bad writing, difficulty arises in proof, witnesses alone are to be depended upon.[5] Here it is implied that otherwise the document itself could be relied upon. The Mānava (VIII. 168) says that Manu has declared all transactions, based on force, as those which have not been entered into, *e.g.*, gifts made by force, documents executed by force (*lekhita*). The general term used for documents in the Artha-Śāstra is lekha.[6] Technical documents of Government had already acquired long established forms. That is proved by

---

1 *Ibid.*, Ch. 65, p. 166. सामन्तप्रत्यया वास्तुविवादाः ।

2 Cf. *Manu*, VIII., 253-258, Y. II. 150-52.

3 *AS.*, Ch. 58, p. 149. पथि भक्तमर्थविशेषतः । तदुभयं नियम्यो दद्यात् ।

4 *Ibid.*, Ch. 68, p. 177. देशकालविदूरस्थान् साक्षिणः प्रतिपादयेत् ।
दूरस्थानप्रसारान् वा स्वामिवाक्येन साधयेत् ॥

5 *Ibid.*, p. 176. बालिश्यादभियोक्तुर्वा दुःश्रुतं दुर्लिखितं प्रेताभिनिवेशं वा समीक्ष्य साक्षिप्रत्ययमेव स्यात् ।

6 *Ibid.*, Ch. 31, p. 71. The later term *patra* is used by Manu in IX. 219 (*Smṛiti-chandrikā*, App. 643-5).

Aśoka's inscriptions and the Chapter on Śāsanādhikāra in the Artha Śāstra. Legal documents are mentioned even in the Jātakas. An instrument of gift on a metal plate executed in the days of the Buddha (*c.* 575 B.C.) was seen by Fa-Hien. Aśoka speaks of 'permanent' documents, and 'copies' in his inscriptions. It seems that documents must have been in vogue at least as early as about 700 or 800 B.C. Yet in sculptures and the Pāli canon, when a gift of land is described, it is the ceremony (of pouring water) which is represented, and not executing a deed.[1] Style of legal documents is seen in the inscriptions of about 150 B.C., where names of mother and father are given in describing kings. Documents, according to Nārada, mentioning king should name his mother also.

By the time of Yājñavalkya, the stage was reached when writing was deemed necessary in a transaction of immovable property. When the king made a gift of land or granted a pension (*nibandha*), he had to execute a deed (*lekhya* Y. I. 317). It was to be done on cloth or copper-plate, and to be sealed with the royal arms, 'for the information of future kings' (II. 318). The king's dynasty, and his own name, had to be mentioned, as well as the details of property transferred (II. 319). The document had to be signed and dated in his own regnal years (*sva-hasta-kālasampannaṁ*, II. 320). Dating in regnal years is implied by the Artha-Śāstra (ch. 27, p. 60, *rājavarshaṁ, māsaḥ ......iti kālaḥ*). Vishṇu (III. 82) repeats the directions of Yājñavalkya (II. 317-320) almost in his very words. We have ample examples in actual copper-plates of such royal deeds of transfer. Private deeds were essentially on similar lines. Marīchi lays down that transfer of immovable property and partition must be effected by a written instrument.[2]

---

[1] Cf. the anonymous text cited in the *Mitāksharā*, VIII. '*hiraṇyodakadānena.*'°

[2] See quotation in the *Vīramitrodaya*, p. 188:

स्थावरे विक्रयाधाने विभागे दान एव च ।
लिखितेनाप्नुयात् सिद्धिमविसंवादमेव च ॥

Yājñavalkya and, like him, Vishṇu, treat *lekhya* as a special kind of evidence, with separate rules of proof (Yājñ., II. 84-94; VI., vi. 23, 25, 26; VII). A document attested would be proof by itself. The onus was on the defendant to disprove it. If he alleged force or fraud, the plaintiff was put to proof.[1]

A document was properly executed when it was attested by necessary witnesses (presumably three, Y. II. 90), and signed by the executant (86). Attestation and the signature of the executant had to be in proper form. He should sign at the bottom: "Agreed to what is written above by me, son of N., I, N. N." (86). Witnesses signed: "Here son of N., I, N. N., a witness" (87). The scribe also attested at the request of both parties: "This is written by me N., son of N.N." (88). If a document was in the hand-writing of the executant, it need not be attested (89). If the document was torn, burnt, lost, or inaccessible by being in a foreign country, the court could compel a defendant to execute another deed (91). If the execution was denied, the plaintiff had to rebut it by direct evidence, comparison of hand-writing, and by circumstantial evidence and argument (92). Receipt was endorsed in the hand-writing of the debtor on the back of the document, or an acquittance taken from the creditor (93).[2] When the whole amount was paid off the document was torn in two, or an acquittance taken (94). It seems that documents executed in the time of Yājñavalkya were mostly simple bonds, mortgages and usufructuary mortgages (II. 90). The body contained details of parties and date etc., as prescribed for a plaint. It seems that when the executant was dead and the claim was sought to be proved against his heirs, it was the witnesses to the

---

[1] *Yājñ.*, II., 91. विनापि साक्षिभिर्लेख्यं स्वहस्तलिखितन्तु यत् ।
तत्प्रमाणं स्मृतं लेख्यं बलोपधिकृतादृते ॥

[2] [For a Sanskrit acquittance see JBORS, 1929 p. 63.]

fact of the transaction who proved the contract, and not the document, according to Kauṭilya.[1] According to Vishṇu, it could be proved by comparison of handwriting, the onus being on the plaintiff.[2] Presumption of genuineness of ancient documents is mentioned in later works.

§ 18. It is extraordinary that the law of Yājñavalkya about the endorsement of the executant and that of witnesses, except the detail about the father's name, still survive in the country. We all have seen the practice of tearing in the middle a money bond when it is paid off. This is done by the creditor in the presence of the debtor.

---

[1] *AŚ.*, p. 176.

[2] *Vishṇu*, VII. 13, यद्यर्णी धनिको वापि साक्षी वा लेखकोऽपि वा ।
म्रियते तत्र तल्लेख्यं तत् स्वहस्तैः प्रसाधयेत् ॥

LECTURE VIII.

CRIMINAL LAW.

Defamation—Blasphemy—Slander of Assembly—of Country—Assault—Assault on Trees and Animals—Constructive Assaults—Theft—Early Definition of theft by Dharma Lawyers.

§ 1. Yājñavalkya paid special attention to the reform of the laws of the Code of Manu on the criminal side. It was here that Sumati Bhārgava's work was most out of date. The country had been accustomed for centuries to the mild punishments instituted by the policy of the early Maurya rulers, who substituted fines for tortures, amputations and capital sentences. The Buddhist rule of the later Mauryas would have still toned down the severity of criminal law. The Mānava Code, with a ferocious puritanism and a blood-thirsty religious zeal, remained a controversy, rather than the law, on the subject of crimes. Yājñavalkya sat down to remedy this defect, and he succeeded in giving a workable code of criminal law. He defines crimes with reference to the older law which had been in force before the Code of Mānava, classified offences and laid down the old punishments in milder forms. He gave a code without any controversy, unlike the object and reasons of the so-called Manu on the law about the Śūdra, without citing any opinion, without any fear of the name of Manu and even of contradicting him. He does not deserve credit for originality as he had the Code of Kauṭilya before him. Yet he deserves a greater credit than that of originality. He boldly cured the injury done to the society by the Code of Manu. He prescribed uniform laws, removed the weight of social depression off the limbs of the nation. Even Brahmins by birth, like A ś v a-g h o s h a, revolted from the very claim of superiority preached, asserted and legalised by the Mānava Code in favour of Brahmin birth, and declared it unproven and unprovable, absurd and preposterous.[1] What Aśvaghosha did as a preacher, Yājñavalkya silently did as a legislator, and even so as an orthodox legislator. He was one of those men of the second and third centuries of the Christian era who overhauled and rearranged the social system, and saved society from becoming a furious ocean of battering interests and views, and, who, rising to the occasion, solved the problems and sowed the seed which grew and blossomed into the majesty of peace, progress and culture of the Gupta period. Legal genius of the race kept pace with other activities and reached the pinnacle of glory in the latter period, but in criminal law it found nothing to add; it accepted Yājñavalkya as final.

'Word-assault.'

§ 2. Let us take some examples. The term which has been translated by modern writers on Hindu Law as 'D e f a m a t i o n' is V ā k-p ā r u s h y a which literally means *force used through language* or *assault by language.* It consists of, as Kauṭilya[2] defines: (*a*) Calumny (Apavāda, 'slander'), (*b*) Contemptuous talk (Kutsana), or (*c*) Intimidation (Abhibhartsanā) and [(*b*) covers what we call to-day *sacrilege*].

Kauṭilya treats the *Vāk-pārushya* offences after *Sāhasa,* with which he begins the law on crimes,[3] while the Mānava and Yājña-valkya[4] begin the subject with *Vāk-pārushya.* Kauṭilya first provides against calumny, while Sumati (Mānava) against the

---

[1] *Vajrasūchî.*

[2] *AŚ.*, Ch.75, p. 193. वाक्पारुष्यमपवादः कुत्सनमभिभर्त्सनमिति ।

[3] *Ibid.*, Ch. 74.

[4] *Manu,* VIII. 267-278; *Yājñ.*, II. 204-211.

contemptuous talk towards Brahmins.[1] Yājñavalkya follows Kauṭilya.[2] He says (204) :

"*He who by true or untrue or ironical* (statements) *attacks* (or insults) *persons* (as) *wanting in limb* or *faculty* or *as diseased, shall be fined* 12½ *paṇas.*" (12½ was the one-fourth of the lowest, *i.e.*, the 'first' class of Sāhasa fines).

Slander may be, according to Kauṭilya, of (*a*) the person (*śarīra*), (*b*) temperament (*prakṛiti*), (*c*) learning (*śruta*), (*d*) occupation (*vṛitti*), or (*e*) nationality (*janapada*) of a man. Taking first the slander of person, he enjoins :

i. "Slander of person—such as 'blind', '*khañja*' (wanting in limbs, cripple)—will be fined 3 paṇas ; if untrue, 6 paṇas." "Irony shall be fined 12 paṇas ; irony : such as 'he is of beautiful eyes', 'he is of beautiful teeth'."

ii. "In cases of contemptuous talk with respect to leprosy, impotency etc., the fine shall be 12 paṇas."[3]

§ 3. Yājñavalkya has given the two provisions together. Kauṭilya has a lighter punishment for 'true slander.' But Yājñavalkya regards true or untrue slander equally blameworthy.[4] Likewise, he does not think that irony should be more culpable. Punishments here, as elsewhere, is the maximum provided, unless expressly denoted to be otherwise ; and in accordance with the principle already discussed, the judge had the discretion as to the quantum of punishment to be inflicted.

---

[1] *Manu*, VIII. 267. शतं ब्राह्मणमाक्रुश्य क्षत्रियो दण्डमर्हति ।
वैश्योऽप्यर्धशतं द्वे वा शूद्रस्तु वधमर्हति ॥

[2] *Yājñ.*, II. 204. सत्यासत्यान्यथास्तोत्रैर्न्यूनाङ्गेन्द्रियरोगिणाम् ।
क्षेपं करोति चेद्दण्ड्यः पणानर्धत्रयोदश ॥

[3] *AŚ.*, Ch. 75, p. 193. शरीरप्रकृतिश्रुतवृत्तिजनपदानां शरीरोपवादेन काणखञ्जादिभिः सत्ये त्रिपणो दण्डः । मिथ्योपवादे षट्पणो दण्डः । शोभनाक्षिदन्त इति काणखञ्जादीनां स्तुतिनिन्दायां द्वादशपणो दण्डः । कुष्ठोन्मादक्लैब्यादिभिः कुत्सायां च ।

[4] *Yājñ.*, II. 204, *supra.*

§ 4. The Mānava has the first law in VIII. 273-274, following closely the language of Kauṭilya, only changing it in later terms, *e.g.*, for *Janapada* he gives *Deśa* and *Jāti*, for *vṛitti*, he gives *karma*. Instead of 'person' and 'temperament,' he has 'personal' (*śārīram*).

"If one talks with arrogance about the learning (*śruta*), country and birth (nationality), occupation, or about the body-matters (of another), untruly, the fine shall be two hundred. "If a one-eyed man or a *khañja* (man of a defective person) and others (similar ones) are spoken about in that way (*i.e., arrogantly*), even if truly, the talker (slanderer) shall be fined at least one Kārshāpaṇa."[1] We see that the fine in the first case is raised to two hundred, while in the latter it has a tendency to be reduced by Sumati. Yājñavalkya rejects these high punishments and goes back to the Maurya law as much as possible. All the same he does not agree with either Kauṭilya or Sumati that a true slander deserves mitigation of sentence.

§ 5. Kauṭilya next deals with Kutsā—contemptuous language or abuse in general. "Whether *Kutsā* be true, untrue, or ironical (stuti-nindā), the punishment shall be

(*a*) about 12 paṇas, provided that it is towards equals,

(*b*) double, if it is to one of higher position, and

(*c*) half, if towards men of lower position ;

"provided further that in case it is towards women, except one's wife, the fine shall be doubled (in each of the above cases) ; "provided further that if abuse is due to mistake, intoxication, stupefication etc., the punishment shall be halved."[2]

---

[1] *Manu*, VIII. 273-274. :

श्रुतं देशञ्च जातिञ्च कर्म शारीरमेव च ।
वितथेन ब्रुवन् दर्पाद्दाप्यः स्याद्विशतं दमम् ॥
काणं वाप्यथवा खञ्जमन्यं वापि तथाविधम् ।
तथ्येनापि ब्रुवन् दाप्यो दण्डं कार्षापणावरम् ॥

[2] *AS.*, p. 193. सत्यमिथ्यास्तुतिनिन्दासु द्वादशपणोत्तरा दण्डाः तुल्येषु विशिष्टेषु द्विगुणः । हीनेष्वर्धदण्डः । परस्त्रीषु द्विगुणः । प्रमादमदमोहादिभिरर्धदण्डाः ।

The above provision will apply to the case of "calumny" as well, for Kauṭilya treats the two together. It should be noticed that Kauṭilya does not base his law on caste-orders, but uses a term which denotes position in life. Sumati Mānava, versifying, puts it in this way :

> "One who refers with moral reproach (āksharayan) to the father, wife, brother, or son of another, and one of superior position (gurum), shall be fined a hundred, also one who does not give the way to a superior."[1]

The punishment here (100 paṇas) refers to an offence from the inferior to the superior, and not between equals. It is there a degree higher. According to the law of Kauṭilya, it ought to be 25 (double of '12', really 12½, fractions being evidently left out in realising fines in Maurya times). But 'Manu' fixes it at 100 : Yājñavalkya however reduces it to 25 :

> "From one who abuses, 'I am seducer of your sister, your mother,' shall be realised by the king, a fine of 25,
> and only half, if the abuse was to an inferior, and a double amount if to a superior."[2]

Having laid down the law on A p a v ā d a and K u t s ā, Kauṭilya gives explanations on them. One is about the proof of impotency by expert evidence and evidence of those having personal knowledge.[3] This is with reference to the plea of true slander. The second explanation is on *Apavāda* of *prakṛiti* (caste or origin).

§ 6 In the case of Slander of *prakṛiti* (caste or origin) when between Brahmin, Kshatriya, Vaiśya, Śūdra, and the lowest, if it is by the latter of the former, the fine shall be three paṇas and

---

[1] *Manu*, VIII. 275 : मातरं पितरं जायां भ्रातरं तनयं गुरुम् ।
आक्षारयञ्छतं दाप्यः पन्थानञ्चाददद्गुरोः ॥

[2] *Yājñ.*, II. 205-206 : अभिगन्तास्मि भगिनीं मातरं वा तवेति च ।
शपन्तं दापयेद्राजा पञ्चविंशतिकं दमम् ॥
अर्धोऽधमेषु द्विगुणः परस्त्रीषूत्तमेषु च ।

[3] *AŚ.*, p. 193 : कुष्ठोन्मादयोश्चिकित्सकाः सन्निकृष्टाः पुमांसश्च प्रमाणम् ।

upwards in the increasing order; if by the former of the latter it shall be two paṇas and lower in the decreasing order." "It shall be the same also in k u t s ā (abuse) *e.g.*, 'a low Brahmin'."[1]

§ 7. Yājñavalkya, as above, following Kauṭilya both in the order of the provisions and the provisions themselves, prescribes: In prātilomya-apavādas (slander of caste inversely) punishment shall be administered on the Varṇa (caste) consideration of superiority and inferiority—the fine shall be double and treble of 25; where apavāda (defamation) of varṇas is in the reverse (ānulomya) order, the punishment shall decrease by half.[2] It was impossible to catch the sense of this passage of Yājñavalkya without the corresponding passage of the Kauṭilya, and it is no wonder that Vijñāneśvara and Mandlik found the passage obscure.

The fine is high in comparison with Kauṭilya's law, but very low when we look at that fixed by the Mānava: "The discerning judge, in the cases of Brahmin and Kshatriya, shall impose the punishment of first amercement (250) on a Brahmin, when he refers with reproach (*ākshārayan*, 275) to one's caste (svajāti, 277), and the middle amercement (500) on a Kshatriya (so doing); on Vaiśya and Śūdra slandering one's caste, it will be the same respectively (250 or 500). Here the punishment of the cutting off (of the tongue) does not apply (as in abuse hurled directly, 270), this being the law"[3] (277). In direct abuse, Sumati Bhārgava has his own ferocious laws which he treats of separately, just in the beginning (267-269; 270-272):

---

[1] *Op. cit.*, p. 194. प्रकृत्योपवादे ब्राह्मणक्षत्रियवैश्यशूद्रान्तावसायिनामपरेण पूर्वस्य त्रिपणोत्तरा: दण्डा:। पूर्वेणापरस्य द्विपणाधरा। कुब्राह्मणादिभिश्च कुत्सायाम्।

[2] *Yājñ.*, II. 207. प्रातिलोम्यापवादेषु द्विगुणास्त्रिगुणा दमा:।
वर्णानामानुलोम्येन तस्मादर्धार्धहानित:॥

[3] *Manu*, VIII. 267-277.

ब्राह्मणक्षत्रियाभ्यान्तु दण्ड: कार्य्यो विजानता।
ब्राह्मणे साहस: पूर्व: क्षत्रिये त्वेव मध्यम:॥
विट्शूद्रयोरेवमेव स्वजातिं प्रति तत्त्वत:।
छेदवर्ज प्रणयनं दण्डस्येति विनिश्चय:॥

"A Kshatriya deserves a fine of 100 when he has abused (talked contemptuously to) a Brahmin, a Vaiśya, 150 or 200 respectively, and a Śūdra, torture."

"A Brahmin shall be fined 50 in abusing a Kshatriya ; 25 in abusing a Vaiśya, 12 in abusing a Śūdra."

"Also in offences between equals in caste, 12."

"In case of unspeakable abuses, the fine shall be double in each case."

"When the once-born man of Śūdra and of the mixed, Śūdra-like, castes attacks a twice-born with terrible language, his tongue deserves to be cut off, for he is of vile influence."

"If he mentions the personal name and caste (in opposition), an iron nail, ten inches long, shall be thrust into his mouth, red-hot."

"If he arrogantly preaches dharma to Brahmins, burning oil the king shall have poured in his mouth and ears" (272).[1]

§ 8. It is evident that the Śūdra here is the 'dharma'-preaching learned Śūdra, *i.e.*, the Buddhist or Buddhist Śūdra, and a Śūdra who claims equality and who mentions the epithet 'Brahmin' itself with contempt. The king is to suppress by 'law' these Śūdras. He is of 'vile influence.' His controversy is to be gagged.

Yājñavalkya rejects and repeals such laws. It should be noticed that no such law exists in Kauṭilya. His Kutsā law is based on social status, not caste. Caste comes in only when caste-defamation is the cause. In personal defamation, he makes no distinction whatsoever ; Sumati places his new law quite apart and then takes up the subject in the order and language of Kauṭilya.

---

[1] Manu, VIII. 267-277.

The third explanation of Kauṭilya is "that the same provision applies to the laws of slander of learning; in the cases of occupation e.g., of bards, artists, artizans, actors (etc.), and in the cases of slander of one's nationality e.g., 'he is a Prājjūṇaka.' (Cf. Gupta inscription: *Prārjuṇaka*) 'He is a Gandharian'.[1] (Evidently these nations who were in the empire were reproached by the Magadha people for some custom of theirs).

§ 9. Kauṭilya and Yājñavalkya lastly take **Intimidation**. For intimidating with language, punishment laid down by Kauṭilya was half the punishment of the commission of the injury threatened. "If provocation, intoxication, or ignorance is pleaded, 12 paṇas he shall pay, provided he is incapable of carrying out the threat. Where he is capable of doing the injury and there is enmity, he shall give security for his whole life."[2]

It seems that threats very generally were not idle in those days.

The Mānava as a code is not exhaustive and here is an illustration It omits the point of verbal intimidation. Yājñavalkya remedies it:

> "Let a fine to the amount of a hundred paṇas be inflicted for language threatening injury to the arm, neck, eyes or thigh; and half of it for the like to the foot, nose, ears, hand, etc."
>
> "If this was uttered by an incapable man, he shall be fined 10 paṇas. If he is capable, he shall furnish surety for the safety of the man threatened."
>
> "If the threat is of a sinful act of the higher kind, the offender shall be punished with the first Sāhasa

---

[1] *AŚ.*, Ch. 75, p. 194. तेन श्रुतोपवादः, वाग्जीवनानां कारुकुशीलवानां वृत्त्युपवादः; प्राज्जूणकगान्धारादीनां च जनपदोपवादा व्याख्याताः।

[2] *Loc. cit.* अशक्तः कोपं मदं मोहं वाऽपदिशेत्, द्वादशपणं दद्यात्। जातवैराशयः शक्तश्चापकर्तुं यावज्जीविकावस्थं दद्यात्।

punishment (imprisonment or fine), if the threat is of a sinful act of the lesser degree, he shall be fined with the first amercement."[1]

Kauṭilya finally provides punishments for language of contempt towards objects of patriotism and reverence. They are :

(*a*) 1. One's own country,
2. One's own town, or
3. Nationality or birth,
4. One's national assembly.

(*b*) 1. Gods,
2. Monuments of worship.[2]

For (1) and (2) of (a) division, the punishment was of the first class sāhasa (felony) punishment (imprisonment or fine) ; for (3) and (4) the middle class sāhasa punishment, or (*b*) the highest class of the felony punishment.

§ 10. The Mānava again is deficient here, Yājñavalkya is again complete. The latter includes in this (II. 211) the defamation of the king.[3] This must be of a personal character, for treason is provided for elsewhere (II. 302).

"Attack of language against a Vedic Brahmin, the king, and the gods is an Uttama (highest) sāhasa crime ; that against (one's) *jāti* (nationality or caste) and one's own guild (*pūga*) is the middle sāhasa crime, and against one's town and country is the first sāhasa crime."

An analysis of the law in the three works illustrates how our law subsequent to the Maurya times is based on the Artha-Śāstra of Kauṭilya. It also shows that without the latter, we can

---

1 *Yājñ.*, II. 208-210.

2 *AS.*, Ch. 75, p. 194. स्वदेशग्रामयोः पूर्वं मध्यमं जातिसङ्घयोः ।
आक्रोशाद्देवचैत्यानां उत्तमं दण्डमर्हति ॥

3 त्रैविद्यनृपदेवानां क्षेप उत्तमं साहसः ।
मध्यमो जातिपूगानां प्रथमो ग्रामदेशयोः ॥

Cf. *Manu*, VIII. 312-313.

not fully understand the two Codes. Unfortunately, the fact of debt was not noticed by the Hindu commentators; otherwise the interpretation of the Mānava and Yājñavalkyan Codes would have been different. The commentator, whom I find nearest the sense of the ancient law as now disclosed, is Medhātithi. The authorities, on whom he drew, must have lived in Gupta times, up to which period the tradition of the old law was fully alive (see the last lecture below).

§ 11. A similar state exists in respect of the law on the subject of assault (daṇḍa-pārushya). Both Codes mainly depend on the pre-Śuṅga law as it appears in the Artha Śāstra. The modifications in the Mānava and the improvement in Yājñavalkya are of the same nature as we have seen in analysing the law on the Word-Assault.

Battery.

Let us now deal with the points of difference with reference to the new light which is thrown by Kauṭilya.

§ 12. *Daṇḍa-pārushya*, lit., 'assault by beating' was a common law offence, probably exclusively in the Artha School. It is not found in Āpastamba, Vasishṭha, Gautama or Baudhāyana. Only Vishṇu gives it (Ch. V), and Vishṇu is later than the Mānava and probably also than Yājñavalkya. It being a common law offence it was gradually extended, and several offences were constructively brought under it. Originally it denoted 'battery' as its name implies, *pārushya*, cruelty, 'rough behaviour.' On its analogy, 'word-assault' or 'word-cruelty' (defamation etc.) was created an offence, and the original *Pārushya* was distinguished by the addition of *Daṇḍa*, 'stick.'

Kauṭilya defines Daṇḍa-pārushya : "*Daṇḍa-pārushya* is
(1) touching,
(2) hurt, and
(3) severe hurt (prahata)."[1]

[1] *AS.*, Ch. 76, p. 194. दण्डपारुष्यं स्पर्शनमवगूर्णं प्रहतमिति ।

As the description of the offence shows that the (3) consisted of severe hurts, inflicted with the means of 'wood,' 'brick bat,' 'iron' etc., or other dangerous agencies as rope, which may not cause an open wound, up to mutilation, and injuries short of causing death.

Avagūrṇa which literally means 'roaring', technically denoted beating with hand, feet, with materials causing scratching and simple hurts, even with dangerous weapons.

Touching consisted of actual and constructive touching as 'with mud, ashes, or dust, thrown.' Offence against women was aggravated. Plea of mistake, intoxication and want of discrimination could be taken in Touching.

§ 13. Some Artha-Śāstra jurists fixed a period in which complaint for simple assault (*kalaha*, dispute) must be lodged, but Kauṭilya rejected this principle on the ground, that there cannot be a bar by efflux of time in a criminal offence. "There can never be impunity acquired by a criminal."[1] (p. 196).

No period of Limitation.

§ 14. Yājñavalkya starts with 'Touching'-with-ashes etc. (II. 213), gives the plea of defence in the very terms, deals with *Udgūrṇa* in the same order as Kauṭilya, and passes on to severe hurt (218) without giving the technical name (220).

§ 15. There is a remarkable rule of procedure, which Yājñavalkya gives before he takes up the law, in the order of the Artha-Śāstra. The rule is therefore his own. In cases where assault is alleged, and the only direct evidence offered are the allegation of the complainant and the marks of injury, great caution is to be exercised in drawing an inference from circumstantial evidence, 'as there is the danger of fabricated wounds.'[2] Another improvement by Yājñavalkya is in II. 214, where he excuses

[1] *Op. cit.*, p. 196. "नास्त्यपकारिणो मोक्ष" इति कौटिल्यः।

[2] *Yājñ.*, II. 212. असाक्षिकहते चिह्नैर्युक्तिभिश्चागमेन च।
द्रष्टव्यो व्यवहारस्तु कूटचिह्नकृतो भयात्॥

totally an offence committed under intoxication and want of intelligence (‘*moha*’).

§ 16. Yājñavalkya adopts the Artha-Śāstra law, that, when many men inflicted hurt on one man, the offence should be regarded serious and punishment doubled (221).

§ 17. In II. 216, on the subject of battery (*Udgūrṇa*), he lays down a very important rule from the point of view of social history. In assault, if both parties threaten with arms, the punishment would be the same “to all.”[2] In other words, no distinction in punishment would be made on the ground of caste inequality. The Artha-Śāstra does not make any distinction there, though in ‘Touching’ by throwing impure things, he makes the offence more blameworthy if it is committed against men of superior rank and women.[3] There also the position of the offender is not taken into consideration. But Yājñavalkya (II. 214) makes the position of the aggrieved party relative to that of the offender. He does not mention caste, but probably that is included in the term.[4] In II. 215 he, just before taking up the point of *Udgurṇa*, says generally—‘A non-Brahmin causing pain to a Brahmin shall be deprived of his limb.’ Then in II. 216 he says, that where both parties take up arms, the punishment would be the same ‘for all.’ It thus seems that provision in II. 215 is not an interpolation.

§ 18. In the Artha-Śāstra, at the end of the ‘Touching’ section, a provision appears:

‘That limb of a Śūdra with which he hammers a Brahmin (*abhihanyāt*) shall be cut off.’[5]

Mr. Sham Sastry thinks that it is an interpolation. Its appearance in a position which corresponds with its position in

---

[1] मोहमदादिभिरदण्डनम् ।

[2] परस्परन्तु सर्वेषां शस्त्रे मध्यमसाहसम् ।

[3] *AŚ.*, Ch. 76, p. 195. विशिष्टेषु द्विगुणाः । हीनेषु अर्धदण्डाः । परस्त्रीषु द्विगुणाः ।

[4] *Yājñ.*, II. 214. समेष्वेवं परस्त्रीषु द्विगुणास्तूत्तमेषु च । हीनेष्वर्धदमो etc.

[5] *AŚ.*, *loc. cit.* शूद्रो येनाङ्गेन ब्राह्मणमभिहन्यात्तदस्य छेदयेत् ।

Yajñavalkya excludes this idea. Then, the passage in Yājñavalkya is so cryptic that without a known law it could not be understood.[1] The relation of the 'limb' is not mentioned there, nor the caste of the striker except as non-Brahmin. The real explanation seems to be that it was a pre-Mauryan repressive law which Kauṭilya gives, but he modifies it by laying down in the Chapter on commutation, that where a Śūdra is condemned to have his eyes destroyed for 'rivalling a Brahmin,' for stealing property of gods, for treason and for blinding, his sentence can be commuted to a fine of 800.[2] Yājñavalkya, in the corresponding place, has 'living with Brahmin-hood' *i.e.*, claiming equality. The law about a Śūdra hammering a Brahmin is connected with the claim of equality, and evidently the punishment of maiming remained a mere name for a heavy fine. Since the rise of Buddhism, severe punishments against Buddhist Śūdras and Śūdra ascetics, 'Bhikkhus', had come into existence. Āpastamba in a solitary passage (II. 27) shows this. In connection with penance and those refusing to undergo it, he enjoins upon the king that a Śūdra, who has reviled an Ārya religious man, should be deprived of his tongue.[3] This and similar provisions are modified by the general commutation allowed in Kauṭilya's Code. Yet Kauṭilya punished people who entertained at ceremonies Ājīvakas, Śākyas, (Buddhist) and similar "Śūdra ascetics."[4]

§ 19. The Mānava begins the subject (VIII. 279-289) with the punishments for the Śūdra offending against the 'Head of Society' (Brahmin). It seems, as if he sat down primarily to write a crusading code for the suppression of the Śūdra, and for raising the dignity of the Brahmin. The Śūdra here is the 'Śūdra' *i.e.*,

---

[1] *Yājñ.*, II. 221. विप्रपीडाकरं छेद्यमङ्गमब्राह्मणस्य तु ।

[2] *AŚ.*, Ch. 87, p. 225. शूद्रस्य ब्राह्मणवादिनो देवद्रव्यमवस्तृणतो राजद्विष्टमादिशतो द्विनेत्रभेदिनश्च योगाञ्जनेनान्धत्वमष्टशतो वा दण्डः ।

[3] *Āp.*, II. 10, 27, 14. जिह्वाच्छेदनं शूद्रस्यार्यं धार्मिकमाक्रोशतः ।

[4] *AŚ.*, Ch. 77, p. 199. आजीवकादीन् वृषलप्रव्रजितान् देवपितृकार्येषु भोजयतः शत्यो दण्डः ।
Cf. Yājñ., II. 235.

Buddhist, lay man and ascetic. They are not called ascetics, as they were no ascetics in the orthodox eyes. In VIII. 284, he deals with severe hurt, and, as usual, prescribes severe punishments. On general law, this is the only one-verse section. Then he adopts the Artha-Śāstra law which is a glory of Hindu law. Kauṭilya (p. 197), Manu (VIII. 285) and Yājñavalkya (II. 227-229), all unanimously bring trees and plants under the protection of law. Injury to them was assault. No one of the vegetable kingdom according to Manu should be pained (*hiṃsā*). One inflicting pain on them was to be punished according to the position of the injurer. Cutting branches was a cruelty to their limbs (Y. 227). Cruelty to animals is likewise treated in the law of assault in both the Codes, which borrow it from the earlier law of Kauṭilya.

§ 20. The law of assault was extended constructively to the injuries done by one's animals to men.[1] Men driving animals under a vehicle, came under the law of assault if they caused injury to the public on the road. If the driver was 'killed,' the master was not blamed; if the offence was committed by a driver whose master was a minor, the minor was held innocent, but his car was forfeited or, the guardian fined. If the animal ran amock, or mischief up to death was caused by an accident over which the driver had no control, he was excused totally; and similarly when there was no negligence on his part. Kauṭilya gives the rules about offences on the road in a separate place, and Yājñavalkya accordingly treats it separately. But the Mānava Code puts the whole law on assault in one and the same place. Needless to say that he follows the old law.

§ 21. Injury to one's residence, in *kalaha* ('quarrel'), was taken to be equivalent to injury to the owner himself.[2]

---

[1] See *Manu*, VIII. 291-295; *Yājñ.*, II. 298-299.

[2] *AŚ.*, Ch. 76, p. 196. परकुड्यमभिघातेन क्षोभयतस्त्रिपणो दण्डः। छेदनभेदने षट्पणः प्रतीकारश्च।

His sacred right of ownership was disregarded, and the owner felt insulted. The mischief, though not on his person, fell on his mind by violation of Dharma, and as force was openly used, it amounted to assault, all the elements being present. Mental pain is an element in Hindu law of assault. If a man was 'touched' through ashes falling on his head—a cause of great annoyance—the crime was aggravated. The Mānava omits this constructive assault by mischief to residence. But Yājñavalkya adopts it.[1]

Theft.

§ 22. Theft is one of the great sins and it attracted attention of all classes of jurists. The king, if he failed to protect property, was not true (to Coronation Oath), and was fit to be given up, the tie of loyalty was to be cut off by the subject.[2] He ceased to be a Hindu king, and was as bad as an atheist.[3] The Mānava Code refers again and again to this theory which had become an axiom of Hindu constitutional law. It seems that during the reign of the last Maurya, the 'atheist', 'the untrue king', property was not safe. It was not safe politically, certainly, but it seems not to have been safe internally as well.

§ 23. Theft is defined by Kauṭilya as seizing of property stealthily. It is distinguished from robbery, the latter being perpetrated openly.[4] (A. Ś., p. 191). This very definition in the very language of Kauṭilya is given in 'Manu' VIII. 331.[5] Robbery sāhasa includes much more than the present

---

[1] *Yājñ.*, II. 223. अभिघाते तथा छेदे भेदे कुड्यावपातने ।
पणान् दाप्यं पञ्चदश विंशतिन्तद्द्वयं तथा ॥

[2] *Manu*, VIII. 308. अरक्षितारं राजानं बलिषड्भागहारिणम् ।
तमाहुः सर्वलोकस्य समग्रमलहारकम् ॥

[3] *Ibid.*, 309. अनपेक्षितमर्यादं नास्तिकं विप्रलुम्पकम् ।
अरक्षितारमत्तारं नृपं विद्यादधोगतिम् ॥

[4] *AŚ.*, Ch. 74, p. 191. साहसमन्वयवत्प्रसभकर्म । निरन्वये स्तेयमपव्ययने च ।

[5] *Manu*, VIII. 332. स्यात् साहसन्त्वन्वयवत् प्रसभं कर्म यत् कृतम् ।
निरन्वयं भवेत् स्तेयं हृत्वापव्ययते च यत् ॥

robbery in law; there could be robbery of property or person. Open abduction thus came under it. Likewise theft was extended to cover d e c e i t. Theft, in Hindu law, is taking away property not openly, but by fraud. If loss of property is caused by trick or deceit, it is theft. Men and women could be stolen (M. VIII. 323). 'Theft' covered cases of loss of property.

§ 24. The king was not allowed to grant pardon to a thief (M. VIII. 317). He is asked to punish even his own parents, preceptor, wife, friend, and son, generally, but in case of theft especially.[1] Brahmin thief was fined sixtyfour-fold, while Kshatriya for the same offence thirtytwo-fold, Vaiśya sixteen-fold and a Śūdra eight-fold.[2] Punishment for theft was in reverse order as Kauṭilya prescribes punishment in many other offences. Where intention of theft was absent, it was not theft (VIII. 341). Punishment was sought to be deterrent (pratyādeśāya, VIII. 334).

§ 25. Yājñavalkya makes many new cases of c o n s t r u c t i v e t h e f t s: selling goods with undisclosed defect, (II. 257), a thing sold and not delivered by the vendor (254), combination by tradesmen to raise prices and to cause loss to the public and the state (249, 250); substitution in a sealed deposit (247); representing articles for sale to be superior to what they are (246). All these offences had been treated by Kauṭilya under the heading 'Miscellaneous.' In his opinion, they were not theft proper. Yājñavalkya transferred them under theft. There is not a single case of theft, by the time of Yājñavalkya, where capital punishment was inflicted. It had been abolished in all cases under the Mauryas.

---

[1] *Ibid.*, 335. पिताचार्यः सुहृन्माता भार्या पुत्रः पुरोहितः ।
नादण्ड्यो नाम राज्ञोऽस्ति यः स्वधर्मे न तिष्ठति ।

[2] *Ibid.*, 337-33. अष्टापाद्यन्तु शूद्रस्य स्तेये भवति किल्बिषम् ।
षोडशैव तु वैश्यस्य द्वात्रिंशत् क्षत्रियस्य च ॥
ब्राह्मणस्य चतुःषष्टिः etc.

Early Dharma definition by theft.

§ 26. *Kautsa*, *Hārīta*, *Kaṇva* and *Pushkarasādi* had defined theft (before *Âpastamba*): 'coveting property in possession of another man, under any condition, is theft.' *Vārshyāyaṇi* made an exception—'ripening crop, taken by man or draught-ox.' *Hārīta* said, that without permission, it would be theft. *Âpastamba* limited such taking to a small quantity.[1]

---

[1] *Âp.* I. 9. 27. 1—5.

यथा तथा च परपरिग्रहमभिमन्यते स्तेनो ह
भवतीति कौत्सहारीतौ तथा कण्वपुष्करसादी । १ ।
सन्त्यपवादाः परिग्रहेष्विति वार्ष्यायणिः । २ ।
शम्योषा युग्यघासो न स्वामिनः प्रतिषेधयन्ति । ३ ।
अतिव्यपहारी व्यृद्धो भवति । ४ ।
सर्व्वत्रानुमतिपूर्व्वमिति हारीतः । ५ ।

LECTURE IX.

CRIMINAL LAW (*continued*).

Plea of Self-defence—Sāhasa—'Strī-saṁgrahaṇa'—Five High Offences—Śūdra and Penance—Brahmin and Tonsure—Corporate bodies—Quacks—Brahmin v. Śūdra—Treason—Regulations—Capital Punishment —Prison.

Plea of Self-defence.

§ 27. A great conquest of the Dharma School is the evolution of the law of self-defence. As I have shown it in an earlier lecture, they took it from the Purāṇa, which was the origin of the theory (Āp. 1. 29, 7). The Dharma School took it over in connection with penances. If a man killed or wounded another 'in repelling force by force,' no guilt attached to him.[1] The reason seems to be that (1) the mental element to do harm is absent, and that (2) what the repeller does is moral, acting in protection of life. Both considerations operated with the Dharma lawyers. Both principles, for instance, are present before their mind, when they discuss theft as already noticed by us. If a hungry man took a handful from a field it was no theft.[2]

After a controversy, ranging over centuries, the Dharma lawyers decided definitely that, for want of '(bad) intention', there was no sin. Yet, even remote negligence they held to be punishable, though lightly. The theory gradually migrated into law proper. We have seen that Kauṭilya's Code provides a plea of mistake, intoxication and *moha* in defence of abuse and assault.[3]

---

[1] *Manu*, VIII. 348-351 ; *Gaut.* VII.25 ; *Vas.* III. 15-18, 24 ; *Baudh.* I. 18-23 ; *Vi.* V. 189-192. Viśvarūpa would attribute the principle to the Artha-Śāstra. See his remarks on *Yājñ.* II. 21 : यथार्थशास्त्रे व्यवहारप्रकरण उक्तं—'नाततायिवधे दोषी हन्तुर्भवति कश्चन' इति। पुनर्धर्म्मशास्त्रे प्रायश्चित्तप्रकरणे 'कामतो ब्राह्मणवधे निस्कृतिर्न विधीयत' इति। Āpastamba (I. 28, 17, 29. 2, 7, 8) did not accept the Purāṇa view.

[2] This is a living law in the villages up to this time. A man walking by a field can uproot a handful of stalks and start eating the grains therefrom without any objection from the man keeping watch.

[3] *AŚ.*, Ch. 65, p. 193. प्रमादमदमोहादिभिरर्धदण्डाः। The same about assault, see *ibid.*, Ch. 66, p. 195.

Kauṭilya, however, does not admit it in slander, where the very act shows wilfulness, intelligence and spite ; and excludes all possibility of such defence. Kauṭilya, likewise, makes trespass excusable, if committed by a lunatic.[1]

§ 28. Yet the difference is marked between the two Schools. While the plea would only mitigate the offence in the Artha-Śāstra law, Yājñavalkya accepts it as entitling total excuse.[2] The plea of self-defence in murder and grievous hurt, is totally absent in the Artha-Śāstra, and, strange enough, also in Yājñavalkya. The omission might have been due to his closely following, from the beginning to the end, the arrangement of the Artha-Śāstra. But, it was an important law repeated prominently in the Dharma Śāstras and the Mānava. A careful lawyer like Yājñavalkya could not have made a mistake on the question. It seems that the law as administered did not accept the theory fully. The Artha-Śāstra School probably thought that there is an element of intention present ; and it is unscientific and dangerous to accept the theory as a ground for total excuse. They relegated it to the domain of ordinary Nyāya or consideration of justice and equity by the court. According to their system, an act in self-defence was a ground for mitigation, and had to be examined in each case on merits. A general law on the subject was impossible. Even the lawyers of the Dharma School felt the difficulty of a cut and dried law on the subject. Sarvajña Nārāyana commenting on Manu VIII. 350, says, that the defender must not wound such a man 'excessively,'[3] and Kullūka, that the condition is that one must be unable to save himself by running away.[4] In other words, exceptions to this law of exception had to be made—

---

[1] *AŚ.*, Ch. 90, p. 232. मत्तोन्मत्तौ प्रवृत्तप्रवेशाश्चादण्ड्याः ।

[2] *Yājñ.* II. 214. मोहमदादिभिरदण्डनम् ।

[3] आततायिनं हननप्रवृत्तं हन्यादेवाङ्गच्छेदादिरूपघातेन नत्वत्यन्तं अन्यत्र गोब्राह्मणात् । (citing Gautama).

[4] पलायनादिभिरपि स्वनिस्तरणाशक्तौ etc. Cf. Bṛihaspati, II. 15–17 (S.B.E. xxiii. p. 235) VM., pp. 24, 25.

a course which has been followed by our present-day courts. The Dharma law extends the exception to the defence of (*a*) Property (Kshetra), and of (*b*) Wife, evidently as she is part of the defender's body.[1]

§ 29. The Mānava gives it the greatest extension (VIII. 348-351). He extends it to a national revolt and revolution (348), when the Āryas are not allowed their common and religious liberty; to the protection of a Brahmin by an outsider (349); and to 'a battle of dakshiṇā', the significance of which is not clear.[2] He expounds that even a preceptor, a minor, an elder, or a Brahmin could be killed with impunity in the exercise of the right of private defence; no one was too sacred when the right was concerned, no sin, no guilt, *i.e.*, no penalty of penance or law—followed the result: 'fury recoils on fury.' The right is not affected, whether it is exercised in an open place or otherwise (351).[3]

Sāhasa.

The section *Sāhasa* (VIII. 344 ff.), modern scholars have translated as 'Robbery'. The correct translation of Sāhasa would be "(offences of force to person and to property)." That is how Kauṭilya defines it: '*Sāhasa is an act of force in sight of defenders.*' "Theft is (an act of force) not in sight and with deceit."[4] Nārada defines it similarly. '*Sāhasa* is an injury coupled with force,[5] while theft is coupled with fraud. The *act of force* may be directed to person or property. Hence Kauṭilya mentions

---

[1] See *Manu*, VIII. 349. स्त्रीविप्राभ्युपपत्तौ च घ्नन्धर्मेण न दुष्यति ।

[2] It is generally understood to mean a sudden affray between priests over sacrificial fees. But I think that the reference is technical which has become obscure.

[3] *Manu*, VIII. 350-351:

गुरुं वा बालवृद्धौ वा ब्राह्मणं वा बहुश्रुतम् ।
प्रकाशं वाप्रकाशं वा मन्युस्तन्मन्युमृच्छति ॥

[4] *AS.*, Ch. 74, p. 191. साहसमन्वयवत् प्रसभकर्म निरन्वये स्तेयमपव्ययने च ।

[5] Nārada, XIV. 12. See quotation in VM., p. 498.

सहसा क्रियते कर्म यत्किञ्चिद्बलदर्पितैः ।
तत् साहसमिति प्रोक्तं सहो बलमिहोच्यते ॥

illegal imprisonment as a Sāhasa. Nārada makes theft only a species of Sāhasa.

§ 30. Likewise the term which scholars translate as 'adultery' is not properly rendered. Strī-Saṁgrahaṇa, *lit.*, means 'seizing women to oneself', which covers both rape and adultery. It ought to be rendered as 'offences regarding women.' 'Seizing' is against the husband or guardian when it is adultery, and against both husband and wife or guardian and woman when rape. Strī-Saṁgrahaṇa has been regarded as one of the heinous sins from the earliest times. In early Hindu law it constituted a genus by itself. Only Bṛihaspati, in later times, classes it under Sāhasa. Various penance-penalties were devised with reference to various degrees of the gravity of the offence. Law proper also distinguished shades of guilt, and it tended to be less severe than the Dharma, in cases of adultery proper. As we have seen, the Artha-Śāstra abolished tortures in all adultery cases, except in respect of the Queen.[1] In case of an unmarried but marriageable girl, it made the offender marry the girl and pay a dowry.[2] Rape was always visited with the severest punishment—imprisonment, torture, maiming and death.

Strī-Saṁgrahaṇa.

§ 31. The puritanical Mānava revolts from mild punishments in adultery. Its tone is of a lofty clergyman, a reformer, and his law consequently suffers. His punishments are inordinately severe; death is a general sanction,[3] which causes no small trouble to commentators, who have to reconcile contradictory provisions of other authorities. Only in case of the 'willing maiden', he follows the Maurya law.[4] For adultery in defiance of the husband, the woman was to be torn to pieces by dogs—

---

[1] *AŚ.*, Ch. 90, p. 234. सर्वत्र राजभार्यागमने कुम्भीपाकः ।

[2] *AŚ.*, Ch. 89, p. 230. अकामायाः शत्यो दण्डः, आत्मरागार्थं शुल्कदानं च ।

[3] *Manu*, VIII. 359. अब्राह्मणः संग्रहणे प्राणान्तं दण्डमर्हति ।

[4] *Ibid.* 364. सकामां दूषयंस्तुल्यो न वधं प्राप्नुयान्नरः ।

an archaic punishment (known to the Jātakas)—and the adulterer was to be roasted and consumed slowly on an iron bed by putting logs of wood underneath it[1] (372). For this severe punishment the Mānava in its statement of reasons, in the beginning, says:

"The wives of all the four Varṇas must be kept pure."[2]

These severe laws find no place in Yājñavalkya.

§ 32. Kauṭilya, Sumati (Manu) and Yājñavalkya make a distinction between adultery with a 'guarded woman' and that with an 'unguarded woman'. The word in Manu is *guptā*, 'concealed' or 'guarded', whereas Yājñavalkya uses the term *avaruddhā*.[3] Kauṭilya's term gives the real meaning: '*avarodha*' or inner apartments. This probably explains the passage in the Mahā-Bhārata where women are described 'whom the sun and the moon have not seen.' Bhāsa gives another detail; these Avarodha women in going out kept a veil which covered the face and probably the whole body (*avaguṇṭhana*). But on all ceremonial and public occasions they kept their faces uncovered.[4] This explains why the Avarodha ladies of royal households are seen in the balcony without a covering, in sculptures.

§ 33. Circumstantial evidence was allowed in case of adultery by Kauṭilya,[5] which has been adopted by Yājñavalkya.[6] Caste, in offence of adultery, was an element which decided the amount of punishment according to Kauṭilya. This was within all reasonable bounds in Kauṭilya, while it was converted by 'Manu' into a terror for the Śūdra, a depressor for the

---

[1] In., VIII. 371: भर्तारं लंघयेद्या तु स्त्री ज्ञातिगुणदर्पिता ।
तां श्वभिः खादयेद्राजा संस्थाने बहुसंस्थिते ॥.

The reading of Mandlik and Gharpure has been followed, Jolly's reading is faulty.

[2] *Ibid.* 359: चतुर्णामपि वर्णानां दारा रक्ष्यतमाः सदा ।

[3] Cf. *Manu*, VIII. 374, 376-378, 382-385, etc.; *Yājñ.* II. 290. For अवरोध in Kauṭilya see *AŚ.*, p. 42.

[4] *Pratimā*, Act I, p. 25 (1915).

[5] *AŚ.*, Ch. 89, p. 231: कैशाकेशिकं संग्रहणं उपलिङ्गनाद्वा शरीरोपभोगानां तज्जातेभ्यः स्त्रीवचनाद्वा ।

[6] *Yājñ.*, II. 283: पुमान् संग्रहणे ग्राह्यः केशाकेशि परस्त्रिया ।
सद्यो वा कामजैश्चिह्नैः प्रतिपत्तौ द्वयोस्तथा ॥.

Vaiśya and the Kshatriya as against the Brahmin, and immunity for the Brahmin. Non-Brahmins of Aryan descent became subject to corporal punishment for offending with a willing Brahmin woman (377), while the Brahmin went off with a fine, or was exiled, in rape (378). Yājñavalkya follows generally Manu. He lays down a general law for all without distinction : torture for all when the offence was 'prātilomya' and imprisonment or fine when 'ānulomya.'[1] The effect is the same ; there was no one higher than the Brahmin, so he could not be tortured. But the form of the law is excellent. It shows that there is no partiality, while that of Manu appears to be a law by an interested party. The real question remains—was the Brahmin culprit given the punishment, as in Kauṭilya (p. 234), of living death, the 'branding' ?[2] Or, was he made immune from it by the Mānava (VIII. 380 ;[3] IX 241) ?

§ 34. The evidence of V i s h ṇ u shows that branding was done in all cases prescribed, after the Mānava Code.[4] Only 'in other cases', where he would have been liable to a penalty of torture, the Brahmin was banished with 'all his property' and without being branded[5] (Vishṇu V. 8). Branding was current as late as the time of the C o d e s of N ā r a d a[6] and B ṛ i h a s p a t i (XVII. 11).[7]

---

[1] Y., II. 286 : सजातावुत्तमो दण्ड आनुलोम्ये तु मध्यमः ।
प्रातिलोम्ये वधं पुंसो नार्याः कर्णादिकर्तनम् ॥

[2] *AŚ.*, Ch. 90, p. 234 : श्वपाकीगमने कृतकबन्धाङ्कः परविषयं गच्छेत्, श्वपाकत्वं वा ।
Here no exception is made in favour of the Brahmin.

[3] न जातु ब्राह्मणं हन्यात् सर्वपापेष्वपि स्थितम ।
राष्ट्रादेनं बहिः कुर्यात् समग्रधनमक्षतम् ॥

[4] *Vishṇu*, v. 3. स्वदेशाद्ब्राह्मणं कृताङ्कं विवासयेत् ।

[5] *Ibid.* 8. अन्यत्रापि वध्यकर्मणि तिष्ठन्तं समग्रधनमक्षतं विवासयेत् ।

[6] Nār. XIV. 10 : शिरसो मुण्डनं दण्डस्तस्य निर्वासनं पुरात् ।
ललाटे चाभिशस्ताङ्कः प्रयाणं गर्दभेन च ॥

In the translation of the preceding verse Jolly has wrongly rendered the word 'vadha' by 'corporal punishment.'

[7] महापातकयुक्तोऽपि न विप्रो वधमर्हति ।
निर्वासनाङ्कनं मौण्ड्यं तस्य कुर्यान्नराधिपः । See quotation in Vivāda-Ratnākara, p. 634.

§ 35. Yājñavalkya on his part seems to abolish branding for all in rape and adultery and to prescribe in its place a uniform law:

(*a*) in adultery, other punishments than torture, *i.e.*, imprisonment and fine, when by one of higher caste with a lower woman;

(*b*) in rape by one of higher caste on lower woman, the second class imprisonment and fine for all;

(*c*) in rape and adultery by one of lower caste on a higher woman, torture;

(*d*) in adultery and rape amongst equals, the highest class of punishment of fine and imprisonment.[1]

The punishment is severer than that prescribed by Kauṭilya. It is lighter than the punishment laid down by 'Manu,' except in the case of the Brahmin, who is not allowed by Yājñavalkya to go free with a mere shaving of the head.

§ 36. The offence of *Strî-Saṁgrahaṇa* included unauthorised talking with women, sending of presents of flowers etc., to them, touching of their clothes or person, by a stranger. In the matter of constructive offences under this head the three Codes are of the same view.[2] Offence of force is presumed to be absent, when the complainant is a woman of the town. The guilt when established was lightly punished. The position of the Buddhist nun is curious in this respect. She does not occupy any definite legal position. She is punished if she is a willing party, while the offender is punished in either case with a small fine.[3] This is the position in all the three Codes. It seems that two causes operated in creating this anomalous position. The nuns were probably recruited from the lowest classes; then,

---

[1] *Yājñ.* II. 286-287: स्वजातावुत्तमो दण्ड आनुलोम्ये तु मध्यमः ।
प्रातिलोम्ये वधः पुंसो नार्याः कर्णादिच्छेदनम् ।
अलङ्कृतां हरन् कन्यामुत्तमं त्वन्यथाऽधमम् ।
दण्डं दद्यात् सवर्णासु प्रातिलोम्ये वधः स्मृतः ॥

[2] *Manu*, VIII. 354-358; *Yājñ.* II. 284; *AŚ.* pp. 155, 158.

[3] *Manu*, VIII. 363; *Yājñ.* II. 293; *AŚ.* p. 234.

in the eye of the law they were, like monks, mere Śūdra, and an unauthorised fraternity. As they had left home, in the eye of the law, they became 'king's women,' women without protection of the family, public women. The law strained every nerve to stop the growth of these legal outcasts of 'wandering females.'

§ 37. We should note the theory of Dharma, that an offending woman after penance was free from blame. The husband refusing to accept her was deemed blameworthy. The Dharma law said 'marriage is a tie created by Dharma',[1] and Dharma has declared her pure after penance. This was a common theory that punishment and penance cured an offender. The later law-givers make an exception to this in cases of people convicted of the Five High Offences.

Five High Offences.

§ 38. The five mahāpātakas are : slaying a priest, drinking *surā*, theft, adultery with preceptor's wife, and associating with the high sinners.[2] The High Sins have had a fluctuating history. At first there were seven such offences, as evidenced by the description of Yāska.[3] Abortion was amalgamated with the killing of a Brahmin. Theft was finally narrowed down to the theft of gold (Manu, IX. 235 ; XI. 55 ; Y.III. 257). Murder of man was converted into the murder of Brahmin. About 400 B. C. they were limited to four—(1) Theft, (2) human murder, (3) adultery with preceptor's wife, and (4) surā-drinking. "Human murder" and "theft", not Brahmin murder and theft of gold, are mentioned by Āpastamba (II. 27. 16). In the same place, he mentions adultery in general (II. 27. 1. ff).

§ 39. The great offenders, even after undergoing punishment, were not fully admitted into society. They did not, for instance, become competent witnesses.

---

[1] *Âp.* I. 6, 13, 11. धर्माद्धि संबन्धः ।

[2] *Yājñ.* III. 227 : ब्रह्महा मद्यपः स्तेनस्तथैव गुरुतल्पगः ।
एते महापातकिनो यश्च तैः सह संवसेत् ॥

[3] *Nirukta*, Ch. VI., 27.

§ 40. Yājñavalkya admits the Śūdra to penance[1], and thereby removes a great incapacity from him. By this admission, many of his punishments at common law were commuted. He could perform penance for the great offences.

Śūdra and Penance.

§ 41. The Mānava (VIII. 379) subjects the Brahmin to the punishment of 'Tonsure'. This was inflicted in many cases under the Kauṭilya. Vincent Smith, the historian, has suggested that it was a form of punishment borrowed from the Persian Empire. But before the birth of the Persian Empire it existed in India. The Jātakas bear testimony to it. When inflicted on a culprit, it meant that he was expelled from society. The Buddha's order adopted 'shaving' as a mark of giving-up society.

Brahmin and Tonsure.

§ 42. The Mānava after providing for defamation, assault, theft, sāhasa, and adultery (386), gives miscellaneous rules which occur at the end of the Dharmasthîya book of Kauṭilya and the first two chapters of the next book (pp. 198 ff.). Yājñavalkya gives them under Sāhasa (232—258). Yājñavalkya follows on, step by step, the law of Kauṭilya. The Mānava parts company at the end of its Ch. VIII. with Kauṭilya at his Ch. II. of the book of Kaṇṭaka Śodhana. It gives then the laws about husband and wife and inheritance.

§ 43. Yājñavalkya's section on *Saṁbhūya Samutthāna* ('United Undertaking') dealing with "Merchants who, for profit, trade by forming corporations (Samavāya II. 259)," is entirely new (II. 259—265). This shows that corporate trading had developed much more since Kauṭilya and the Mānava. Verses 259—260 deal with the private rights of their members. Why they should have been

Corporate Bodies.

[1] *Yājñ.* III. 262: चान्द्रायणं चरेत् सर्वानवकृष्टान्निहत्य तु ।
शूद्रोऽधिकारहीनोऽपि कालेनानेन शुध्यति ॥

placed under criminal law is not explicable, unless we take that they were enforced by the Kaṇṭaka Court, as the Artha-Śāstra says about the guilds of artizans. The guild merchants or companies also probably came under the jurisdiction of the magisterial courts.

The Marine Officer was punished if he exacted the land tax from the companies. A crooked partner could be expelled and his share of profit could be declared forfeited to the other members.[1] Trade by sea with foreign countries seems to have been brisk. These provisions would have protected both the Hindu and the foreigner.

Quacks.

§ 44. In the miscellaneous laws, there is one which deserves notice, about quacks. If a man, not qualified to treat men or animals, declared himself as an expert, he was liable to punishment.[2] This was a Maurya law come down to the time of Yājñavalkya. The medical art had been long specialised in the country and there was no room for the quack. Quacks for doctoring even animals were not allowed.

Brahmin *vs.* Śūdra.

§ 45. The Mānava, upto verse VIII. 403, follows the Artha-Śāstra, IV. 2. Then it gives (404—409) some rules about ship-owners and dock-dues. Then it reverts to the duties of castes (410—411), only to come down on the Śūdra again as a peroration to his chapter on criminal law, with which it concludes the subject (412—420). Sumati says that the Śūdra's position was that of the slave, which historically was probably correct. From these equations he deduces that the Śūdra could not hold as his own anything, which could not be confidently taken away.

---

[1] *Yājñ.* II. 263. तरिकः स्थलजं शुल्कं गृह्णन्दाप्यः पणान्दश । *Ibid.* 265. जिह्मं त्यजेयुर्निर्लाभमशक्तोऽन्येन कारयेत् ।

[2] *Ibid.* II. 242. भिषङ्मिथ्याचरन्दाप्यस्तिर्यक्षु प्रथमं दमम् ।
मानुषे मध्यमं राजमानुषेषूत्तमं दमम् ॥ Cf. *AS.*, p. 202.

All that belongs to him belongs to his master.[1] It was therefore lawful that the Brahmin may dispossess the Śūdra (417). Here again, there is a reference to the seizure of the throne of the Śūdra Maurya by the Brahmin Pushyamitra. It also probably legalises seizure of property of the Buddhist Saṅgha who had been enormously rich. He, the Brahmin, in verse 418, is asked to keep the Vaiśyas and Śūdras in order (as a ruler)[2], and in verses 419-420 the identity of "the Master" with the Brahmin of verse 417 and the king is complete!

Treason.

§ 46. Secondary acts of Treason (Y. II. 295; 302-303) are comparatively lightly punished and here again Yājñavalkya follows the Maurya law. But he does not mention the alternative commutative fine for the cutting off of the tongue. It seems, that was a part of the procedure of criminal execution, as indicated by the Artha-Śāstra. This shows that many of the torture-punishments (*vadha*), mentioned in the Code of Yājñavalkya, were mere technical names for the punishment, and in fact they meant only fines or imprisonment. Such was the actual state which Fa-hien found in 400 A.C., when the Code of Yājñavalkya (probably with the Code of Nārada) must have been the existing authority. In that view the Code would be an extremely kind code of criminal law, even a great improvement on the Kauṭilya, for the Kauṭilya is still a severe code in matters of state offences, in which destruction of irrigation works is also included.[3] The irrigation works built by Chandragupta and his predecessors were great constructions. His government had to fight sedition and treason, for a section of the population remained attached to the old dynasty. Mischief

---

[1] *Manu*, VIII. 417. विस्रब्धं ब्राह्मणः शूद्राद्द्रव्योपादानमाचरेत् ।
न हि तस्यास्ति किंचित् स्वं भर्तृहार्यधनो हि सः ॥

[2] *Ibid.* 418. वैश्यशूद्रौ प्रयत्नेन स्वानि कर्माणि कारयेत् ।
तौ हि च्युतौ स्वकर्मभ्यः क्षोभयेतामिदं जगत् ॥

[3] *AŚ.* Ch. 88, p. 227.

to the irrigation works was a loss to the Government, and paralysing the great system would bring discredit on the new administration. Those laws were necessary as political measures in the time of Kauṭilya. But they had no justification in the time of Yājñavalkya, and Yājñavalkya consequently does not incorporate them into his Code, or modifies them greatly.

Regulations not Laws.

§ 47. A number of rules against anti-sanitation acts are found in Kauṭilya.[1] They however do not form part of his Code of Law. They are placed in the chapter on the administration of the capital. All those rules which do not find place in Kauṭilya's Code but are important, do not appear in the two Dharma Codes. This indicates that they were regulations and not laws, and that there existed a sharp division between the two.

Belief in sorcery seems to have been dead since Kauṭilya's time[2]. Laws about it in the last chapter of the Kaṇṭaka book are omitted by Yājñavalkya.

Capital punishment.

§ 48. It seems that the general tendency of the country in the early centuries of the Christian era had been to look at capital punishment with disfavour. The reason, amongst others, was the spread of Buddhism. The discussion in the Mahā-Bhārata on the undesirability to continue capital punishment is very important.[3] Such a theory must have influenced the policy of punishment both with regard to Brahmins and non-Brahmins. The discussion does not make any distinction. The discussion in the Mahā-Bhārata is as follows.

The discussion starts with the stock, adverse argument that if capital punishment was abolished, all the distinction between virtue and vice would disappear. 'This is mine,' 'That is not his', distinctions like these would prevail no more, 'rights and obliga-

---

[1] *AŚ*. Ch. 57, p. 145. Cf. the other regulations of social and semi-political nature in that Chapter.

[2] *Ibid.*, pp. 233-234.

[3] *MBh.*, XII. Ch. 267, 10-16.

tions', would be in abeyance, and 'society' would come to an end. The fallacy is obvious; the argument assumes that total cessation of punishment has been promised. And the reply opens with an emphasis on the desirability of punishing offence. But the punishment should be inflicted "without destroying the person" of the offender. In support of this, four reasons are advanced—

(*i*) Capital punishment operates hardship upon the innocent dependants. "By killing the wicked, the king kills a large number of innocent men; (for instance) by killing a single robber, his wife, mother, father, children, (etc.) are (sometimes) killed." (10).

(*ii*) The offender may be capable of improvement. "Sometimes a wicked man is seen to imbibe the right mode of life." (11).

(*iii*) Capital punishment takes away the possibility of good members being added to society. "It is again seen that good people do spring from wicked ones." (11).

(*iv*) A historical reason: "The offender should not be uprooted for it is not in consonance with the traditional law." (16). The end of punishment which the traditional law had in view is assumed to be a mental cure, "and for mental cure, non-capital punishments are prescribed (in ancient law)—mental pain, imprisonment, disfiguring etc., (some readings also include confiscation)." (12-13).

The theory never found its way in the law books and writings of Hindu lawyers. But that does not exclude its effect on actual administration. As a fact, Fa-hien does find capital punishment abolished in India in actual administration.

§ 49. In the Artha-Śāstra and in the inscriptions of Aśoka, the Prison appears as a well-known institution, but if we look at the translations of the two Codes it would seem that there is not a single case where imprisonment is awarded. Translations here are faulty. "The First amercement," "the Middle amercement" and "the Highest amercement" are really the First,

Prison.

the Middle and the Highest "Sāhasa punishments." They are punishments both of imprisonments and fines ; there were the first class (etc.) Sāhasa fine and the first class Sāhasa imprisonment. When the codes prescribe a fine they say *dāpya* (to be 'given') and similar terms, or mention the amount. When they mean imprisonment, they do not qualify it.

Bandhana or imprisonment was to be served either in the j a i l, *Bandhana-āgāra*, or at the m i n e s (AS.) which meant hard labour. The Mānava, by a provision, directs that if the culprit failed to pay the fine he would have to do labour, or in other words, in default the man had to undergo imprisonment.[1]

---

[1] *Manu*, ix. 229. क्षत्रविट्शूद्रयोनिस्तु दण्डं दातुमशक्नुवन् ।
आनृण्यं कर्मणा गच्छेद्विप्रो दद्याच्छनैः शनैः ॥

LECTURE X.

CONTRACT.

Importance of the subject in Hindu Law—Void and voidable contracts—Public Policy—Definiteness—Acts of God and State —Debts—Interest—rule of 'dandupat'—Gautama on rules about interest—Kauṭilya's rule of limitation in debts—Manu's rule—Rule of Priority—Bonds—novation—attestation and registration—Liability of heirs for predecessor's debts—'Pious' duty of son and grandson—*Srîdhara* v. *Mahîdhara*—Vasishṭha's rule of interregnum in interest—Later rules on interest —Lex loci in contracts—Execution against the person of the debtor.

§ 1. In Hindu Law on the whole the largest space is devoted to contract. It is found so in the Artha-Śāstra, and since Yājñavalkya this has been a still more pronounced feature. The Mānava, being the first Dharma-Vyavahāra-Śāstra, leans to the tradition of the Dharma-Sūtras, and devotes greater attention to Inheritance, yet its law on contract preponderates over all other subjects in bulk.

Importance.

§ 2. Contracts had been differentiated already before the time of the Artha-Śāstra, and subtle principles distinguished. Almost all the principles of contract which we know to-day are to be found in the laws of the Artha-Śāstra. A more scientific classification was made by Yājñavalkya, and several technical terms, *e.g.*, 'act of God' and 'act of State', introduced. Nor did the subject stop there. Nārada still improves upon the law as left by Yājñavalkya.

§ 3. This shows a growing economic prosperity of the country since the Maurya times. Even in the Mānava which has no claims to be a scientific treatise, we find new provisions on contract—

e.g., about s e a-c a r r i e r s and s h i p - o w n e r s—which represents the ever-increasing commerce and adventure of the Hindus of the third century B.C.

§ 4. The word for contract in the Artha-Śāstra is v y a v a-h ā r a. It is significant that the civil law begins with vyavahāra in the A r t h a-Ś ā s t r a. It first gives those vyavahāras which were v o i d and v o i d a b l e. The D h a r m a-Ś ā s t r a s on the other hand begin with the r e c o v e r y of d e b t s. Debts had attracted the attention of the Dharma lawyers, as it was sin not to pay off debts. It was this name *vyavahāra* of the Artha-Śāstra lawyers which gave the name to the whole system of law evolved by their school. The Kauṭilîya places even s l a v e r y under contract, because, as we shall see, slavery in the eye of the Artha lawyers depended on elements of contract either express or implied.

§ 5. In classification Yājñavalkya stands unique in the history of the legal literature of the country in regarding g a m b l i n g as a species of contract. Except him no other authority yet known assigns that place to d y ū t a and s a m ā h v y a, g a m b l i n g and w a g e r i n g. Both before and after him, gambling never attained that position in Hindu jurisprudence.

Void and Voidable Contracts.

§ 6. According to Kauṭilya[1] the contracts which cannot be enforced in Court (*na sidhyeyuḥ*) are divided into five classes :

(*a*) those entered into in s e c l u s i o n or s e c r e c y (*e.g.*, in the interior of a house, in the dead of the night, in forests, *unless* they be subsequently acknowledged to the knowledge of others, or *unless* they be by nature such as had to be kept private, *e.g.*, those relating

---

[1] *AS'*., ch. 57, pp. 147-148. तिरोहितान्तरगारनक्तारण्योपध्युपह्वरकृतांश्च व्यवहारान् प्रतिषेधयेयुः। ···परोक्षेणाधिकर्णग्रहणमवक्तव्यकरा वा तिरोहिताः सिध्येयुः। दायनिक्षेपोपनिधिविवाहयुक्ता स्त्रीणाम निष्कासिनीनां···अगारकृताः सिध्येयुः। साहसानुप्रवेशकलहविवाहराजनियोगयुक्ताः···सिध्येयुः।···आश्रमव्याधचाराणां···सिध्येयुः।

to division of family property, deposit put in trust, those relating to marriage, to conspiracy, or to political undertakings ordered by the State, etc., (entered into at night), or contracts by hermits (entered into in forests), etc.;

(*b*) those entered into by f r a u d (upadhikṛitāḥ.)—(Fraud, involved in the procedure of a detective police officer authorised by court, was excepted, *e.g.*, when they were asked to make enquiries in disguise about trust deposits having had no witnesses);

(*c*) those entered into by m e m b e r s of an u n d i v i d e d f a m i l y, m i n o r s, c o n v i c t s, c r i p p l e s, etc., 'l e g a l l y i n c a p a c i t a t e d', *unless* authorised;[1]

(*d*) those entered into by a person in anger, distress, intoxication or lunacy;[2]

(*e*) those entered into by a person under illegal domination (*apagraha*) or duress.[3]

(1) "G o o d c o n t r a c t s were those which were made between proper parties, in proper place, at proper time, with free will and power."

(2) "Contracts made with full procedure, in proper place, with ascertainment of the quality, peculiarities and measure of the object of contract, are enforceable contracts."

(3) "D o c u m e n t s executed in evidence even afterwards in respect of such contracts are admissible—except an Ā d e ś a ['order'] and a m o r t g a g e d e e d."[4]

The Mānava sums up these principles in VIII. 163-168:

---

[1] *Ibid.*, p. 148. अपाश्रयवद्भिश्च कृताः,...कनिष्ठेन...अभिशस्त...व्यङ्गव्यसनिभिश्च, अन्यत्र निसृष्टव्यवहारेभ्यः।

[2] *Ibid.* क्रुद्धेनार्तेन मत्तेनोन्मत्तेन...वा कृता व्यवहारा न सिध्येयुः।

[3] *Ibid.* अपगृहीतेन वा कृता न ... सिध्येयुः।

[4] *Ibid.* स्वे स्वे तु वर्गे देशकाले च स्वकरणकृताः सम्पूर्णचाराः शुद्धदेशा दृष्टरूपलक्षणप्रमाणगुणाः सर्वव्यवहाराः सिध्येयुः। पश्चिमं त्वेषां करणमादेशाधिवर्जं सिध्येयुः।

(*i*) a contract (‘*vyavahāra*’) made by a person intoxicated, insane, distressed,

(*ii*) not legally independent (family members etc.), a minor, or one in dotage, or an unauthorised person, cannot be enforced (163).

“Even if the plaint be proved, it does not become valid, when the cause alleged is o u t s i d e t h e l a w o f c o n t r a c t.” (164).

In other words, the above contracts do not furnish a valid cause of action.

(*iii*) F r a u d—in mortgage, sale, gift, acceptance—wheresoever detected shall make the contract invalid and cancelled. (165).

(Verses 166-167 give the exception to the law on contracts by members of an undivided family. If benefit of the contract has accrued to the family or the contract is for the good of the family, the head and the family are bound by the contract.)

(*iv*) Contracts evidenced by documents executed under f o r c e are regarded as never made (168).

As to the last, the Mānava says that Manu has laid it down. This Manu was either the author of the Mānava Artha-Śāstra or a mere shield for a new provision to be introduced in a Dharma code. The exception under (*iii*) is a distinct improvement on the law of Kauṭilya. Yājñavalkya in II. 31-32 gives greater details than the Mānava, and these are verbally taken from the Artha-Śāstra. According to him force (*bala*), fraud (‘*upadhi*’), secrecy etc., want of capacity (in ‘women,’ ‘minor’), enmity, intoxication, lunacy, distress, fear, and want of authority, make contracts incapable of giving cause of action.[1]

[1] *Yājñ.* II. 31-32. बलोपधिविनिर्वृत्तान् व्यवहारान्निवर्तयेत् ।
स्त्रीनक्तमन्तरागारबहिः शत्रुकृतांस्तथा ॥
मत्तोन्मत्तार्तव्यसनिबालभीतादियोजितः ।
असम्बद्धकृतश्चैव व्यवहारो न सिध्यति ॥

§ 7. Medhātithi commenting on Manu VIII. 164, interprets it as meaning that contracts against the spirit of law and good practice can have no legal force. In illustrating it he gives 'a sale of wife and children,' or 'giving away one's whole property, when there are children.'[1] This leads to a very important discussion. We find the Mīmāṁsā emphatically deciding, on its own arguments, that one cannot give away '*sarvasva*', 'one's whole property,' because it belongs to the family, and that one cannot give away or sell one's wife and children because one has no property in children.[2] This is one of the most important contributions of the Mīmāṁsā to Hindu law. History was against the doctrine, and the Dharma lawyers felt indecisive. The basis of their argument was their doctrine of Hindu marriage. Was marriage a sale of the bride ? Old Vedic texts, refering to the archaic practice, indicated that it was so. The Dharma lawyers were perplexed. Vasishṭha leaned to the view deduced from the Vedic texts.[3] If the bride was bought, the children, the fruit, derived from an object bought (slave) became legally the property of the father. Then, there was the story in the Vedic literature of the sale of Sunaḥśepa. Āpastamba, on the other hand, argued, 'the only thing which creates marriage is Sacrament.' Hence wife and children cannot be objects of transfer.[4] But I was surprised to find it as a definite law, stated without reference to any controversy, in the Kauṭilīya. It seems that the law anticipated the philosophy of the Dharma and the Mīmāṁsā. The sword of the State had cut the knot of the Vedic text. Kauṭilya proudly asserted :

Contracts against Public Policy.

---

[1] *Medh.* on *Manu,* VIII. 164. बहिश्चेद्धर्माद्धर्मबाह्यं यदुच्यते शास्त्राचारविरुद्धं पञ्चकादधिकाद्वृद्धिः भार्यापत्यविक्रयादिरन्वयिनः सर्वस्वदानमित्येवमादि ।

[2] See Nîlakanṭha, *Vyavahāra-mayûkha,* (*Dāya* Section), pp. 31-32.

[3] *Vas.* I. 36. तस्माद्दुहितृमतेऽधिरथं शतं देयमितीह क्रयो विज्ञायते ।

[4] क्रयशब्दः संस्तुतिमात्रम् । धर्माद्धि संबन्धः (II, 6.13.11)। दानं क्रयधर्मश्चापत्यस्य न विद्यते (10)।

"Sale and mortgage of children is a legal institution amongst the Barbarians [Mlechchhas]. But slavery is not for the Hindu [Ārya]."[1]

Kauṭilya threw contempt on the Dharma theory defending the Vedic text. After Kauṭilya, all literature is unanimous that a Hindu could not be a slave. Kauṭilya abolished enslavement of captives in war if they were Hindus [Āryas]. In the law of contract it was prescribed by him that one could not sell even oneself.

Even a Śūdra who had Aryan breath in him, "Ārya-prāṇaḥ," could not be a slave.[2] Megasthenes refers to these laws, when he says that slavery was not allowed in India.

A contract for sale or transfer of wife and children, therefore, was a contract opposed to public policy, as Medhatithi says[3] (although the verse, to which he attributed this doctrine, seems to be connected with the previous verse and is not an independent section).

§ 8. Kauṭilya in the same place says that an agreement for an immoral undertaking would be set aside. Similarly, an agreement for transfer of property under fear of a criminal case or any other sort of fear would be illegal, liable to punishment. An agreement for sedition was to be similarly treated. (p. 189).[4]

§ 9. Yājñavalkya gives the law on the illegality of sale of wife and children in II. 175.[5] In the Mānava (VIII. 412), enslavement of the upper Varṇas is punishable even in case of a Brahmin offender,[6] but the Code omits the law on the

---

1 *AS.*, Ch. 70, p. 181. म्लेच्छानामदोषः प्रजां विक्रेतुमाधातुं वा । न त्वेवार्यस्य दासभावः ।

2 *Loc. cit.* उदरदासवर्जमार्यप्राणमप्राप्तव्यवहारं शूद्रं विक्रयाधानं नयतः स्वजनस्य द्वादशपणो दण्डः ।

3 *Medh.* on *Manu*, VIII. 164.

4 *AS.*, Ch. 73, p. 189. धर्मदानमसाधुषु कर्मसु...कामदानमनर्हेषु च।...दण्डभयादाक्रोशभयादर्थभयाद्वा भयदानं प्रतिगृह्णतः स्तेयदण्डः।...राज्ञामुपरि दर्पदानं च। तत्रोत्तमो दण्डः।

5 स्वं कुटुम्बाविरोधेन देयं दारसुतादृते ।
दास्यं तु कारयँल्लोभाद्ब्राह्मणः संस्कृतान् द्विजान्।

contract of transfer of wife and children. This was probably purposely done out of respect to the Dharma Śāstra. After Yājñavalkya, Nārada and other Code-writers invariably embody it in the law on transfer.

Definiteness.

§ 10. Kauṭilya says that a contract to be valid must be d e f i n i t e about the subject-matter. Kauṭilya's laws throughout emphasise the necessity about stating t i m e and p l a c e, stipulated for the performance of the contract. And regarding cause of action in the plaint, it had to be stated as to when and where the cause of action arose.[1] The contract must be definite regarding time and place. Some contracts, according to Kauṭilya, were not "limited by time and place." These were exceptions. But as to the measure, etc., of the subject-matter, he requires the contract to be definite.[2] These rules imply that there must be mutuality, and the parties should have understood each other, there should not be any room for the plea of mistake. The rules about definiteness are implied by Yājñavalkya (II. 5, 6), though not independently stated. The fault of Yājñavalkya is his brevity. He, of course, omits principles as he gives only provisions as a regular code.

Acts of God and State.

§ 11. Kauṭilya's laws state various grounds on which a party may be excused from fulfilling certain contracts, *e.g.*, when the performance had been prevented by a revolution, by fire, flood, shipwreck, or invasion, etc.[3] Yājñavalkya, in the corresponding place (II. 66, on Nikshepa), sums up these grounds as 'r ā j a-d a i v i k a' "State or Divine."[4] Other contracts, according to Kauṭilya, could be similarly rendered impossible, *e.g.*, when fire, theft,

---

[1] *AŚ.*, Ch. 58, p. 149. संवत्सरमृतुं मासं पक्षं दिवसं करणमधिकरणमृणं......चाभिलिख्य ...निवेशयेत् ।

[2] *AŚ.*, Ch. 68, p. 175. असंख्यातदेशकालं तु पुत्राः......

[3] *Ibid.*, Ch. 69, p. 177. ...दुर्गराष्ट्रविलोपे...ग्राममध्याग्न्युदकाबाधे...नावि निमग्नायां...नोपनिधिमभ्याभवेत् ।

[4] *Yājñ.* II. 66. न दाप्योऽपहृतं तत्तु राजदैवकतस्करैः ।

flood, or Government has made delivery of the goods sold, impossible. There an action for recession would lie to have the contract set aside.[1]

The Mānava adopts the exception, *e.g.*, in VIII. 189, but couples it with the proviso—unless the party (seeking relief) was a party (to the factor bringing about the condition of impossibility *i.e.*, negligence in destruction by fire, etc.).[2] Both 'Manu' and Yājñavalkya, however, omit the rule while writing about contracts of sale.

Debts and Interest.

§ 12. Debts were either secured or unsecured. Hindu codes treat of unsecured debts under the title 'Ṛina'. The Mānava has a curious Dharma doctrine which he opposes to the Vyavahāra law. He, at some length (VIII. 48-50), discusses and decides that a creditor, seeking to realise debt after it has been established in law court, should not be blamed by the king. He might adopt the Dharma method of realisation (*e.g.*, by sitting in '*dharnā*') or by self-help. This of course had not been allowed by the Artha-Śāstra. Yājñavalkya also sanctions the Dharma procedure of execution.[3] We have here a retrograde step, but probably it was not put into practice. Evidently, what the Dharma lawyers did not approve of, was the punishment for self-help. The Dharma School themselves discouraged sitting in '*dharnā*'. Āpastamba enumerates a creditor who sits at his debtor's (*pratyupavishṭa*) amongst those whose food is not to be accepted by a Brahmin [I. 6. 19 (1)].

§ 13. Unsecured debts bore two sorts of interest, with reference to commercial and non-commercial debts. The commercial interest included in it the insurance risk. Mer-

---

[1] *AŚ.*, Ch. 72, p. 187.

[2] चौरैर्हृतं जलेनोढमग्निना दग्धमेव वा ।
न दद्याद्यदि तस्मात् स न संहरति किंचन ॥ *M.*, viii. 188.

[3] *Yājñ.* II. 40., प्रपन्नं साधयन्नर्थं न वाच्यो नृपतेर्भवेत् ।

chants took long voyages and journeys by land and sea entailing great risks. The traders by land-route passed through jungles, which in those days constituted semi-independent buffer states, and had to pay interest, according to the Artha-Śāstra, at 10% per month. The sea-traders paid as high as 20% per month.[1] On the other hand, from ordinary people only 2% per month could be realised at Law, and 1¼ at Dharma. The tendency of the Dharma was to lower the rates. Yet Gautama allows the maximum (the 'Sea') rate 20%.[2] Originally the Dharma School looked upon money-lending with disfavour. Āpastamba forbids food to Brahmins from 'those living by lending' [I. 6. 18 (20-22)]. Baudhāyana cites [I. 5 (2)] that all the Dharma authorities condemn the usurer as a great sinner.

§ 14. The Mānava introduced a new set of laws on interest (VIII. 140-142). He accepts the vyavahāra rate of 5%, but makes the increase binding on castes other than Brahmins. He grades even interest by caste. Accordingly, the Śūdra had to pay the most. Evidently, the rate increased to five from two per centum since Kauṭilya's time. The Mānava mentions the rate of Vasishṭha under his name, but 1% to 5% he finds as the established legal rate. It seems that capacity to pay higher interest increased with the prosperity and wealth of the country. Yet the Mānava, by allocating caste to rates of interest, sought to stop the tide of the economic law in favour of the Brahmin. The Kshatriya who had the least necessity of borrowing had to pay 3%, while the Vaiśya paid the real current rate 4% and the Śūdra 5%. Yājñavalkya, here again, follows the Mānava (II. 37). Vishṇu repeals the caste rates (II. 2-3).

As to the interest on commercial debts, the Mānava leaves it entirely open (VIII. 157). The commentators explain that 'the

[1] *AŚ.*, Ch. 68, p. 174. सपादपणा धर्म्या मासवृद्धिः पणशतस्य । पञ्चपणा व्यावहारिकी । दशपणा कान्तारकाणां । विंशतिपणा सामुद्राणां । *Cf. Yājñ.*, II. 38.

[2] *Gaut.*, XII. 29. कुसीदवृद्धिर्धर्म्या विंशतिः पञ्चमाषी मासम् । And so does the revised Baudhāyana (1. 5. 22. 25).

sea-voyage' includes trade routes by land. This is confirmed by Yājñavalkya who gives the Artha-Śāstra rates of 10% and 20% and in the alternative leaves the commercial rate to free contract.[1]

Yājñavalkya allows only the Dharma rate $1\frac{1}{4}\%$ in case of debts secured by pledges, and allows the caste rate of 'Manu' in other cases.[2] Interest above the legal rates was regarded as usury, and not recoverable.[3] A further limit was placed by not allowing interest to accumulate above d o u b l e t h e a m o u n t o f t h e p r i n c i p a l.[4] 'In loans, interest paid at one time shall never exceed the double (of the principal).' Yājñavalkya reiterates it (II. 39), with some variations tending towards an increase about 'interest' in kind.[5] He is followed by Vishṇu in clear terms: *hiraṇyasya parā vṛidhdhir dviguṇā*, 'on cash, the highest interest is two-times' (*Cf.* Gautama, XII. 29-31). This law is in conformity with the law of the Artha-Śāstra, which throws light on the meaning of *dviguṇa*, 'double', used here. The Artha-Śāstra in Ch. 68, p. 174, gives the law: "If (interest) is allowed to accumulate owing either to intention (*stambhapravishṭa*) or the absence abroad, double the capital (*mūlyadviguṇaṁ dadyāt*), shall be paid. A creditor, who sues for four times the amount lent, shall pay a fine of four times the total amount under the debt (*bandha*)." The last passage shows that the creditor could sue for upto three times the capital lent. That is, he could sue for the capital plus twice the amount as interest. And this is also the natural meaning of the words of Manu and Yājñavalkya.

---

[1] *Yājñ.*, II. 38. कान्तारगास्तु दशकं सामुद्रा विंशकं शतम् ।
दद्युर्वा स्वकृतां वृद्धिं सर्वे सर्वासु जातिषु ॥

[2] *Ibid.* 37. अशीतिभागो वृद्धिः स्यान्मासि मासि सबन्धके ।
वर्णक्रमाच्छतं द्वित्रिचतुष्पञ्चकमन्यथा ॥

[3] *Manu.*, VIII. 152. कृतानुसारादधिका व्यतिरिक्ता न सिध्यति ।

[4] *Ibid.*, 151. कुसीदवृद्धिर्द्वैगुण्यं नात्येति सकृदाहृता ।

[5] *Yājñ.*, II. 39. सन्ततिस्तु पशुस्त्रीणां रसस्याष्टगुणा परा ।
वस्त्रधान्यहिरण्यानां चतुस्त्रिद्विगुणा तथा ॥

But the commentators of Manu, commencing with Medhātithi, unanimously hold that 'the double' covers both the principal and interest. Medhātithi expressly rules out the other interpretation: "if it is said that the 'two-fold' ('double') character applies to interest, and that with the capital debt the amount becomes three-fold, it will not be admissible. (In 'two-fold,') 'fold' is part of the whole......" This latter interpretation is recognised by our law-courts to-day.

§ 15. The Mānava does not allow compound interest (VII. 154); nor does it allow Kāyika ('corporal') interest, that is, in the shape of labour. The 'corporal' interest was evidently already an archaic form; it is not found in the Artha-Śāstra, nor is its prohibition repeated in Yājñavalkya. Compound interest does not seem to have prevailed, for Yājñavalkya does not mention it. Penal interest, called *Kāritā Vṛiddhi*, 'stipulated interest', that is, a rate contracted for but not allowed by law, was illegal.[1] Compound interest, if agreed to in a different place (foreign place), was illegal outside that place and beyond the time agreed upon (VIII. 156).

§ 16. The Mānava is unusually full on interest. It seems that the question was still in controversy owing to changing economic conditions.[2] By the time of Yājñavalkya the rates had settled down.

§ 17. The rule of limiting the amount is of present interest.

Rule of '*Dandupat.*'

It is known as the rule of *Dandupat*, and is held binding on all Hindus in the presidency of Bombay by the Bombay High Court, and in the presidency town

---

[1] *Manu*, VIII 153. नातिसांवत्सरीं वृद्धिं न चादृष्टां विनिर्हरेत् ।
चक्रवृद्धिः कालवृद्धिः कायिता कारिका च या ॥

[2] A work, called *Kusîda-Sûtra*, is mentioned in the *Mahābhāshya*, (P. IV. 4. 9). Was it a treatise on *Interest*, or by *Kusîda*? A Sûtra on currency is mentioned in the Pāli books.

of Calcutta by the Calcutta High Court, as the Hindu law of contract is still held applicable in the absence of a provision in the Indian Contract Act, the Interest Act or the Transfer of Property Act, on the point.

"Dandupat" applied to secured debts only.

The Artha-Śāstra proves that the laws about interest, which we find in the Mānava, had already been introduced by the Artha School, except a few exceptions. For instance, (*a*) Interest in kind had been limited, though its rates were greatly reduced in the time of the Mānava. (*b*) The rule of d o u b l e d a c c u m u l a t i o n had become definite. It is, however, noticeable that it r e l a t e d o n l y t o s e c u r e d d e b t s, and it again appears with the same definiteness in Yājñavalkya.[1] It must be therefore taken that the rule in the Mānava similarly refers to secured debts, which is indicated by the preceding verse of 'Manu.'[2]

Gautama on interest.

§ 18. Interest was payable e v e r y y e a r, unless the debtor was abroad. This settles the great controversy of the commentators on the meaning of the word *sāṁvatsarī* in VIII., 153 of the Mānava.[3] G a u t a m a quotes this rule as enjoined by some.[4] As the rule is in Chapter 12 of Gautama dealing with king's laws, evidently he refers to Kauṭilya. Gautama knows the rule of double accumulation as well.[5] Gautama is the only Dharma-writer who mentions these new rules on interest. This is another indication of the date of Gautama's sūtras in their present edition.

---

1 *Yājñ.*, II. 58. आधिः प्रणश्येद्द्विगुणे धने यदि न मोच्यते ।
काले कालकृतो नश्येत् फलभोग्यो न नश्यति ॥

2 *Manu*, VIII. 150. यः स्वामिनाननुज्ञातमाधिं भुङ्क्तेऽविचक्षणः ।
तेनार्धवृद्धिर्मोक्तव्या तस्य भोगस्यनिष्कृतिः ॥

3 See *supra* p. 185, *n.* 1.

4 *Gaut.*, XII. 30. नातिसांवत्सरीमित्येके ।

5 *Ibid.* 31. चिरस्थाने द्वैगुण्यं प्रयोगस्य ॥

§ 19. The Artha-Śāstra gives some other rules which are not found in the Dharma codes. For instance, interest was not allowed to accumulate against minors, bachelors, students while away from home for study, the poor, and those engaged in long sacrifices.[1] The rules approved by the Mānava were selected few. Others, *e.g.*, the last set, were rejected by it. The tendency was to remove disabilities from capital. Otherwise, the Mānava would not omit the rule in favour of long sacrifices. It may be that the Mānava's one-year law was interpreted to mean, as it literally does, "interest exceeding one year shall not be claimed"; and this would have been a sufficient protection. But this interpretation will make the law about accumulation nugatory. It seems that, the creditor was compelled to sue every year; he, on his part, was not allowed to court accumulation. The rule of yearly realisation was to be slackened when the debtor wanted it.

Other rules on Interest.

§ 20. A remarkable rule exists in the Kauṭilîya. When the debt has become due, and money has been tendered, but the creditor has failed to take it back, he cannot claim it after 10 years.[2] The Mānava which is generally against the bar of time (VIII. 145),[3] seems to accept the Artha-Śāstra law, for in case of chattel the Mānava also allows a limitation of 10 years (VIII. 147-148). The conditions for the fulfilment of the rule is perfect:

Limitation by time.

"(But in general) whatever (chattel) an owner sees enjoyed by others during ten years, while though present, he says nothing, that (chattel) he shall not recover. If (the owner) is neither an idiot nor a minor, and if (his chattel) is enjoyed (by another) before

[1] *AS.*, Ch. 68, p. 174. दीर्घसत्रव्याधिगुरुकुलोपरुद्धं बालमसारं वा नर्णमनुवर्धेत ।

[2] *Ibid.* दशवर्षोपेक्षितमृणमप्रतिग्राह्यम् ।

[3] आधिश्चोपनिधिश्चोभौ न कालात्ययमर्हतः ।

his eyes, it is lost to him by law, the enjoyer shall retain it." Yājñavalkya has also the rule of 10 years' adverse possession for chattel (II. 24)

Priority.

§ 21. Kauṭilya, and following him Yājñavalkya, says that the debtor would be sued in order of the date of debts, debts owed to Government and priest (*'Srotriya'*) holding priority by law.[1] The Mānava does not adopt this rule. Probably it is a case of omission. In Kauṭilya there is a second part to this rule which seems to me to be a law of *insolvency*. We have already seen that interest, in case of a poor creditor, was not allowed by him to run. Here he says that when a debtor is leaving the country the total debts due should be claimed by the aggregate of the creditors.[2] A recorded case in the *Rājataraṅgiṇī*, which we shall discuss later in this lecture, shows that a man, who wanted to turn insolvent, cleared his debts to the best of his ability by selling off his properties, and left the country (VI. 16). It seems that suits by all the creditors would have entitled them to a rateable distribution, and the rule of priority was suspended.

The law on debtors, unable to pay their debts, seems to have become hard with the supremacy of the Dharma law. The Mānava and Yājñavalkya not only omit the above rule, but make pauper debtors work for their creditors.[3]

---

[1] *AŚ.*, Ch. 68, p. 175. नानार्णसमवाये तु नैकौ द्वौ युगपदभिवदेयातां ।… तत्रापि गृहीतानुपूर्व्यां राजश्रोत्रियद्रव्यं वा पूर्वं प्रतिपादयेत् ।

Yājñ., II. 41. गृहीतानुक्रमाद्दाप्यो धनिनामधमर्णिकः ।
दत्वा तु ब्राह्मणायैव नृपतिस्तदनन्तरम् ॥

[2] *AŚ.*, *loc. cit.* अन्यत्र प्रतिष्ठमानात् । Kauṭilya—"Excepting the case of a debtor going abroad, no debtor shall be simultaneously sued for more than one debt by one or two creditors." *'Going abroad'* was an act of insolvency.

[3] *Manu*, VIII. 177. कर्मणापि समं कुर्याद्धनिकायाधमर्णिकः ।

Yājñ., II. 43. हीनजातिं परिक्षीणमृणार्थं कर्म कारयेत् ।

§ 22. In mortgages, bonds were executed, according to the Artha-Śāstra, as soon as the agreement was complete.[1] It is called karaṇa in the Artha-Śāstra. The same term is used by the Mānava.[2] When the stipulated time was run through, both in simple and usufructuary mortgages, the cause of action arose and a suit became due.

Bonds

Novation

This could be put off, according to the Mānava, by renewing the contract through a new deed.[3] If interest was not paid up-to-date, it was included in the bond debt and 'the sum' was changed.[4] This was the only case where compound interest is allowed by the Mānava. Here it formed part of the consideration of novation. The question of the compound interest in the bond was limited by the stipulation of time and place, 'beyond which it would cease to be of value to the creditor.' (VIII. 156).[5]

§ 23. Yājñavalkya describes a new sort of bond. In this the charitra, 'character,' of the debtor was mortgaged (bandha).[6] This was a bond of honour, that is, only word of honour was pledged there and no property. There is yet another kind of deed mentioned in the same verse of Yājñavalkya : it is Satyaṅkara, 'Instrument of Oath (or Truth).' In this no interest was mentioned and the money recoverable was double the sum paid, while the Honour Bond carried legal interest.[7]

---

[1] *AŚ.*, Ch. 8, p. 148.

[2] *Manu*, VIII. 154. ऋणं दातुमशक्तो यः कर्तुमिच्छेत् पुनः क्रियाम् ।
स दत्वा निर्जितां वृद्धिं करणं परिवर्तयेत् ॥ (In Jolly's ed. it is कारणं)

[3] *Ibid.*, VIII. 155. अदर्शयित्वा तत्रैव हिरण्यं परिवर्तयेत् । (to be read with the previous verse).

[4] *Ibid.* यावती संभवेद्वृद्धिस्तावतीं दातुमर्हति ।

[5] चक्रवृद्धिं समारूढो देशकालव्यवस्थितः ।
अतिक्रामन्देशकालौ न तत्फलमवाप्नुयात् ॥

[6] *Yājñ.*, II. 61. चरित्रबन्धककृतं सवृद्ध्या दापयेद्धनम् ।

[7] *Ibid.* सत्यङ्कारकृतं द्रव्यं द्विगुणं प्रतिदापयेत् ॥

Attestation and Registration.

§ 24.* As to the necessary contents and the number of witnesses necessary to attest the document, we have already discussed the details. Between the time of the Mānava and Vishṇu a system of registering bonds had grown up. Vishṇu says that a document is called *'attested by the king'* when it is initialled by the Registrar of the Adhi-karaṇa,[1] which here seems to be a technical term, connected with *karaṇa*, 'deed', and probably not the general term denoting 'Government Office.' The same officer under the same name is met with in the Rājataraṅgiṇī.[2] King Yaśaskara of Kashmir heard a forgery case on appeal. There the letter *r* had been changed into *s*, which converted *rahitaṁ*, 'without,' into *sahitaṁ*, 'with.' The document was registered, and the appellant lost his case in all the lower courts, 'step by step.' The king sent for the books of account of the defendant and looked into the entry under the date of the deed. It was found in the debit column (*vyaya-madhye*) that Rs. 1,000 was paid to the Registrar (adhikaraṇalekhaka). The Registrar was entitled only to a small fee. The judges of the King's Council would not yet be convinced by this evidence. The Registrar was summoned, and he confessed his guilt. The change was made in the Registry Office (VI. 1-41).

Other codes also mention alternative registration either at the 'King's office' or at the office of the Jānapada, and also at the Registrar's office of the Paura.[3] The last two were corporate associations with great constitutional powers.[4]

Liability of heirs for predecessor's debts.

§ 25. Yājñavalkya, II. 50-51, deals with the liability of the heirs for the debts of the deceased. The general law had been that no member of the family was bound to pay a debt contracted by

---

1 *Vishṇu*, VII. 3. राजाधिकरणे तन्नियुक्तकायस्थकृतं तदध्यक्षकरचिह्नितं राजसाक्षिकम्।

2 *Rājataraṅgiṇi*, VI. 38.

3 Vyāsa and Bṛihaspati cited by Aparārka, p. 691, and p. 683 (*sub* Y. II. 92 and 84). Führer, *Vasishṭha*, p. 84 (*chīrakaṁ°*).

4 See *Hindu Polity*, II, Chs. XXVII-XXVIII.

the chief of the family unless it were for family necessity.[1] Kauṭilya (p. 174) makes an exception in the case of a debt contracted by the father and the duty of the son and the grandson to pay it after the death of the father. He qualifies that debt as being for his life, marriage, land, or suretyship,—provided the debt was unlimited with respect to time and place, otherwise it would have been barred by the covenant itself. In these cases the son and the grandson, as such, were bound to pay the debt.[2] As to interest, Kauṭilya limits the liability to sons and does not extend it to grandsons. Similarly, 'heirs (which will include sons etc., as a matter of course) or others who succeeded to the assets of the deceased, or the surety who joined in the debt, were liable for the interest.'[3]

This, according to the rule for construing sūtras, relates to a debt which was 'limited with regard to time and place.' The 'unlimited' debt was to be paid only by 'sons, grandsons, and heirs, provided they received (corresponding) assets of the deceased.' Without receiving assets only sons and grandsons had to pay the debt in case the debt was as qualified above.

Kauṭilya distinguishes those taking assets from 'dāyāda' or heirs. The distinction is made to denote a stranger *e.g.*, one who married the widow of the deceased; with the widow he would receive the property to which widow had succeeded and would become liable for the debts of the deceased. It would also denote the king in case of an escheat.

The son, the grandson, the *dāyāda* (heir), the *riktha-hara* (stranger receiving the estate), and the surety were not bound to

---

1 *Manu*, VIII. 166. ग्रहीता यदि नष्टः स्यात् कुटुम्बे च कृतो व्ययः ।
दातव्यं बान्धवैस्तत् स्यात् प्रविभक्तैरपि स्वतः ।

2 *AŚ.*, Ch. 68, p. 175. असंख्यातदेशकालं तु पुत्राः पौत्राः दायादा वा रिक्थं हरमाणा दद्युः । जीवितविवाहभूमिप्रातिभाव्यमसंख्यातदेशकालं तु पुत्राः पौत्रा वा वहेयुः ।

3 *Ibid.*, p. 174. प्रेतस्य पुत्राः कुसीदं दद्युः दायादा वा रिक्थहराः सहग्राहिणः प्रतिभुवो वा ।

pay the following debts: (*a*) the "useless" and (*b*) "suretyship" debts, and (*c*) "minor's suretyship" debts of the deceased.[1]

The latter law of Kauṭilya is expressed by the Mānava, VIII, 159-160: (*a*) "suretyship debts," (*b*) "idle," "gambling," or "drinking" "gifts," and the "balance of a fine or toll"—'the son is not bound to pay'[2]; 'the suretyship referred to is for appearance of parties in court.'[3]

§ 26. The Mānava does not saddle the son and the grandson with the 'pious duty'. It gives VIII. 166 which negatives the theory: "If the debtor be dead and (the money borrowed) were expended for the family, it must be paid by the relatives out of their own estate, even if they are divided." In other words, the members of the family of the late *kartā* or manager are liable for the debt, only if it was for the benefit of the family. The following law of Yājñavalkya has been interpreted by Aparārka and Vijñāneśvara to mean that there is a duty on the son to pay up his father's debt even when he does not receive any assets from the father:—

'Pious duty'

"The son shall not pay the paternal (debts) contracted for wines, lust, and gambling, or due on account of the unpaid portion of a fine or toll, or idle promise" (II. 47). "When the father has left the country (*i.e.*, become insolvent), or died, or become afflicted (physically), his debts proved by witnesses, if disputed, should be paid by the son" (II. 50).

"He who has received the estate or the wife of the deceased should be made to pay his debts. The son in whom has the property vested [of the deceased father] to the exclusion of others (*putro'nanyāśritadravyaḥ*) [shall be made to pay his father's debt]. Of a sonless debtor, those who hold his estate (shall be made

---

[1] *AŚ.*, Ch. 68, pp. 174-175. न प्रातिभाव्यमन्यदसारं बालप्रातिभाव्यम् ।

[2] *Manu*, VIII. 159. प्रातिभाव्यं वृथादानमाक्षिकं सौरिकं च यत् ।
दण्डशुल्कावशेषं च न पुत्रो दातुमर्हति ॥

[3] See *Manu*, VIII. 160.

to pay his debts)" II. 51.[1] This by itself, or read with the law of Kauṭilya[2] which Yājñavalkya, as a rule, closely follows, means that the son to be liable must have inherited property from the father. This is supported by Vishṇu who agrees with our codes generally. Vishṇu in VI. 27, 29, 34, 35, 36, makes it clear that the liability depends on inheritance or benefit. But Vijñāneśvara, the author of the *Mitākshara* commentary, and Aparārka interpreted it differently. King Aparārka, commenting on verse II. 51, said that *riktha-grāha* ('one who has received the estate,') does not apply to the 'son' (न पुत्रपरो रिक्थ-ग्राह-शब्दः), and relying on a text (पुत्रपौत्रैर्ऋणं देयम्, 'debt is to be discharged by sons and grandsons') Aparārka leans to the view that grandsons, in the absence of sons, should pay the debts of a wealthless grandfather (तेन निर्धनस्य पितामहस्य पुत्राभाव एव पौत्रा ऋणापकरणेऽधिक्रियन्ते, p. 653). But the text of Yājñavalkya qualifies the son with 'in whom has vested the property to the exclusion of others' (अनन्याश्रितद्रव्यः), which clearly contemplates the condition of inheriting and possessing assets from the father. This has been explained away by Aparārka as meaning an 'independent' son (स्वाधीनधनः; यस्तु स्वातन्त्र्येण वर्त्तते, p. 652). Viśvarūpa, an earlier authority, however, takes the expression to mean just as I have translated above, and says, 'the son of one who has left no property shall not be liable' (नत्वद्रव्यस्य पुत्रो दद्यात्), 'for debt follows assets (ऋणस्य द्रव्यानुसारित्वात्). He cites the definite text of Kātyāyana that unless a son inherits property from his father *in presenti* he cannot be made

---

[1] सुराकामद्यूतकृतं दण्डशुल्कावशिष्टकम् ।
वृथादानं तथैवेह पुत्रो दद्यान्न पैतृकम् । (II. 47).
पितरि प्रोषिते प्रेते व्यसनाभिप्लुतेऽपि वा ।
पुत्रपौत्रैर्ऋणं देयं निह्नवे साक्षिभावितम् ॥ (II. 50).
रिक्थग्राह ऋणं दाप्यो योषिद्ग्राहस्तथैव च ।
पुत्रोऽनन्याश्रितद्रव्यः पुत्रहीनस्य रिक्थिनः ॥ (II. 51).

प्रेतस्य पुत्राः कुसीदं दद्युः । दायादा वा रिक्थहराः सहग्राहिणः प्रतिभुवो वा ।... असंख्यातदेशकालं

to pay, even if the son were very rich.[1] But Vijñāneśvara in his Mitāksharā interpreted this provision of Yājñavalkya against its express text, ignoring though not misinterpreting *ananyāśritadravyaḥ*,[3] on the basis of the 'pious duty' texts cited by Aparārka, which in reality do not lay down what they are alleged to do. However, that has become the interpretation of the Mitāksharā School, although the Anglo-Indian law by its independent process has in effect restored the law of Yājñavalkya by limiting the pious duty of the son and the grandson to the measure of the assets inherited.

Our Codes do not contemplate any liability of a son to pay his father's debts during the latter's life-time. Yājñavalkya (II. 50) and Vishṇu (VI. 27) mention death or civil death.[2]

§ 27. Bṛihaspati preserves the law that a grandson was not liable to pay interest on the debt of his grandfather.[4] Nārada (I. 4) says that if a lawful debt is unpaid by the son, it must be discharged by the grandson. "The liability does not descend to the fourth."[5] This is confirmed by Vishṇu (VI. 27-28). There is an *artha-vāda* (explanatory) verse in Nārada

---

पुत्राः पौत्राः दायादा वा रिक्थं हरमाणा दद्युः । जीवित-विवाह-भूमि-प्रा तमाव्यसंस्थात-देश-कालं तु पुत्राः पौत्राः वा वहेयुः । (pp. 174-175).

It should be noticed that in respect of the former class of debts, the sons and the grandsons are exactly in the same position as any other successor to the estate of the deceased debtor. The latter class are debts benefiting the family, and for them the sons and the grandsons are liable for an independent reasoning, not any pious duty.

1 यथाह कात्यायनः यावन्न पैतृकं द्रव्यं विद्यमानं लभेत् सुतः ।
सुसमृद्धोऽपि दाप्यः स्यात् तावन्नैवाधमर्णिकः ॥

2 The law interpreted by our Courts and the Privy Council makes a son liable even in the father's life-time on the doctrine of pious obligation for which there is no sanction in the Codes.

3 *Vijñāneśvara* on *Yājñ.*, II. 51.

4 *Bṛihaspati*, X. 49 (Jolly). See quotation in VM., p. 341 :

ऋणमात्मीयवत् पित्र्यं पुत्रैर्देयं विभावितम् ।
पितामहं समन्देयन्न देयन्तत्सुतस्य तु ॥

5 *Nār.*, I. 4. क्रमादव्याहृतं प्राप्तं पुत्रैर्यन्नर्णमुद्धृतम् ।
दद्युः पैतामहं पौत्रास्तच्चतुर्थान्निवर्तते ।

(1. 6) which says that one's three ancestors are to be worshipped.[1] This is, like the last (1. 5), a quotation emphasising the moral liability of descendants and the hope of the ancestors for religious benefit from the descendants. Verse 1. 6 gave rise to some ambiguity as to whether the liability in debts extends to the great-grandson. This happened at a time when the Code of Nārada was the ruling authority in Magadha. The following case of *Srīdhara* vs. *Mahīdhara* noted in A s a h ā y a 's commentary on Nārada's Code proves it.[2] "Three deceased ancestors, *i.e.*, the father, grandfather, and great-grandfather, may claim the discharge of their terrestrial and celestial liabilities from the fourth in descent. This rule is illustrated by the history of an action which was brought before the court in Patna (Pāṭaliputra). A merchant of the Brāhmana caste, by the name of Śrîdhara, had lent the whole of his wealth, consisting of 10,000 drammas (drachmas), which he had gained through great labour, to a trader, by the name of Devadhara, on condition that interest amounting to two per cent, per mensem, on the principal should be paid to him. The interest was duly paid to Śrîdhara at the end of the first month. In the second month, however, Devadhara met his death through an accident. His son died of an attack of cholera. Devadhara's great-grandson alone was left. His name was M a h î d h a r a. As he was addicted to licentious courses, the management of the estate was undertaken by his maternal uncles. They got into the hands of a cunning Brāhmaṇa called S m ā r t a D u r d h a r a, who advised him not to pay a single rupee to Śrîdhara, as he could prove from the law-books that he had no claim to the money The uncles of Mahīdhara, much pleased with this piece of advice,

Srīdhara v. *Mahīdhara.*

---

[1] पूज्यनीयास्त्रयोऽतीता उपजीव्यास्त्रयोऽग्रतः ।
एतत्पुरुषसन्तानमृणयोः स्याच्चतुर्थके ॥
According to Jolly it is of doubtful authenticity, not being found in the shorter text. Jolly, *S.B.E.*, XXXIII, p. 44, *n.*

[2] Jolly's translation of Asahāya on *Nār.*, I. 6, S.B.E., XXXIII., pp. 43-44.

promised to give 1,000 drammas to the Brāhmaṇa if they had not to pay the money to Śrîdhara. Thus, when at the close of the second month, the uncles and guardians of Devadhara's great-grandson, Mahîdhara, were asked by Śrîdhara to pay 200 drammas, being the amount of interest due on the sum lent to Devadhara, they refused payment. They said, 'We do not owe you the principal, much less any amount of interest. The Brāhmaṇa Smārta-Durdhara has pointed out to us that the obligation to pay stops with the fourth in descent.' Śrîdhara was struck dumb with grief and terror, on hearing this announcement made to him. When he regained his senses (*i.e.*, recovered from the shock), he repaired to the court of justice, attended by his family, friends, and servants, and impeached Mahîdhara, together with his uncles, for their dishonesty. Both parties took sureties. The uncles of Mahîdhara engaged Smārta Durdhara to plead for them. After pretending that his clients were connected with his family by a friendship of long standing, he went on to refer to a text of Nārada (I. 5), as proving that the obligation to pay the debts of ancestors stop with the fourth in descent. All his arguments, however, were refuted and held out to derision by a learned Brāhmaṇa, by the name of Smārta-Śekhara, who, at the end of his address, charged him openly with having taken a bribe from his clients. The consequence was that Mahîdhara and his uncles lost their cause."

The case was not decided on merits. And therefore it does not decide the point. Vijñaneśvara is of opinion that the liability does not extend to the great-grandson.[1] And this is correct, as it is confirmed by other Smṛitis. Asahāya was misled by the case of Mahîdhara and misconstrued verse 6. Probably the case would have been decided otherwise, if the etiquette of the Hindu Bar was not in issue[2]. We should notice that Yājñavalkya has extended the law from 'death' (Kauṭilya) to 'absence abroad.'[3]

[1] Vijñāneśvara on *Yājñ.* II. 15.
[2] See Lect. XI below.
[3] See *Yājñ.*, II. 50, quoted p. 193, *n*, 1 above.

Leaving the country was an act of insolvency. The later Codes define the period of absence which would entitle the creditor to call upon the son and the grandson to pay : 20 years' absence was made equivalent to death or refusal for the purpose.[1] Vishṇu includes in 'death' 'taking to ascetic life' as well,[2] for it was a civil death like insolvency.

Vasishṭha's rule of legal interregnum for interest.

§ 28. The law of interest was the subject of minute discussion and juristical development. It was carried much further than our two Codes, by Nārada, Bṛihaspati and Kātyāyana. Between the two Codes, or of a time earlier, a remarkable doctrine is found quoted in Vasishṭha (II. 49).[3] When the king dies, the running of interest ceases until the coronation of the new king. This unnecessarily puzzled Bühler.[4] All official and legal transactions were dated in regnal years of the ruling kings, counted from his coronation. With this we are familiar from Aśoka's inscriptions as well as documents in Sanskrit. The period between the two points of time—the death of the ruling king and his successor's coronation—was a legal interregnum. It was non-existent in the eye of the law, and no interest, therefore, argued the Dharma jurist, was to be counted for the period. We, however, do not find it in our Codes or the Codes subsequent to them. It seems that the doctrine never found approval with practical legislators.

Later laws.

§ 29. Nārada provides for a case which was left out by the two Codes. Interest does not run unless there be an agreement. But even in the absence of an agreement, when debt is demanded and is

---

1 See *Vishṇu*, VI. 27. धनग्राहिणि प्रेते प्रव्रजिते द्विदश समाः प्रवसिते वा तत्पुत्रपौत्रैर्धनं देयम् ।

2 *Ibid.*

3 राज्ञा तु मृतभावेन द्रव्यवृद्धिं विनाशयेत् ।
पुना राजाभिषेकेण द्रव्यमूलं च वर्धते ॥ (Führer, p. 9) II. 49.

4 Bühler. *S.B.E.*, XIV., p. 15 *n.* : "it gives a rule ordering all money transaction to be stopped during the period which intervenes between the death of a king and the coronation of his successor. I am, however, unable to point out any parallel passages confirming this."

not paid, interest accrues from the date of demand, at five *per centum* (which had been the legal rate). In friendly loans, in the absence of an agreement, no interest was chargeable, but such a loan was presumed to have been advanced for six months only.[1]

Interest awarded as damages where no contract.

Kātyāyana provides further for cases where a debtor has taken a loan called *yāchitika* (payable on demand), and goes abroad before a demand is made, (there being no contract for payment of interest), interest will run after the expiry of a year, and where demand has been made before the debtor's departure, the debtor is allowed a free grace of three months whereafter interest begins to run. While the debtor is in the country, interest will date from the demand.[2] On the authority of these texts of Nārada and Kātyāyana, the author of the Mitāksharā has deduced the rule that in cases of absence of a stipulation for interest, interest will be payable from the date of demand.[3] It is interesting to note that this part of the Hindu law of contract, in the absence of provisions in the Indian Contract Act and the Interest Act, was held to be applicable between Hindus by the High Court of Bombay.[4] Cases may still arise where the Hindu law of contract may yet be found providing for situations unprovided for by modern legislation.

§ 30. The immense foreign trade of the period necessitated Nārada to say that contracts of loan entered into foreign countries were to be governed by the laws of the place of contract (I. 105-106).

Lex loci in loans.

---

[1] I. 108-109 : न वृद्धिः प्रीतिदत्तानां स्यादनाकारिता क्वचित् ।
अनाकारितमप्यूर्ध्वं वत्सरार्धात्प्रवर्धते ॥
प्रीतिदत्तं तु यत्किंचिन्न तद्वर्धत्ययाचितम् ।
याच्यमानमदत्तं चेद्वर्धते पञ्चकं शतम् ॥

[2] See citations in the *Mitāksharā* under Y. II. 39, 'दद्युर्वा' etc.

[3] *Mitā.* on Y. II. 39 (in some editions, numbered II. 38).

[4] *Saunadanappa* vs. *Shivabasawa*, 31 B. 354.

Personal liberty of debtors.

§ 31. The royal law was very jealous with regard to its jurisdiction in cases of loans. As Kauṭilya put it, 'the nature of the transactions between creditors and debtors on which the welfare of the kingdom depends, shall always be scrutinised' (Ch. 68, p. 174). The Artha-Śāstra law discouraged interference by the creditor with the personal liberty of the debtor. We have seen the attitude of our Codes on the subject. The later Codes, however, followed the policy of the Artha-Śāstra. The Artha-Śāstra, for instance, prohibited the arrest of cultivators and Government servants while at their work, for debts. Nor was a wife, although party to a contract by her husband, to be arrested. Bṛihaspati forbids self-help by a creditor—'where the claim is disputed, whosoever attempts (to recover his debt) without reporting to the king (the law-court), shall be taken prisoner and punished.'[2] Nārada directs that realisation of a debt from a solvent debtor, refusing to pay, is to proceed through the king.[3] According to Kātyāyana, force was not to be employed in realising debts from the king, master, a Brahmin, heir, friend (surety ?), merchants, cultivators and artists. The only exception was 'the wicked' (*i.e.*, *malafide* debtors).[4] The Dharma doctrine about the position of the debtor, well-nigh that of a slave, was not accepted in the law courts. The old right of the creditor with regard to personal attachment was reduced to a vanishing point.

§ 32. There is no provision in our two Codes which corresponds to Kauṭilya's "Interest on debts due from persons engaged in long sacrifices, or who are suffering from disease, or who are detained for study, or who are minors or too poor, shall not accumulate" (Ch. 68, p. 174).

---

[1] 'Cultivators or government servants shall not be caught hold of for debts in times of their work'. [P. 175 (Ch. 68)].

[2] अनावेद्य तु राज्ञे यः सन्दिग्धेऽर्थे प्रवर्तते ।
प्रसह्य स विनेयः स्यात् स चाप्यर्थो न सिध्यति ॥ Cited by Nîlakaṇṭha in V. Mayūkha, p. 70.

Kātyāyana has a similar provision. *Ibid.* Yama (*ibid.*) also directs intervention of the Court. 'A solvent debtor who does not pay through wickedness shall be made to pay by the king.'

[3] Nîlakaṇṭha's quotation in *V. Mayūkha*, p. 69. राजानं स्वामिनं etc.

[4] Nîlakaṇṭha, p. 69.

LECTURE XI.

CONTRACT (*continued*) AND TRANSFER OF PROPERTY.

Surety—joint and several liability—heir's liability—Agency—torts by agents—Contract of Carriage—Contract of Service—Slavery—Maurya law of slavery—Partnership—Corporations—Transfers—Mortgage—Pledge—Mortgage and doctrine of Trust—Redemption—limitation—Conditional Sale—Registrar of Adhi—Trust Deposits—Title and Possession—Purchase in market overt—Law of finder—Rescission of contracts—Warranty—Contract of Marriage—Divorce—Specific performance.

Surety.

§ 1. Suretyship (prātibhāvya) in the Mānava is of two kinds: (1) for appearance of a party in court, (2) for payment of debt.[1] The obligation of the surety in the first case ceased when he produced the party in court. The court took sureties from both sides for the appearance of the parties and for court-fees. Class (1) refers to that, and also probably to a surety promising to the creditor to produce the debtor in court at the time a suit was brought. Class (2) was the regular surety who stood guarantee at the time of the loan for repayment in default by the debtor. An heir was not bound for the first class of suretyship but he was so for the second.[2] Yājñavalkya gives a third surety, *prātyayika*, who, according to other Codes, was surety at the ordeal proceeding. The liability of this too did not descend to the heir.[3]

---

[1] *Manu*, VIII. 158-160.

[2] *Ibid*. VIII. 159. प्रातिभाव्ये···न पुत्रोदातुमर्हति। दानप्रतिभुवि प्रेते दायादानपि दापयेत्।

[3] *Yājñ.*, II 54. दर्शनप्रतिभूर्यत्र मृतः प्रात्ययिकोऽपि वा।
न तत्पुत्रा ऋणं दद्युर्दद्यु र्दानाय यः स्थितः॥

The Mānava lays down :

> 'The surety who has paid off the debt shall be sufficiently recompensed. It shall be paid by him who has been discharged by the payment of the surety'.[1]

This means that both the debtor and the co-surety, if any, shall make good the payment made by the surety.

On liability of sureties Yājñavalkya, II. 55-56, says :

> "When there are many sureties they shall pay proportionately. But when they have taken up the liability severally (*lit.*, 'when each one has become the picture of the debtor'), the creditor has the option (as to realisation)." "When (one) surety has been publicly made to pay the amount, those liable to pay the debt shall have to pay double."[2]

The law in the two Codes is substantially the same. But unfortunately the section in the Mānava (VIII. 161) had been misunderstood by the commentators. The law of joint and several liability of surety, so clearly enunciated in Yājñavalkya was known to the time of the Mānava.

§ 2. The law on suretyship is greatly developed in the Codes. Kauṭilya in this respect is far behind. The Codes distinguished two sorts of liabilities (M. VIII. 160-161) which had been known to the Artha-Śāstra, but they proceed further and distinguish between joint and several liabilities. Later authorities further develop the distinction and declare, as rightly pointed out by Vijñaneśvara, that the several liability contemplated is of personal character and that when it descends to the heirs it becomes joint.

---

[1] *Manu*, VIII. 162. निरादिष्टधनश्चेत्तु प्रतिभूः स्यादलंधनः ।
स्वधनादेव तद्दद्यान्निरादिष्ट इति स्थितिः ॥

[2] *Yājñ*. II. 55-56. बहवः स्युर्यदि स्वांशैर्दद्युः प्रतिभुवो धनम् ।
एकच्छायाश्रितेष्वेषु धनिकस्य यथारुचि ॥
प्रतिभूर्दापितो यत्तु प्रकाशं धनिनां धनम् ।
द्विगुणं प्रतिदातव्यमृणिकैस्तस्य तद्भवेत् ॥

§ 3. In view of later authorities[1] it seems certain that the two Codes use the word 'son' designedly to limit the suretyship liability to the son only and not to extend it to the grandson. Here the 'pious duty' liability is thus limited to one generation only. 'Manu' gives a general term '*dāyāda*' (heirs) who are made liable, and does not mention the son in VIII. 160 (which is the substantial section), while in 159 only son is mentioned and no heir. Similarly Yājñavalkya makes all who take from the deceased, liable, and finally son in default of others.[2]

Liability of heir limited to son.

Here the liability arising from suretyship and from ordinary debt parted company with regard to the grandson. Originally, as in Kauṭilya, both for debts and suretyship the grandson was liable,[3] but debt arising from suretyship came to be treated differently. It seems that the Hindu lawyers did not regard a liability arising out of suretyship as a debt proper. It was a debt created by law and not by the man himself. The lawyers of 200 B.C. and later were free to speculate about it as their hand had not been tied by the Dharma law on the subject. The Dharma law had taken note only of debts proper.

§ 4. Kauṭilya says that there can be no relationship of debtor and creditor amongst members of the undivided family, *e.g.*, between father and son, brothers, husband and

---

[1] *Kātyāyana* quoted by Aparārka on *Yājñ*. II. 54:

प्रातिभाव्यागतं पौत्रर्दातव्यं न तु तत्क्वचित् ।
पुत्रेणापि समं देयमृणं सर्वत्र पैत्रिकम् ॥

Vyāsa, Ibid. ऋणं पैतामहं पौत्रः प्रातिभाव्यागतं सुतः ।
समं दद्यात्तत्सुतौ तु न दाप्याविति निश्चयः ॥

In the printed edition of Aparārka it is said on this verse of Vyāsa: "अधमर्णपौत्रप्रतिभूपौत्रयोः पुत्रावृणं प्रातिभाव्यागतं च न दाप्यौ ।" But it must be अधमर्णपौत्रप्रतिभूपुत्रयोः etc.

[2] *Yājñ*. II. 51. रिक्थग्राह ऋणं दाप्यो योषिद्ग्राहस्तथैव च ।
पुत्रोऽनन्याश्रितद्रव्यः पुत्रहीनस्य रिक्थिनः ॥

[3] Cf. AŚ., Ch. 68, p. 174. प्रेतस्य पुत्राः कुसीदं दद्युः । दायादा वा रिक्थहराः सहग्राहिणः प्रतिभुवो वा ।

wife.[1] Yājñavalkya applies this principle to suretyship as well as to lending.[2]

Agency.

§ 5. The principles of agency are applied, as early as the times of Kauṭilya and his predecessors, to acts done by members of the family on behalf of the family. There agency, both express and implied, is clearly recognised. Agency of servants, agency of commercial agents, sales through agents, and tort through agents become subject of law. The Codes further discuss agency between husband and wife, of partners, and in commercial transactions. Any member of the family could be authorised to contract on behalf of the family. A servant or even a slave could act as an agent in the matter of contract. Even a minor, if authorised to act as agent, would bind by his act the principal: the contract entered into by him on his behalf would be valid.[3]

Commercial Agency in Kauṭilya.

§ 6. An agent selling goods of the principal was bound to render all profits to the principal. He was not responsible for the rates, and was expected to sell at the market-rate.[4] His position, however, was that of a trustee.[5] The agent must exercise due diligence of a prudent man. If, for instance, owing to distance and time the price fell down, the principal was entitled to the

---

[1] *AŚ.*, Ch. 68, p. 175. दंपत्योः पितापुत्रयोः भ्रातॄणां चाविभक्तानां परस्परकृतमृणमसाध्यम् ।

[2] *Yājñ.* II. 52. भ्रातॄणामथ दम्पत्योः पितुः पुत्रस्य चैव हि ।
प्रातिभाव्यमृणं साक्ष्यमविभक्ते न तु स्मृतम् ॥

[3] Cf. *AŚ.*, Ch. 58, p. 148. अपाश्रयवद्भिश्च कृताः, पितृमता पुत्रेण, पिता पुत्रवता निष्कुलेन भ्रात्रा, कनिष्ठेनाविभक्तांशेन, पतिमत्या पुत्रवत्या च स्त्रिया, दासाहितकाभ्यां, अप्राप्तातीतव्यवहाराभ्यां··· अन्यत्र निसृष्टव्यवहारेभ्यः ।

[4] *Ibid.*, Ch. 69, p. 179. वैय्यापृत्यकरा यथादेशकालं विक्रीणानाः पण्यं यथाजातमूल्यमुदयं च दद्युः ।
(See the next footnote below for the reading वैय्यापृत्यकरा) ।

[5] And under the Chapter dealing with 'Trust' (*Aupinidhikam*, Ch. 69) he treats the subject of commercial agency, between *vaiyyāapṛitya* (Hindi *vaipārî*) and *vaiyyāpṛitya-kara* (Hindi *aṛhatiyā*) and between master and servant. [See Gaṇapati Sāstrin, *AŚ.*, p. 75, for the reading *vaiyyāpṛi°*].

[6] *AŚ.*, Ch. 69, p. 179. देशकालातिपातने वा परिहीणं सम्प्रदानकालिकेन अर्घेण मूल्यमुदयं च दद्युः ।

market-rate of the time when the goods reached the agent. An agent, even if the price be named by the principal, could not take the profit which accrued by selling at a higher rate; if price came down he would only render account at the lower rate of sale and the price realised.[1]

Commission agents (Sāṁvyavahārikas) and "Guarantor-Agents" were free from all liability even in case of total or partial destruction of the goods by accident or decay. On goods despatched by them to another place and clime the commission agents were entitled to make deductions for cost and damage borne by them and the commission which they paid to other merchant companies. "The rest of their duties are to be considered on the basis of the law of deposit (trust)."[2]

Implied Agency in the two Codes.

§ 7. In these laws of Kauṭilya we practically find all the principles of commercial agency developed. The Codes mainly devote their attention to implied contract of agency. Thus Yājñavalkya under contract (II. 31-33) deals with property recovered by the king. He is to restore the property to the owner,[3] who is evidently regarded as the principal. Manu, VIII. 34, 40, provides similarly in the corresponding place. Unless we take that the finder of the property is looked upon as an agent, we cannot explain the position of the provision in the two Codes.

Husband and wife are not liable for the debts of each other, according to Yājñavalkya, unless they contract as implied agent of the family.[4] The Mānava also implies agency when

---

[1] *Ibid.* यथासम्भाषितं वा विक्रीणाना नोदयमधिगच्छेयुः मूल्यमेव दद्युः । अर्घपतने वा परिहीणं यथापरिहीणमूल्यमूनं दद्युः ।

[2] *Ibid.*, p. 180. सांव्यवहारिकेषु वा प्रात्ययिकेष्वराजवाच्येषु भ्रेषोपनिपाताभ्यां नष्टं विनष्टं वा मूल्यमपि न दद्युः । देशकालान्तरितानां तु पण्यानां क्षयव्ययशुद्धमूल्यमुदयं च दद्युः । पण्यसमवायानां च प्रत्यंशम् । शेषमुपनिधिना व्याख्यातम् ।

[3] *Yājñ.*, II. 33. प्रणष्टाधिगतं देयं नृपेण धनिने धनम् ।

[4] *Ibid.*, 46. न योषित्पतिपुत्राभ्यां न पुत्रेण कृतं पिता ।
दद्यादृते कुटुम्बार्थान्न पतिः स्त्रीकृतं तथा ॥

contract is made for the benefit of the family even unauthorised by other members.[1] It is on the same principle that contracts by the manager of the family are held binding against the whole family estate.

Tort by agents.

§ 8. Injuries of civil nature have been treated both as tort and crime. This feature is found in the law on assault commencing from Kauṭilya down to our second Code. Injury to another's animal, mischief to property, etc., are both torts and crimes. Injury to human person is, as a rule, treated exclusively as crime. The old law of w e r g i l d or V a i r a n i r y ā t a n a, remembered in the Dharma Sūtra of Āpastamba[2], became obsolete before 500 B.C., and probably before 700 B.C., the period of the rise of the Artha law. T o r t s b y a g e n t which drew special attention of the first Dharma codes were those which had been the subject of speculation in the Dharma Schools. These were the ones committed by hired herdsmen. The origin of the law about herdsmen is the administration of the so-called 'Forest areas' of hermitages. The earliest Dharma Sūtra deals with the subject only in connection with hermitage. Out of respect to the Dharma law the Mānava devoted an inordinate space to it (VIII. 229-243). The Artha Śāstra discusses the subject as cattle-trespass, not as a section of contract (p. 172). The subject of master and servant is discussed under the law relating to Slaves and Servants. The Mānava expressly says that the subject is dealt with from the point of view of the Dharma (dharmatatvataḥ).[3] Yājñavalkya follows the Mānava and takes the "Master and Herdsmen" as a separate title (II. 159-167).

For the damage done by cattle the master was responsible and not the herdsman.[4] The measure of the damage done was the

---

1 *Manu*, VIII. 166-167. Cf. *Yājñ.*, II. 45.

2 Cf. Āpastamba, I. 24, 1 ff.

3 *Manu*, VIII. 229. पशुषु स्वामिनाञ्चैव पालानाञ्च व्यतिक्रमे ।
विवादं संप्रवक्ष्यामि यथावद्धर्मतत्त्वतः ।

4 *Yājñ.*, II. 161. गोपस्ताड्यस्तु गोमी तु पूर्वोक्तं दण्डमर्हति ।

cost of the crop eaten.[1] For cattle doing damage under the influence of an Act of God or State, no liability attached to the owner (163). The Mānava gives fewer rules on tort (VIII. 238-243). If the fields are not protected, the liability will be lessened.[2] For torts by drivers of vehicle and by minors, Kauṭilya makes the master and the head of the family responsible.[3]

Contract of Carriage.

§ 9. Contract of carriage is a subject which grew mainly in the two Codes (M. & Y.). The growth proves the growth of trade and commerce on so great a scale that the carrier's business becomes distinct and important.

In "long voyages" the freight depends upon 'punctuality as to time and destination.' This is the rule in river navigation. There is, however, no fixed law as to freight at sea.[4] For Act of God and in the absence of fault on the part of the crew, the ship-owner was not to blame.[5]

The question of freight depended upon the condition of "proper place and time" *i.e.*, time and destination were of essence. But the conditions could not be insisted upon with regard to a "sea voyage."

Verse 405 seems to lay down that empty receptacles of merchandise, brought back in ships, paid a nominal freight.[6] New laws were necessary for sea-trade. Merchants forming companies for sea-trade and going abroad are treated in new laws by Yājñavalkya (II. 259-264). Custom of trade had been recognised as early as the 4th century B.C. (Kauṭilya). Yājñavalkya

---

1 *Yajñ.*, II. 161. यावत् सस्यं विनश्येत्तु तावत् स्यात् क्षेत्रिणः फलम् ।

2 *Manu*, VIII. 238. तथापरिवृतं धान्यं विहिंस्युः पशवो यदि ।
न तत्र प्रणयेद्दण्डं नृपतिः पशुरक्षिणाम् ॥

3 *AŚ.*, Ch. 90, p. 233.

4 *Manu*, VIII. 406. दीर्घाध्वनि यथादेशं यथाकालं तरो भवेत् ।
नदीतीरेषु तद्विद्यात् समुद्रे नास्ति लक्षणम् ॥

5 *Ibid.* 409. दाशापराधतस्तोये दैविके नास्ति निग्रहः ।

6 *Ibid.* 405. रिक्तभाण्डानि यत् किंचित् etc.

says: 'A carrier is to make good the loss of commodity, except that caused by an Act of State or an Act of God.' This shows that the carrier's fee included insurance charges against theft, robbery etc., and must have been high. Failure to start on journey at the appointed time entitled the merchant to recover damage as much as double the carrier's fee.[1]

Contract of Service.

§ 10. Contract of service is considered with reference to contract by artizans, artists, priests, guilds of skilled labour, contract of slavery, pupilage etc. An a r t i z a n, if physically unable to do the work, was excused.[2] Breach of contract was an actionable wrong, the recoverable damage being limited to the immediate and not a remote damage, extending upto double the amount of the wage.[3] The Mānava gives these principles, with the difference that it limits the liability of the workman to forfeiture of wage for the work done, and to a nominal fine in refusal to take up the work.[4] Yājñavalkya makes an exception: when the contract becomes impossible of performance on the part of either party, the wage shall be paid for the work already done, and the contract will be at an end.[5] As to breach by a priest of his contract with the head priest, the same rules are applied (M. VIII. 206).

§ 11. A remarkable rule is given by Yājñavalkya for such contracts where wages are not fixed. The law would presume an i m p l i e d p a r t n e r s h i p between the entrepreneur and the

---

[1] *Yājñ.*, II. 197. अराजदैविकं नष्टं भाण्डं दाप्यस्तु वाहकः ।
प्रस्थानविघ्नकृच्चैव प्रदाप्यो द्विगुणां भृतिम् ॥

[2] *AŚ.*, Ch. 71, p. 184. अशक्तः कुत्सिते कर्मणि व्याधौ व्यसने वा अनुशयं लभेत ।

[3] *Yājñ.*, II. 193. गृहीतवेतनः कर्म त्यजन्द्विगुणमावहेत् ।
अगृहीते समं दाप्यो etc.

[4] *Manu*, VIII. 215-216. भृतो नार्तो न कुर्याद्यो दर्पात् कर्म यथोदितम् ।
स दण्ड्यः कृष्णलान्यष्टौ न देयं चास्य वेतनम् ॥
आर्तस्तु कुर्यात् स्वस्थः सन् यथाभाषितमादितः ।
सुदीर्घस्यापि कालस्य तल्लभेतैव वेतनम् ॥

[5] *Yājñ.*, II. 196. उभयोरप्यसाध्यं चेत् साध्ये कुर्याद्यथाश्रुतम् ।

artizan in such cases. The latter will get a share of the profit.[1] This principle, although not found in the Mānava, is very old. Kauṭilya has it.[2]

§ 12. In the case of skilled labour and professional artists, doctors etc., in work done by them on their own accord, the law implied a contract of service, and wages at the market rate and on the evidence of 'experts' (*kuśalas*) were awarded by the Court, according to the same authority.[3]

§ 13. There had been a view earlier than Kauṭilya that the contract being mutual the employer was not at liberty to get the work done by others as long as the workman was willing to do the work, and on breach on the part of the employer the workman was entitled to the whole wage.[4]

Slavery.

§ 14. Where wage was wanting, the Hindu lawyers regarded the case to be one of slavery. Hence the contract of apprenticeship by a novice, who worked with his master and received only food, is treated under the subject of slavery (Yājñavalkya II. 184).

§ 15. A promise of slavery to a rescuer by the rescued for himself and his dependants was held invalid, and the rescuer was awarded some compensation to be fixed by the evidence of experts.[5]

Maurya laws on Slavery.

§ 16. Kauṭilya gives rules on slavery which throw a flood of light on the subject. He makes "Ārya" synonymous with "free," which he uses primarily to denote the Hindu race. His principle is that

---

[1] *Yājñ.*, II. 194. दाप्यस्तु दशमं भागं वाणिज्यपशुशस्यतः ।
अनिश्चित्य भृतिं यस्तु कारयेत् स महीक्षिता ॥

[2] *AŚ.*, Ch. 70, p. 183. कर्षकः सस्यानां, गोपालकः सर्पिषां, वैदेहकः पण्यानामात्मना व्यवहृतानां, दशभागमसम्भाषितवेतनो लभेत ।

[3] *AŚ.*, Ch. 70, p. 184. यथा वा कुशलाः कल्पयेयुः ।

[4] *Ibid.*, Ch. 71, p. 185. "उपस्थितमकारयतः कृतमेव विद्यात्" इत्याचार्याः ।

[5] *AŚ.*, Ch. 70, p. 184. नदीवेगज्वालास्तेनव्यालोपरुद्धः सर्वस्वपुत्रदारात्मदानेनार्तस्त्रातारमाहूय निस्तीर्णः कुशलप्रदिष्टं वेतनं दद्यात् ।

an Ārya can never be a slave. Under this principle he brings the free Śūdra also, whom he calls "Ā r y a-p r ā ṇ a," "breathing the breath of the Ārya" (*i.e.*, the freeman). Except a born-slave of the Śūdra caste, if one sold an Ārya-prāṇa Śūdra or a minor, he was heavily punished.[1] Chancellor Kauṭilya introduced a policy of making his countrymen a nation of freemen. Under the Code of Kauṭilya, a slave, if ill-treated, *e.g.*, made to carry a dead body and leavings of food, acquired freedom, and so a female slave with whom the master committed adultery.[2] Rape on a slave woman was punished as a crime. Offsprings of all self-sold slaves became "Hindu" (free) on birth.[3] Inheritance to those who had 'mortgaged' themselves was open ; and free earning, when not opposed to the work imposed on him, was also made available to the slave. He had to attain "Hindu-hood" (āryatva) by paying off the bond money.[4]

"All these laws applied to the born and *āhitaka* ('pledged'), slaves as well."[5]

Property of a slave was inherited by his own kinsmen.[6]

If a female slave became wife of the master, all her relatives became free. No "Ārya," taken captive in war, could be a slave.[7]

§ 17. All these laws are repealed by the Mānava (VIII. 415). A slave could not hold any property of his own (VIII. 416). Nor could he earn anything for himself (VIII. 416). Slaves' children were accretion to the master (IX. 55). The Maurya law of slavery meant abolition of slavery in India. Megasthenes, a contemporary,

---

[1] AŚ., Ch. 70, p. 181. उदरदासवर्जमार्यप्राणमप्राप्तव्यवहारं शूद्रं विक्रयाधानं नयतः स्वजनस्य द्वादशपणो दण्डः

[2] *Ibid.*, p. 182. प्रेतविण्मूत्रो···अतिक्रमणं च स्त्रीणां मूल्यनाशकरं।

[3] *Ibid.* आत्मविक्रयिणः प्रजामार्यां विद्यात्।

[4] *Ibid.* आत्माधिगतं स्वामिकर्माविरुद्धं लभेत, पित्र्यं च दायम्। मूल्येन चार्यत्वं गच्छेत्।

[5] *Ibid.* तेनोदरदासाहितकौ व्याख्यातौ।

[6] *Ibid.*, p. 183. दासद्रव्यस्य ज्ञातयो दायादाः।

[7] *Ibid.* स्वामिनस्तस्यां दास्यां जातं समातृकं अदासं विद्यात्।
आर्यप्राणो···कर्मकालानुरूपेण मूल्यार्धेन वा विमुच्येत।

could rightly say, as he did, that there was no slavery in India in his time. But the reaction came under the Dharma-law, and the *Dāsa-kalpa*, ('Rules made about slaves') of the Mauryas were set aside. To a Dharma lawyer it was preposterous to call a Śūdra and a slave "Ārya." The slave had been regarded as chattel in Dharma. It is to the great credit of Yājñavalkya that in part he reverted to the Maurya policy, and applied principles of contract to slavery. Force avoided the contract of slavery ; a slave who saved the life of his master was held to have completed his service and was free ; if he paid his price or the cost of maintenance he was entitled to obtain liberty.[1]

Re-action in Manu against Maurya laws.

Yājñavalkya on Slavery.

§ 18. The law Codes distinguished a guild from partnership. Partnership (Sambhūya-samutthāna) was a body (unity, 'samavāya'), formed to work for profit (Yājñavalkya, II. 259).[2] A guild was a corporation which was not temporary and which existed as a legal person. In the latter case, the body corporate contracted debts, etc. (II. 185-192), while in the case of partnership, the partners acted (II. 259-265). Partnership is already known to Kauṭilya. Partnership of priests had been a standing example. In big sacrifices several partners worked conjointly, while the fees paid were joint.[3] The Artha Śāstra takes the case of the priests' partnership first ; the Mānava does the same (VIII. 206-210) and says that the same principles will apply to other sorts of partnership.[4] The law court could divide the shares of partnership.

Partnership,

---

[1] *Yājñ.*, II. 182. बलाद्दासीकृतश्चौरैर्विक्रीतश्चापि मुच्यते ।
स्वामिप्राणप्रदो भक्तत्यागात्तन्निष्क्रयादपि ॥

[2] समवायेन वणिजां लाभाय कर्म कुर्वताम् ।
लाभालाभौ यथाद्रव्यं यथा वा संविदा कृतौ ॥

[3] *AŚ.*, Ch. 71, pp. 186-187.

[4] *Manu*, VIII. 211. सम्भूय स्वानि कर्माणि कुर्वद्भिरिह मानवैः ।
अनेन विधियोगेन कर्तव्यांशप्रकल्पना ॥

A partner could give a proxy (M. VIII. 207), and he could retire after receiving profits upto the date of his retirement (206). A partner could be expelled on good ground (AŚ.)[1]. Yājñavalkya, found the centre of the law of partnership shifted from priest to trade. It had shifted in the time of the Mānava, and probably earlier. Yājñavalkya corrected the order : his law of partnership is for merchants and foreign traders, and 'the same principles apply to priestly partnership and that of agriculturists and artizans' (II. 265).[2] Apart from guilds and other corporations, the latter two classes and the merchants had been by then thoroughly used to this form of contract. They joined for profit. A partner was liable for tort against other partners, acting beyond authority or negligently (II. 260). For extra exertion of the nature of insurance, *e.g.*, preserving partnership property against robbers etc., he became entitled to a fee of insurance (II. 260). Partners had to take notice of the laws of the country (261). Only the offending partner was liable for his illegal act (262-263). A partner's heir succeeded to the assets of a dead partner, or in the alternative one who took up the vacant share ; otherwise the king was entitled to the assets of the deceased's share (264). Dishonesty, and uselessness (incapacity in making gain) were reasons for dissolution of partnership, but an incapable partner could give a proxy to work for him. (265).

§ 19. Corporations. Corporate bodies in internal matters were regulated by their own laws (M. VIII. 41). The court only punished a member who would not obey a 'resolution' of the body.[3] The law implied a contract on the part of the members undertaking to obey the decision

---

[1] *AŚ.*, p. 186. (Cf. *Yājñ.* II. 265.)

[2] *Yājñ.* II. 265. अनेन विधिराख्यात ऋत्विक्कर्षककर्मिणाम् ।

[3] *Manu*, VIII. 219. यो ग्रामदेशसङ्घानां कृत्वा सत्येन संविदम् ।
विसंवदेन्नरो लोभात् तं राष्ट्राद्विप्रवासयेत् ॥

of the majority.[1] The members were agents of the body corporate, and whatever they received, *e.g.*, from the king, belonged to the whole body. Appropriation of common property by a member was theft in the case of a corporation.[2]

§ 20. Kauṭilya gives laws on the subject only with reference to the village corporation, which he calls the 'village', where disobedience of members to the resolution of the body was fined by the court. If a member did not co-operate, *e.g.*, in putting up a public show, he was not allowed the benefit of the work. "The same laws apply to the corporation called 'the country', 'of caste'," etc.[3]

§ 21. We have seen that both Codes recognise the laws of corporations. Before them Gautama knows them.[4] Vasishṭha will fine 'the village'.[5] The Jātakas, the Buddhist sūtras, and the inscriptions of the second century B.C. bear witness to the flourishing condition of corporate life. Yājñavalkya in particular recognises the body corporate as a *legal persona.* Debt could be contracted by such a body as one man, according to Yājñavalkya. It could hold property (II. 187), and employ agents (II. 190). Yājñavalkya's law upholds the existence and rights of corporate bodies of even heretics (II. 191 and 192). It seems that there was a special royal court for corporations in the time of Yājñavalkya, presided over by three judges (II. 185).

Transfer of Property.

§ 22. Transfer has three technical terms in Hindu law: (1) *Ādhi*, 'placing with', is employed to denote all transfers by way of mortgage. The *ādhi* may be, as Bṛhaspati and others say, of movable or

---

[1] *Yājñ.*, II. 188. कर्तव्यं वचनं सर्वैः समूहहितवादिनाम् ।
यस्तत्र विपरीतः स्यात् स दाप्यः प्रथमं दमम् ॥

[2] *Ibid.*, 187. गणद्रव्यं हरेद्यस्तु संविदं लंघयेच्च यः ।
सर्वस्वहरणं कृत्वा तं राष्ट्राद्विप्रवासयेत् ॥

[3] *AŚ.*, Ch. 67, p. 173. कर्षकस्य ग्राममभ्युपेत्याकुर्वतो ग्राम एवात्ययं हरेत् ।... प्रेक्षायामनंशदः सस्वजनो न प्रेक्षेत ।... तेन देशजातिकुलसंघानां समयस्यानपाकर्म व्याख्यातम् ।

[4] *Gautama*, XI. 21.

[5] *Vasishṭha*, III. 4.

immovable property,[1] *i.e.*, an article put in pawn or a mortgage. Probably the earlier in history was the movable *ādhi*, the pledge, as the word denotes the function of actual delivery with the physical possession of another. Nārada however gives another explanation: *adhikriyate iti ādhiḥ*, '*ādhi* is so called because the property is placed *under* (another).[2] The second term is (2) vikraya ('the reverse of *kraya* or purchase), that is, sale, a very ancient word.[3] (3) Dāna, 'gift', is the act of giving away, and is of course as old as the world.

Mortgage, Pledge and Trust.

§ 23. *Ādhi* is treated by Kauṭilya along with 'Trust-Deposit'. From the Artha Śāstra down to the later codes the clear principle upon which the Hindu lawyers base the law of mortgage (Ādhi) is the principle of trust. The Mānava (VIII. 149) makes an Ādhi as sacred as the property of a minor in the hands of a stranger and a trust-property (*nikshepa* and *upanidhi*). Ādhi, therefore, like trust-property, cannot be lost, (says 'Manu',) by limitation of time or by adverse possession (VIII. 145, 149).

§ 24. It is necessary to take the law of trust first. *Upanidhi*, which is a technical term in Kauṭilya for property put in pure trust, is defined by Nārada:

> "When a man entrusts any property of his with another in confidence and without suspicion (it is *upanidhi*)."[4]

Upanidhi is of two sorts: *Nikshepa* where the trustee knows the subject of the trust, and *Upanidhi* where the trust-property is sealed, the trustee not knowing what the value of the

---

[1] *Bṛihaspati*, XI. 17. See quotation in VM., p. 305: आधिर्बन्धः समाख्यातः स च प्रोक्तश्चतुर्विधः। जङ्गमस्थावरश्चैव गोप्यो भोग्यस्तथैव च।

[2] *Nārada*, I. 124. अधिक्रियत इत्याधिः etc.

[3] See *AŚ.*, Ch. 69, p. 179, *avakrī*, 'hiring' for another secondary formation.

[4] *Nār.*, II. 1. स्वं द्रव्यं यत्र विश्रम्भान्निक्षिपत्यविशङ्कितः।

property is or to whom it will finally go. These two terms are known to both the Mānava (VIII. 149) and Yājñavalkya (II. 65), while Kauṭilya has only *upanidhi* as a general term. Kauṭilya uses also four other technical terms denoting classes of trusts: *Yāchitaka, Avakrī'aka, Ādeśa* and *Anāvadhi*. Yāchitaka is the property borrowed for an occasion, *e.g.*, a horse by a friend. Avakrītaka is property on hire. Anāvadhi is property entrusted to a carrier. Ādeśa is not known, but the corresponding term, which later authorities give is, *Nyāsa*, *i.e.*, property placed in the hand of some one for some particular purpose *e.g.*, gold in the hand of a smith to be converted into an ornament. Nārada gives another illustration of Upanidhi: a wealthy minor under the guardianship of a stranger (Nārada II. 15). Yājñavalkya knows *upanidhi* (II. 65), *yāchitaka, anvahita, nyāsa, nikshepa* 'and others' (II. 67). The Mānava evidently includes the other classes in Nikshepa (VIII. 190-197). The Hindu lawyers take into consideration two characteristics common to Ādhi and Ūpanidhi: transfer of the property and the position of the transferee as that of a trustee. In both cases ownership in their eyes lie with the real owner. Both the Ādhi- and Ūpanidhi-holders, using the property without authority, were liable to the punishment for theft.[2]

§ 25. Ādhi is divided by Kauṭilya in two classes, *sthāvara* (non-moving) and non-*sthāvara* (the latter by implication), *i.e.*, immovable and movable. The rules applicable to both are the same in the Mānava (VIII. 143-145) and in Yājñavalkya (II. 58-64), for they make no distinction between the two, while they clearly have in view both classes. They, however, divide Ādhi in another two divisions: usufructuary, and non-usufructuary, which the others call 'usufructuary' (*bhogya*) and 'secret' (*gopya*).[3] The latter class in the case of immovable property would be what we call today simple mortgages.

---

[1] See *AŚ.*, Ch. 69, p. 179.

[2] *Manu*, VIII. 144, 190-197; *Yājñ.*, II. 67.

[3] Cf. *Manu*, VIII. 144; *Yājñ.*, II. 59; *Bṛi* (VM., p. 305).

Right of redemption and limitation.

§26. The point of difference between Kauṭilya and the Mānava and between the Mānava and Yājñavalkya is about l i m i t a t i o n. Kauṭilya says that an *ādhi* with use to the obligee is never lost to the owner. The right of redemption always exists.[1] Yājñavalkya has the same law (II. 58).[2] In the other case, says Kauṭilya, the interest shall accumulate, that is, the consequence will be as laid down in the law on debts.[3] This is expressed by Yājñavalkya thus (II. 58): the pledge, if not redeemed until the principal is doubled, shall forfeit to the obligee. Yājñavalkya further lays down (*ibid.*) that if contracts depend on time (the time for redemption is fixed), redemption would be barred after the date appointed. Similarly it is laid down both in the Artha Śāstra with regard to immovable property (p. 178) and in Yājñavalkya generally (II. 64), that when from the mortgaged property the net profit accumulated is double the amount of the mortgage money, the property shall become automatically free.[4] The Mānava is silent, but the latter rule is deducible from its law on debt and interest. It, however, expressly demurs to the corresponding rule in favour of the mortgagee. It says that there can be no limitation against the ownership by lapse of time in the case of Ādhi (VIII. 143), or in the case of trust of Upanidhi (VIII. 145) or in Yāchitaka which it does not name but describes ('things used by permission, *e.g.*, a riding horse' etc., VIII. 146).

Conditional sale.

This causes great confusion amongst the commentators, as the Mānava is quite opposed to other Dharma Śāstras, the others having followed the law of Yājñavalkya. The

[1] *AŚ.*, Ch. 69, p. 178. नाधिः सोपकारः सीदेत्।

[2] आधिः प्रणश्येद्द्विगुणे धने यदि न मोक्ष्यते।
कालेः कालकृतो नश्येत् फलभोग्यो न नश्यति ॥

[3] *AS.*, *loc. cit.* निरुपकारः सीदेन्मूल्यं चास्य वर्धेत।

[4] *AŚ.* Ch. 69, p. 178.

Mānava, as observed above, sets its face against the law of limitation.

§ 27. Other rules on Ādhi are given which emphasise the trustee character of the mortgagee. If he uses the Ādhi (when he ought not to do so) he would be fined and lose his interest. He would be liable for loss, except in case of Act of God or State. He was bound to hand over the property when mortgage-debt was tendered. He had to employ due care in using the property, and forfeited his rights (in proportion) when the property deteriorated owing to his negligence.[1] These rules are taken from the Artha Śāstra. Yājñavalkya in addition gives a new rule. No contract of Ādhi could be established unless acceptance by the obligee was proved.[2]

Where security became insufficient the mortgagor had to give additional security, otherwise the debt became due at once.[3] This latter rule is also found in the Artha Śāstra which says that on deterioration the mortgagee shall bring a suit for permission to sell the property.[4]

Court-officer for Ādhi.

§ 28. There was a special officer of the Court called Ā d h i - p ā l a, who supervised the sale proceedings etc., of the mortgaged and pledged property. He was, according to Asahāya, the Mortgage and Pledge Registrar who can even take the pledge in his own deposit. The designation which Kauṭilya gives to him (Ādhi-pāla)[5] ('the Protector of Ādhis') indicates that.

Secret trust deposits.

§ 29. In matters of t r u s t d e p o s i t s which were all secret transactions, at times even without a single witness, Kauṭilya gives some executive authority to the judges.

---

[1] *Yājñ.* II. 59. गोप्याधिभोगे नो वृद्धिः सोपकारेऽथ हापिते ।
नष्टो देयो विनष्टश्च दैवराजकृतादृते ॥

[2] *Ibid.*, 60. आधेः स्वीकरणात् सिद्धिः ।

[3] *Ibid.* रक्ष्यमाणोऽप्यसारतां । यातश्चेदन्य आधेयो धनभाग्वा धनी भवेत् ।

[4] *AŚ.*, Ch. 69, p. 178. विनाशभयात्···धर्मस्थानुज्ञातो विक्रीणीत ।

[5] *Ibid.* आधिपालप्रत्ययो वा ।

They can employ detectives to find out the real truth and their evidence will be valid.[1] The Mānava confirms this procedure.[2]

Title and Possession.

§ 30. No possession, in the view of the Mānava, gave any valid title, (except ten years' possession of chattel other than slave VIII. 145-149; 199-200). The Code lays down the general proposition :

> "When possession (sambhoga) is proved but no title (*Āgama*) produced, title being the source (of ownership), possession in that case is no valid cause. This is the definite law."[3]

To this rule of law, the Code proceeds to give, the following exception :

> "If a man takes any chattel from the market before the Government office (*kula*),[4] he acquires that property with a clear legal title by that purchase."

"If the real owner (afterwards) claims the property which by reason of overt (*prakāśa*) purchase is untainted, the price shall not be lost. The king shall acquit him as innocent. The owner who had lost the chattel gets back his property from the king"[5] (202). The commentators make the purchaser lose his money. Kullūka however on the authority of Bṛihaspati[6] says that the owner had to pay half the price paid. The text here is clear and the meaning given by me is in accordance with the spirit of the

---

[1] *AŚ.*, Ch. 69, p. 180.

[2] *Manu*, VIII. 182. साक्ष्यभावे प्रणिधिभिर्वयोरूपसमन्वितैः ।
अपदेशैश्च संन्यस्य हिरण्यं तस्य तत्त्वतः ॥

[3] *Ibid.*, VIII. 200. सम्भोगो यत्र दृश्येत न दृश्येतागमः क्वचित् ।
आगमः कारणं तत्र न सम्भोग इति स्थितिः ॥

[4] Cf. Bṛihaspati's *rāja-purusha* quoted by Kullūka on M. VIII. 202. It was a constitutional law that the king made good any theft in the kingdom. See *Hindu Polity*, II. p. 98.

[5] *Manu*, VIII. 201-202. विक्रयाद्यो धनं किञ्चिद्गृह्णीयात् कुलसन्निधौ ।
क्रयेण स विशुद्धं हि न्यायतो लभते धनम् ॥
अथ मूलमनाहार्य प्रकाशक्रयशोधितम् ।
अदण्ड्यो मुच्यते राज्ञा नाष्टिको लभते धनम् ॥

[6] Quoted by Kullūka on Manu VIII. 202 : स्वामी दत्वार्धमूल्यन्तु प्रगृह्णीयात् स्वकं धनम् ।

previous verse which gives the purchaser 'a clear title'. By the time of Bṛihaspati a change came about, and the purchaser got back only half the money.

§ 31. The whole outlook of earlier and subsequent law is different on the main issue. Yājñavalkya makes possession a valid piece of evidence (II. 22) except in cases of trust and government property (II. 25 ; 26). It is inferior to title as a proof, but even there the relative superiority of title suffers from the onerous condition that title without a title of possession was useless. Yājñavalkya throws the onus expressly on the party alleging ownership to prove his case by title and possession against the man in possession (II. 171),[1] but the Mānava principle which does not admit possession as evidence, consequently, throws the onus on the man in possession to prove his title (VIII. 200).[2] The man, whose possession was alleged to be without title was at once converted into the position of a man with a stolen property who must clear his character.[3] Stolen property of which the owner could not be traced went to the king.[4]

Purchase in market overt.

§32. The law of the Artha Śāstra on possession we have already discussed. Its laws on purchase from a non-owner (VIII.197-202) 'asvāmi-vikraya,' are reproduced in Yājñavalkya (II. 168, 174).[5] The doctrine of purchase in market overt is however peculiar to the Mānava. It is an equitable doctrine of purchase in good faith, introduced by the Mānava from some Dharma work defining theft. The doctrine that the purchaser's money was safe was a doctrine created by the author of the Mānava Code. The credit for that is his. Yājñavalkya borrows it from the Mānava and fails to put it so well by reason of his framing the law in the negative :

---

1 आगमेनोपभोगेन नष्टं भाव्यम्

2 See *supra*.

3 Cf. *Yājñ.*, II. 171 ; *Nār.*, I. 87.

4 *AŚ.*, p. 190.

5 *Manu*, VIII. 201. See *supra*.

"A man shall get back his property, sold to another, whose guilt will be found, if he bought not overtly; and he shall be considered a thief, if he bought secretly, at low price, out of time, and from an inferior man."[1]

§ 33. A sweeper finding a *res nullius* was to be confirmed in his possession according to Kauṭilya, the king taking a share out of it on the principle of the treasure-trove law.[2] The government finding a lost property deposited in the office of lost properties, which was a branch of the Toll Office, and took it (as finder or heir to the community) if no one claimed it for three fortnights.[3] This law is rendered in verse II. 173 of Yājñavalkya, who, however, extends the period of waiting to one year.

Law of finder.

§ 34. The form of action known as 'Rescission of Sale and Purchase' was open to both parties. It was a declaratory suit, primarily for the cancellation of an executory contract. When the contract became impossible of performance the vendor sought relief. The suit had to be brought within a limited time for obtaining *anuśaya* (cancellation).[4] If the contract was obtained under force and duress (*e.g.*, 'criminal proceedings'), the vendor had his contract set aside and the offender was also punished.[5]

Rescission of contract.

When property of the owner had passed to another by an unlawful sale, the owner had to bring a suit in the Civil Court (Dharmasthîya) under the same form of action to get the sale set aside and to recover his property.[6]

---

[1] *Yājñ.*, II. 168. स्वं लभेतान्यविक्रीतं क्रेतुर्दोषोऽप्रकाशिते ।
हीनाद्रहो हीनमूल्ये वेलाहीने च तस्करः ॥

[2] *AŚ.*, Ch. 78, p. 202. भरकपांसुधावकाः सारत्रिभागं लभेरन् । द्वौ राजा रत्नं च etc. Cf. *Yajñ.*, II; 34-35.

[3] *Ibid.*, Ch. 73, p. 190. शुल्कस्थाने नष्टापहृतोत्पन्नं तिष्ठेत् । त्रिपक्षादूर्ध्वमनभिसारं राजा हरेत् स्वामी वा ।

[4] *AŚ.*, Ch. 72, p. 187. वैदेहकानामेकरात्रमनुशयः etc.

[5] *Ibid.*, Ch. 73, p. 189. दण्डभयात्…भयदानं प्रतिगृह्णतः स्तेयदण्डः ।

[6] *Ibid.* नष्टापहृतमासाद्य स्वामी धर्मस्थेन ग्राहयेत् । Cf. *Yājñ.*, II. 169-170.

According to the Mānava (VIII. 197-199) the sale would be declared (vijñeya) null and void when made by a non-owner, unless by an agent (197). Witnesses were not to be produced by the plaintiff against 'that thief', though he considers himself not a thief.[1] His punishment was to be considered on the ground whether he had a valid excuse for his conduct and whether he acted alone; his accomplices (anvaya) were also punished (198). It should be noticed that the provision is directed against one who bases his right on long possession ('he who thinks himself not to be a thief but really is a thief'. VIII. 197). Yājñavalkya could not approve of it and does not adopt it in his Code. But the general principle embodied in VIII. 199[2] ought not to have been omitted. The Verse itself, however, is of doubtful authority, some of the commentators do not know it, although Medhātithi has it.

Breach of Warranty.

§ 35. In breach of warranty, contract was set aside and damages awarded. The Mānava, VIII. 203, lays down that if the same commodity as sold or meant to be sold is not delivered, the contract is not made good. It must be of the same quality as contracted for. A contract for a commodity at a distance and beyond the sight of the parties does not prevail.[3] Yājñavalkya deals with the subject from the point of view of the crime involved. (II. 245 ff). On this point the Yājñavalkya Code is different. It gives only one rule on warranty, which is far from covering the whole ground.[4]

---

[1] *Manu*, VIII. 197. न तं नयेत साक्ष्यन्तु स्तेनमस्तेनमानिनम् ।

[2] अस्वामिना कृतो यस्तु दायो विक्रय एव वा ।
अकृतः स तु विज्ञेयो व्यवहारे यथा स्थितिः ॥

[3] *Manu*, VIII. 203. नान्यदन्येन संसृष्टरूपं विक्रयमर्हति ।
न सावद्यं न च न्यूनं न दूरे न तिरोहितम् ॥

[4] *Yājñ.*, II. 177. दशैकपञ्चसप्ताहमासत्र्यहार्धमासिकम् ।
बीजायोवाह्यरत्नस्त्रीदोह्यपुंसां परीक्षणम् ॥

§ 36. Marriage contract is a very interesting topic. I would not have adopted this title if I had not the authority of the Artha-Śāstra. The Dharma school, it should be remembered, regarded marriage as a sacrament. But the Artha regarded it as a contract, whether entered into by parties themselves or vicariously through guardians (mostly, guardians for the brides). The consequences which flowed from the contract view find expression in the Artha laws. There could be a divorce between the parties. There could be a forced dissolution by the State. [Probably there could be a legal unity by the decree of the Sovereign.[1]] There is a great opposition offered on the point in our Dharma codes.

Marriage contract.

§ 37. A marriage contract, according to Kauṭilya, was open to an action for rescission. If it was discovered that the bride had known another man, the marriage would be set aside. If the blemish had been announced before the marriage, the plaintiff was out of court. Likewise for unannounced blemishes of the bridegroom, a marriage was liable to be set aside, and when the marriage was set aside the *śulka* and *strīdhana* remained with the bride. In the former case the śulka and strīdhana were returned to the ex-husband.[2] It is remarkable how the Mānava meets the situation. "If a girl is given in marriage without announcing her blemishes, and the girl is mad, a leper or has already lost her virginity, the giver shall be liable to punishment" (VIII. 205).[3] [The punishment was a fine according to the Artha-Śāstra.] As to the marriage itself, if another girl was shown to the bridegroom, as it must have been done in many cases, specific performance

Divorce.

---

[1] *Mrichchhakaṭika*, Act X.

[2] *AS.*, Ch. 72, p. 188. कन्यादोषमौपशायिकमनाख्याय प्रयच्छतः षण्णवतिर्दण्डः शुल्कस्त्रीधनप्रतिदानञ्च। वरयितुर्वा वरदोषमनाख्याय विन्दतो द्विगुणः, शुल्कस्त्रीधननाशश्च।

[3] नोन्मत्ताया न कुष्ठिन्या न च या स्पृष्टमैथुना।
पूर्वं दोषानभिख्याप्य प्रदाता दण्डमर्हति॥

was decreed and the other girl married to him. The śulka of the first marriage was lost, according to the Artha-Śāstra. But the first bride, according to the Mānava, remained a wife: "If one girl was shown and another given in marriage, the bride shall marry both for one śulka. So ordained Manu."[1] And thus a new law was attributed to Manu. The first marriage is not to be set aside, for, how could, in view of the Dharma lawyer, a marriage, which was created by sacrament and not by contract, be set aside?

The passages VIII. 226-228 are interpolations, as they are not known to all the commentators and they are out of place and incoherent. They at the same time are not contradictory to the law we have reviewed. Yājñavalkya in the Āchārakāṇḍa (I. 66-67) deals with the subject and not under law proper. In other words, he removes it from contract to sacrament. He says that for not announcing the blemish, punishment would lie. The girl shall not leave her husband, otherwise she will become a fallen woman; she is a wife with sacrament, though of the *punarbhū* re-married class.[2]

Yājñavalkya as a Dharma lawyer has given the best explanation: she retains the wife-hood, a lawful position (*saṁskṛitā*). By the dissolution of 'the contract' she would be lowered. She cannot marry a third time, as it is not recognised. It seems that marriage of this sort of women became probably difficult in the time of Yājñavalkya. In the time of Kauṭilya marriage of such girls was quite easy as shown by a dozen provisions of Kauṭilya under different heads, *e.g.*, a maiden who was

---

[1] *Manu*, VIII. 204: अन्यां चेद्दर्शयित्वान्या वोढुः कन्या प्रदीयते।
उभे ते एकशुल्केन वहेदित्यब्रवीन्मनुः॥

[2] *Yājñ.*, I. 66-67: अनाख्याय ददद्दोषं दण्ड्य उत्तमसाहसम्।
अदुष्टां तु त्यजन् दण्ड्यो दूषयंस्तु मृषा शतम्॥
अक्षता च क्षता चैव पुनर्भूः संस्कृता पुनः।
स्वैरिणी या पतिं हित्वा सवर्णं कामतः श्रयेत्॥

seduced had to be given a śulka and strīdhana so that she can easily find a husband, and so forth.[1] In any case the view that marriage was a contract and śulka was the consideration, was deposed for ever in Hindu Law by the two Dharma Codes.

Specific performance.

§ 38. In the above topic we have seen a case of specific performance. But Hindu Law, as a rule, did not favour it. It preferred to award damages. To this policy the two Codes adhere.[2]

---

[1] E g., *AŚ.*, Ch. 89, p. 230. दासस्य दास्या वा दुहितरमदासीं प्रकुर्वतः शुल्कावध्यदानं च ।

[2] Cf. *Manu*, VIII. 223; *Yājñ.*, II, 176—177. For specific performance in respect of a contract for sale, and on promised gift, see Lecture XIII.

LECTURE XII.

FAMILY LAW.

History of Marriage—Dharma and Artha Schools on Marriage—Mānava Code revises Kauṭilya's Law—Yājñavalkya on Marriage Law—On woman's inheritance—Forms of Marriage—Āsura Marriage—Its present importance—Consequences of non-sacramental marriages—Marital relations between Dvija and Śudrā Sons—Adopted Son—His inheritance—Primogeniture—Partition—Early Doctrine of Dāyabhāga—Mitākshara Doctrine—Growth of Son's right—Succession to Strīdhana-Daughter Rise of her right—Mother—Partition by Father—Self-acquisitions—Exclusions—Order of Succession—Succession to Son—Escheat.

History of Marriage.

§ 1. Hindu literature has it that historically there was no institution of marriage at first. The introduction of the institution is referred to a Vedic period. A particular Rishi, who found his mother leaving his father and taking to another man, questioned the conduct, and the mother replied that it was lawful. Thereupon he discussed the question with the Rishis, who came to a decision and abolished the stage of non-marriage. This is the history of marriage given in the Mahā-Bhārata.[1] It is probably supported by a *mantra* of the K. Yajurveda.[2] The literature of this country is unique in this respect. Other national literatures do not remember or do not like to admit that originally the sacred tie of marriage did not exist. Here the matter is related quite historically, and the persons connected with it are historical Vedic personalities. The origin of the institution is known and recorded. Even if

[1] Cf. the story of Uddālaka Śvetaketu in MBh. I. 122, 4ff.
[2] Cited in *Manu*, IX. 19-20.

this history of the origin be not quite accurate and we take it as a theory, it is still unique, as shewing the courage and boldness of the ancient nation in stating a truth, which the modern world was loath to admit for their society as recently as the last generation. They used to say that the theory was true only of non-Aryan races. But here the ancient literature of the Aryans confirms the theory.

Dharma and Artha Schools on Marriage.

§ 2. Marriage, according to the Dharma School, is a duty, and, as already pointed out, a sacrament. Without son the Śrāddha could not be offered to the manes, and, to have sons, marriage was necessary.[1] Now we see from the Artha-Śāstra that both religion and State united in having a policy of population. The desire for progeny, from the political point of view, is as ancient as the Ṛigveda. Kauṭilya sanctions that a young woman, whose husband went abroad, after waiting for ten months, should petition to the Dharmastha Court for permission to marry another man, for, says Kauṭilya, 'to nullify ability to be mother is against law.'[2] It seems to me that for early marriage, the political laws are to be blamed, and not the Dharma laws. While the Mānava, as a rule, contemplates late age-limits for men, at 24 or 30, for marriage,[3] Kauṭilya seems to imply the limit at 16 for men and 12 for girl.[4] It seems from

---

[1] Cf., *M.* IX. 96.

[2] *AŚ.*, Ch. 61, p. 159. दत्तशुल्कां दशतीर्थान्यश्रूयमाणं ; दशश्रूयमाणम् । अतः परम् धर्मस्थै विसृष्टा यथेष्टं विन्देत । तीर्थोपरोधो हि धर्मवध इति कौटिल्यः ।

[3] *Manu*, IX. 94. त्रिंशद्वर्षो वहेत् कन्यां हृद्यां द्वादशवार्षिकीम् ।
त्र्यष्टवर्षोऽष्टवर्षां वा धर्मे सीदति सत्वरः ॥

Manu's IX 94, mentioning the age of 30 and 24 for man and 12 and 8 for girls comes last, after the discussion of marriage assuming the bride to be of the marriageable age, as if the author was incorporating a new rule into the general and an earlier law (IX. 88-93). In both cases (30 and 24) even in IX. 94, the policy is to put off a man's conjugal life above 30. The Gṛihyasūtras' occasional misreading of *anagnikā* into *nagnikā*, is now checked and corrected by Kauṭilya's 12 years age-limit for girls. As Kauṭilya was distinctly lowering the age-limit, for which he gives his reason, we may assume that before his time, it tended to be higher.

[4] *AŚ.*, Ch. 60, p. 154. द्वादशवर्षा स्त्री प्राप्तव्यवहारा भवति षोडशवर्षः पुमान् । (read with विवाहपूर्वो व्यवहारः Ch. 59, p. 151).

the inscription of King Khāravela (c. 160 B.C.) that he probably married at the maximum limit, in the 31st year.

§ 3. The Dharma law gave a sacred position to marriage, while the Artha law had made it, as we have seen (Lecture X), a contract and a contract easy for dissolution. They were at one with regard to the policy that opportunity to make the numerical strength of the nation should not be lost, but the Dharma avoided the weakening of the marriage tie.

§ 4. What gave opportunity to the politician was the early Vedic and post-Vedic custom or law which was nearer to the time of the No-Marriage stage and which was really a remnant of that stage. In the Jātakas we find the practice stated, without any abhorrence, that ladies of the royal household were allowed by their husbands to raise issues by strangers. Kauṭilya takes the practice as absolutely lawful, that is, established, although some controversy arose since the time of the Jātakas as to who would be supposed to be the legal father of the child so raised, whether the husband of the mother, or the natural father. The former view, Kauṭilya says, was that the 'owner of the field' was the owner of the crop, while some differed and asserted that the man who sowed the seeds had the right to the son. Kauṭilya had his own theory and he held that the son raised, belonged both to the seed-owner and the mother. As through the mother the legal father claimed him, he became the heir to both the fathers.[1] These lax practices, which were undoubtedly ancient, could entitle the Artha lawyers to deduce the principle that "obstruction to the ability to become mother is transgression of law (Dharma)."[2]

§ 5. The Dharma-lawyers, in view of the consequence, fought against the very law which gave rise to such deductions. Āpas-

[1] AS., Ch. 64, p. 164. "परपरिग्रहे बीजमुत्सृष्टं क्षेत्रिणः" इत्याचार्याः । "माता भस्त्रा ; यस्य रेतस्तस्यापत्यम्" इत्यपरे । "विद्यमानमुभयम्" इति कौटिल्यः ।

[2] AS., Ch. 61, p. 159 तीर्थोपरोधो हि धर्मवधः ।

tamba, in bold and open disregard of the ancient law, pronounced it inapplicable in his time. No levirate was allowed by him though he admitted it as an ancient law.[1] But the real fight was taken up in the Mānava, which by itself is a direct attack on the political principles of the Artha on the question of marriage. In spirited and emphatic language it condemned levirate and its consequential laws. It deals with the subject under law proper (IX. 32 ff), that is, the place where Kauṭilya has it. He gives two opposite theories of the Dharma School, (33-34) which resembled the two theories cited by the Artha. They were evidently common to both. But the Mānava gives also the opinion of Kauṭilya :—

> "In the opinion of some the seed is important; in the opinion of others, the origin through women. In the opinion, where both are equally important, the issue looked from that point is praised."[2]

The last was the opinion which was the exclusive opinion of Kauṭilya according to his Artha-Śāstra.

From IX. 35 ff. the Mānava gives its own opinion. If you sow vrīhī rice, you won't get śālī rice, or beans. Hence the seed is the factor (IX. 40). The son born does not belong to the family of the legal husband. The Code gives the opinion of the Purāṇa-author V ā y u, which the 'historians'[3] recite (42-44). It adds that a man is a unity of himself, the wife and the son (45). The wife being part of the husband's body,

> "neither by price in return, nor by repudiation, the wife can be separated from the husband."[4]

This, as usual, the author in giving his own view attributes to

---

1 Cf. *Âp.*, II. 10, 27, 2-7.

2 *Manu*, IX. 34. विशिष्टं कुत्रचिद्बीजं स्त्रीयोनिस्त्वेव कुत्रचित् ।
उभयन्तु समं यत्र सा प्रसूतिः प्रशस्यते ॥

3 *Ibid.*, IX. 42. अत्र गाथा वायुगीताः कीर्तयन्ति पुराविदः etc.

4 *Ibid.*, 45-46. एतावानेव पुरुषो यज्जायात्मा प्रजेति ह ।···
न निष्क्रयविसर्गाभ्यां भर्तुर्भार्या विमुच्यते ।

the primeval authority (46). The theory has a double significance: (*a*) that once a wife, always a wife, and (*b*) that union with another man is excluded owing to this conjugal unity. The trinity of husband, wife and son excludes a stranger. Further, once more stating his reasons (47-51), the author quotes the old theory and the sanction on Niyoga (52-63), and then overrules and forbids the sanction (64), and finally refutes the theory (65-68). He says—

"The sacred texts of marriage have no reference to *niyoga*."[1] Medhātithi is puzzled, as the Ṛigveda (X.40.2) does refer to *niyoga*. Without knowing the history of the controversy, without knowing that the Mānava was fighting the Artha laws of Kauṭilya, the whole treatment of the subject by the Mānava Code is a puzzle to everybody. Why should the Mānava author go to the length of denying the fact of the ancient practice? Why should he call the ancient practice 'a law for cattle'?[2] The answer is that he had to fight the law of the last régime on the d i s s o l u t i o n of m a r r i a g e. At every step he must say that marriage was indissoluble. He would not leave any loop-hole for the deduction that a woman may not lose an opportunity to become a mother. He would fill up the one breach afforded by ancient history, explaining away the texts, by pointing out that the *mantras* which create the marriage-tie do not mention *niyoga*, do not sanction *niyoga*. As to history and literature, there too the Mānava was alive to the difficulty. The literature was full of instances of *niyoga*. This he met by confession and avoidance. There was in ancient time that rascally king, that Vena, who did not follow law and was therefore deposed. The stories about *niyoga* refer to his reign (66-67):

'That chief of royal sages (ironical) caused a confusion of varṇas'. 'Since that time foolish people having been

---

[1] *Manu*, IX. 65. नोद्वाहिकेषु मन्त्रेषु नियोगः कीर्त्यते क्वचित् ।

[2] *Ibid.*, 66. अयं द्विजैर्हि विद्वद्भिः पशुधर्मो विगर्हितः ।

following the custom, only to be condemned by the good people.'[1]

Mānava Code revises Kauṭilya's laws.

§ 6. Controversy is followed by law. From verse 69 onwards the Code gives laws closely pursuing the Artha-Śāstra law, modifying and revising or repealing them, and where so necessary, recording its reasons, its own principles. (1) A widow may not remarry any one except the younger brother of her husband (69). But even their new conjugal relation should be within certain bounds (70). This was a modification of the Artha-Śāstra law which had laid this very law for a wife with children by the late husband. And for the wife who was young and without children, the law had been that she may marry any one she liked.[2] (2) If the husband went abroad, she must live loyally when maintenance is provided for by the husband. When not so provided for, she may live by blameless work (75), and she shall wait for 8 years, 6 years or 3 years, according to the nature of the business on which the husband went abroad (75-76). If the husband provided her maintenance, she had to remain loyal. Otherwise she waited for so many years. The Mānava does not say what she should do after the waiting period, and this gives rise to difference of opinion amongst the commentators. Nandana gives the correct meaning that a remarriage was allowed, but Medhātithi, though he knows this interpretation by his predecessors, disallows a remarriage even in face of the direct permission by Nārada and Parāśara. Other commentators, according to the view of their time, say that after the period of waiting she should go out to search the husband ![3]

This law was a modification of the Maurya law : (1) When a wife has given birth to children, she should wait for the return

---

[1] *M.*, IX. 67. स महीमखिलां भुञ्जन् राजर्षिप्रवरः पुरा ।
वर्णानां संकरं चक्रे कामोपहतचेतनः ॥

[2] *AŚ.*, Ch. 61, p. 159. सवर्णतश्च प्रजाता नापवादं लभेत ।...अन्यतः पर...दृष्टं विन्देत

[3] See Bühler's note on *Manu* IX. 76.

of the husband for over a year, the utmost being 8 years. When she has not been a mother, for 4 years, and then she could marry another ('in *dharma-vivāha*'). (2) If the wife was a virgin, she waited only for a few months after puberty, and then could marry with the permission of the Court any one she liked.[1]

The main difference is that if the husband provided the wife with maintenance, she could never be free. The law was too well established to be ignored altogether. The Mānava therefore gave the law, but with an effective rider.

§ 7. Similarly the Mānava in IX. 72-73 gives the very law of Kauṭilya about blemishes discovered in the wife after marriage, but it modifies it by saying that the husband could do unto her *tyāga*.[2] *Tyāga* in Kauṭilya is a technical term denoting 'separation from conjugal intercourse' as opposed to *moksha* ('freedom'), the technical divorce. In other words, she remained a legal wife, according to the Mānava, though given up by the husband. As to the effect of the transaction on the 'giver of the girl,' he was not entitled to the śulka, which, according to the Artha Śāstra appears to have accompanied every marriage and was recoverable by the father by suit. This is expressed by the Mānava, "as far as he was concerned, the transaction had no effect."[3]

§ 8. Kauṭilya says that if the wife was ill-treated beyond a mild abuse and three slaps, or similar beating, she could bring action for defamation or assault, and likewise if the wife beat the husband, he could also seek the shelter of the Court.[4] The Mānava gives this and almost all other laws of Kauṭilya

---

[1] See *AŚ.*, Ch. 61, pp. 158-159.

[2] *Manu*, IX. 72 विधिवत् प्रतिगृह्यापि त्यजेत् कन्यां विगर्हितम् ।
व्याधितां विप्रदुष्टां वा छद्मना चोपपादिताम् ॥

[3] *Ibid.*, 73. यस्तु दोषवतीं कन्यामनाख्याय प्रयच्छति ।
तस्य तद्वितथं कुर्यात् कन्यादातुर्दुरात्मनः ॥

[4] *AŚ.*, Ch. 60, pp. 154-155. "नग्ने विनग्ने न्यङ्गेऽपितृकेऽमातृके" इत्यनिर्देशेन विनयग्राहणम् । वेणुदलरज्जु-हस्तानामन्यतमेन वा पृष्ठे त्रिराघातः । तस्यातिक्रमे वाग्दण्डपारुष्यदण्डाभ्यामर्धदण्डाः । तदेव स्त्रिया भर्तरि प्रसिद्धदोषाया ईर्ष्याया, बाह्यविहारेषु द्वारेष्वत्ययो यथानिर्दिष्टः ।

with many slight modifications, unless there is a cause for difference in principles. The Code finally sums up the subject by saying :

(1) wife is a divine institution 'given by gods' ; one should not think 'I have obtained her by choice' (IX. 95) :

(2) here unity is established by the Veda (96) :

(3) the *śulka* (which the Artha-lawyers regarded as essential—as the consideration—in marriage) ought not to be taken, as it degrades marriage to the position of sale (98). The śulka is an archaic institution, it is a covert price of the bride (100) :

(4) The summary of the Dharma (law) on marriage is—**'Let Mutual Fidelity continue until death'** (101).

There should not be severance between the two (*i.e.*, no divorce) (102.)

In many respects the Code of Sumati Bhārgava was a distinct reaction. But on marriage the Code was a factor for raising its status to a sacrament—a moral ideal of the highest type. The Code rescued it from contract, which in the last analysis resolved into a sale. At the same time, the Mānava has all the vices which the monkish ideas of the Buddhists and the Jainas had circulated about women. The Mānava was for marriage, but not for women ; Kauṭilya was for women, but not for marriage.

Yājñavalkya on marriage laws.

§ 9. Yājñavalkya is not concerned with all the controversy. That had been already done by the Mānava. He records the result of the fight. The girl after puberty can select her husband.[1] This law is given by Yājñavalkya in full agreement with the law before the Mānava. The Mānava would make the girl wait for three years.[2] Yājñavalkya removes this condition. A girl promised is equal to a girl married.[3] Here Yājñavalkya

---

[1] *Yājñ.*, I. 64. कन्या कुर्यात् स्वयं बरम् ।

[2] *Manu*, IX. 90. त्रीणि वर्षाण्युपासीत कुमार्यृतुमती सती ।

[3] *Yājñ.*, I. 65.

follows the Mānava, and not Kauṭilya. This was a question of principle. In I. 67-69, he, however, confirms the old law of *Niyoga*, in spite of 'Manu's' dictum to the contrary. A wife (73-74) with defects could be superseded, but she should be given a solatium.[1] This unique provision is again adopted from the older law. It is exactly the same in Kauṭilya. Again, when a question of principle comes up, as here, he follows Manu : he exhorts not to remarry whether as a widow or as an ex-wife.[2]

§ 10. A great change is to be read in the provisions of Yājña-valkya (II. 77) where absolute obedience to the husband is laid down as the highest duty of the wife. It was not the wife of the time of Kauṭilya who would bring an action for defamation or assault and become a defendant in court for beating the husband. It was not the wife of the time of the Mānava who regarded "m u t u a l fi d e l i t y" to be the highest duty. It was the wife of Yājñavalkya's age, permeated to the core, like pickle, with the new morals of Buddhism—with the '*dharma*' of abject obedience and unnatural tolerance. The Hindu law-books—the Dharma Śāstras like the Yājñavalkyan—have bequeathed that wife, it seems, to all ages, undoubtedly to the great satisfaction of the Hindu husbands.

§ 11. From 83-87 Yājñavalkya is dealing with the question of wife's duty on husband's disappearance. She has to remain loyal and ascetic ; relatives must protect her. That is all. Not a word about divorce.

§ 12. Yājñavalkya, at the same time, introduces a curious new rule. He prohibits widowerhood. A widower should 'without delay take another wife.'[3]

---

[1] *Yājñ.*, I. 74. अधिविन्ना तु भर्तव्या महदेनोऽन्यथा भवेत् ।

[2] *Ibid.*, I. 75. मृते जीवति वा पत्यौ या नान्यमुपगच्छति ।
सेह कीर्तिमवाप्नोति मोदते चोमया सह ॥

[3] *Ibid.*, 89. दाहयित्वाग्निहोत्रेण स्त्रियं वृत्तवतीं पतिः ।
आहरेद्विधिवद्दारानग्नींश्चैवाविलम्बयन् ॥

§ 13. Yājñavalkya's name must be always remembered for endowing women with the right of inheritance. He heads the list of the heirs of a sonless deceased, with wife and daughter.[1] Without his law, daughters and widows could not have been heirs to-day in this country. The Mānava does not admit either of them in its list (IX. 185-187). Whence this change in the law and why? Was the source foreign or indigenous? The credit of Yājñavalkya is greatly diminished when we see that the very provision existed as a definite law in the time of the Mauryas regarding daughter:

Yājñavalkya on woman's inheritance.

"The movables of the sonless deceased, his own brothers or those living with him (re-united) shall take; also, the maiden daughters."[2]

"If one has sons, they shall take the property; otherwise, daughters, born of the four lawful marriages. In their non-existence, the father, if alive, in his non-existence, brothers of the deceased and his sons."[3]

It should be noticed that the Maurya law gives the daughter absolute inheritance. This is a very important point, not only as throwing light on the right of daughter but also that of widow. There is no doubt that the law was taken by Yājñavalkya, like so many other laws, from the Maurya laws. Now Yājñavalkya places 'wife' and 'daughter' in the same position without making any difference as to their respective rights. If the daughter took absolutely, the wife also was intended to take absolutely. The plain meaning of the verse and the previous law on which it is based prove that Yājñavalkya's law

---

[1] *Yājñ.*, II. 135. पत्नी दुहितरश्चैव पितरौ भ्रातरस्तथा ।
तत्सुता गोत्रजा बन्धुःशिष्यः सब्रह्मचारिणः ॥

[2] *AŚ.*, Ch. 62, p. 160. द्रव्यमपुत्रस्य सोदर्या भ्रातरः सहजीविनो वा हरेयुः कन्याश्च. Shama Sastry wrongly reads *riktham* with this sentence. It belongs to the next section. [The above interpretation of mine is now fully supported by Gaṇapati Śāstri's text, p. 32].

[3] *Ibid.* पुत्रवतः पुत्राः दुहितरो वा धर्मिष्ठेषु विवाहेषु जाताः ।

gives the daughter an absolute inheritance. The Artha-Śāstra settles the question.

§ 14. It would have been noticed that Kauṭilya does not enfranchise the w i d o w. On the other hand, he has expressedly enjoined that the widow has no claim to the property. She was only entitled to maintenance from it.[1] Nor does he enumerate the m o t h e r in the list of successors. Yājñavalkya's glory is thus enhanced. He not only enfranchises the w i f e whom he places before the d a u g h t e r, but also the m o t h e r, coming after the father.[1]

§ 15. The reason of the change in the policy of law towards women is, in my opinion, two-fold: Social and Juridical. Buddhism had conquered the Hindu mind. Its influence on the Buddhists and the non-Buddhists was alike in the matter of outlook towards men and women and their mutual rights. Buddhism had enfranchised women. The nun was an equal of the monk. The gates of the spiritual and religious rights were equally open to the despised woman as to the self-styled god of the earth. Nuns' sisterhood could and did hold property as much as monks' brotherhood. The conscience of the lawyers questioned, 'why should not women hold property at law?' Again, we have seen that the new laws took away all independence from the woman in seeking a new alliance for herself and her support. What was she to do when the husband died? The lawyers who laid the life-long obligation on her to remain true to one man, must also think of prescribing some new right in return. If the law had been matured in the time of the Mānava, and Sumati Bhārgava had been as great a lawyer as Yājñavalkya, he would have anticipated Yājñavalkya's law, to make his desired policy well-rooted. The conclusion to which Yājñavalkya came as a lawyer, was one from which there was no escape, considering the basic principle on which the Dharma lawyers founded their theory of indis-

---

[1] *AŚ.*, Ch. 59, pp. 1[illegible]2-153.

solubility of the marriage-tie. Women became half the person of the husband by the sacrament of marriage. Can, then, as Bṛihaspati put it later, anybody take the property of the dead man when his half-body was still alive ?[1] On the same principle the mother being half of the father's self, must inherit in the order she was placed by Yājñavalkya. As to the daughter the history was different and the principle was different (see below § 40.)

§ 16. There is a controversy amongst the commentators : whether the law of Yājñavalkya refers to the estate of a sonless deceased person, divided from his agnates, or otherwise. As we have seen in numerous matters, Yājñavalkya presumes, so to say, a knowledge of the Artha Śāstra laws in men dealing with his Dharmaśāstra. It is only when we read the two together that we fully understand Yājñavalkya's Code. His is like an amending Code to the Code of Kauṭilya. Contemporary people knew and understood what was meant by his law. They knew the other law, the Maurya law which was cited even centuries later. It is not improbable that reference to the Artha Śāstra, with regard to these laws, is implied by verse II. 21, which says that 'the Dharma Śāstra' is stronger than 'the Artha Śāstra.' If we take it to mean that *the* Dharma Śāstra (*i.e.*,the Yājñavalkyan) is stronger than *the* Artha Śāstra (*i.e.*, the Kauṭilîya), the Code of Yājñavalkya is to be read with the 'weaker' (the amended) Artha Śāstra. Now if we read the two together,[2] we will have

[1] *Bṛihaspati* quoted by Aparārka (p. 740) on *Yājñ.*, II. 136 :

आम्नाये स्मृतितन्त्रे च लोकाचारे च सूरिभिः । शरीरार्धं स्मृता भार्या पुण्यापुण्यफले समा ॥

यस्य नोपरता भार्या देहार्धं तस्य जीवति । जीवत्यर्धशरीरेऽर्थं कथमन्यः समाप्नुयात् ॥

[2] Kauṭilya (Ch. 62, p. 160) lays down the law for the reunited (*sahajīvan'aḥ*), 'Those who have been *living together* shall *re-divide* their property whether they had already divided their ancestral property before, or they had received no such property at all' (Shama Sastry's translation). (Mr. Shama Sastry has missed the technical meaning of 'those living together.' Kauṭilya is using the expression for the reunited family). After this the next section says, 'the property of a sonless man, his uterine brothers, or those reunited with him, shall take, and also unmarried daughters.' Here there is *or* between 'uterine brothers' and 'the reunited ones', which means, the law-giver is contemplating inheritance of a

to say that Yājñavalkya refers to the individual, divided estate, and that Vijñāneśvara[1] and others are right, and Aparārka[2] and Sūlapāṇi[3] are wrong in their interpretation.

But all the commentators are equally guilty in reducing the right of the widow to a limited interest.

§ 17. The Mānava (III. 21 ff.) gives eight classes of marriage which are too well known to be repeated here. It is sufficient to remind ourselves that the Code allows six out of them and excludes Āsura and Paiśācha. The Āsura it condemns on the plea, already noticed, that no consideration for marriage ought to be taken. The Paiśācha is condemned on account of moral repulsion.

Forms of Marriage.

§ 18. There is some new light to be focussed on the subject. There was originally only one form of marriage. The Mānava Gṛihya Sūtra is aware of only two forms—Brāhma and Śaulka.[4] They mean 'priestly' (brāhma) and 'contractual' (*śaulka*). *Śulka* latterly meant a 'tax', a 'fee', but in its original sense it seems to have implied a condition. In the Mahā-Bhārata it is used to denote a *prize* or *bet*. Bhāsa employs it in that sense in connexion with the marriage between Daśaratha and Kaikeyī.[5] Kaikeyī's śulka at the time of the marriage was that her son was to succeed to the throne. When it means a tax, it means the toll at the gate of the city, the condition which must be fulfilled before entry was permitted. The underlying idea seems

divided person. (*Cf.* Y. II. 139). In each case the estate is burdened with the share of the unmarried girls. It should be noticed that the provision comes after Kautilya has started the subject of division. After the last provision, follows the order of inheritance (*dāyakrama*, indicated by the heading of the chapter)—sons, daughters, etc. It is thus evident that Kauṭilya is speaking of the inheritance of a man who had separated from his agnates. Similarly we can say now that both Aparārka (p. 943) and Mitra Miśra, (com. on Y. in MS) had the right appreciation of the law when they said that the word for wife being *patnī*, only a wife married in one of the approved forms is meant. This is clearly deducible from Kauṭilya's law.

[1] *Vijñaneśvara* (ed. Gharpure, 1914) p. 92. The explanation of Vijña. is evidently founded on his comparative study of Kātyāyana and others. Kātyāyana is clear: see text cited in the *Mitāksharā, ibid.*).

[2] *Āparārka*, pp. 743-744.

[3] *Śūlapāni* (MS.)

[4] *Mānava Gṛihaya Śūtra*, I. 7-8.

[5] *Bhāsa* Pratimā, I. 15. *cf*

to be a condition, a conditional security or consideration. If the girl is given up, the *śulka* would be forfeited, otherwise it would go to the girl and her husband. 'If one damsel has been shown and another be given to the bridegroom, he may marry both for the same *śulka*' (M. VIII. 204). The Artha School, as pointed out above, attached importance to śulka. According to the Mānava, śulka was returned to the bridegroom. A pair of oxen was the śulka. The Brāhma form had no śulka. Marriage was completed only by Brāhma or Vedic text. It seems that śulka was not a part of the sacrament. The Mānava rightly attacks śulka, in the sense of consideration, as unlawful; legally it was the text which completed the legal tie.[1] This is asserted by the Mānava, although it says further on (probably a later addition) that the Seven-Steps completed the sacrament.[2] This was a later view which attached more importance to the ceremonial than the words of the solemn utterance. Śulka charged was comparatively nominal. It was symbolical. The Greek writers mention the custom of exchange of bride by a couple of oxen. They also mention the sale of young women in open market whom people bought to make wives.[3] This refers to the purchases and sales which the Artha Śāstra makes penal ('to take men or women to the market for sale').[4] The śulka, in the form of a pair of oxen, came to be associated in men's mind with the sale of the woman. 'A covert price' of the bride is the name given to it by the Mānava, who regarded it as no part of the Vedic ritual. The Vedic references are very probably to slaves bought, and the author of the Mānava was not wrong when he said that no former usage warranted a purchase of the *patnī*.

---

[1] Cf. *Manu*. III. 53-54; *Āpastamba*. II. 6, 13, 12 and Govinda's comment on *Baudhāyana*, I. 11, 20, 4. *Manu*, IX. 100:

नानुशुश्रुम जात्वेतत् पूर्वेष्वपि हि जन्मसु ।
शुल्कसंज्ञेन मूल्येन छन्नं दुहितृविक्रयम् ॥

[2] *Ibid.*, VIII. 227.

पाणिग्रहणिका मन्त्रा नियतं दारलक्षणम् ।
तेषां निष्ठा तु विज्ञेया विद्वद्भिः सप्तमे पदे ॥

[3] Strabo, quoted by Jolly, *Recht und Sitte*, § 16 McCrindle, *Arrian*, p. 222.

[4] *AŚ.*, ch. 70.

31

§ 19. The Saulka was the Ārsha form. On the analogy of the Brāhma, which was open to priests, the Prājāpatya was introduced with the popular element Śulka. This was a later invention: Āpastamba and Vasishṭha do not know it. Nor do they know the Paiśācha. The Artha Śāstra is the first work to give this name. Either the form was prevalent in the Piśācha country (Chitral) and the name was derived from there, or it was a mere creation of the lawyers. Kauṭilya in his laws prescribes punishment for it as an illegal act, and forced the violator to marry the girl and to pay Śulka to the parents. But nowhere he repeats the term. The Rākshasa, as Yājña-valkya says, was the form permitted in war.[1] It had nothing to do with the Demons. The Āsura in which the parents took a large amount from the bridegroom was substantially a sale. This shows that the Ārsha was not so regarded when the classification came into existence. The Āsura is called Mānusha ('popular' or 'human') in Vasishṭha,[2] which shows that this form was common amongst the vulgar. This form, too, the Mānava Code, on the same principle—to stop marriage being regarded as a sale—condemns. But it does not bring about a drastic change. It allows inheritance to the son of the Āsura marriage. In the early centuries of the Christian era India imported women from Persia for marriage. Under these conditions Yājñavalkya does not make the Āsura marriage illegal. By doing so many women would have been degraded from wives into slaves. Hence the old law was preserved.

Present importance of Āsura Marriage.

§ 20. The Āsura marriage has continued upto this day, and the people who are party to it do not think for a moment that they are doing anything blame worthy. No one can say that the provision of 'Manu' against it is a *vidhi* when he himself recognises it later

[1] *Yājñ.*, II. 61. राक्षसो युद्धहरणात्

[2] See *Vas.*, I. 35.

and in inheritance. The later Code, the Mitāksharā on it, and all later authorities tacitly accept it as legal. Under such conditions, it would be wrong to look at the Āsura marriage from the point of view of the English law and apply the principles of marriage brocage to it. Unless by legislation the Āsura marriage is declared illegal, the Courts ought to uphold transactions connected with it. The Hindu law does not abolish it. The disabilities it places on the nuptial rights are sufficiently penal. No other penalty without express legislation would be fair.

§ 21. The term which is responsible for the names Ā s u r a (converted from M ā n u s h a) and R ā k s h a s a and P a i ś ā c h a is 'G ā n d h a r v a.' It seems that it has reference to the practice of some people or even mythical people who were believed to be given to love-making. Other names were given by analogy after it. The G a n d h a r v a s are associated with the A s u r a s and the R ā k s h a s a s. We know the other names of the Āsura and the Rākshasa marriages. The R ā k s h a s a is not known to Vasishṭha who has in its place K s h ā t r a.[1] The P a i ś ā c h a was the last to come in the list.

Classification of Marriages.

§ 22. The Artha Śāstra defines the B r ā h m a as making over of the bride with ornaments.[2] It seems that by 'B r ā h m a' was signified a "complete" or absolute marriage (like *brahma* in *brahma-deya*). The P r ā j ā p a t y a arises from sacred rites to be performed jointly (by the bridegroom and the bride).[3] This was the highest ideal of the Hindu marriage. It is really this form which obtains to-day as a normal and respectable form. It partakes of the nature of the Brāhma also, as brides are generally given, with ornaments, by the parents. "By giving a pair of bullocks is Ārsha." "By mutual unity is Gāndharva." "Gift to

---

[1] *Vasishṭha*, I. 34.

[2] *A.Ś.*, Ch. 59, p. 151. कन्यादानं कन्यामलङ्कृत्य ब्राह्मो विवाहः।

[3] *Ibid.* सहधर्मचर्या प्राजापत्यः।

a priest at sacrifice is Daiva." "By payments of Śulka is Āsura." "Taking by force is Rākshasa." "Taking a woman who is asleep is Paiśācha."[1] The introduction of the nomenclature *Gāndharva* or *Paiśācha* produced this technical classification—of the Deva, Ṛishi, Gandharva, Asura, Rākshasa, Piśācha marriages. Brāhma, Prājāpatya, Ārsha and Daiva, according to the Artha Śāstra, are called *Dharma-Vivāhas* or marriages completed by sacrament. In them, says Kauṭilya, the father alone was the authority.[2] While the others (by Sūtra implication) were not accompanied with sacred rites. They became lawful when both father and mother agreed to the man and the woman remaining as husband and wife. In all these non-dharma marriages the śulka which would have finally gone to the girl, was taken by the parents.[3] Inheritance was open to the children of the first four marriages (of sacrament), not to the children born of the last four marriages.

Consequences of non-sacramental marriages.

§ 23. For wives a *vṛitti*, 'settlement,' was made by the husband, of at least 2000 1.[4] This settled property and her ornaments constituted her strīdhana, according to Kauṭilya.[5] The part of the śulka called *śulka-śesha*, to be given later, went also to the wife.[6] Strīdhana in the Rākshasa and the Paiśācha marriages could not be touched by the husband on pain of criminal prosecution.[7] If he took, for a time, the strīdhana of the Āsura or the Gāndharva marriage, he was liable to restore it with interest.[8] But the strīdhana of wives of other marriages could be utilised by the husband when he needed it.

1 *AŚ.*, ch. 59.

2 *Ibid.* पितृप्रमाणाश्चत्वारः पूर्वे धर्म्याः ।

3 *Ibid.*, p. 152. तौ (मातापितरौ) हि शुल्कहरौ दुहितुः ।

4 *Ibid.* परद्विसाहस्रा स्थाप्या वृत्तिः ।

5 *Ibid.* वृत्तिराबध्यं वा स्त्रीधनम् ।

6 *Ibid.* मृते भर्तरि धर्मकामा...शुल्कशेषं च लभेत ।

7 *Ibid.* राक्षसपैशाचोपभुक्तं स्तेयं दद्यात् ।

8 *Ibid.* गान्धर्वासुरोपभुक्तं सवृद्धिकमुभयं दाप्येत ।

Thus the union under the latter four forms was never regarded as perfect. Their children did not acquire the status of full heirs, and the wives never became part of the husband's spiritual self.

Marital relations between Dvija and Śūdrā.

§ 24. This exposition of the different marriages in the Artha Śāstra and the rights thus conferred, explains many obscure points in the law of inheritance. Marriage with a Śūdrā woman by all the upper three castes is allowed in the earlier law. Only in case of priests, the earlier Dharma Sūtras prohibit a Śūdrā wife as the chief wife.[1] It seems that the priestly class was especially fond of 'the black beauty' as a Dharma Sūtra calls her : *krishṇa-varṇā yā rāmā* . . . . (Va., XVIII. 18). When the Brahmin married a wife, he performed his religious rites in her company. He gave her his own status, as admitted by the Mānava,[2] and pointed out by Aśvaghosha. That the fair-haired, fair-eyed Brahmin (and also probably the fair Vaiśya) should be especially fond of 'black beauties' is a problem that belongs to Psychology. Its legal and social affects were enormous. A Brahmin, if he married in form a Śūdrā woman and made her his *patnī*, a *crishalī-pati* in the language of the Sūtra-kāras (*e.g.*, Va., XIV. 11), must have a different attitude to his Śūdra relatives. He must perforce come to regard them as fellowmen. This, partially, if not wholly, may explain the existence of the learned Śūdra and the Śūdra talking Sanskrit. It was only when religious controversies of a bitter and revolutionary nature came on the stage that the Brahmins, or for the matter of that the orthodox community, tried to suppress the Śūdra. Marriage with their women by the Brahmin came to be questioned and the law revised. In discovering the date of this revolution the Artha Śāstra is highly important. The

---

[1] *Cf. Gautama*, XV. 18, where the शूद्रापति has been explained as one whose only wife (*dharmapatnī*) is Śūdrā. See also *Manu*, III. 155.

[2] *Manu*, IX. 23-24.

marriage is fully allowed, and the issue gets a share in inheritance against the sons from wives of superior castes, though he is evidently not to offer oblations. The process had begun, but it was far from being an object of attack. The Śūdra with the "Aryan breath" of Kauṭilya was probably a Śūdra with Aryan blood in him—son of a Śūdrā woman and an Aryan father. He was the Śūdra who had become part of the Aryan society. The process would have resulted in a complete fusion but for the social revolution of which the Mānava was the Code Napoleon.

§ 25. The Mānava, as in every case of a new policy of law, discusses and condemns the Śūdrā-wife of a Brahmin, but he does not make a drastic change. The effect, however, was great, as Yājñavalkya could and did totally prohibit it.[1] The prohibition from the thnic point of view was of no value. The mixture of blood had already been complete. The 'fair-hair' of the Brahmin and the 'fair-skin' of the Vaiśya had ceased to be the external sign. And the time had come when Aśvaghosha had to say that there was no difference in complexion of the Śūdra and the non-Śūdra. The law only succeeded in making the caste system immutable and hide-bound, but after nearly a full fusion.

§ 26. The social revolution divided the Vedic India from the present Hinduism beginning about the year 188 B.C. The Mānava Code carried caste into every law, and every institution, and carried caste into marriage also: such and such marriage was only open to such and such caste.[2] The Artha Śāstra contemplates a Śūdra marrying according to Vedic rites. But he was no more entitled to any rite under the Mānava Code. No trace of a division of marriages on caste is found in the Artha Śāstra or earlier.

---

[1] *Yājñ.*, I. 56. यदुच्यते द्विजातीनां शूद्राद्दारोपसंग्रहः ।
नैतन्मम मतं यस्मात्तत्रात्मा जायते स्वयम् ॥

[2] See *Manu*, III. 24 ff.

§ 27. All the classes of sons are already known to the Artha Śāstra. As a consequence of the theory of Kauṭilya, the kshetraja son of a wife by another man inherits the immovable property of both the fathers as expressly laid down (*AŚ.* p. 164), likewise the son secretly born (gūḍhaja). But the cast-off son (*apaviddha*) belonged to the one who performed his necessary ceremonies, and so did the adopted son, the kānīna and the sahoḍha, and the paunarbhava.[1] These as well as the kṛitaka and the parikrîta—the constructive sons—received only ⅓ when a natural (aurasa) son was born. This law applied only when the latter were "savarṇa" sons—sons from wives of equal in caste. Otherwise, they received only food and clothing.[2] An aurasa son even from a Śūdrā woman would exclude artificial sons, according to Kauṭilya. The son, equal in rights to the aurasa, was the son of the appointed daughter.[3]

Sons.

The Mānava discourages a kānīna (son of a maiden), a sahoḍha (son come with a wife to her new husband), a son bought, a *paunarbhava* (from a widow re-married), an *upagata* (self-given), and a son of a Śūdrā wife[4]—the first two, owing to the legal view against the kshetraja and the paunarbhava because of the Mānava theory about remarriage. The Śūdrā's son is excluded on account of the prohibition of the Mānava against the marriage with

The Mānava and Yājñavalkya on sons.

---

1 *AŚ.*, Ch. 64, p. 164.···क्षेत्रजः पुत्रः। असति अन्यस्मिन् पुत्रे स एव द्विपितृको द्विगोत्रो वा द्वयोरपि स्वधारिक्थभाग्भवति। तत्सधर्मा···गूढजः, बन्धुनोत्सृष्टोऽपविद्धः, संस्कर्तुः पुत्रः कन्यागर्भः कानीनः, सगर्भोढायाः सहोढः, पुनर्भूतायाः पौनर्भवः।

2 *Ibid.* औरसे तूत्पन्ने सवर्णास्तृतीयांशहराः। असवर्णा ग्रासाच्छादनभागिनः।

3 *Ibid.* तेन तुल्यः पुत्रिकापुत्रः।

4 *Manu*, IX. 159-160. औरसः क्षेत्रजश्चैव दत्तः कृत्रिम एव च।
गूढोत्पन्नोऽपविद्धश्च दायादा बान्धवाश्च षट्॥
कानीनश्च सहोढश्च क्रीतः पौनर्भवस्तथा।

Śūdrā women. The bought and the volunteer sons differ from the adopted on account of the absence of sacrament.

§ 28. Amongst the former sons the k s h e t r a j a is excluded by the Mānava against the a u r a s a (IX. 162). When the latter does not exist, the kshetraja will inherit his real father's estate. The Mānava does not allow the kshetraja anything except maintenance (163). An exception is, however, made: if there be disruption of the joint family estate, the charge of maintenance will be commuted by giving him $\frac{1}{6}$ or $\frac{1}{5}$ of the property (164). He evidently cannot claim partition, as he could under the Maurya law. He, at the same time, is the sole heir when there is no a u r a s a son (165). In the absence of these two, the other ten come in the Code in the order they are placed (165). Y ā j ñ a - v a l k y a follows Manu except with regard to the order, more particularly about the adopted son which we shall examine in detail presently.

§ 29. The main difference between the earlier law and our Śuṅga Code (Mānava) is that the latter does not allow a share in every case where the constructive sons are *Savarṇa*. They are heirs, but they become entitled to the "paternal" estate (according to 'Manu') on the contingency of successive failures. The difference was due to the changed attitude towards the old form of raising sons on the 'soil' and towards the status of the wife. Here Yājñavalkya, of course, follows Manu.

Before the Mānava Code, according to the Artha Śāstra all these secondary sons, if *savarṇa* (of the same caste as the father), became coparceners. The share on partition was two-thirds to the *aurasa* and one-third to the others (*aurase tûtpanne savarṇā-stritīyâṁśaharāḥ* | *asavarṇā grāsâchchhādana bhāginaḥ*). The lower caste sons received maintenance in the presence of higher caste sons (*AS.*, 164). The Dharma School limited the coparcenary to the first six, the other six being heirs. This is clearly stated by S a ṁ k h a-L i k h i t a as cited in the Vivāda-Ratnākara (pp. 547, 552). Probably this is what is intended by Gautama's *rikthabhājaḥ* and *gotra-bhājaḥ*. Śaṁkha-Likhita define the shares of the first six (which do not include *dattaka*, they being aurasa, kshetraja, putrikāputra, paunarbhava, kānīna, and gûḍhotpanna): 'they are *bandhu-dāyādas*, of the same gotra as the father and the grandfather, having in the coparcenary property coparcenership (*riktha-piṇḍau sāpindyaṁ cha*). Amongst them divide the property in ten parts—two parts for the father, two for the aurasa, three for the kshetraja and the putrikāputra, one for each of the others (V. Ratnā. p. 547). Hārîta (V. Ratnā. p. 545) also gives a scheme for a partition between the aurasa and five secondary sons (kānîna, pau°, son of two fathers, kshetraja and putrikā°).

The Mānava and, following him, Yājñavalkya reduce the secondary sons into mere heirs. But the Artha Śāstra law is restored with verbal accuracy by Kātyāyana:

उत्पन्ने त्वौरसे पुत्रे तृतीयां शहराःस्मृताः सवर्णास्त्ववर्णास्तु ग्रासाच्छादन-भागिनः (Ratnā. p. 544).

Devala also repeats it (cited by Raghunandana in the Dāyatatva, II. 37, and Jagannātha, 2 Cole. 332).

Bṛihaspati gives shares to 'the kshetraja and others'—*i.e.*, kānîna, paunarbhava, according to Chaṇḍeśvara (V. Ratnā., p. 545). (क्षेत्रजाद्याः सुताश्चान्ये पञ्चषट्-सप्तभागिनः ।)

But Bṛihaspati's explicit text, cited by Chaṇḍeśvara, a little earlier (p. 541) allows only maintenance to the others in the presence of the aurasa and the putrikā.

§ 30. Both Yājñavalkya (II. 130) and Manu (IX. 168) say that the adopted son may be given either by the father or by the mother, while according to Kauṭilya[1] and Vasishṭha (XVII. 29) he must be given by both.

Adopted son.

[1] *AŚ.*, Ch. 64: मातापितृभ्यामद्भिर्दत्तो दत्तः ।

His position in Manu and elsewhere.

The old Dharma theory that there should not be a substitute of a son, mildly recalled by Manu (IX. 161), is traceable as early as Yāska (III.) where a son of the body alone rests on Vedic authority[1]. It was after a great struggle that the adopted 'son' was admitted as a son by the Dharma-lawyers. Gift of a son was based on the doctrine of sale, that the father can sell his son. This was questioned even before Yāska's time who cites the controversy (स्त्रीणां दानविक्रयातिसर्गा विद्यन्ते न पुंसः। पुंसोऽपीत्येके। शौनःशेपे दर्शनात् III. 4). That the father can sell his son was itself based on Vedic passages suggesting that the wife herself was purchased on account of the śulka. The interpretation of those passages was challenged by Āpastamba (II. 6. 13. 12) and he said that marriage was based on sacrament and not on consideration. Hence, he held that there could be no gift of a son. Vasishṭha opposed these arguments. He pointed out that sale of sons are mentioned in the Veda (XVII. 31-32). But Vasishṭha could not give a text for the gift of a son, which the Dharma-lawyers distinguished; such an abnormal thing was to be supported by a definite text. Vasishṭha had to fall back upon the Vedic passage regarding marriage (I. 36). Gautama (XXVIII. 32) and Baudhāyana (II. 3. 20, 31; VII. 5) without any discussion mention the gifted son. The 'son bought' was a separate class by himself. 'Manu', as he condemns the doctrine of purchase in the case of wife and bases marriage on sacrament, similarly, bases the adoption of the gifted son (*datrima*, i.e., what is later known as the d a t t a k a) on sacrament—*dadyātāṁ yam adbhiḥ* (IX. 169). 'With (libations of) water' (*adbhiḥ*) which, to quote D e v a n a B h a ṭ ṭ a (Smṛitichandrikā, Vy. II. p. 669) refers to the *vidhāna* or sacrament, or to quote V i ś v a r ū p a, to *dharma* (Y. II. 134), was 'essential' (R ā g h a v ā n a n d a, *adbhirityavaśyaṁ*). His affiliation is so complete, owing to this new doctrine introduced by Manu, that the *datrima* son, unlike all other fictional sons, does

[1] *Nirukta*, III. 3, अन्योदर्यो मनसापि न मन्तव्यः ।

not any longer belong to his natural family, and he is not allowed to offer oblations to his natural ancestors (M. IX. 142). He adopts the family of his sacramental father, and is completely severed from his natural family. It was a natural corollary that the position of the *dattaka* son should go up in Manu. He is placed in the Mānava Code (IX. 158-160) as the third in the list of the twelve sons, coming after the *aurasa* and *kshetraja*, while he comes very low in the Artha-Śāstra which gives him the ninth place. The Artha-Śāstra order is followed by Nārada (XIII. 45-46), who in turn is followed by Devala (cited by Mitra-Miśra, p. 620, Chaṇḍeśvara, p. 550, and others), and Yama (similarly cited). We have already seen that Nārada is always faithful to Kauṭilya. Baudhāyana (II. 2, 10-23) and Gautama (XXVIII. 32-33)—I think, under the influence of the Mānava Code – give *dattaka* the same order as the Mānava. The agreement with Baudhāyana and Gautama puts the genuineness of the text of the Mānava beyond doubt. Mayne (who says "No doubt Manu is one of the five who thus favours the adopted son. But it may be questioned, whether his text has not undergone an alteration in that respect"—*Hindu Law and Usage*, 7th ed., p. 130) does not take note of that agreement, nor does he notice the fundamental doctrine enunciated and relied on by the Mānava. Bṛihaspati who keeps faithful to Manu, gives the same order as Manu (Jolly's trans. of Bṛi., XXV. 39-40, SBE. XXXIII, p. 376, 3 Colebrooke, 162-171). Vasishṭha who has a different doctrine on marriage and the right of the father in his children, assigns naturally a low position—the eighth—to the '*dattaka*' (XVII. 12-28, 28-39). This is repeated by Vishṇu (XV. 1-27). Āpastamba on account of his theory that there is no property of the husband in the wife and of the father in the son or daughter, does not recognise adoption of son or daughter, nay he does not accept any substitute whatsoever, holding that a son is the son of the progenitor only (II. 6. 13. 5-11).

The origin of the enumeration, for the Dharma School, was the Purāṇa, as specifically stated by V a s i s h ṭ h a (*dvādaśa ityeva putrāḥ Purāṇa-dṛishṭāḥ.* XVII. 12). Their order in H ā r î t a (cited in the Vîramitrodaya, p. 619), V a s i s h ṭ h a, and V i s h ṇ u (XV) on the one hand, and K a u ṭ i l y a, N ā r a d a (XIII. 45-46) and D e v a l a (V. Mitrodaya, p. 620) on the other, is as follows :—

	H.	V.	Vi.	K.	N.	D.
1)	aurasa, (born in wedlock)	aurasa,	aurasa,	aurasa,	aurasa,	1) aurasa,
2)	kshetraja,	kshetraja,	kshetraja,	putrikā-putra,	kshetraja,	2) putrikā-putra,
3)	paunarbhava,	putrikā,	putrikā,	kshetraja,	putrikā-putra,	3) kshetraja,
4)	kānîna,	paunarbhava	paunarbhava,	guḍhaja,	kānîna,	4) kānîna,
5)	putrikā-putra,	kānîna,	kānîna,	apaviddha,	sahoḍha^{0}	5) guḍho^{0}
6)	gūḍhotpanna,	gūḍho^{0}	gūḍho^{0}	kānîna,	guḍho^{0}	6) apaviddha,
7)	*datta,*	sahoḍha,	sahoḍha,	sahoḍha,	paun^{0}	7) sahoḍha,
8)	krîta,	*datta,*	*dattaka,*	paun^{0}	apaviddha,	8) paun^{0}
9)	apaviddha,	krîta,	krîta,	*datta,*	*labdha,*	9) *dattaka,*
10)	sahoḍha,	svayamupagata,	svay^{0}	kṛitaka,	krîta,	10) svay^{0}
11)	svayamupagata,	apaviddha,	apaviddha,	krîta,	kṛita,	11) kṛitaka
12)	sahasā-dṛishṭa.	śūdrāputra.	natural, ('procreated on any')	pratilomas and antarālas,	svay^{0}	12) krîta.

Manu (IX. 158-160), Baudhāyana (II. 2. 10-37) and Gautama (XXVIII. 32-33) have the order thus :—

	M.	B.	G.
			a) 'those who are inheritors' :—
1)	aurasa.	aurasa,	aurasa,
	('putrikā-putra' treated separately)	putrikā-putra,	
2)	kshetraja,	kshetraja,	kshetraja.
3)	*datta,*	*datta,*	*datta*
4)	kṛitrima.	kṛitrima,	kṛitrima.
5)	gudhoº	gudhaja,	gudhoº
6)	apaviddha,	apaviddha,	apaviddha.
			b) 'those who bear (both) gotras' :—
7)	kānîna,	kānîna,	kānîna,
8)	sahodha,	sahodha.	sahodha,
9)	krīta,	krīta.	paunº
10)	paunº	paunº	putrikā-putra,
11)	svayº	svayº	svayº
12)	śaudra.	nishāda, (from śūdrā)	krīta.
		pāraśava, (illegitimate, without marriage—not an heir.)	

There is a complete, verbal and substantial, agreement between Manu and Baudhāyana, while Gautama has his own view on the position of the putrikā-putra and the purchased son. The paunarbhava comes down in the Mānava owing to its hostility to remarriage. This is certain that Gautama implies that the *datta* occupies the same status as the aurasa, born out of dharma wedlock. It is implied that the *datta* is cut off from his natural gotra. Before the Mānava, only in Kauṭilya we have the high position of the putrikā-putra who is placed next to the aurasa and above the kshetraja. Devala follows Kauṭilya completely. Baudhāyana, Gautama and Manu are in agreement regarding the high position of the apaviddha, while Manu with his statement of object and reason raises up the *datta,* in which respect Vasishṭha is nearer Kauṭilya than others. Hārîta has a less ancient order.

Now let us see the attitude of Yājñavalkya (II. 128-133) on the question of the right and the order of precedence of these sons. His order is: (1) aurasa, (2) putrikā-putra, (3) kshetraja, (4) gūḍhaja, (5) kānîna, (6) paunarbhava, (7) dattaka, (8) krîta, (9) kṛitrima, (10) svayaṁdatta, (11) sahoḍhaja and (12) apaviddha ('the son of Śūdra by concubine is also an heir' II. 133). Except for bringing down the sahoḍha and the apaviddha to the bottom, Yājñavalkya follows, as in so many other matters, the Kauṭilîya. He does not agree with any one else. He found the law of the royal law courts still following the tradition of the Kauṭilîya, except regarding the sahoḍha and the apaviddha who must have become extremely rare or nearly obsolete. The position of the dattaka, in spite of the Mānava laws, in actual life had not improved. This explains the attitude of D e v a l a and N ā r a d a and Y a m a (3 Colebrooke 154). It seems that in the later Gupta time, juristic opinion ultimately crystalised in favour of the higher position for the dattaka son as advocated by the Mānava Code, for B ṛ i h a s p a t i does give him that position. K ā t y ā y a n a is not quoted to prove a contrary opinion. We should therefore take it that the Hindu law's definite and ultimate resolve was in favour of the dattaka, as far as the codification goes. After Bṛihaspati and Kātyāyana, we get the Hindu jurisprudents. They, from V i ś v a r ū p a and V i j ñ ā n e s v a r a, down to M i t r a M i ś r a, accept the order of Manu and Bṛihaspati, and disregard Y ā j ñ a v a l k y a and others. The only dissent sounded by J î m ū t a v ā h a n a (Dāyabhāga, X. 7) is discounted by J a g a n n ā t h a and others who were familiar with the living opinion in Bengal.

Inheritance by the Dattaka.

§ 31. The Code of Manu, (IX. 158-160) and all earlier and later codes, except the Code of Yājñavalkya, divide the twelve sons into two classes—'*bandhu-dāyādas*' and '*abandu-dāyādas*', literally 'those succeeding to the bandhus' and 'those not succeeding to the bandhus', which has a far-reaching consequence on the inheritance of the fictional (*gauṇa*) sons including d a t t a k a. That the 'bandhus' here are meant the bandhus of the artificial father is now made clear: the Mānava adopts the two technical terms invented by K a u ṭ i l y a who defines them, while others use them as well-established. K a u ṭ i l y a (III. 7. 60)[1] says:—

> svyamjātaḥ pitṛi-bandhūnāṁ cha dāyādaḥ | paraṁ-jātas saṁskartureva, na bandhūnāṁ | tat-sadharmā.. .. .. .. dattaḥ.

"The son produced by the father inherits also the relatives of the father; that one produced by another, inherits (the father) who performs his sacrament, and does not inherit the relatives (bandhus). Such (the latter) is the status of the *datta* (son)."

The M ā n a v a classes aurasa, kshetraja, datta, kṛitrima, gūḍhotpanna and apaviddha in the *bandhu-dāyāda* class (IX. (158-159), and the latter six—kānîna, sahoḍha, krīta, paunarbhava, svayaṁdatta, and śaudra—as the *a-dāyāda-bandhus* (IX. 160). G a u t a m a calls his two groups of six each as '*riktha-bhājaḥ*' and '*gotra-bhājaḥ*' (XXIX. 32-33) *i.e.*, 'inheritors' and the 'bearers of (both) gotra (names)'. B a u d h ā y a n a does not know any such division, but H ā r î t a (VM., p. 619) uses the term *bandhu-dāyādāḥ* and *a-bandhudāyādāḥ* and places *datta* as the first in the latter. N ā r a d a (XIII. 47; VM., p. 620) and D e v a l a (VM., p. 620) divide their enumerations of the twelve sons into two divisions (1 to 6 and 7 to 12) under bandhu-dāyādas and a-bandhu-dāyādas. Bṛihaspati calls *datta*, *apaviddha*, *krīta* and *kṛita*, '*riktha-sutāḥ*', 'inheriting-sons.'

The two terms denote that the first class of sons will succeed to collaterals, while the latter will inherit lineally or more strictly their artificial fathers only. By counting the dattaka son below the first six, all the metrical dharma-śāstras, except Manu and Bṛihaspati, exclude the collateral succession of the *dattaka* and *kṛitrima* amongst others. Yājñavalkya, however,

---

1 *AS.*, Ch. 64, p. 164. स्वयं जातः पितृबन्धूनां च दायादः। परं जातस्संस्कर्तुरेव न बन्धूनाम्।

ignores the distinction of *bandhu-dāyādas* and *non-bandhu-dāyādas*, and so does Vishṇu.

§ 32. The commentators met the problem, and all over India except Bengal, unanimously rejected that limitation on the dattaka's capacity. A s a h ā y a, the oldest known commentator, in spite of his being the commentator of N ā r a d a who places the *dattaka* son amongst the non-bandhu-dāyādas, counts the *dattaka* as the third (A s a h ā y ā c h a r y a cited by C h a ṇ ḍ e-ś v a r a in the V. Ratnā, p. 544). Asahāya expressly holds that he inherits both his adoptive father and that father's relatives (*jñātis*). V i ś v a r ū p a, the oldest commentator of Yājña-valkya and a high authority, writing on Y. II. 136, cites Manu in preference to others and bases his opinion on his text. Similarly V i j ñ a n e ś v a r a (on Y. II. 132, Mit., I. II. 30-35) refuses to recognise the distinction even of Manu, and the difference between Manu and others he explains away 'as founded on the difference of (the sons) being endowed with quality.' This interpretation is adopted by all subsequent writers of every school—*e.g.*, D e v a n a B h a ṭ ṭ a (Smṛiti-Chandrikā, X), C h a ṇ ḍ e ś v a r a (Vivāda-Ratnākara, p. 551), V ā c h a s p a t i (XVI., p. 230, pūrvapūrvā-bhāve°, etc., ignoring Nārada). M i t r a-M i ś r a (VM., pp. 618-621) after a masterly review of the different authorities notices the conflict—'Here is a conflict with Manu clearly'........ 'This is to be removed by referring the (opposing, contrary texts) to a difference in caste or to local custom,' that is, the other texts being contrary to Manu, they have to be taken as referring to the adoption of a lower caste son or to a local custom contrary to Manu. The D a t t a k a - C h a n d r i k ā (V. 22-24) says 'the doctrine of one holy saint that the son given is heir to kinsmen, and that of another that he is not such heir, are to be reconciled by referring to the distinction of his being endowed with good qualities or otherwise).'

The author of the S a r a s v a t î-v i l ā s a (§ 386, Setlur's trans., p. 161) counts him as the fourth. Similarly Mādhava rejects Hārîta (§ 52, Setlur, p. 330) and the Madana-Pārijāta follows the order given in the *Subodhinî* on the Mitāksharā (Setlur, p. 521).

Jîmūtavāhana, on the other hand, clearly holds (X. 7-8) that a dattaka is not entitled to succeed collaterally. But he has not been followed by Jagannātha and his contemporaries (Mayne, 7th ed., p. 216). The High Court of Calcutta in *Puddokumaree* v. *Juggut Kishore* (5 C. 630), it is submitted, have misinterpreted Devala and unwarrantably brushed aside the interpretation of Devala's text by Jîmūtavāhana. Jîmūtavāhana could be, and was rightly, superseded on the ground of a contrary opinion current in Bengal after him and the decided cases of the Bengal Courts (Mayne, p. 216). In fact, the widening of the rights of the dattaka was a necessary result of the disappearance of the favourite artificial son, the kshetraja. In view of the non-acceptance of Manu's distinction by Yājña-valkya, Hindu commentators and jurists were perfectly entitled to say that the distinction was no more binding. This provision of Manu about collateral succession may still come into play if a man adopts an *a-savarṇa* son.

§ 33. There was an early view which asserted that only the eldest son was entitled to succession, to the exclusion of the others. This view is cited by Āpastamba.[1] This was, of course, perfect lineal primogeniture as we call it. This was very early regarded as inequitable, as it is asserted in the Vedic text cited by Yāska and Āpastamba that Manu Svāyambhuva himself made an equal division of property in favour of his sons (आविशेषेण पुत्राणाम् दायो भवतिधर्मतः).[2] But the trace of primogeniture lingered for a long time. The eldest son in the Artha-Śāstra is allowed an extra-

Primogeniture.

[1] *Āp.*, II. 6. 14, 6. ज्येष्ठोदायाद इत्येके ।
[2] *Āp.*, II. 6. 14, 11. Yāska, III. 4.

chattel as the right of the first-born.[1] The Mānava cites opinions on the subject and begins by saying, 'the eldest may take the whole estate' (IX. 105). His treatment shows that the property tied to primogeniture would have had a charge on it for the maintenance of the other brothers; that is, it remained a joint-family property[2]; while the view cited by Āpastamba shows that the eldest took the whole estate to himself (ज्येष्ठो दायाद इत्येके). The Mānava in the next verse (106) gives the latter view, and the reason he quotes in IX. 107. This right, the Mānava by giving its reasons, couples with the duty of maintaining the cadets of the family (108-110). This shows that the real p r i m o g e n i t u r e was in force in some families or in some part of the country, although it was not looked upon with favour, as indicated by the opinion of Āpastamba that there should be partition and a partition in equal shares amongst all the brothers.[3] The Mānava did not seek to abolish the law, as there was an express Vedic text in favour of primogeniture. But in IX. 111 it gives the general rule and the policy of law: division is better on the Dharma principle. He allows him an extra (112-118) share in chattel as in Kauṭilya, but even here he introduces as exception (115): if all the brothers are equally clever the partition should be in equal shares.[4]

§ 34. Both the Kauṭilīya and the Mānava, being, what Nārada implies his own law in one place to be "Sārvabhauma," "imperial," had to take into consideration the existing laws both in Magadha and outside, and initiated a policy of law where a general law was not possible. Now the policy of the Mānava worked out so satisfactorily that Yājñavalkya could abolish the relic of the *Jyeshṭha*-share altogether (II. 117). It is remarkable that in

---

[1] See *AŚ.*, Ch. 63, p. 162.

[2] *Manu*, IX. 105. ज्येष्ठ एव तु गृह्णीयात् पित्र्यं धनमशेषतः ।
शेषास्तमुपजीवेयुर्यथैव पितरं तथा ॥

[3] *Āp.*, II. 6, 14, 1. जीवन् पुत्रेभ्यो दायं व्यभजेत् समं ।

[4] *Manu*, IX. 115. उद्धारो न दशस्वस्ति सम्पन्नानां स्वकर्मसु ।

some Aryan families, the *Jeṭhāṁsa* rule still survives in the United Provinces, but now it is called a "custom." What was once really a law has been converted on account of the law of Yājñavalkya and the commentators into a custom. That each Vidhi section in these Smṛitis was real law is now evident. Even passages like Yājñavalkya's I. 80 on conjugal life are shown to have been law proper by corresponding passages in the Artha-Śāstra, when, for instance, a breach in that matter was punishable by the law-court on the petition of a wife of a man who had several wives.[1] The exceptional law of primogeniture in ruling families and government officers, the later text-writes treated under *R ā j a n ī t i*, independent of the law proper.

Partition.

§ 35. The Artha-Śāstra starts the l a w of p a r t i t i o n with the clear statement that sons have no right of ownership as long as the father is alive, and that the partition cannot take place as long as 'they,' *i.e.*, the father and mother, are alive.[2] The same thing we find in Manu, IX. 104 and Yājñavalkya, II. 117. The general rule of the Artha-Śāstra refers to *dravya*, which is generally understood to denote chattel but lower down immovable property of the father is mentioned. It seems that *dravya* was used to mean 'property' in general. When the father made a partition himself, he was not to make any difference between the shares to the sons.[3] The same law is given by the Mānava, IX. 215.

Early history of the Dāyabhāga doctrine.

§ 36. It is to be marked that we get the germ of the theory of the Bengal School in the law of the Artha-Śāstra that the sons were *anīśvara*, 'without authority' or 'right of ownership,' as long as the father was alive. Likewise at the same time, when he made a division he could not pass over any without a lawful cause.

---

[1] *AŚ.*, p. 153 (Ch. 59).

[2] *AŚ.*, Ch. 62, p. 160. अनीश्वराः पितृमन्तः···तेषामूर्ध्वं पितृतो दायविभागः ।

[3] *AŚ.*, Ch. 62, p. 161. जीवद्विभागे पिता नैकं विशेषयेत् । न चैकमकारणान्निर्विभजेत ।

Mitāksharā doctrine in Yājñavalkya and earlier.

§ 37. Yājñavalkya's law is prominently different on the point: the son became joint-owner in the ancestral property, both real and personal.[1] This new law is the basis of the M i t ā k s h a r ā right. Vijñaneśvara gives the principle that the right is acquired the moment the son is born. It seems that it was deduced from the earlier law that the sons (and descendants) took "according to descent, (pitṛitaḥ)"[2] *i.e.*, per stirpes, as the grandson was joined in his share with his father in division, it followed that he and his father were jointly owners. The son had been acquiring independence slowly: s e p a r a t e a c q u i s i t i o n of the son is an established fact in the Artha-Śāstra. Then, 'sons or grandsons till the fourth generation from the first parent shall also have prescribed shares.'[3] This is the basis of the law of Yājñavalkya. Probably Yājñavalkya meant only to reproduce the law of Kauṭilya, but the form in which it is stated had a far-reaching effect.

Growth of Son's right.

Succession to Strīdhana.

§ 37A. On son's right to mother's s t r ī d h a n a, the Mānava has the same law as Kauṭilya: sons and daughters divide equally on her death (IX. 193), and if she had no child, the husband would succeed (196). The only difference is that according to the Kauṭilīya the property of a woman married in any of the four unapproved forms went to her father's family,[4] while according to the Mānava, the āsura wife's strīdhana followed that rule, but the gāndharva wife's property followed the same course as the wife married in an approved form.[5] The Mānava does not say anything about the Rākshasa and the Paiśācha wives'

---

[1] *Yājñ.*, II. 121. भूर्या पितामहोपात्ता निबन्धो द्रव्यमेव वा।
तत्र स्यात् सदृशं स्वाम्यं पितुः पुत्रस्य चैव हि॥

[2] *AS.*, Ch. 62, p. 160. पितृतो दायविभागः।

[3] *Ibid.* पुत्राः पौत्रा वा चतुर्थादित्यंशभाजः।

[4] *Ibid.*, Ch. 59, p. 152. मातापितृप्रमाणाः शेषाः। तौ हि शुल्कहरौ दुहितुः।

[5] *Manv*, IX. 196-197.

strīdhana. According to the Artha-Śāstra the husband was the heir of the wife wedded in the approved form in the absence of children, but only to the extent of the śulka he gave (as security). The rest went to the woman's father's family.[1]

Different rule laid down by Yājñavalkya.

§ 38. Yājñavalkya (II. 145) adopts the rule of Kauṭilya, making the distinction between the four approved and the four unapproved forms of marriages, with, however, this prominent difference that the daughters succeed exclusively and not the sons.[2] Here he differs both from Manu and Kauṭilya. This is again a marked tendency of partiality in Yājñavalkya for the enfranchisement of woman. He is compensating her for the absence of her right in the father's estate as against brothers. Vijñāneśvara extends the right by including the daughter's daughter in "the daughter."

§ 39. An illegitimate son in the codes is the son of the 'dāsī' which denotes a female slave and a prostitute or a concubine.[3] Yājñavalkya gives him inheritance only when he is the son of a Śūdra (II. 134). It should be noticed that the son from a female slave became a full citizen (Ārya) according to Kauṭilya, and would have inherited if a savarṇa.[4] It would have been regarded as a gāndharva union. But the policy of law as to slavery having been changed, distinction was made and the slave woman became a distinct class. Probably it is he who is intended by 'Śūdra woman's son' of the Mānava (IX. 179)[5] who is excluded and who is made a class by himself. The Mānava had limited even this limited right of the slaves' son of a Śūdra to the condition of the option

[1] *AŚ.*, Ch. 59, p. 153. तदभावे भर्ता। शुल्कमन्वाधेयमन्यद्वा बन्धुभिर्दत्तं बान्धवा हरेयुः।

[2] *Yājñ.*, II. 145. अप्रजः स्त्रीधनं भर्तुर्ब्राह्मादिषु चतुर्ष्वपि।
दुहितॄणां प्रसूता चेच्छेषेषु पितृगामि तत्॥

[3] *AŚ.*, pp. 181-184 (Ch. 70), pp. 123-125 (Ch. 47) *Cf.* 1 Bom. 97 (*Rahi v. Govinda*).

[4] *AŚ.*, Ch. 64, p. 164, *cf.* Ch. 63, p. 163.

[5] As understood by Nandapaṇḍita (on Vishṇu, XV. 27).

[6] *Manu*, IX. 179. दास्यां वा दासदास्यां वा यः शूद्रस्य सुतो भवेत्। सोऽनुज्ञातो हरेदंशम् etc.

of the father.[6] Yājñavalkya adopts his view in II. 133. Earlier Hindus abhorred illegitimacy and legalised every son. But for the controversy on the right of the slave and Śūdra raised by the Mānava, this difference about the dāsi-putra would not have become so marked in law, and his total disinherison in case of the three upper varṇas would not have resulted. Vishṇu, in XV. 27, which is an original Sūtra, recognizes 'a son born of any woman whomsoever' as the last son in the list of sons.

Daughter.

§ 40. Although in the Mānava d a u g h t e r is not an heir in the list of heirs, yet her position is very high. She is equal to son (IX. 130), the object of the dearest tenderness (IV. 185), and even the picture of the father (IV. 185), nay, the very self of the father : '*in her he lives*' (IX.130). Nowhere in Hindu law her legal position is so tenderly defined. On no other subject the severe author of the Mānava spends so much sentiment. For a moment he forgets that daughter is a woman—the object of frown of all masculine thinkers from Buddha down to Nietzsche. He knows her only as daughter. She is, he says, to be always excused (IV. 185). It would have been strange that the Mānava with these ideas about daughter left her out of inheritance, and especially so when the former law had been in her favour. More so, again, when we remember that in earlier literature she just missed being an equal of her brother in inheritance in all cases. Yāska, citing a Vedic mantra, says that those who hold that daughter is a dāyāda (heir) quote it in support but others quote it to support the (exclusive) right of the son.[1] Her right is shrouded in later times in the Dharmasūtras. 'While in her he lives, how can another man take the property?"[2] (Manu). What is the sense in saying that there is no difference between the daughter and the son, if he is not going to say that she is to take like the son ? The 'a p p o i n t e d d a u g h t e r'

---

[1] *Yāska*, III. 3. अथैतां दुहितृदायादा उदाहरन्ति । पुत्रदायादा इत्येके । 4. न दुहितर इत्येके ।
[2] *Manu*, IX. 130.

is not an heir, but her son certainly is both in Kauṭilya and Sumati. The argument that she is not mentioned in the list of the heirs is of no force, for it does not include even the son of the appointed daughter. Both are already treated separately, hence they are not repeated. The Mānava in fact abolished all difference between the son of a daughter appointed and the son of a daughter unappointed, and makes both equally heirs to the maternal grandfather.[1] He has laid the law which Yājñavalkya adopts. Here Sumati (Mānava) had laid down a new law—separating the law of the past history with a deep line of demarcation. The law of daughter's appointment was made useless. The formality was practically abolished. The present was cut off from the past. This was a result of the high regard for the daughter in the author of the Mānava. 'Between a son's son and a daughter's son there exists in this world no difference' (M. IX. 139). On this definite point the Maurya law was made absolute for all ages.[2] Manu introduced this Artha law into Dharma. As he was having a new thing, he gives his reasons as usual. The law of putrikā-putra was really a law of adoption by contract. If a son to the putrikā was born after appointment, half the property went back to the family of her father (IX. 134-135). Although the *putrikā* was an adopted son (*putra*), yet the father could never become heir to that daughter.[3]

§ 41. One more forward step was taken by the Mānava in favour of the daughter. An unmarried daughter was given the Yautuka property of the mother to the exclusion of the brothers.[4] What was this *Yautuka* property is not clear.

---

[1] *Manu*, IX. 136. अकृता वा कृता वापि यं विन्देत् सदृशात्सुतम् ।
पौत्री मातामहस्तेन दद्यात् पिण्डं हरेद्धनम् ।

[2] *Ibid.* 139. पौत्रदौहित्रयोर्लोके विशेषो नोपपद्यते ।
दौहित्रोऽपि ह्यमुत्रैनं संतारयति पौत्रवत् ॥

[3] Putrikā-putra is known to Yāska III. 5 ff.

[4] *M.* IX. 131. मातुस्तु यौतकं यत् स्यात् कुमारीभाग एव सः ।

This is not known to the Artha-Śāstra, nor is it defined by the Mānava. Nor is it one of the six strîdhanas of the Mānava (IX. 194). It seems that it was her private hoard or some sort of earning. On this law of exception Yājñavalkya improves and makes a general rule that the daughter should take first the strīdhana of the mother.[1]

§ 42. There is yet one further provision in favour of the favourite of the Mānava. Daughter's daughter should also get 'some thing' out of affection from the estate of the maternal grandfather.[2] Son's daughter has no place in the laws of the Mānava Code.

§ 43. That maintenance and cost of marriage was a charge on the estate of the father, was already settled law before the Mānava.[3] This obligation had been established even before the time of Yāska. Yājñavalkya (II. 124) makes the brothers contribute $\frac{1}{4}$ from each share to the "uninitiated sisters." This Vijñāneśvara regards as a right to that share, and the wording does show that. The Mānava gives this law in IX. 212 where the commentators explain 'sisters' as 'unmarried sisters.' According to Manu, they take an equal share with the brothers. She gained a settled position by the law of Kauṭilya. This was, however, settled on the authority of the state, the Dharma law had not come to that decision. Hence the Mānava gives his statement of 'object and reasons' (IX. 129 ff). With his lofty preface, to what conclusion does he come? Accepted authority of the commentators makes the whole section refer to 'the appointed daughter.' I venture to differ. I say that the plain meaning

---

[1] Cf. *Yājñ.*, II. 145.

[2] *Manu*, IX. 193. यास्तासां स्युर्दुहितरस्तासामपि यथार्हतः ।
मातामह्या धनात् किञ्चित् प्रदेयं प्रीतिपूर्वकम् ॥

[3] *AŚ.*, Ch. 62. p. 161. कन्याभ्यश्च प्रदानिकम् ।

of IX. 130 should be taken. In the light of the Artha Śāstra its plain meaning is to be accepted as referring to the inheritance of a daughter as such.

§ 44. About mother's right on partition the Code of Yājña-valkya gives a new direction. The old law (Kauṭilya, Ch. 59, pp. 152-153, 160-161, and Manu, IX. 194-200) provided her with śtrīdhana and finished the subject. The śtrīdhana in part had been fixed by law, and she could realise that amount from the estate of the husband. It was sacred (AŚ. p. 152, M. VIII. 29). Yājñavalkya, however, contemplates a case of no strīdhana. This may arise in irregular marriages or in a priestly marriage. Yājñavalkya with his usual policy for the independence of woman, provides against the contingency of her penury (II. 115). One share equal to that of the sons was to be given to her. This was to be done where nothing had been given to her from the family of the husband, *i.e.*, without any consideration of her wealth received from her father's family.[1] The question amongst the commentators arose whether she took as a share or only maintenance, *i.e.*, if the property was large, could the sons give her only just enough for maintenance. Śrīkara, a predecessor of Vijñāneśvara, was of the view that maintenance was intended. But Vijñāneśvara opposes this. No doubt he is right. Looking at the general policy of Yājña-valkya and the plain meaning no room remains for controversy. It is plain that a share is intended. A very ingenious objection is taken by the lady writer Lakshmī-devī (authoress of the *Bālama-Bhaṭṭī* commentary on the *Mitākshara*), who says that no partition can be made between husband and wife 'both being one', and hence only maintenance is intended. An equally clever answer is offered in anticipation by that acute lawyer Mitra-Miśra, who says that it is not to be taken as partition but as a gift of

Mother.

---

[1] *Yājñ.*, II. 115. यदि कुर्यात् समानंशान् पत्न्यः कार्याः समांशिकाः ।
न दत्तं स्त्रीधनं यासां भर्त्रा वा श्वशुरेण वा ॥

love. The right of the mother in a partition by sons after their father's death was the same (II. 123).

§ 45. Yājñavalkya has been followed in establishing the mother's share, by Brihaspati and Vyāsa (V. Ratnā., p. 484). There is no trace of this law earlier. We have it also in V i s h ṇ u (XVIII. 34), but we cannot be sure that V i s h ṇ u has not borrowed it from Y ā j ñ a v a l k y a, for it is quite unconnected with the Dharma-sūtras. We may even say that it is opposed to the general policy of the Sūtras which expressly hold that women can have no property or share in any estate: **न दायं निरिन्द्रियाह्यदायाश्च स्त्रियो मता इति श्रुतिः** (Bodhāyana), and **तस्मात् स्त्रियो निरिन्द्रिया अदायादीः इति तैत्तिरीयकश्रुतिः** (cited in the Smṛiti-Chandrikā, p. 623), **तस्मात् पुमान् दायादोऽदायादा स्त्री** (Yāska, III. 4). 'A wife is declared to have no property' (Manu, VIII. 416). The amount of share might have been suggested by a text like that of Ś a ṅ k h a-L i k h i t a (V. Ratnā. p. 547) which says that a father making a division shall keep two shares to himself.

Partition by Father.

§ 46. The A r t h a-Ś ā s t r a (Ch. 61, p. 160) declares that sons cannot call for partition as long as the father and mother are alive, and that sons and grandsons upto the fourth degree in the undivided ancestral property have shares, and continuous *piṇḍa*. Now it is clear that the prohibition to partition here refers to ancestral property and not to self-acquisitions which is known to Kauṭilya (*svayamārjitamavibhājya°*, p. 160), although employed in the case of the sons. The Mānava in IX. 104 repeats the law of Kauṭilya almost with verbal accuracy :—

ūrdhvaṁ pituścha mātuscha sametya bhrātaraḥ samam |
bhajéran paitrikaṁ rikthamanīśāste hi jīvatoḥ ||

against Kauṭilya's :

anīśvarāḥ pitṛimantaḥ, sthitapitṛi-mātṛikāḥ putrāḥ ; *teshāṁ ūrdhvaṁ pitṛito dāya-vibhāgaḥ pitṛi-dravyāṇāṁ* (p. 160).

M a n u, read with Kauṭilya, gives the law that the sons are *anîśvara*, 'non-proprietors', in the life-time of the two parents with regard to ancestral property. J î m ū t a v ā h a n a alone, who generally goes back to the ancient texts and finds out the original meaning, was right in interpreting the texts in his masterly review of the Smṛiti law on the right of the father and the time of partition (*Dāya-bhāga*, Chapters II, III. 1, 1-14). Ś a ṅ k h a-L i k h i t a note that the sons are 'not independent' (*asvatantrāḥ*) to call for partition both at Artha and at Dharma (*Artha-Dharmayoḥ*, V. Ratnā. p. 456), and use the very term of the Artha Śāstra (*piṭri-mantaḥ*, translating the archaic *aniśvarāḥ* by *asvatantrāḥ* (V. Ratnā. p. 460). Saṅkha-Likhita's sūtra was composed in the Śuṅga period. They, amongst other things, enjoin an *aśvamedha* sacrifice by a *sārvabhauma* king (Vîramitrodaya-Rājaniti, p. 252). Reference to 'Dharma' by Ś a ṅ k h a-L i k h i t a would have been to the Dharma-sūtras like G a u t a m a (XXVIII. 1-2), V a s i s h ṭ h a (XVII. 40-41), B a u d h ā y a n a (II. 2. 3, 8), H ā r î t a (V. Ratnā. p. 459) and to Manu (IX. 104). But except Ś a ṅ k h a-L i k h i t a (V. Ratnā. p. 460) no sūtra-kāra has the rule for postponing partition until the death of the mother. And when Ś a ṅ k h a-L i k h i t a say that both at A r t h a and at D h a r m a (mentioning Artha first as weaker in authority) partition cannot be claimed by a son, they limit it there (p. 456) to the life-time of the father (*jivati pitari*). Hence it is perfectly clear that Manu borrowed the rule prohibiting partition until the death of both parents from the Artha. Śaṅkha-Likhita give reasons for including the mother in their rule (*riktha-mūlaṁ hi kuṭumbaṁ*), a proof that they were for the first time including it in the Dharma-sūtra.

Yājñavalkya (II. 117) follows Kauṭilya and Manu and lays down the time for partition by sons at the death of both parents.

Exception in regard to self-acquisitions are given both by Kauṭilya (p. 160) and Manu (IX. 205, 206, 208).

A father, making a division, is ordained in the Artha-Śāstra (p. 161) not to favour one son against the other, and not to disinherit any without reason. Manu embodies the rule in IX. 215 (न पुत्रभागं विषमं पिता दद्यात् etc.) which was in conformity with the views of both the Artha and Dharma Schools (*Cf.* Baudhāyana, II. 3, 2-3).

Yājñavalkya in II. 114 and 116 gives the rules about partition by a father. The verses II. 114 to 116 read together. It is recommended to the father to make an equal division, adhering, if he likes, to the ancient practice of honouring the eldest with special favour. The latter rule was falling into desuetude, primogeniture being repulsive to Hindu lawyers. If an equal division is made by the father, the mothers should be given shares. But, Yājñavalkya notes in 116, if an unequal division, as a matter of fact, is made by the father it is valid (*dharmyaḥ smṛitaḥ*). Kauṭilya's law that where there are several sons by different fathers (cousins) and brothers and nephews or grandsons, division is to be made per stirpes (*pitṛitaḥ*; *piturekamaṁśaḥ hareyuḥ*, p. 160), is reproduced by Yājñavalkya in 120-121: 'amongst sons of different fathers the allotment of shares is according to the fathers. The ownership of both the father and the son is the same in land, income from pension, or wealth received from the grand-ancestor."

The lawyers of Western India, that is, the author of the Mitākshara and his followers, construe II. 116 of Yājñavalkya sanctioning unequal division, as referring to the self-acquired property of the father, a case which required no law. In other words, the text is made nugatory by the explanation. Mistranslation of '*dharmyaḥ*' by Mandalik ('if just') is a result of that interpretation. The same school of Hindu-lawyers interpret verse 121 as an independent provision, meaning a declaration of equal right of the father and the son in the ancestral property, while in comparison with the older law the text refers to denote the shares *per stirpes* as opposed to shares *per capita*.

From this verse Vyāsa, one of the latest smṛitikāras, deduces the rule that the proprietary right being equal, the son can demand a partition of the ancestral property (Aparārka, p. 728). In view of Vyāsa's authority the Mitākshāra lawyers were justified in their interpretation, though Jîmūtavāhana alone was historically correct in maintaining the contrary view. Vyāsa, in spite of the whole of the previous legal literature being against him, succeeded, he being on the side of justice; the previous law was hard. Cases of perverted, angry, diseased and unorthodox fathers are pointed out by Nārada (XIII. 16) where he suspends the law after stating it as in Yājñavalkya (XIII. 15: that the father had the right to make an unequal division). Nārada (followed by Bṛihaspati, XV. 1) engrafted exceptions on the law that division cannot be demanded during the life-time of the father, after stating it (XIII. 2-3) namely, when the father could expect no more sons, and sisters had been married, partition during father's life was possible. Thus the way had been already prepared to drive out the ancient law. Hindu juridical and judicial conscience wanted advance, and Vyāsa put that desire into law. Nîlakaṇṭha boldly says (on Nārada XIII. 15, citing him in his Mayūkha, p. 35) that the law prohibiting partition at the instance of sons, had force in former ages only.

Partition was favoured by the Dharma School before Manu. Āpastamba [II. 6. 14 (1) enjoins: 'he should, during his life-time, divide his wealth equally amongst his sons'], Baudhāyana (II. 2.3, 2-3) and Gautama (XXVIII. 4: *vibhāge tu dharma-vṛiddiḥ*) indicate it. Manu also mentions the favourable doctrine of the Dharma School (IX. 111). The Artha School seems to have been particularly against partition in the parents' life-time, and it was under that influence that Manu provided IX. 104. For we find that H ā r î t a, as cited by Vijñaneśvara (*sub.* Y. II. 114) and Nilakantha (p. 34), had already laid down, anticipating N ā r a d a that when the father is old, perverted, and suffering from a lingering disease, partition may be had by sons in spite of the father's unwillingness (**जीवन्पुत्रेभ्यो दायं विभजेत् समं अकामे पितरि रिक्थभागी वृद्धे विपरीतचेतसि दीर्घरोगिणि च**). It must be this sort of forced partition to which G a u t a m a refers in XV. 19: he declares those men who separate from their father on partition against his will, degraded (**पित्रा चाकामेन विभक्तान्**). It was under the influence of the actual Artha Śāstra law that the Mānava (IX. 104) and Yājñavalkya (II. 116-117) had to adopt the severer attitude.

The tradition of the father's power of making an unequal division persists in N ā r a d a and B ṛ i h a s p a t i (see Jîmūta-vāhana, *Dāya-bhāga*, C. II. § 75). K ā t y ā y a n a, however, versifies the direction of the Artha Śāstra (p. 161) that the father should not be partial to one son, nor disinherit any without sufficient cause (*Dāya-bhāga*, III. 84). The verse provision, as J î m ū t a v ā h a n a points out (*DBh.*, C. II.), presupposes the power. With V y ā s a the tide turns. Before Vyāsa, V i s h ṇ u (XVII. 1-2, if the text is not later), had interpreted, so to say, the texts of Manu and Yājñavalkya in a different way—that is, in a way anticipating Vijñāneśvara, but that construction was never accepted by any other Smriti-writer. N ā r a d a, B ṛ i h a s-p a t i and K ā t y ā y a n a, all read Manu and Yājñavalkya with the Artha Śāstra, on the question. With the interpretation of V y ā s a the matter ended in favour of Vishṇu, until it was questioned by U d y o t a and J î m ū t a v ā h a n a (*BDh.*, II. 9).

V i j ñ ā n e ś v a r a, in the introduction to the subject beginning with Y. II. 114, notes that he found the law as understood by the public to be that it was by birth that sons and grandsons acquired right to property (*loke cha putrādīnām janmanaiva satvaṁ prasiddhataraṁ*). Under II. 114 he says that the text refers to self-acquisitions of the father (*svārjitadravya-vishayaḥ*), but when he comes to II. 117, he, finding Nārada (XIII. 16) against him, does not take his stand on Vyāsa or Vishṇu, but says a thing which is stronger than any text. He says that the law giving power to the father for making an unequal division was a dead law, the society being against it (*śāstra-drishṭastathāpiloka-vidvishṭatvān nānushṭheyaḥ*), like the direction on the offering of beef to a priest guest (**महोक्षं वा महाजं वा श्रोत्रियाय**°), and he cites Y. I.156 that a law abhorred by the society is not to be followed. It is thus evident that the law of the absolute power of the father had ceased to be in force in Western India when Vijñāneśvara flourished, like the practice of the sacrificial cow-killing (*gavalambhana*) and *niyoga* which he cites. Thus Vyāsa merely codified the law as he found it, while Vishṇu was anticipating it, if his text is uncorrupted (for his XVII. 23 is the real corresponding and equivalent provision to Y. II. 120-121 and which is given at the end of the chapter). The sūtras XVII. 1-2 of Vishṇu are not quoted by Aparārka who cites Vyāsa and others. If they existed in the present form, the early Mitāksharā writers would not have omitted to cite them in their favour.

§ 46. The subject of self-acquired property called *svayamārjita*, 'self-acquired', in the Artha Śāstra (p. 160), is dealt with by Manu in IX. 204-209, and by Yājñavalkya in II. 118-119 and in the first-half of II. 120. The only trace of the doctrine of self-acquisition in the Dharma-sūtras is found in Gautama, XXIX. 30 (*svayamarjitamavaidyebhyo vaidyaḥ kāmaṁ na dadyāt*) ; 'a learned (coparcener) may not, if he likes, give his self-acquisition to 'the unlearned ones'. This is what came to be called the *vidyādhana* ('gains of science') self-acquisition in later writers. As defined by Bṛihaspati and Kātyāyana, that is, the final code authors, it meant the fees and honoraria of the Brahmin, earned

Self-acquisitions.

by him as a priest and as a lawyer[1]—both as a debater or a giver of opinion (Smṛiti-Chandrikā, pp. 638, V. Ratnā. p. 502). Beyond this the Lharma School had not gone. The law about the self-acquisition proper, the economic acquisitions, was evolved by the lawyers of the Artha School and the royal law Court. The Kauṭilîya, Ch. 62, p. 160, lays down:

> 'Self-acquisition with the exception (of that property) which is raised by means of the paternal wealth is not partible' (*svayamārjitamavibhājyaṁ anyatra piṭri-dravyādutthitebhyaḥ*).

It is noteworthy that Gautama employs the very term of Kauṭilya (*svayamarjitaṁ*). The Mānava, IX. 204, gives the law of Gautama, turning the negative into the positive form and extending it much further. Share in the acquisition from learning should be given to the younger brothers, if they all live by learning (*vidyā*). Manu is giving here the economic aspect of the question which is clearly brought out by Bṛihaspati and Kātyāyana. When the *vidyā* is in the sense of 'art', and the whole family lives by the 'art,' the exemption of Gautama is not to apply. Where *vidyā* is not a training in art, but lawyers' and priestly *vidyā* and the earnings are a tribute to intelligence; those earnings are exempted from the net of coparcenary. This Manu terms *vidyā-dhana* proper in IX. 206, where he classes it with gifts from friends, gifts at marriage, and customary presents of honour. Manu, IX. 208, deals with the general self-acquisition of economic nature. 'What one member acquires by his exertions without using paternal wealth, that self-acquisition of his own effort, he shall not share unless by his own will'. Here he is codifying the law of Kautilya. This is the general law. Sections IX. 205 and IX. 209 give explanations in favour of the sons against the father and the father against the sons respectively. When the sons—ordinary, 'uneducated' ones, *i.e.*, without any special

[1] On these special texts a vakil's or a professor's earnings should be considered as ovided for specifically.

training, obtained at the expense of the father—unite their labour, that wealth is not the father's property, but is to be divided equally amongst the brothers (205). Conversely when the father alone recovers a lost paternal property (*pitṛikaṁ dravyaṁ*), it becomes a self-acquisition (*'svayamarjita'*) of the father, and the sons cannot have a share therein unless the father allows it (209).

The necessity for these provisions arose on account of a Dharma view which was against the actual law as administered in the law-courts, the Artha-Śāstra law. The Mānava here does not favour the Dharma view and adopts the Artha law. Vasiṣṭha, XVII. 51, says "And if one of the sons has himself gained something (*svayamutpāditaṁ*), he shall receive a double share." This was against the Artha law. The Mānava, to meet this, inserted the explanatory section IX. 205. And section 209 was necessitated probably by another Dharma doctrine, the original sūtra for it is not available to us to-day, but the doctrine is found preserved in a verse cited by Vijñāneśvara (*sub.* Y. II. 119), under the name of Śaṅkha (not Śaṅkha-Likhita), that if ancestral land is recovered by one member the others get it, subject to giving an extra one-fourth share to the recoverer. Manu, following the law of the royal court, is superseding these two Dharma provisions by his two explanations.

Now let us see what Yājñavalkya does. Yājñavalkya, in II. 118-120, first gives the general law that whatever is self-acquired without injury to paternal wealth, gifts from friends and wedding presents, do not belong to coparceners. This is the general law of Kauṭilya and Manu (section 208 with one portion of § 206). The doubtful and controverted topics—hereditary property recovered by one member, gains of vidyā, and the case 'where common wealth is put to commercial (or, industrial) use (called) *samutthāna*'— are dealt with in §§ 119 and 120. The first two are self-acquisitions and are not to be shared by coparceners, and the last is divisible equally amongst the owners of the common wealth put to economic or commercial use. Yājñavalkya is supporting Manu's § 205 on the analogy of partnership. About *vidyā-dhana* Yājñavalkya gives no qualification and treats it as settled law. The tendency of N ā r a d a to limit the application of the doctrine of self-acquisition to such cases where the family has not supported the member in his student days, and of V y ā s a even to limit its operation in the wealth acquired by valour if the member uses the chariot or the sword of the family (*Smṛitichandrikā*, pp. 637-641) is carried to the farthest limits by the commentators. V i j ñ ā n e ś v a r a is particularly ungenerous while interpreting the generous provisions of Yājñavalkya (II. 118-119). He says that whatever is gained without detriment to paternal estate in the cases mentioned here alone are exempted ; anything outside them, *e.g.*, accepted charity, is partible (*sarva-śeshatvāt*. . . . *pratigraha-labdha-mapi vibhajanīyaṁ*) ! A p a r ā r k a gives the natural meaning (p. 723). V i j ñ ā n e ś v a r a is carried away by his enthusiasm for the joint family. J ī m ū t a v ā h a n a (VI. 14-22) sums up after discussing the later restrictive texts :

> "Since it appears from these and other texts that partition does or does not take place in the case of wealth acquired by science, valour or the like, according to as joint property is or is not employed ; and since this alone is the reason, a sacred maxim containing that only must be inferred........this is the object of holākā interpretation (of the Mīmāṁsā). [21-22]

It is not necessary to say that every modern lawyer will agree here with this talented jurist.

V i j ñ ā n e ś v a r a limits the law of Yājñavalkya by explaining 'without any injury to paternal wealth (*pitṛidravya*), to mean the wealth of the father and mother (*mātā-pitror dravyā-vināśena*). But Yājñavalkya had used it in the sense of the *paitrika* of Manu (IX. 209), meaning ancestral in the male line.

There is a special prejudice in the commentators against the operation of the doctrine of self-acquisition with regard to immovable property. A p a r ā r k a, for instance, on Y. II. 119, says that if the *dravya* be land, garden, etc. (क्षेत्रारामादिकं द्रव्यं), the rule of self-acquisition applies only when the recoverer is permitted by the coparceners to recover the property; if without their consent he recovers, he gets only an extra one-fourth share. Thus he makes the provision of Yājñavalkya almost nugatory. For his authority, A p a r ā r k a quotes a text which he attributes to R i s h y a-Ś ṛ i ṅ g a, and Vijñāneśvara to Ś a ṅ k h a, to limit the text of Yājñavalkya to movable property, but there is no warrant for this as Kauṭilya, Manu and Yājñavalkya use d r a v y a in the sense of property in general. And so does even Aparārka himself. Hindu lawyers, however, looked upon landed property with special partiality. By interpretations tenable or otherwise, they took their stand on an obscure text. V i j ñ ā n e ś v a r a goes so far as to say that self-acquired immovable property should not be alienated without the consent of the sons (स्थावरे तु स्वार्जिते पित्रादिप्राप्ते च पुत्रादिपारतन्त्र्यमेव, *Introduction*, ed. Gharpure p. 75). And for this he finds authority in a text, subsequently attributed to V y ā s a, with whom really the Mitāksharā School begins. M i t r a-M i ś r a, however, explains it away saying that the consent here is mere attestation. (*Vīramitrodaya*, p. 585, trans., II. i, § 22).

Cases of exclusion from shares in coparcenary.

§ 47. The A r t h a Ś ā s t r a excludes the following from a ṁ ś a ('share') which means share in coparcenary :—(1) the *patita* or degraded and (2) "the children, born thereof", (3) the impotent (*klība*), (4) the idiot, (5) the lunatic, (6) the blind, and (7) the leper.

There are three riders to this disinheritson.

(*i*) If these are married, and their children (*apatya*) are not like them, the children get their (the father's) share.

(*ii*) All of these (evidently including their wives)—except the degraded—are entitled to maintenance ('grāsā-chhādana', 'food and clothing').

(*iii*) The wives of all these (not excluding the *patita*), if past the capacity to procreate, should raise children, who will inherit in their place. (AŚ., the last two paragraphs of V. 59, Ch. 62, pp. 161-162).

The explanation (*iii*) has an important bearing, as we shall see, on the present-day law of adoption.

M a n u, IX. 201-202, reproduces the law of Kauṭilya :—

"These have no *aṁśa* (share) : (1) the *klība* and (2) the *patita*, (3) the born blind and the (born) deaf, similarly, (4) the mad, (5) the idiot and (6) the dumb, also (7) those who are wanting in a limb or any organ (*nirindriyāḥ*).

All of them have to be well maintained up to the end (202). If they married ('*arthitā tu dāraiḥ*', in place of Kauṭilya's '*bhāryārthe*'), the children (*apatya*) born of their body (*tantunāṁ*) become entitled to the heritage (203).

We can easily detect the difference and the reason for it. The children are not disinherited, but 'the issues of the body' alone are let into inheritance. The reason for this is that Manu is against the *kshetraja*. This distinction of Kauṭilya that a son born of the *patita* is not to inherit but a son raised by his wife was to inherit, seemed absurd to the author of the Mānava, and he did not include the *patita*'s son in the *aṁśa*-less list, and also removed the bar to maintenance to the *patita*, not to drive him to beggary and further degradation. Further, he prescribed expiation and a procedure to reclaim the *patita* by XI. 187-189 (read with 182-186, the latter being the old law). K a u ṭ i l y a with regard to the *patita*'s son of the body had only followed the old law which was in consonance and in common with the Dharma law, *e.g.*, B a u d h ā y a n a in II. 2. 46 gives the exception in the very term which is found in Kauṭilya—'*patita-tajjāta*' (*varjaṁ*). Baudhāyana's whole enumeration being *andha, jaḍa, klība, vyasanin* (perverse), *vyādhita* (diseased), *akarmaṇin* ('not following religious acts') *patita* and those 'born of him.' The last two were not to be maintained, according to B a u d h ā y a n a (43-45), except when the *patita* was a mother (48). According to G a u t a m a, the *jaḍa* and the *klība* received no inheritance (XXVIII. 43), and were merely maintained; only the son of the *jaḍa* received share (44); and a man not following religious acts was disinherited (40). According to Ā p a s t a m b a (II. 6. 14. 1), the *klība*, the *unmatta* (lunatic) and the *patita* received no share from the father. Those, not following religious acts are included by Manu in his IX. 214. B a u d h ā y a n a by excluding only the born son of the *patita* evidently let in the sons of the others, while G a u t a m a had allowed share only to the son of the idiot, and Ā p a s t a m b a had made no such provision.

'M a n u' by making the change in favour of the *patita* and his son went against Baudhāyana, and by allowing all the sons (except kshetraja) went beyond the Dharma School and followed the Artha-Śāstra. He was, however, consistent with his own view and consistent in his general policy of accepting the law prevalent in the law-courts at the cost of the Dharma School. The status of the *patita*, which was dreadful at Dharma, improved; it became humane and workable in the law-court. This was a good result of the attempt of preparing a combined Code of Artha and Dharma. The Dharma lawyer Sumati had to become reasonable and a practical man.

The position implied by Manu that a *patita*, unless he performs religious expiation, is not entitled to property, should be still held to be living Hindu law, especially when the process is not unreasonable. In the United Provinces and in Bihar it is a living practice that a man after serving his sentence for a criminal offence undergoes some purification.

Y ā j ñ a v a l k y a ' s (II. 140) list of the *shareless* (*niraṁśakāḥ*) is :--

(1) *klība*, (2) *patita*, (3) his born son, (4) *paṅgu* (cripple), (5) lunatic, (6) *jaḍa* (idiot), (7) *andha* (blind), (8) and those with incurable diseases.

He has followed Kauṭilya in respect of the first three, the idiot and the lunatic, and combined Kauṭilya's leper and the diseased of B a u d h ā y a n a and the deaf and the dumb of Manu in his 'incurables.' His *paṅgu* is Manu's *nirindriya* taken from the Dharma School, as a maimed man or one wanting in a limb cannot perform the ceremonies. Y ā j ñ a v a l k y a omits the non-religious. The practice of having *kshetraja* son was still living, and Y ā j ñ a v a l k y a reproduced the K a u ṭ i l î y a law, instead of the idealised provision about the son of the *patita* of Manu. Yājñavalkya and Kauṭilya were here more of a Dharma-śāstrin than Manu. Yājñavalkya being a practical lawyer could not afford to go against the conservative laws and a living practice.

Now on the texts of Y ā j ñ a v a l k y a and B a u d h ā y a n a, who exclude the born son of the *patita*, and in view of the express text of Kauṭilya, the adopted sons of the 'share-less', excluded men, should step into their shoes. According to Y ā j ñ a-v a l k y a, N ā r a d a, B ṛ i h a s p a t i and K ā t y ā y a n a, the A r t h a Ś ā s t r a is an authority where it is not in conflict with the Dharma-śāstras. Here it is not against Baudhāyana and Yājñavalkya. The passage of M a n u is not to exclude an adopted son, but a kshetraja ; Manu is himself most favourable to the adopted son. Unless there be an express Dharma text interdicting the right of the adopted son of an excluded co-sharer, the interpretation of the M i t ā k s h a r ā is not admissible on the point.[1]

[1] Mayne, § 598, 7th edition, p. 811. *Mita.* II. 10, § 11

In the history of the extension of this law of exclusion, there is a remarkable controversy. Nārada includes in the list of exclusion 'one who is gone out' (*apatrāyita*). This was a technical term denoting a man of whom the family had washed their hands clean by certain ceremonies.[1] Madana said that 'the man gone out' meant a man convicted of sedition or treason (*rājadrohādyaparādhena*, Mayūkha, p. 64). That is to say, a man convicted of offences against the State was excluded from heritage, evidently on the analogy of a hostile son who is included in the list of Nārada. This political interpretation is, however, rejected by Nîlakaṇṭha, with no small amount of criticism. What Nārada meant was an unreclaimable *patita* man. There is no authority that a political offender was in that class. The nearest approach is Kauṭilya's law of a forced divorce in case of treason. This was, evidently, in favour of the wife, not to let her lose her source of maintenance. The interpretation of Nîlakaṇṭha is, however, not less offensive. He says that the term means people going in ships to foreign countries!

Order of Succession

§ 48. The order of succession had a gradual growth. It very much developed after Kauṭilya and 'Manu.' The order given in the Artha-Śāstra is limited to

(1) Son, daughter, father, brothers, brothers' sons (the last, *per stirpes*)—each inheriting on the failure of the preceding one.

(2) Property without dāyāda goes to the King, except despicable property of the dead man, and the property of the Vedic priest which goes to the Traividyas (probably their guild).[2]

[1] See Sankha-Likhita on it, cited by Nîlakaṇṭha, V. Mayū. p. 64.

[2] AŚ, Ch. 62, pp. 160-161

(3) Properties in 'the forest', of hermits, ascetics, and bachelors of learning, goes to the Āchārya, Śishya, and dharmabhrātā ('brother in religion').[1]

It is evident that after the brother's sons the succession ceases and the property escheats.

Sons included grandsons and great-grandsons, for in dealing with partition Kauṭilya says :—

'Putrāḥ (sons) or pautrāḥ (their descendants) upto the fourth are sharers. Upto the fourth the *piṇḍa* is one.' ('Those who are of the broken-up piṇḍa shall take equally').[2]

In other words, the *piṇḍa* is the family tie making one group, like one unity ; the four, from propositus, constitute one p i ṇ ḍ a. This is exactly what the M ā n a v a says :

To the three water libation should be given. The *piṇḍa* exists in the three. The fourth is the giver. The fifth has no connection.'[3]

Manu's order of succession (IX. 185—89) is : sons, father, brothers. the nearest (amongst the sapiṇḍas) to the (deceased) *Sapiṇḍa,* then a *Sakulya,* the Spiritual Teather, a Pupil, the Traividyas, the King (except in case of a Brahmin's estate). [Daughter has been separately dealt with.[4]]

The Dharma School, evidently subsequently to Kauṭilya's time, developed the theory of inheritance further. Before him Ā p a s t a m b a has this order :

(1) on the failure of sons the nearest Sapiṇḍa takes (inheritance) ;

[1] AŚ., Ch. 73, p. 191. वानप्रस्थयतिब्रह्मचारिणामाचार्यशिष्यधर्मभ्रातृसमानतीर्थ्या रिक्थभाजः ।

[2] AŚ., Ch. 62, p. 160. पुत्राः पौत्रा वा चतुर्थादित्यंशभाजः, तावदविच्छिन्नः पिण्डो भवति । विच्छिन्नपिण्डाः सर्वे समं विभजेरन् ।

[3] *Manu*, IX., 185-187.

[4] M. IX. 130.

(2) on the failure of the latter the Spiritual Teacher (Āchārya), on his failure, the pupil should employ it to his religious needs, or the daughter may take,

(3) 'on the failure of all, the King shall take the inheritance.'[1]

This is practically the same as the order of Kauṭilya :

(1) father,
(2) sons,
(3) grandsons,
(4) great-grandsons,
(5) daughters.

The only difference is that the daughter is postponed to the brothers and the nephews. The preceptor and the pupil (in case of Brahmins only) come in to do his funeral ceremonies and not as heirs proper.

Gautama gives the following order (XXVIII, 1, 18, 21—23) :

(1) sons,
(2) son of appointed daughter,
(3) sapiṇḍas, ('those connected with the piṇḍa')
(4) those connected with the *gotra*.
(5) those connected through the Rishi.
(6) wife of sonless man who may raise an issue. [Woman's strīdhana goes to unmarried daughter and poor daughter] (24).

The inclusion of the wife probably was with the condition to raise a son for the deceased and to hold the property for that prospective son.

The author of the Mānava Code must have been conscious of his view that marriage constituted husband and wife into a unity. Yet the provision of law having been

---

[1] *Ap.*, II., 6, 14, 2-5. पुत्राभावे यः प्रत्यासन्नः सपिण्डः। तदभाव आचार्य आचार्याभावे अन्तेवासी हृत्वा तदर्थेषु धर्मकृत्येषु वोपयोजयेत्। दुहिता वा। सर्वाभावे राजा दायं हरेत्।

against the inheritance by wife, the M ā n a v a law-giver does not include her. He adheres, as far as possible, to the current laws. As regards succession after the order laid down in the law of the last régime, the author of the Mānava finds himself free and introduces the theory of the Dharma School, who now try to put off the King's inheritance as much as possible. The M ā n a v a extends the inheritance to the 's a k u l y a', the spiritual teacher, the pupil or any Brahmin (in the inheritance of a Brahmin's estate).[1]

The s a k u l y a corresponds to 'those connected with the g o t r a' of Gautama. These would be the a g n a t e s generally, 'of the same k u l a or family' who remain outside the Sapiṇḍas and the receivers of the water-libations (IX. 186). These, about the time of the Mānava, appear as a class by themselves, introduced no doubt from the Śrāddha literature which had been growing independently. V a s i s h ṭ h a[2] speaking of *niyoga* counts relatives as those (1) united in property, (2) or by birth, (3) or by p i ṇ ḍ a, (4) or by water-libation, (5) or by g o t r a. When these are not in existence, outsiders, i.e., Sapiṇḍas and secondary sons, inherit.[3] G o t r a here has the significance of the actual family of the members living together as in Manu, IX. 190, for the section of Vasishṭha deals with niyoga, like Manu IX. 190. They are men who are equal to the husband.

In Baudhāyana's Dharma-Sūtra (present version) Sakulya and Sapiṇḍa are given technical interpretation. Relations from great-grandfather to great-grandson are termed Sapiṇḍas,

---

[1] *Manu*, IX. 187-188. अतऊर्ध्वं सकुल्यः स्यादाचार्यः शिष्य एव वा ।
सर्वेषामप्यभावे तु ब्राह्मणा रिक्थभागिनः ॥

[2] *Vasishṭha*, XVII. 79-80. अतऊर्ध्वं समानार्षजन्मपिण्डोदकगोत्राणां पूर्वः पूर्वो गरीयान्। न तु खलु कुलीने विद्यमाने परगामिनी स्यात्। Here piṇḍa, as in Manu, IX. 186, means the funeral cake, and not the family unity or coparcenary.

[3] *Ibid.*, 81.

and those beyond are called Sakulyas,[1] that is, what we call now *samānodakas* (not Jīmūtavāhana's Sakulyas). The Baudhāyana-Sūtras lay down the order of succession in this way :—

1. Sapiṇḍas,
2. Sakulyas,
3. Teacher and pupil,
4. King.[2]

The teacher is now regarded as included, for the reason that he stands on thefooting of the father. By analogy, the pupil would be regarded as son. Their former vicarious utility as performers of śrāddha is now converted into a reason for inheritance—constructive blood-relationship, like constructive sonship.

Yājñavalkya, having this development in the Dharma books, fixes the order which comes down to us and by which we are bound to-day :—

1. son,
2. wife (applying probably the theory of oneness of husband and wife),
3. daughter,
4. both parents,
5. brothers,
6. 'and likewise their sons,'
7. gotrajas,
8. bandhus,
9. pupil,
10. fellow-student ;

---

[1] *Baudh.*, I. 5, 11, 9-10. अपि च प्रपितामहः पितामहः पिता स्वयं सोदर्या भ्रातरः सवर्णायाः पुत्रः पौत्रः प्रपौत्रस्तत्पुत्रवर्जं ; तेषां च पुत्रपौत्रमविभक्तदायं सपिण्डानाचक्षते । विभक्तदायानपि सकुल्यानाचक्षते ।

[2] *Baudh.*, I. 5, 11-15. असत्स्वन्येषु तद्गामी ह्यर्थो भवति । सपिण्डाभावे सकुल्यः । तदभावे पिताचार्योऽन्तेवास्यृत्विग्वा हरेत् । तदभावे राजा...

"on the failure of the each preceding one, the next following."[1]

For the succession to the property of the hermits, ascetics and the bachelors of science, he adopts the law of Kauṭilya in his own terms (II. 137). To this succession the preceptor is relegated. The fellow-student, as a constructive brother, is a new addition. It is based, I think, on Gautama by whom Yājñavalkya has been very much influenced on inheritance. Gautama places last the *Rishi-sambandhins*—'those connected through the Ṛishi.' Besides the gotra, one became connected with the *Rishi-kula* of one's Teacher. The 'Ṛishi-sambandha' corresponds to the Teacher and Pupil of the others. Yājñavalkya expresses this connection as 'pupil' and 'fellow-student' (son and brother). They, however, inherit as heirs to all the Varṇas, as the law is expressed by him for all the Varṇas.[2] A law which was originally intended for the Brahmin's inheritance becomes applicable to all. The pupil and fellow-student of a Śūdra, Vaiśya or Kshatriya would be thus secular pupils and class-mates. They come in for inheritance before the King. It may be of some use to make a note of one's Hindu tutors and fellow-pupils! One is a potential heir to them! The point is yet to be contested in an escheat case. And one who contests ought to succeed, if Hindu Law is applied.

A class is introduced in the list by Yājñavalkya which is entirely new and for which no precedent exists in previous literature: it is the B a n d h u s or cognates. Did Yājñavalkya mean all the Bandhus whom we find, for instance, in the Mitāksharā, or, only a few as Aparārka contends for? This I propose to answer by reference to the source upon which Yājñavalkya drew.

Yājñavalkya had in view the following Bandhus whom he found in Manu:

---

[1] *Yājñ.*, II. 135-136. पत्नी दुहितरश्चैव पितरौ भ्रातरस्तथा । तत्सुता गोत्रजा बन्धुः शिष्यः सब्रह्मचारिणः ॥ एषामभावे पूर्वस्य धनभागुत्तरोत्तरः । *etc.*

[2] *Yājñ.*, II. 136. सर्ववर्णेष्वयं विधिः ।

1. sister,
2. daughter's daughter.

Yājñavalkya does not mention the 'Sapiṇḍas' of Manu in his list, as he has already prescribed the law on the subject by a previous section, II. 121. His *Gotrajas* therefore correspond to Manu's 'Sakulyas' which he does not use, on account of the extension given to it by the definition in Baudhāyana. He had a convenient term supplied by Gautama—*Gotra-Sambandhin*. The meaning of *Gotra* in the Mānava (IX. 190) was limited to the actual family members. Yājñavalkya uses it in the same sense and in the real, not the technical, sense of *Sakulya*, 'those of the family' (not 'stock'). They meant those immediate members of the family living at the time beyond the four coparcener Sapiṇḍas. 'Manu' and Yājñavalkya never meant the Sakulya of Baudhāyana or Samānodaka of the present law. Utmost what they meant was what the far-sighted Jīmūtavāhana says: the three descendants beyond the great-grandson and the ascendants beyond the great-grandfather.[1] Even that is too much because the highest and the lowest could not be in existence in all human probability, unless the descending generations are multiplied through adoptions by minors—a thing which would have been held invalid in those days as offending against the principle of gift.

That the interpretation offered here of Yājñavalkya's *gotraja* is correct is borne out by an evidence which is conclusive. Vishṇu, who follows so closely Yājñavalkya and Manu, gives this order of succession in XVII. 2-16. The order of his provisions should be noticed in comparison with the order of the verses of Yājñavalkya:

Sūtra 2. 'Of paternal estate from grandfather, both father and son are equally owners' (*Cf.* Y. II. 121).

S. 3. Sons separated from father should give a share to a brother born after (*Cf.* Y. II. 122).

[1] *Dāyabhāga*; XI. 1. 38.

S. 4. The estate of a sonless man goes to his wife (*patnī*) (*Cf.* Y. II. 135),
S. 5. in her non-existence, to the daughter (*Cf.* Y. II. 135),
S. 6. in her non-existence, to the pitṛi [or pitṛis] (*Cf.* Y. II. 135),
S. 7. in non-existence thereof, to the mother (*Cf.* Y. II. 135),
S. 8. in her non-existence, to the brother (*Cf.* Y. II. 135),
S. 9. in his non-existence, to the brother's son (*Cf.* Y. (II. 135),
S. 10. in his non-existence, to the Bandhu,
S. 11. in his non-existence, to the Sakulya,
S. 12-16. in his non-existence, to the fellow-pupil, then to the King. The property of a hermit goes to the teacher or the pupil (*Cf.* Y. II. 135-137).

Now we get here the Bandhu and the Sakulya against Yājñavalkya's Gotrajas and Bandhus. Why should the order be changed and *Bandhu* placed before *Sakulya*? 'Sakulya' is not to be found in Yājñavalkya. It is taken from Baudhāyana[1] in the technical sense of all agnates traceable, that is, many more, unlimited, agnates were let in. In this new classification, the Bandhus *i.e.*, the Bandhus named (sisters, daughter's daughter, etc.), must naturally come first, as their inheritance is already settled. The Bandhus of Yājñavalkya, therefore, are the Bandhuc as discussed above, otherwise it would be impossible to explain the preference of the Bandhus over the Sakulyas.

The commentators have changed the substantive law. The Bandhus who ought to come in much before the Sakulya strangers are unjustly postponed. The mistake was due to taking Sakulya of Manu as the technical S a k u l y a. *Kulya* is a frequent term in the Artha Śāstra, meaning one of the family. If, as by Govinda[2], the real sense of S a k u l y a had been accepted by

[1] The lateness of Baudhāyana's law of inheritance is shown by II. 23. 43, which gives the whole Strīdhana of mother to daughters. *Cf. Vasiṣṭha*, XVII. 46.

[2] Govinda on *Baudh.*, I. 5, 11, 10: सम्बन्धविशेषज्ञाने सति सपिण्डा उच्यन्ते । सम्बन्धमात्रज्ञाने कुल्याः । अतश्च सपिण्डा अपि सकुल्याः । (*See* Bühler, SBE, Vol. XIV, p. 179, *n.*).

the commentators, they would have rejected the view that all the Bandhus (many of whom are really much nearer and have a better claim) are to be postponed to the Samānodakas, as being opposed to Manu, and, therefore, illegal. I hope this mistake will be rectified one day by the Privy Council or legislature.

Nārada goes back to the old law and terms in their old sense. His order is (XIII. 51) :—

1. daughter,
2. sakulyas,
3. bāndhavas,
4. sajātis—those from common descent.
5. King.

Here Sajātis stand for the stranger agnates, the Sakulyas for the father, son, brother, nephew and the sapiṇḍas generally, then come in the Bandhus, quite in keeping with the old law and Vishṇu, and after them appear the non-descript distant agnates. Lastly, comes the King. Sajāti, as the commentators say 'descended from the same ṛishi', probably also covers the case of pupilage constructively.

Succession to Son's estate.

§ 49. On the question of succession to the son's estate, the Mānava (IX. 185) and Yājñavalkya (II. 135-136) differ only inasmuch as the latter makes 'both parents' heir. Now, in view of Yājñavalkya, II. 136, the question arises,

(*a*) whether they take jointly,

(*b*) or, if separately, whether the father comes in before the mother, or, *vice versa*.

Vijñāneśvara, on a quotation of Vishṇu, places the mother first; but the text is wrongly given; it was taken from a quoted passage. Vishṇu, XVII. 6-7, gives *pitṛi-gāmi tadabhāve mātṛigāmi*. This makes the interpretation of Vijñāneśvara inadmissible. But the real difficulty yet remains, for *pitṛi-gāmi* means both 'devolving on parents' and 'devolving on father.' Śrīkara is of opinion that both parents are meant to take jointly. This on general principles seems to be sound. A wife is the joint-owner, since her marriage, of all that belongs to the husband, according to Āpastamba.[1] Bṛihaspati also says that she inherits her husband by survivorship, the half body of the husband still remaining.[2] Manu, IX. 217, which cuts into the connected verses 216 and 218, is absolutely out of place. No mention of the mother's inheritance is made where it ought to be, and here it is thrown into partition. This seems to me a later addition, an interpolation, and is not to be treated as a verse of the original Mānava and not even of the edition which was before Yājñavalkya. The verse makes the mother the next heir of a childless son, and is thus contradictory to all other sections. Then it adds the paternal grandmother as the heir next to the mother.[3] Of this order no trace is found either in Yājñavalkya or Vishṇu (Ch. 17). The commentators writing on it give contradictory orders of succession. They are naturally puzzled. Except in Mithilā (Vāchaspati), the law as interpreted by the Mitākshara lawyers (Aparārka, Nîlakaṇṭha, the authors of the Smṛitichandrikā, the Madanaratna, the Kalpataru, the Pārijāta, and lastly the Vîramitrodaya who reviews all the authorities) is that the father succeeds before the mother. They all contradict Vijñāneśvara who is only supported by Vāchaspatimiśra, the Maithila lawyer, and Kamalākara whose authority is inferior to that of Mitra-Miśra, Nîlakaṇṭha and Devana Bhaṭṭa. Jîmūtavāhana is with the majority of the Mitākshara lawyers, and places the father first.

§ 50. We have seen the position of the King as the last successor. The Hindu reasoning about his right is that he succeeds to all "master-less" property. This is found as early as the Jātakas (I. 398) as a definite principle. He gets the benefit of *res nullius*.

Escheat.

---

1 *Āpastamba*, II. 11. 29. 3. कुटुम्बिनौ धनस्येशाते ।

2 See *Bṛihaspati*, XXV. 47.

3 *Manu*, IX., 217. अनपत्यस्य पुत्रस्य माता दायमवाप्नुयात् ।
मातर्यपि च वृत्तायां पितुर्माता हरेद्धनम् ॥

LECTURE XIII.

MISCELLANEOUS TOPICS.

The Law of Gift—Gifts in Perpetuity—Examples of Appeals and Original Cases—Security for Costs in Appeal—Court-fees—Professional Lawyers—Pardon by Crown—Eugenic Rules—Sapinda Doctrine—Prohibition in Selection—Age to be Parents—Telegony—Sex in Embryo—Commentators—Later Smriti Codes—Megasthenes and Hindu Law.

The Law of Gift.

§. 1. The texts which treat of sale and contract of sale treat also of gift. In the eyes of Hindu lawyers gift is a mutual contract. Therefore, there can be an agreement for gift which would be enforceable at Hindu Law. Kauṭilya and the Codes enjoin specific performance of a legal agreement for gift. If the agreement is for a subject which cannot be given, for illegality, impossiblity, force, fraud, or duress, the agreement would not be enforced. Likewise an executed gift would be set aside by the Court for any of the reasons which would avoid a sale or an ordinary contract. A property which cannot be sold, cannot be given as a gift. As sale is mutual, so gift is implied to be complete by mutuality. Hence acceptance is necessary, actual or constructive, but not delivery. As Yājñavalkya lays down, in case of immovable property, acceptance had to be made openly.[1]

§ 2. A promise for gift even of a religious nature could not be enforced if the object of the gift did not remain any more in the same condition (M., VIII. 212-213). But when a gift had been actually made, except for illegality and other valid causes, it was irrevocable (M., IX. 47). The fact which completed it, was the statement of the donor, 'I give' (Manu, IX. 47).[2] This was

[1] *Yājñ.*, II. 176 ; see also *Manu*, VIII. 159, 164, 161, 212-214 ; X. 75-77.

[2] सकृदंशो निपतति सकृत् कन्या प्रदीयते ।
सकृदाह ददामीति त्रीण्येतानि सकृत् सकृत् ॥

joined with the condition imposed by Yājñavalkya that a gift 'should be publicly made, and especially so in the case of an immovable property.' This implies that acceptance in each case was necessary.

Even an acceptor of a gift could seek redress and get the gift set aside on the ground of fraud practised on him. (Manu, VIII, 165 ; Y., II. 176). This probably would have been an onerous gift. Conditional gifts are allowed by later authorities, and seem to be implied by Manu, IX. 47. Sarvajña Nārāyaṇa interprets Manu, IX. 47, extending it even to a promise of gift. In gifts made to gods, the god must have been regarded as accepting vicariously or tacitly. The property of gods was most sacred, as implied by M., XI. 20.[1] M e d h ā t i t h i says that when a property is metaphorically called D e v a s v a ('god's property'), it is meant that it cannot be taken. A gift made to gods would probably be complete even without actual acceptance, on the analogy of Manu, IX. 47. According to Kātyāyana, a property promised to gods could be sued for, *e.g.*, after the death of the promisor his son could be sued for the property. This shows that the promise here was regarded as a contract *in rem*.

Perpetuity.

§ 3. Gifts are all regarded as transactions *in rem* by the Mānava Code. But it is not so with regard to the other contracts. It thus follows that the question of perpetuity can arise in Hindu Law only with regard to a gift. No covenant of perpetual nature can be imposed on a subject of sale, as the contract is personal in the eye of Hindu Law. In gifts especially when they are of the nature of a religious trust, a perpetual covenant can be imposed, the contract being *in rem*. But when the takers are not gods, but human beings, the gift is absolute (originally with water poured in the donor's hands, to signify clear severance of interest), and no covenant taking away from the full right of ownership would be valid in Hindu Law, for the transfer would not then be complete in its eyes.

---

[1] *Manu*, XI. 20, यद्धनं यज्ञशीलानां देवस्वं तद्विदुर्बुधाः ॥

Examples from History of Appeals and Original Cases

§ 4. I have already alluded to the texts allowing appeal and revision.[1] On appeal, further and fresh evidence could be taken of the same or new witnesses, and new materials examined. A case of appeal is recorded in the Rājataraṅgiṇī under the reign of King Yaśaskara. There with the judges who had determined the case on appeal the King in his Council heard the appeal, admitted fresh evidence and reversed the judgment.[2] Another case is mentioned in the same history which arose out of a decision of executive officers. This was probably more of an original case, as no previous step is described. This case was brought by an unnamed cobbler whom we may call the Cobbler of Kashmir. King Chandrāpīḍa was building his famous temple of Keśava Deva.[3] The house of the Cobbler fell in the designed area and the officer measured it, preparatory to its acquisition. The Cobbler told the officer that he had no right to do it, but he would not listen. The Cobbler called at the palace and asked the King to hear his case. The King heard his case sitting in Council. The Cobbler of Kashmir argued that the King had no right to acquire his house ; it was his private property and no law allowed acquisition of the private property of a subject by the king. His right in his house was as sacred as the King's right in his palace. The King and the Council decided that the law really did not allow the procedure. The next morning, the King of Kashmir walked up to the house of the Cobbler of Kashmir and with folded hands begged of him the house for the sake of the intended temple. The Cobbler proudly

---

[1] M., IX. 234. Y., II. 305-6. Mitramiśra is of opinion that appeal is not allowed by Manu (V.M., p. 122 citing तीरितं etc.). Cf. AS. ch, 86, pp. 222-223. See also Nārada, *Intro. on Judicial Procedure*, 7, 11, 43, 50, 65 ; Bṛihaspati, 1, 29 ; Kātyāyana, V.M., p. 123. Asahāya describes the appeals in his time : 'whatever is decided in a town goes to the capital, what has been decided in the capital goes before the king, what has been decided by the king, though wrongly decided, cannot be tried anew,' on NS., *Procedure*, 11, Text, p. 7 : "ग्रामे दृष्टः पुरे याति पुरे दृष्टस्तु राजनि। राज्ञा दृष्टः कुदृष्टो वा नास्ति पौनर्भवो विधिः।"

[2] *Rājataraṅgiṇī* VI. 14ff.

[3] *Ibid.*, IV. 55ff.

made a present of it to the King. It is impossible to decide whether to admire more the Cobbler of Kashmir or King Chandrāpīḍa. The former vindicated the right of private property, the latter vindicated the majesty of Hindu law.

Security for Costs in Appeals

§ 5. Heavy security for furnishing costs to be decreed and the court-fee costs were taken before an appeal was heard. There was presumption in favour of the correctness of the judgment; abuse of appeal was discouraged. If the party's appeal failed, the costs to the court and the costs to the respondent decreed against the appellant were heavy, generally double of those in the original trial.[1]

Court-Fees

§ 6. Court-fees were taken both from the plaintiff and the defendant. Security was taken before-hand from both parties for court-fees which were calculated after the judgment, as the winning party paid at a lower, and the losing party at a higher, rate and the calculation could not be made until decision was pronounced (Manu, VIII. 170: Yājñavalkya, II. 42). In cases of perverse judgment the jury and the judge were punished[2], for no one was above the law.

Professional Lawyers

§ 7. Manu, VIII. 169, shows that professional lawyers were already in existence in the time of the Mānava Code.[3] The verse says that the people who suffer for the sake of others are witnesses, sureties and the judges, but that those who are benefited by litigation, are the king ('who gets court-fees', the creditor ('who gets his decree'), the merchant ('the speculator who supplies money for defence to the defendant and acquires his property in return'), and the Brahmin.[4] This Brahmin

---

[1] See references under § 6.

[2] *Yājñ.*, II. 306-307; *Manu*, VIII, 12-19; IX. 231, 234; *AŚ.* ch. 86.

[3] The Burmese Code of Manu gives also scale of fees.

[4] *Manu*, VIII. 169:

त्रयः परार्थे क्लिश्यन्ति साक्षिणः प्रतिभूः कुलम् ।
चत्वारस्तूपचीयन्ते विप्र आढ्यो वणिङ् नृपः ॥

is the Brahmin who advised each party on law. Medhātithi says that the latter four derive advantage from law suits. The definition of *vidyā-dhana*, with its history going back to the Dharma-sūtras, presupposes the existence of the profession much earlier.[1]

§ 8. The position of our Hindu predecessors-in-profession with regard to their remuneration is illustrated by a recorded case which we have already noticed.[2] As late as about the seventh century of the Christian era, they were probably not supposed to take a commercial fee. Apparently, that case was decided against the defendants on the ground of the illegal agreement between the client and the lawyer to give and recieve a 'present' of 1000 dr. on the conclusion of the case in favour of the defendants. The agreement savoured of champerty. It is possible that only champerty was condemned, while a reasonable Brahminical fee (*dakshiṇā*) was allowed at the time. The passage about Counsel Durdhara's statement that he was appearing for the sake of an old friendship, is, in any case, significant on remuneration at the time when the *Nārada-Bhāshya* was composed.[3] The profession seems to have been honorary in principle.

§ 9. There is evidence that as early as the first century A. C. professional lawyers in India were a class by themselves and that they formed a characteristic feature of a capital. For, in the *Milinda-Pañho*, Bk. V., where the chief features of a typical Hindu city have been described in detail, lawyers also figure. But they figure under a nick-name which is indicative of the uncharitable lay view taken of the profession at the time. Lawyers were called '*Sellers-of-Law*' or '*Traders-in-Law*.' (*Dhammapaṇikas*). Before them there figure in the description the "Keepers-of-Law" (*Dharma-rakshas*) who seem to have been a class of lawyers

[1] See Lecture XII, Section on self-acquisition,

[2] See Lecture XI, *ante*.

[3] The *Nārada-Bhāshya* of Asahāya could not be later than the seventh century, for about the middle of that century Pāṭaliputra was found deserted, and Asahāya speaks of Pataliputra as a living town where in the court Nārada's law was quoted and discussed.

known and referred to for their knowledge of correct texts, and then come in criminal judges, *Rūpa-dakshas*[1] ('those skilled in judging appearances') who were 'skilled in detecting the source of offences, skilled in deciding whether any act is offence or not, whether the offence is grievous or slight...... skilled in deciding questions as to the rise, the acknowledgment, the absolution, or the confession of an offence, the defence of an offender.' After the sellers of different luxuries, and the police (*nagara-goptas*) the writer describes the '*sellers-of-law*', "who according to the spirit and according to the letter, according to justice (*nyāyataḥ*) and according to reason (*kāraṇataḥ*), according to logic and by illustrations, *explain and re-explain, argue and re-argue.*"[2]

Hindu advocates were known for repeating themselves as early as about the first century B. C.[3] Virtue is often hereditary!

§ 10. A text of Nārada, which I cite below (§16), also testifies to the practice of lawyers who could address the court even 'unappointed by their clients.'

§ 11. It appears that about the eighth century A.C., at all events, scales of fees for advocates were established in a legalised form in India. The Hindu Law borrowed and adopted by Burma at about that time provides for such fees to be calculated at a percentage of the value of the suit or according to the gravity of the offence. The *Dhammathat* or the *Law* of Manu dictates: "Any good pleader, though the statement of his case may not have been taken down, if he has only just sat

Fees

[1] *Milinda-Pañho*, ed. Trenckner, p. 344 ff. I am giving above the expressions of the text restored into Sanskrit.

[2] Translation by Rhys Davids, *Sacred Books of the East*, XXXVI 236.

[3] "Milinda Pañho" was commented upon in the 5th century A. C. It seems to have been written in the Punjab, before the rise of Northern Buddhism. Its hero, Menander, was a Greek adventurer whose coins are still found bearing characters of the second century B. C. When the work was composed the nationality and the obscure place of birth of Menander were distinctly remembered by the writer, and even names of Greek servants are given. The book may be put down to about 100 B. C.

down, or puts up the sleeve of his jacket, shall have a right to his pay." [1]

§ 12. This is not the only provision of the Burmese *Dharma-śāstra* which would call forth the full approval of our present-day Bar. We have a further provision that having engaged one legal advisor, 'the client shall not call another pleader, unless the client be prepared to fee both fully.' Fees, however could not be recovered after seven months.

§ 13. In the Burmese Code the lawyer has been regarded on the same footing as the physician. It is interesting to note that a patient suffering from a dangerous disease and despairing of his life, would promise, as a matter of form, to become a slave to the physician on recovery, and he would buy himself back, so to say, by making a handsome present.[2] The same principle has been extended with regard to the lawyer's remuneration; when he defended the prisoner "in matters of life and death," he "has the right to a fee of thirty tickals of silver", "the price of his client's body."

§ 14. Two functions, which are distinct and different under Hindu Procedure Law, have been combined in the office of the advocate in the Dhammathats. Under our procedure, both parties at law had to give sureties *(pratibhū)* for prosecution and defence of the case. Sureties were distinct from lawyers. But under the Burmese Code of Manu, an advocate is also a surety for his client.

§ 15. One wonders whether any punishment was prescribed in India or in Burma for the conduct of the advocate who took the fee and would not appear at the hearing. In Burma probably the contingency was avoided by making the fee payable on the conclusion of the case.

§ 16. The employment of Hindu advocates was, as a rule, based on the principle of agency.[3] But it was not always so. The class of agents-at-law (pratinidhi, 'representative') was altogether different.

[1] Richardson, *Laws of Menoo*, p 50.

[2] Cf. "All that I possess, shall be yours, doctor, and I will be your slave." *Vinaya Piṭaka, Mahāvagga*, VIII. 1. 20.

[3] *Nārada*, II (ch. on pleadings), 22.

Their acts were binding on the litigant principals.[1] But apparently the acts of the advocate, if prejudicial to the client, could not be binding on the client.[2] The governing principle was that one learned in law could come in, as such, and assist the Court. This doctrine is expressly laid down: "appointed or unappointed a lawyer (lit. 'knower-of-law') is entitled to speak (before the Court), one who follows the law utters divine voice."[3] As pointed out by Asahāya (on Nārada, III. 2) it refers to lawyers. As the 'appointed' one came and informed the jury (of 7, 5, or 3) to help the Court in dispensing justice,[4] so could an unappointed knower of law come in and address the Court. And the Advocate alone had this privilege, he alone could speak, unasked, before the Court. Any one else attempting to speak 'un-appointed' would have been guilty of one of the 'contempts of Court.'[5]

§ 17. In criminal cases the execution of punishment was the prerogative of the executive.[6] The king could pardon the offender if he so chose. Certain heinous offences—e. g. murder, were expressly excepted from the power of pardon.[7] Nor could an old offender who had repeated the offence be pardoned.[8]

Pardon by Crown

---

1 Śukra-Nīti, IV, 5, 10, 13.

2 Nārada, II. 1-2 Śukra, IV. 5. 23. 'If pleader be bad, the cause he is employed in shall not suffer.' Burmese Code of Manu, p. 20.

3 अनियुक्तो नियुक्तो वा धर्मज्ञो वक्तुमर्हति।
देवीं वाचं स वदति यः शास्त्रमुपजीवति॥ Nārada III. 2 (p. 41) : *Śukra-Nīti*, IV. 5. 28.

4 Brihaspati, I. II; Śukra-Niti, IV. 5. 26.

5 Asahāya, *NS.* 1,2 ; *Parāśara-Mādhavīya* (Bib. Ind), pp. 32-33 (Vya. Ka.) *Śukra-Nīti*, IV. 80-82.

6 Brihaspati, VM. p. 42 ; Trial of Chārudatta in the *Mṛichchhakaṭika* ; V. Mayūkha, p. 92.

7 अन्नादे भ्रूणहा मार्ष्टि पत्यौ भार्य्यापचारिणी।
गुरौ शिष्यश्च याज्यश्च स्तेनो राजनि किल्बिषम्॥ *Manu*, VIII. 317 (see also 316).

8 द्वितीयमपराधं न स कस्यचित् क्षमेत। *Vishṇu*, III. 93.

§ 18. Many laws in our Codes are based on eugenic principles. Modern researches into the problems of eugenics prove that the Hindu race had discovered certain eugenic truths and applied them to their social legislation. Two facts explain those discoveries. The Hindus were great breeders of animals. The royal farms of animals on a huge scale, e. g. under the Mauryas, are historical facts. Vasishṭha expressly says: "Now they quote this also: 'Learning if lost can be recovered. But here when lineage is lost, all is lost (beyond recovery). Even the horse is estimable on account of pedigree, hence a woman of pedigree is taken for wife.'" [1]

Eugenic Provisions in the Codes

In addition to the development of surgery to a very high degree, and a finished knowledge of human anatomy in the periods before the Codes, we find a passion for human culture, for the production of only the handsome, strong and superior type of citizens, especially in a number of republics of the Punjab, which by legislation made it compulsory on every one to devote his best attention to the subject. Weaklings and deformed babies were destroyed by public authority.[2] The republican chiefs were selected not only on the score of political ability but also of good looks and stature. This is known to be the case definitely for one period, *cir.* 325 B. C., that is, the century immediately before our first Code. In that part of the country, where such severe laws about producing the best type of man and woman prevailed, was the seat of Hindu culture. All eyes turned towards Takshaśilā, when culture was mentioned in pre-Mauryan times. The Kāṭhaka, the Pāraskara, the Kapishṭhala, the Charaka and many other schools of the Vedas had their home in the Punjab. The Kāṭhakas themselves had relentless laws on biological development

---

1 *Vasishṭha Dharmaśāstra*, I. 38:

अथाप्युदाहरन्ति—

विद्या प्रनष्टा पुनरभ्युपैति कुलप्रणाशे त्विह सर्वनाशः ।

कुलापदेशेन हयोऽपि पूज्यस्तस्मात् कुलीनां स्त्रियमुद्वहन्तीति ॥

2 *Hindu Polity*, I. pp. 66. 81.

of their fellow-men and women. Under these circumstances it is no wonder that the ancient Hindus made a special technical study of the subject, and embodied the results into their laws. Let us notice some of those laws.

§19. In selecting a bride, the Hindu was free, in one sense, like the modern man. He could take his wife from any caste. Yet his choice was regulated by laws. If we brought to life an ancient Hindu, he would regard the accepted view and practice of the modern world, the absolute freedom of man in matrimonial selections without a check on his choice exercised by any eugenic legislation, as anarchical or primitive. For, his own choice was regulated by a bridal recipe, and if he broke it, he was liable to punishment both at dharma and at law. He must ascertain first about the descent of the girl, lest she should be a Sapiṇḍā on the mother's side or a Sagotrā on the father's side.[1] Mother's piṇḍa or blood-heredity was to be avoided up to the fourth degree, and on the father's side up to the seventh degree, in cognatic relationship, and the whole pedigree (*pravara*) in the agnatic.[2] A marriage in violation of this anti-inbreeding law was null and void, and attracted punishment.

§ 20. On the grounds of heredity the following families were avoided according to the Mānava :[3]

1. where low acts are done (by tendency),
2. which does not produce male children,

---

[1] *Manu*, III. 5,

असपिण्डा च या मातुरसगोत्रा च या पितुः ।
सा प्रशस्ता द्विजातीनां दारकर्मणि मैथुने ॥

[2] *Yājñ.*, I, 53. अरोगिणीं भ्रातृमतीमसमानार्षगोत्रजाम् ।
पञ्चमात् सप्तमादूर्द्ध्वं मातृतः पितृतस्तथा ॥

Gautama, Dh. S. IV. 2. असमानप्रवरैर्विवाहः ॥

[3] *Manu*, III. 6-7 :

स्त्रीसम्बन्धे दशैतानि कुलानि परिवर्जयेत् ॥६॥
हीनक्रियं निष्पुरुषं निश्छन्दो रोमशार्शसम् ।
क्षय्यामयाव्यपस्मारिश्वित्रिकुष्ठिकुलानि च ॥

3. of weak will ('not free will' i. e., where men born are easily led by others),

4. whose members have thick hair on their body, and

5. which suffer from (*a*) hemorrhoids, (*b*) pthisis, (*c*) *āmaya*, (diseases of digestion) (*d*) epilepsy, and (*e*) white or (*f*) black leprosy.

Yājñavalkya put it in a positive form : [1] (1) the family should be distinguished for good acts in ancestry, and (2) the family should not be tainted with hereditary diseases.

§ 21. It is important to notice that the Codes regard a tendency to do good acts or vicious acts as a transmission by heredity, like physical diseases.

§ 22. On personal defects these girls were avoided—maidens with reddish hair, with a redundant member, the sickly, with no hair or with too much hair, and with yellowish eyes [2].

She must be of proper proportions in physique, of thin hair and teeth, and soft body.[3] If the wife is not attractive, (good) children would not be born. [4]

§ 23. These rules seem to have been largely due to the researches of the early Kāma-śāstra thinkers who evidently made a special study of eugenic principles. The rise of the sapiṇḍa theory and prohibition of marriage amongst blood-relations and supersession of the customs of the Vedic period, became part of the social system as a result of their studies—the studies associated with the names of Śvetaketu, his father and other early authorities.

---

1 *Yājñ.*, I. 54: दशपुरुषविख्याताच्छ्रोत्रियाणां महाकुलात् ।
स्फीतादपि न सञ्चारिरोगदोषसमन्वितात् ।

2 *Manu*, III. 8, नोद्वहेत् कपिलां कन्यां नाधिकाङ्गीं न रोगिणीम् ।
नालोमिकां नातिलोमां न वाचालां न पिङ्गलाम् ॥ Cf. *Vishṇu*, xxiv, 9-17

3 *Manu*, III, 10 : अव्यङ्गाङ्गीं सौम्यनाम्नीं हंसवारणगामिनीम् ।
तनुलोमकेशदन्तां मृद्वङ्गीमुद्वहेत् स्त्रियम् ॥

4 *Manu*, III. 61. यदि हि स्त्री न रोचेत पुमांसं न प्रमोदयेत् ।
अप्रमोदात् पुनः पंसः प्रजनं न प्रवर्त्तते ॥

§ 24. Modern statistics have shown that a young man produces the maximum of bad and minimum of good children, while a young woman produces the greatest number of good and the smallest number of bad children.[1] A disparity between the ages of the husband and wife so arranged, that when a man is fully matured and the woman, young, produces the least number of wicked citizens. The Mānava Code fixes the marriage age at 30 for the man and 12 for the girl,[2] *i. e.*, at the age of motherhood the girl would be about 17 or 16 and the man 35. Other age limits are so arranged that a man could not be a father before the age of 32. There is evidence that the girl's age was lowered by Kauṭilya on account of a policy for population.[3] The conflicting texts in the Gṛihyasūtras, with traces of tampering, must be referred to that time. Kauṭilya's law, and the belief in telegony (see § 26 below) made the Mānava adhere to the age 12. But all the same, the experience of having virtuous progeny out of grown-up men and comparatively younger women should be presumed as a basis for the disparity.

Parental Ages

§ 25. A man was not allowed to produce children when he reached the age of 70, or, as some put it, when a grand-child was born he should retire to the hermit life.

§ 26. A point on which the social lawyers became quite

---

[1] *Crime, Its Causes and Remedies*, by Cesare Lombroso, English translation by Henry P. Horton (Modern Criminal Science Series), p. 171.

[2] *Manu*, IX. 94 :

त्रिंशद्वर्षो वहेत् कन्यां हृद्यां द्वादशवार्षिकीम् ।

[3] *AŚ.* ch. 60, p. 154 : *cf.* p. 162 :

तेषां च कृतदाराणां लुप्ते प्रजनने सति ।

सृजेयुर्बान्धवाः पुत्रांस्तेषामंशं प्रकल्पयेत् ॥

[4] Baudhāyana, Dh. S. II chap. 10, (4-6). *Manu*, VI. 2 :

गृहस्थस्तु यदा पश्येद्वलीपलितमात्मनः ।

अपत्यस्यैव चापत्यं तदारण्यं समाश्रयेत् ॥

convinced about the time of the Mānava for the first time, is that one should not marry a widow[1]. 'Once a man's wife, always his wife',[2] had a Dharma principle underneath it. But it also had a eugenic principle underneath it. It says that the husband enters the womb of the wife[3]. She always remains the wife of the first husband. That is a strong conviction in telegony, which arose about 200 B. C. Modern breeders believe in it, and research is on its way to own the theory. Owing to this telegonic theory the law on purification was changed. Formerly adultery with pregnancy could be 'purified' (excused) after a penance. But Yājñavalkya says that no penance can cure a woman after adulterous conception, though ordinary adultery could be cured after monthly illness[4].

Telegony

§ 27. The Mānava Code deals with the causation of sex in the embryo (III. 45-50 ; IV. 128). It is a subject by itself. I may here only draw attention to the fact that research in the matter was conducted in this country, and that results were evidently achieved. Let me quote the testimony of a competent critic. Sir Edward Gait in his Report of Bengal Census [5] says :

Mānava on Causation of Sex

"Many of the modern theories regarding the causation of sex have been anticipated by ancient Hindu writers. The idea under-

---

1 *Manu*, V. 162:

न द्वितीयश्च साध्वीनां कचिद्भर्त्तोपदिश्यते ।

Ibid., IX. 65. न विवाहविधावुक्तं विधवावेदनं पुनः ।

2 *Manu*, IX. 46 :

न निष्क्रयविसर्गाभ्यां भर्तुर्भार्या विमुच्यते ।

एवं धम विजानीमः प्राक्प्रजापतिनिर्मितम् ॥

3 Ibid, IX, 8 :

पतिर्भार्यां संप्रविश्य गर्भो भूत्वेह जायते ।

जायायास्तद्धि जायात्वं यदस्यां जायते पुनः ॥

4 *Yājñ.*, I. 72 : व्यभिचाराद्दतौ शुद्धिर्गर्भे त्यागो विधीयते ।

5 *Census of India*, 1901, vol. VI. *Bengal.* Part I. by E. A. Gait. F. S. S. D. p. 263.

lying many of these theories, both ancient and modern, is that sex is determined by the preponderance of the male over the female principle, or the reverse, at the time of conception. It was stated for example, in an old Hindu work on the subject, that the female principle is weaker on certain days than on others, and that conception on even days following the commencement of the menses tends to result in male, and on odd days in female, children. This general tendency, however, might be counteracted if one sex or the other were specially strong, and a strong and healthy woman is advised to fast, or reduce her diet, at the time when she expects to conceive, if she wishes to be blessed with male offspring. For the same reason it was ordained that the husband should be older than his wife, as he would then ordinarily be more vigorous and have a greater chance of influencing the sex. The great authority on sex amongst the Hindus is the Ādi Śāstra which is attributed to Nāgārjuna but some of the observations in this work, though they indicate an immense amount of research, are not fit for reproduction."

Commentators

§ 28. It is not possible to give a general verdict on the comparative merits of the commentators. M e d h ā t i t h i is probably the best on the whole. He does not refer to parallel passages to find out the real sense of Manu. He is more of a jurist than a commentator, giving his own opinion as to what the law should be, rather than what was intended by the text. N ā r ā y a ṇ a very often gives the correct import where others fail. K u l l ū k a at times refers to parallel passages and ascertains the sense. He is midway between the jurist B h ā s h y a-k ā r a *s* of old and the N i b a n d h a-k ā r a *s* making a comparative study of the subject. Amongst the latter J i m ū t a v ā h a n a and M i t r a-M i ś r a must be given the first position for determining the real import. The value of their works, as well as of the other "D i g e s t s," is very great for a historical student of Hindu Law. In fact unless one has studied the Digests, it is not possible to grasp the spirit of law and to make an historical analysis. For this purpose the commentators of

Yājñavalkya are more misleading than informing. Viśvarūpa, the oldest of the class whose work has come down to us is typical. His occasional citations, however, are useful. :He is anxious to force upon his reader his own views which are at times unsatisfactory. Aparārka, on the other hand, has an individuality and acuteness, and is not given to the vice of interpreting a text in his own way. He tries to find out the object by reference to other texts, and he very often succeeds, while Vijñaneśvara, resembling the jurist Bhāshyakaras and particularly Viśvarūpa, wants to state what the law ought to be, and writes with a masterful and systematising pen. But he is far from being a reliable interpreter historically. Here Aparārka is superior to him. On procedure especially, he is the only reliable expounder of ancient constitution and proceedings. As a commentator of Yājñavalkya, Mitra-Miśra would have stood as the best but for the fact that he is greatly influenced by the authority of Vijñaneśvara. Apparently the ablest and the best commentator of Yājñavalkya, Śrîkara, known only from quotations, we have yet to discover. The commentator who deserves the greatest respect as a faithful interpreter of ancient law is Asahāya. He was near the age when Hindu institutions and traditions were living. He has a respect for the text, and his legal knowledge is indeed great. It is a pity that the best commentary in the history of Hindu Law should remain yet to be critically edited and published.

§ 29. From Kauṭilya up to Kātyāyana there is a continuous descent of codifiers of the Artha-Śastra school. The Mānava leans more to the Artha-Śastra laws than it opposes them.

Later Smṛiti Codes

With the Yājñavalkyan Code the continuity of the Artha-Śastra laws is restored. Nārada, and Bṛihaspati and Kātyāyana, even more than Narada, keep up the traditions of the Artha-Śāstra law. Kātyāyana expressly refers to the laws of the Āmbhîyas and the Mānavas, who are well-known authorities of the Artha School, as we know from Kautilîya. The passage is cited by Chaṇḍeśvara who notes the reading of the *Pārijāta*, viz., *ambhīya-mānavāḥ*, and was puzzled : in quoting the interpretation of the *Pārijāta* (*tan-mānavas tasya śishyāḥ*, he takes 'mānavāḥ to mean 'pupils' (of Ambhi).[1] That is, when the Digest-writers flourished the books of the Artha School were so lost to them that they could not even understand the reference. The Arthaśāstra works of the Āmbhīyas and the Mānavas are cited by Kauṭilya. Kātyāyana always relies on the Kauṭiliya laws. So does Devala, whose chronological position is not yet clear to me. With Vyāsa,[2] in vyavāhara law, however, there is a break. With him the mediaeval school, which came to be known by the name of the Mitaksharā, begins. Vyāsa's law proper was based on the interpretation of the law as it had come into vogue in Western India, in the area where Vijñāneśvara flourished. Vijñāneśvara refers to those notions as current, yet he never cites Vyāsa in his own support when Vyāsa's texts fully support Vijñāneśvara's views, although he cites Vyāsa on Āchāra and Prāyaśchitta. It seems to me that in the metrical smṛiti of Vyāsa, which had originally no vyavahāra part, some lawyer of the period of King Bhoja, Viśvarūpa and Vijñāneśvara (1000—1100 A. C.) put in verses on civil law. Vyāsa's support of *Satī*, which earlier jurists condemn, is another proof of the fact that Vyāsa's book undertook to supply a popular law-book, which was not based on the tradition of the ancient Hindu Law. King Bhoja may be taken as the landmark of this new era. He was a great revivalist and had works written on almost all the subjects of social interest. He found the old world disappearing and wanted to capture and keep it by literature. In legal literature he is cited with respect as Dhāreśvara. We may take his time as the political period of the new legal interpretation and the beginning of the age of Vyāsa and the Mitāksharā school which is still continuing.

---

1 V. Ratnā, p. 652.

2 Some scholars should collect the fragments of Devala and Vyāsa.

Specific Pepformance; *Sudatta* vs. *Prince Jeta*

§30. Specific performance to enforce a promise of gift or a contract for sale is contemplated by our Codes [1] (the provisions for rescession of contract). Some four centuries before the Code of the Mānava, there was a suit for specific performance in the Court of the Lord Justices of Śrāvastī, which was the capital of the kingdom of Kosala. The case is related at length in the ancient Pāli canon. Sudatta, a rich merchant of the capital, wanted to purchase a garden which belonged to Prince Jeta. Sudatta *Anāthapiṇḍika* (Sudatta 'who treated orphans as his coparceners') was a charitable man, and desired to make a gift of a particular garden to Lord Buddha. He enquired from the Prince as to what price he would take for the garden. The Prince named an unreasonable sum, whereupon Sudatta said 'accepted'—'I have taken the garden at that price.' The Prince would not part with the property, and the merchant sued for specific performance. The royal judges (Voharikā Mahāmattā) heard and decided the case, decreeing the suit against the Prince.[2] The garden, thus recovered, was gifted to the Buddha, which remained the property of the Buddhist Saṁgha for a long time. The gift is illustrated in sculputres of the second century B. C. It is also a specimen of the administration of justice in Hindu India. The direction in the law-books (Y., I. 357) [3] that justice was to be dispensed evenly even where the king's relations be parties, had been an old settled principle. The scene in the Mṛichchhakaṭika also illustrates it. The king's brother-in-law has to go to the court of justice just like an ordinary complainant, who also appears before the Judge at the same time, and their position is just the same. A seat given to the accused was successfully objected to by the complainant. The tradition of impartial justice was well-established in Hindu Courts.

---

[1] See *Manu.* IX, 47.

[2] See 17 *Calcutta Weekly Notes*, p. clxii, where the whole case is given by me. *Chhullavagga*, VI. 4, 9.

[3] See foot-note 6, p. 118 *ante*

That principle is put in the mouth of the Judge in the trial of Chārudatta. "How difficult is the work of judges in knowing the mind of men which has to be ascertained for determining causes. People, lost to the sense of justice, state matters here covered with untruths ...As for the judge, abuse (criticism) for even a slight reason comes quitely enough for him, but an appreciation of his merit comes very late indeed. For a judge has to be well-versed in law, expert in following the tracks of cunning and deceit, he must be a good speaker, he must not have a bad temper, and must be impartial to friends and strangers alike."[1]

Megasthenes and Hindu Law.

§ 31. Megasthenes, who visited India several times about 300 B.C. in the time of Chandragupta Maurya and Kauṭilya, has noted several facts concerning law and its administration, which we can identify with the law of the time, in spite of mistaken and faulty observation or statements.

§ 32. We have already noticed that secret deposits on trust, where there were no witnesses, are dealt with by Kauṭilya. The quotation from Megasthenes, given by Strabo (xv. i) and collected by Schwanbeck as Fragment xxvii[2], refers to that when it reads: "They (Indians) have no suits about pledges or deposits, nor do they require seals[3] or witnesses, but make their deposits and confide in each other." Similarly, Megasthenes actualiy refers to Kauṭilya's law when he says, 'for the law ordains that no one among them' (Indians) shall under any circumstances be a slave.[4] This reminds us of the very text of Kauṭilya (*na tvev āryasya dāsabhāvaḥ*, AŚ. p. 181). We find Āpastamba fighting against the theory of slavery in respect of wife,

---

[1] Cf. 16 *C. W. N.* p. iii.

[2] McCrindle, *Megasthenes and Arrian*, 1877, p. 70.

[3] Cf. the 'Open (unsealed) deposits' of Hindu Law.

[4] *Diodorus*, III. 63, McCrindle, p. 40.

daughter and son (II. 6.13, 10-11). The argument, or a similar argument, was evidently extended by the Artha-śāstra thinkers to the question of slavery in general. Probably it is to this tradition that Megasthenes refers as a truly admirable law 'prescribed by their ancient philosophers.'[1] Kauṭilya says that slavery is legal amongst the Mlechchhas, as if here he had amongst others, Megasthenes' countrymen in view. The two passages of Kauṭilya and Megasthenes read together.

When Megasthenes is reported to say that the Hindus had no written law and that they trusted to memory,[2] probably it was a distortion of the meaning of the word Smṛiti. It is probably true that the Hindu seldom went to court, as it is said to be reported by him.[3] Again, Megasthenes says: 'If one is guilty of very heinous offence the king orders his hair to be cropped, this being a punishment to the last degree infamous'.[4] This is of course the tonsure-punishment of Kauṭilya. Tribunals of Justice presided over by royal officers are noticed by Megasthenes,[5] which agrees with the Kauṭilīya. Marriage, after the student life at the age of 37 is mentioned,[6] which proves that the Mānava age for marriage was not an imaginary rule, but had been actually followed by the orthodox before the Mānava Code. Meat-eating after the period of education in the forest, *i.e.* in the life of 'secularity', wearing of fine muslin, and marrying many wives are also noted.[7] 'The active toil' of the *Śramaṇaka* life of those who had their abode 'in a grove in front of the city' is correctly given by Megasthenes.[8] Marriage of girls at the marriage-

---

1 McCrindle, p. 40.
2 *Strabo*, XV. i ; McCrindle, p. 69,
3 *Ibid.*, p. 70,
4 *Ibid.*. pp. 73-74.
5 McCrindle, p. 85. *Strabo* XV. 1 :
6 *Ibid*, p. 99.
7 *Ibid* p. 99,
8 *Strabo*, *ibid.*, pp. 101-102.

able age is recorded.[1] The Śulka of a pair of oxen is known to Megesthenes,[2] which compares with Kauṭilya's *go-mithunadānādārhaḥ* (p. 151); and also the practice that no dowries were given or taken[3] in a *Svayaṃvara.* Punishment for maiming and mutilation[4] corresponds with the Arthasāstra law.[5]

§ 33. This is a very important and direct confirmation of the view that the laws of Kauṭilya, the bases of the laws of Manu and Yājñavalkya, were the laws in actual vogue c. 300 B.C. This also has an indirect confirmation of the authenticity and the contemporary date of the laws of Kauṭilya as come down in his Arthaśāstra.

---

1 *Arrian*, McCrindle, p. 222.
2 *Ibid*., p. 71.
3 McCrindle, p. 222.
4 *Ibid.* pp. 71, 73.
5 *Aś.* ch. 89, pp. 227, 228.

INDEX

INDEX.

A.

abandhu dāyāda—a division of sons not succeeding to bandhu, 250, 251, 252.
abhiśasta patita—persons with marks of the outcaste, not to be called as witness, 111.
abortion, 87, 120, 168.
abduction, 117, comes under theft, 159.
abhāva—vacuum, 71.
abhaya—amnesty, proclamation of no fear, 100.
abhibhartsanā—intimidation, 145.
absence—equivalent to death or refusal to pay, 196, 197.
accomplice. *See* anvaya.
āchāra—related to sacerdotal matters and separate from Vyavahāra, 51, 55, 56, 58, 71, 77. 300.
āchārya—spiritual guide, 7; 46; position of, in the order of succession to the property of his pupils, 276.
acquittance, 142.
Act of God, 175, 206, 207, 216.
act of force, 163.
Act of State, 175, 206, 207, 216.
action, 120-121.
Ādarśas—a Himalayan tribe, 30.
Ādarśa mountain, 29.
ādeśa—same as nyāsa i.e. property held in the hand of some one for some purposes, 214.
ādhi—*lit.m.* 'placing with' i.e. transfer by way of mortgage', 200, 212, 213, 214, 915, 216.
adhikaraṇa—a technical term connected with karaṇa, 190.
adhikaraṇa-lekhaka—registrar of the adhikaraṇa, 190.
ādhipāla—a special officer of the court, the protector of *ādhi*, 216.
adhipati—overlord, 102.
Ādiśāstra—a great authority on sex among Hindus attributed to Nāgārjuna, 298.
adjournment, 122, 137.
adopted son, 245. 246, *See* dattaka.
adultery, 10; law of, 89: 90, 117, 120, 131, 164, 165, 167, 168, 169, 209, 297.
adverse possession, of land permissible by *Kaut.* 128 and not by Dharma lawyers, 129, 130. 188, 213.
advocate, *see* lawyer.
āgama—title; source of ownership, 217.
agency, the principle of, 203; in commercial transactions, 203, 204.
agent, 202; 203, tort by, 204; 205; 212; 220; at law, 291.
agnate, 235, 294.
agreement, for sedition and immoral undertaking, 180, no interest on loan without, 197.
āhitaka—pledged, 209.
Ājīvaka—an order of ascetics, 156.
akarmin—not following religious acts, 273.
ākshārayan—moral reproach, 148, 149.
Alexandrian, 61.
alliance, a vital source of strength or weakness of a state, 95.
ally, an element of the state, 95, 96.
āmaya—disease of indigestion disqualifying marriage of a girl, 295.
Ambhīya—well known authority of the Artha school, 298, 299, 300.
ammercement, 149, 173.
aṃśa—share, 271, 272.
anagnikā, correct reading for *nagnikā*, *n.* 225.
Anāthapiṇḍika—the title of Sudatta, the rich merchant of Kosala for treating orphans a coparceners, 301.
anāvadhi—property entrusted to a carrier, 214.
ancien regime, 109.
Andha—the blind, his incapacity to inherit, 271, 272, 273, 274.
Andhra Kushan period, 61.
Aṅgas—a branch of Vedic literature, 16; separated from Dharma-Sūtra in the time of Gautama 19; essential for the completion of the education of a Brahmin, 51; Dharma-Sūtras last addition to, 66; as sources of Dharma law, 67; one of the seats in the parishad of experts to be held by a person proficient in, 78.

D.

E.

exchequer, 96.
exclusion, law of, 275.
executant, 142, 143.
exposure, a form of punishment, 87.

F.

Fa-hien, 14, 74, 171, 173.
false deposition, 139.
false evidence, 139.
family, not entitled to legislate, 77, 177, 179, 202, 205.
Family law, *n.* 73, 136, 224-284.
famine, 115.
fatalism, condemned by *Kauṭ.* and Manu in politics, 101, 102.
father, name of, to be given describing king in legal documents, 141, 143 ; calumny of, 148 ; 173 ; debt of, 192, 193, 194, 202, 226, 235 ; of kshetraja son, 243 ; position of, in Manu and other legal books, 245, 246, 247 ; position of, in the law of inheritance, 248, 251, 252, 255, 256, 257, 258, 262, 263, 264, 265, 266, 267, 268, 269, 271, 275, 276, 277, 279, 281, 283, 284.
fee, 190, 207, 267 ; scale of, for advocates established in a legalised form, *n.* 288 ; 290, 291.
felony, 85, 152.
fine, 85, 117, 120, 133, 146, 147, 149, 150-151, 166, 174, 192, 207.
first-born, right of, 254-255 ; *see* primogeniture.
five high offences, 168. *See* mahāpātaka.
finder, law of, 219.
Fleet J. F., *n.* 2.
Forest of death, a forest in Bengal, 30, 31.
forfeiture, 85 ; of Majesty, 97.
forgery, of coin, 60 ; of state seals 120, 190.
fraud, in speech, 128 ; 163, 177, 178.
freight, 206.
French Revolution, 20.
funeral impurity, 56.
full procedure, 177.
Führer, *n.* 197.
Gait, Sir Edward, 297.
gambling, to be brought under State control, in *Artha* law 9 ; 108, 109, 116, 176, 192.
gaṇaka—bench-clerk, 112.
gaṇa, republic, 40, the laws of, 107.
Gaṇapati, a Hindu deity, 59.
Gāndharva marriage, marriage by love-making, 239, 240, 257.
Gaṇeśa. *See* Gaṇapati.
Ganges, the river, 132.
Gandharian, a nation reproached by the Magadhans for some custom, 151.
Garga. *See* Garga Saṁhitā.
Garga Saṁhitā, 42, 43.
Gauraśiras, author of a Rājaśāstra, 22.
Gautama, author of a Gautama-Sūtra, the time of, 4, 53-54 ; inheritance in, 6 ; vyavahāra in, 13 ; the rate of interest in, 16, 19, 186, 186 ; the attitude of, towards militant Brahmins, 34, 36 ; non-mention of Mānava Sūtra-Kāra by, 49 ; quoted in Mānava Dharma Śāstra, 50 ; quotes Purāṇa as a source of law, 67 ; recognised Nyāya, as an authority, 68 ; does not accept any country as a seat of authority in legal disputes, 69, 71 ; on the theory of punishment, 84 ; composition of jury, 115 ; non-mention of Daṇḍa-Pārushya in, 153, *n.* 162 ; knowledge of law of corporation by, 212 ; on family law, 245, 246, 247, 249, 263, 267, 273, 280, *n.* 294.
Gautama-Sūtra. *See* Gautama.
gavālambhana—sacrificial cow-killing, 267.
gift, *n.* 1 ; of land, 14 ; verse on, 57 ; prohibition of, in Manu from certain classes of people, 67, jurisdiction of Moffussil Courts in, 116 ; by force, 140, fraud in, 178 ; specific performance of, *n.* 223 ; of son, 246 ; of love, 261 ; principle of, 282 ; law of, 285, 286 ; in perpetuity, 286 ; promise of, 301.
Gītā, 52, 57, 71, 72.
gladiatoring, 9.
gotra, 249 ; those connected with, 277, 279.
gotraja, 279, 280, 281.
gotrabhājaḥ, the right of same caste-sons to the full rights of inheritance, 245, 251.

J.

K.

mentioned in the list of successors by *Kaut.*, 234, 240 ; adopted son can be given by, 245 ; right of, on partition, 261-262, 273 ; in the order of succession, 282.
Mṛichchhakaṭika, a Sanskrit drama, 60, 82, 86, 138.
municipal laws, 3, 106.
murder, 89 ; an offence under mahāpātaka, 168.
mutual fidelity, of husband and wife, 231, 232.

N.

nagara goptā—city police, 290.
Nāgārjuna, the celebrated Buddhist scholar, author and reformer, 298.
nakshatra,—star, reckoning of, from Kṛittikā by *Yājñ.*, 60.
nāma—the description of property in dispute, 122.
nānā, a word marked on the gold coins of Kanishka, 60.
nānaka, the Śivite coins of the later Kushans, 60, 61, 139.
nānaka-mūshikā, *n.* 60.
Nandana, commentator of Manu, 229.
Nārada, for Nārada Smṛiti, the authorship of Mānava Dharma-śāstra attributed by, to Sumati Bhārgava, 44, 45, 49, 55; the age of, 64; the importance of niyoga in, 80 ; records the duty and jurisdiction of Sabhā, 82 ; on the obligation of the King to compensate his subject when theft occurs and the property is not traced, 106 ; technical details about the rules of pleading in, 123, 124 ; on the law of evidence, *n.* 125, 126 ; marks the highest development of the law of evidence, 132 ; discourages ordeals, 134 ; on theft and branding, 164, 166 ; the contract of transfer of wife and children, 181 ; referred to, in the case of Mahîdhara *v.* Śrîdhara, 196 ; on the law of interest, 197, 198 ; the law of debts, 198, 199 ; meaning of *ādhi*, 213 ; *upanidhi*, 214 ; marriage of widows, 229 ; follows Artha-śāstra with reference to *dattaka* in the order of succession, 274 ; the list of sons, in, 248 ; the position of *dattaka* in, 250, 252 ; on the right of father to make unequal division, 265, 266, 267 ; doctrine of self-acquisition, 270 ; the exclusion of *patita*, 274, 275.
Nāradîya Artha-śāstra, *n.* 75.
Nāradîya Bhāshya, 289.
Nāradîya Code, 44, *n.* 75, 75, 82 ; same as Nārada Smṛiti. *See* Nārada.
Nāradîya Rājadharma, 75.
Nāradîya Saṃhitā, 16, 44 ; same as Nārada Smṛiti, *see* Nārada.
Nārāyaṇa, cult of, 54.
Nārāyaṇa Sarvajña. *See* Sarvajña Nārāyaṇa.
Na Siddheyuḥ, contracts which cannot be enforced in law court, 176.
nāstikajana,—heterodox republics, 107.
naśyati—missing, 80.
nation, a constituent element of state, 96.
national assembly, 78.
national revolt, 163.
natural, son, 248.
Nāṭya-Śāstra, a treatise on dramaturgy by Bharata, 27, 28, 41, 51.
Naya-Śāstra (code on polity), 22.
Nero, 43.
Nidāna, 29.
nibandha—pension, 141.
Nibandhakāra, 248.
Nietzsche, 258.
nikshepa—a class of trust, 213, 214.
Nîlakaṇṭha, author of Vyavahāra-Mayūkha, *n.* 199; 265, 266, 275, 284 ; *See* Vyavahāra Mayūkha.
niraṃśaka, shareless, Yājñ.'s list of, 274.
nirindriya—wanting in limbs, excluded from succession, 272, 274.
Nishāda, 249
niyoga, repudiated by Vāyu, 228, 232.
Nirukta—a treatise on Vedic philology by Yāska, *n.* 168.
Non-Aryan race, 225.
Non-Brahmin, 172.
Non-Kshatriya Kings, 64.
non-owner, 220.
non-marriage, stage of, 224, 226.
non-sthāvara movable property, a class of ādhi, 214.
North Bihar, 58.
novation, 189.

Q.

Quack, not allowed to treat men or animals, 170.

R.

S.

T.

U.

V.

W.

Y.